Southern Sounds From The North

Southern Sounds From The North

Richard L. Doran

Library of Congress Control Number: 2008908032
ISBN: Hardcover 978-1-4363-6898-8
Softcover 978-1-4363-6897-1

This book was printed in the United States of America.

To order additional copies of this book, contact:
Xlibris Corporation
1-888-795-4274
www.Xlibris.com
Orders@Xlibris.com
52352

Contents

PREFACE

Having listened to everything from the Beatles to Beethoven and believing music to be amoral, I have learned to listen for the message even when I wasn't necessarily enjoying the music. I realize it doesn't have to be southern gospel to be a good song. Even the great gospel songwriter Bill Gaither once expressed a personal belief that one of the greatest songs ever written was "I'm So Lonesome I Could Cry" by Hank Williams. Yet like everyone else, I do have a preference, and my preferred style of music is southern gospel.

Over the past eighteen years, my heart was repeatedly saddened as I witnessed the passing of many great gospel artists. Starting with Rusty Goodman in 1990 and being followed closely by his brother Sam Goodman, they soon began dropping off like dominos.

In 1998, we lost John Daniel Sumner known to all as J. D. I remember that night at Memorial Hall in Dayton when, as just a teenager, I listened to those low tones coming forth from that giant of a man, and another hero was added to my list. And I still recall the laughter at the Stamps-Blackwood School of Music when our teacher, J. D. Sumner, showed up late for class explaining his tardiness was a result of driving his grandchild around the college campus on their big bus.

Next to go was Brock Speer in 1999. Such a man of integrity, I thoroughly enjoyed the time we spent together at the singing school. And if that wasn't enough, later that same year, I sat emotionally stricken as I listened to Glen Payne of the Cathedrals Quartet sing his last song, over the phone from a hospital bed, to a very attentive crowd at the National Quartet Convention (NQC).

In 2000 we quickly lost Rex Nelon while he was traveling in Europe with the Gaither "Homecoming" group. Soon thereafter in 2001, after a five year battle with lymphoma, Daniel J. "Danny" Gaither went home to be with the Lord where he suffers no more.

Then in 2002, we lost both Howard Goodman and James Blackwood, one of the founders of gospel music, who annually fascinated the crowd as he took off his suit jacket and ran around the baseball diamond during the all-night singing held in Indianapolis, Indiana. In the latter part of 2003, we said good-bye to another old-time favorite as Vestal Goodman waived her handkerchief for the last time down here on earth. Michael W. Smith reminds us in one of his popular songs that, friends are friends forever, yet it can sometimes be difficult to say good-bye even if only for a short while.

In 2004 we said good-bye to that man with the wonderful smile, Jake Hess and we were latter saddened as the health of George Younce progressively declined until in 2005 when he too went home to be with the Lord. Later that same year the pain became more personal as our good friend Charles Feltner departed to join that heavenly choir. Charles left us one comforting thought as he often reminded us, "I'll See You in the Rapture." After speaking with Jim Hill that day at Charles's funeral, I realized that with each passing, another page within the big book of gospel music was being finalized. At which time I acknowledged the need to preserve some of this information but took no further action.

In 2006, my wife, Rita, and I attended a gospel concert at the Canton Palace in Canton along with good friends Tony and Denise Rankin of the Dayton Ambassadors. The concert, a special tribute to the Happy Goodmans, featured the Perrys and the Monument Quartet. As they attempted to sing those old songs in a style that only the Goodmans could produce, my heart was touched, and I was again reminded of the need to preserve some of these precious memories. Within weeks of that concert, we heard news that our wonderful emcee during that Canton concert, Jay Drennan, who was loved by many, had passed away. Upon hearing the news of Jay Drennan, I accepted the challenge to put together a book preserving the history of southern gospel music.

Although separated from the South by the Great Ohio River, the state of Ohio has contributed greatly to the realm of southern gospel music. As such, I determined to direct my focus on those artists who were born or, at some time during their life, lived in Ohio. I labored with great anticipation as I researched the various resources enabling me to bring forth the information within this book. As a result of my research, I realized it was not practical to mention every member of each group. Please understand, I do realize the importance of each group member, and I appreciate the individual accomplishments and sacrifices made by each.

I want to offer a special word of thanks to those groups and individuals who, taking time from their busy schedules, agreed to meet with me, some opening their home and others even taking me out for dinner. Sharing the time with these artists and making new friends along the way has been an inspiration to me, and I will cherish these memories. I trust the information they shared and the stories told will spur a moment of laughter and possibly provide a special blessing to those who venture into the pages of this book.

Acknowledging I could not have completed the task of writing this book without the help of others, I would like to give special thanks to those who, through their hard work, patience, and support, have allowed completion of this book: Barbara Zanhiser, Corky Bebout, Joshua Nelson, Jason Bowles, and especially my wife, Rita, who not only supported my efforts but also stood beside me when discouragement came and gave me the strength to finish the task. I also want to give special thanks to my mother, Pearl (Jordan) Doran, for exposing me to what I consider the greatest music in the world, southern gospel music.

** To avoid repetition, those cities located within Ohio are not followed by the state name.

*** Photos with an (*) at the beginning of the title we taken by Mary Hamilton and are used by permission.

Introduction

In the late 1700s, the Scioto Land Company offered French citizens a chance to leave France and start a new life in America. They presented Ohio as, "the most salubrious [healthy], the most advantageous and the most fertile land known to any people in Europe. The garden of the universe, the center of wealth, and a place destined to be the heart of a great Empire." Since achieving statehood via Thomas Jefferson's signature on February 19, 1803, Ohio, the seventeenth state of the union is right in the middle of what is known as "the Heartland." Making prophets of those early Frenchmen, Ohio's Department of Tourism even displayed the motto, "The Heart of it All," on Ohio license plates for many years.

In 1864, much of the South was devastated by the Civil War. It was a time of emotional chaos in America and a line had been drawn between the North and the South. On December 14 of this same year, in Giles County, Tennessee, James David Vaughan was born to George Washington and Eliza Shores Vaughan. In the late 1880s, young James Vaughan became a student of B. C. Unseld. A few years later, around 1902, Vaughan moved to Lawrenceburg, Tennessee, where he opened the James D. Vaughan Publishing Company and put together the Vaughan Quartet. Soon, through the overwhelming desire and continuing dedication of James D. Vaughan, a new form of music—gospel music—began to grow.

Soon after Vaughan established his quartet, one of his students, V. O. Stamps, formed another group called the Stamps Quartet. By 1927, while Babe Ruth was swinging his way to a record sixty home runs, the Stamps Quartet was captivating audiences everywhere with their matching suits and a new young piano player named Brock Speer. These performances soon caught the attention of a talent scout working with the Victor Talking Machine Company (RCA), and they were offered a contract to record several cuts including their theme song, "Give the World a Smile."

In 1933, the tabletop radio was introduced by the Emerson Radio Company, and by the late 1930s, portable radios and car radios were widely available. Radio ownership had doubled by 1938, and by 1941, a radio could be found in more that 80 percent of American homes. At the time the radio was being introduced, a new type of phonograph record was introduced. This new record, created on disks of up to sixteen inches in diameter, spun at thirty-three revolutions per minute (rpm) and provided fifteen minutes of sound. While these long-play records did not reach consumers until the early 1950s, the new disks provided local radio stations with better music and improved programming flexibility.

In November 1949, despite heavy rains, poor roads, and a football game across the road, more than four thousand delegates crowded into a white-frame Texas gymnasium for the Interdenominational Tri-State (Texas, Louisiana, Arkansas) Singing Convention. For two straight days, they kept the rafters ringing with gospel music. Quartets and soloists from all over the South took their turns on the platform with piano or guitar accompaniment.

During this period in history, eastern Texas averaged about three hundred local singings per week. To feed this growing appetite for gospel music, the newly formed Stamps-Baxter Music & Printing Company produced a monthly magazine entitled the *Gospel Music News* and printed songbooks of gospel favorites—as many as four million copies. Their five songwriters and two song editors created over five hundred new gospel songs every year. Additionally, Stamps-Baxter was paying $5 to $10 for each song published to noncompany writers who submitted more than five thousand songs a year.

The Stamps-Baxter Company also had four traveling quartets that were quickly gaining exposure. One of these quartets, smartly dressed in blue suits and red ties, brought down the house as they sang several of their new songs including a falsetto, blues-style solo of "Swing Low Sweet Chariot." The crowd was captivated with the quartet's close harmony and syncopation resulting in the sale of five hundred songbooks and records.

As the demand for southern gospel music continued to grow, many groups began to travel more extensively across the United States. Improvements to their accommodations came some time later when J. D. Sumner helped in the design of the first custom bus to be used for quartet travel. With the creation of the National Quartet Convention (NQC), gospel music continued to grow, even reaching beyond the boundaries of the United States. As time passed, because of the ever-changing styles of music, that portion of gospel music retaining the traditional style of gospel music was renamed and became what we know today as southern gospel music. It is my desire that you gain a greater appreciation for this special music and capture a glimpse of the hardship, sorrow, and the joy that comes with being part of a gospel music ministry.

Having shared a brief summary of where it all began, including the establishment of Ohio as a state, let's take a look at the roll Ohio has played in the continuation of this great sound we call southern gospel music. Why don't you come along with my wife and I as we travel throughout the state of Ohio on a series of tours? We'll visit the birthplaces and hometowns of many who have given a portion of themselves toward the development, promotion and preservation of southern gospel music. Along the way you will learn some interesting facts about the state of Ohio while we share the stories of some of God's most dedicated disciples. You may experience a warmth within as your own love for southern gospel music is rekindled. So please come along, sit back, and enjoy the adventure of a lifetime.

Chapter I

Toledo Tour

God Delivers Again

Standing there at the Red Sea God's people began to complain
Soon Pharaoh and his mighty army will take us in bondage again
"Stand still and see the Salvation of the Lord!" Moses cried
Then God parted the waters and they crossed to the other side

"We won't bow to your idols," the Hebrew children proclaimed
And so the king gave the command "throw them into the flames"
Then the king said,
"Did we not cast three men into the furnace bound
I see four men loose in the fire unhurt and walking around"

God delivers again! God delivers again!
When it seems all is lost He reaches down His hand
Then all the forces of evil have to flee at His command
Just when things look hopeless, God delivers again

—Michael Payne
(Used with permission)

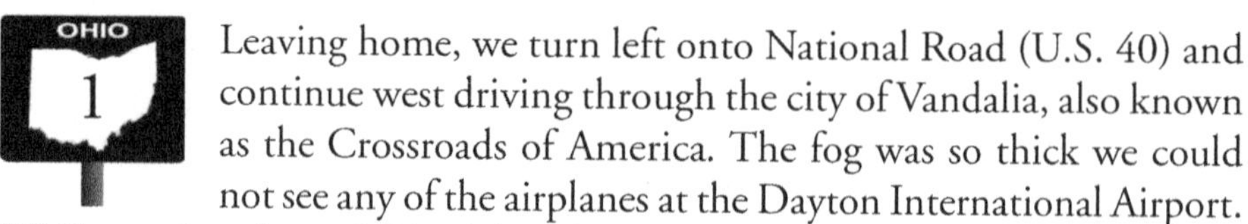

Leaving home, we turn left onto National Road (U.S. 40) and continue west driving through the city of Vandalia, also known as the Crossroads of America. The fog was so thick we could not see any of the airplanes at the Dayton International Airport. While passing through Vandalia, I'm reminded that this was home to Paul Mullins and the Bluegrass Gospelaires. They started singing in the mid-1950s and continued to minister into the 1970s. One of the members, Talmadge Clark, also played with John Burke and the Layman Trio for about two years. He is currently with a group from Kentucky called the Soul Searchers who recently did a television concert on Kentucky channel, WLJC.

Also from Vandalia is a group called the Christian Family Singers. Mitchell and Wilma Jackson formed the group in the 1960s. Wilma's mother, Marie Lawless, was also one of the original members, and they remained primarily a trio as they traveled throughout the Midwest. They have performed at a camp meeting in Oklahoma City, Oklahoma, and as far away as Colorado. Their five children Tina, Denise, David, Mitch, and Mickey were all part of the group at some point in their lives. The group continues today as a duet consisting of the original founders, Mitchell and Wilma Jackson. On the cover of their first album is a picture of Christ sitting down. The person portraying Christ is none other than the well-known Kenny Shiveley and the man kneeling is Mitchell Jackson.

Continuing west along U.S. 40 (Ohio Scenic Byway) we cross Englewood Dam, one of the five dry dams constructed by the Miami Conservancy District as a result of the Great Flood of 1913. Crossing the dam we turn right onto SR-48 and enter the city of Englewood, with its unique brick crossings. Englewood is the home of the Shepherds.

Growing up in the Blue Ridge Mountains of northern Georgia, Ernest DeWaters was exposed to music at an early age. Chatting ladies would sip ice tea while their kids leaped off to one side of the porch, chasing one another in and around the house. The men gathered off to one side, usually picking, strumming, and singing of life's pleasures and woes. Before evenings end, all were drawn to join in on the singing, which usually ended with old gospel hymns.

In high school, he was lead singer for the Shades, a sock hop group out of Dalton, Georgia, and performed solo during his senior year in Dumas,

Texas. While serving in the air force, Ernie performed with the Electras, a group from Abilene, Texas. He was transferred to Vietnam and, after returning from Vietnam, spent time in California performing solo with a group called Bob and Cecil. Ernie then moved to Dayton, where he found Christ. This transformation of his heart also brought a change in his music.

In 1990, Ernie began writing for, and singing with, the Shepherds, a southern gospel quartet in Englewood that is no longer together. In 1997, Ernie formed a group called Ernie DeWaters & Spiritual River, who ministered regionally and even appeared on Christian television in Ashland, Kentucky. Their ministry continued through 2005. Ernie continues today as a soloist in Seattle, Washington.

* * *

The Gibbons Family, also based in Englewood, was formed by Dale and Gayle Gibbons. Gayle (Livingston) Gibbons was born in Dayton on June 20, 1958. She possesses a strong gospel heritage as her father, Norm Livingston, also loves and has promoted gospel music for many years. He plays both the banjo and the fiddle and even played for Lester Flatt and Earl Scruggs years ago. Norm later exposed many big-name groups to the Dayton area, including the original Looper Trio. After concerts, the groups would often stop by his house for refreshments. Gayle remembers some would even spend the night, and her mom would always cook them breakfast. Once they were having a tent meeting and singing at the Livingston County Fairgrounds in Kentucky. One of the special groups for the event was Coleman Looper and the Way Travelers. Dale Gibbons was playing piano for the group at that time, and that is where Gayle met Dale.

Dale Gibbons was born on June 21, 1955, in Pineville, Kentucky. Dale remembers, "My grandmother use to sing all of the time, but she just sang, you know, out on the front porch with no music."

He came from a musical family, and his first encounter with music was singing for years with his mother in church. All self-taught, he learned to play the piano by ear. Someone gave them an old upright piano, and although some of the keys didn't work, Dale banged away on that old piano. At this time, his family was attending the Pontiac Missionary Baptist Church in Pontiac, Michigan, and some boys at the church, using a guitar, taught him when to switch chords on the piano. He nearly drove his parents crazy, but he finally learned to play that old piano.

After living in Michigan, Dale's family moved down to Ozone, Tennessee, where they attended the Ozone Missionary Baptist Church. This is where Dale's singing took place and where he became acquainted with Coleman Looper. Once while Coleman Looper was visiting the church, he heard Dale play the piano, and the next thing you know, Dale, still in his early twenties, was at Coleman's house practicing and soon started playing for the group. Dale tried to sing with them but just couldn't find his harmony part, so Justin, Coleman's son, took the baritone part. Coleman's daughter Cheryl joined the group, and they became a trio.

Once when Dale was with Coleman Looper and the Way Travelers, they sang in Knoxville, Tennessee, at the Civic Auditorium with the Happy Goodman Family—one of Dale's all-time favorite groups. He remembers when he met Howard and Vestal for the first time. He thought they would be "way *up there*," but they were really pleasant, and he considered it an honor to be on the stage with them. Vestal kissed him on the cheek, and he vowed never to wash his face again.

Not all his memories are this good. While driving Coleman's bus one day, Dale had a very bad experience—the air tank blew up! His mother was with them, and she thought somebody had shot them.

After traveling with Coleman Looper and the Way Travelers for four years, the group sang at the Livingston Fairgrounds in Kentucky where Dale met his future wife for the first time.

Married on August 9, 1980, they lived in Tennessee for about six months. After taking a Florida vacation with Gayle's family, they decided to pack their bags and move to Ohio. Giving a two-week notice, they rented a U-haul trailer, packed their stuff and, in January 1981, headed to Dayton. Dale was soon playing piano for the church and took this time to begin to develop his own ministry. On their early projects, Gayle would do recitations and their daughters, Stephanie and Ashley, would sing at least one song. Later Dale started singing some specials with another couple in their church, Roland and Tina VanWinkle. One night in 1999, after hearing them sing, a man from Cincinnati asked them to sing at his church. This was their very first appointment and the beginning of the Gibbons Family.

After Roland left the group, Gayle started singing since then the group has remained a trio. She was nervous and didn't feel that singing was her calling or her forte. She soon learned that God doesn't always call the equipped, but will equip the called. Gayle says, "Of all the songs we sing, I still love to hear those old hymns. And we try to pick a hymn for each project like Page 333,

'I'll Fly Away' and Page 110, 'Heaven's Jubilee' or that great old hymn on Page 50, 'Amazing Grace' as they really go over well."

Once they were singing at an outdoor event in the parking lot of an open strip mall. They had already sung and were just lingering around until it was time to leave. Gayle noticed a dollar store, and she loves to shop—calling it "retail therapy." They would be home the next morning, and Gayle remembered there wasn't any coffee at home, so she ran over to the dollar store to get some. Taking her time, she browsed around in the store. When she got to the counter, the lady who had just checked out opened the door to leave the store. About that time, Gayle heard Dale's voice from the stage, "Has anybody seen my wife?"

She looked at the cashier and said, "That is my husband. Can you check me out in a real big hurry?"

Rushing over to the singing area, Gayle slowly worked her way to the platform. When she was on stage Dale said, "Darling, where were you?"

Dale knew where she had been, but he wanted to embarrass her. So again he asked, "Darling, where were you?"

Realizing there was no way out, she said, "I was at the dollar store."

Their oldest daughter married Rusty Wysong, a drummer. Ironically, Rusty's dad used to play drums for the Southern-Aires. Their youngest daughter married one of the musicians with Eddie Lee and Anointed in Virginia.

In 2006, the group was booked for twelve consecutive weekends, many of them out of state. Gayle became ill very suddenly, leaving Dale to carry most of the equipment. Gayle and Tina could help some, but Dale, having to load most of the equipment by himself, began to question if they could continue another year. Then during their camp meeting, the Lord reacquainted them with some old friends named Ed and Vicki Wright. Ed called Dale indicating God had spoken to him and told him that he wanted him to be a part of their ministry. Ed helps manage the equipment and drive the bus. Vicki manages the product table.

Once they were singing in Springfield in a small church, and the place was packed. The group sang, and Dale also preached for the service that evening. The group had already experienced a difficult day, and when no one came to the altar, Dale questioned in his heart, *Lord, surely in a crowd of this size there is somebody here that needs to know you.* About that time, a gentleman on the very back row got up and walked down the aisle. He had on a pair of bibbed overalls and had a very long beard. When the man knelt down at the altar, Dale knelt down with him and questioned, "Sir, is there anything I can help you pray about?"

The man raised both of his hands up to heaven and said, "Lord, save this old sinner that I am."

The man (Brother Elmer) was seventy-two years old.

Before they purchased their present bus, they traveled using a van and experienced some rough traveling. As the equipment barely fit in their van, they always had to drive two vehicles. If they stayed overnight, to avoid the cost of two hotel rooms, they would often sleep in the van on the seats, or the floor or wherever they could find room to lay down.

When they first got their bus, they parked it at a friend's farm near Tipp City. Later while preparing the bus for an upcoming trip, they had lifted up one of the bay doors. Unaware that their friend's cat has entered the bay, they closed the door. Then on Saturday morning as they headed down the road, they stopped in Franklin for fuel. Some of them were in the store buying food and getting things situated for the trip. Remembering they had some bottled water in the bay, Gayle sent Dale to get the water to put some on the bus. When he lifted the bay door the cat, having been locked in the bay for almost fourteen hours, jumped out right in front of Dale's face and nearly frightened him to death! After recovering, he realized it was their friend's cat. Entering the bus, Gayle asked, "Did you get the water?"

Dale responded, "Well, I got two things to tell you. One, there isn't any water down there, and second, the Collins' cat is riding with us today!"

Quickly exiting the bus, they began their search to find the cat. On his hands and knees, Dale chased the cat through the maze across the parking area running under, through, and around several semitrucks. Finally, they caught the cat and put it in the bathroom of the bus where it would have to stay for the rest of the trip. While traveling down the road, they listened to the continual screeching sounds of the cat. During their stay at the outdoor singing event, Roland's son put a leash on the cat and walked it around like a dog.

They remain very active in the ministry, working full-time jobs and traveling on the weekends. As part of their ministry, they produced a television program entitled *Dayton's Gospel Music Connection.* The program provides quality gospel music in an effort to keep gospel music alive in the Dayton area. In addition to their singing ministry, Gayle has been a professional real estate agent for almost eighteen years. Dale, after working in the medical field at Grandview Hospital for twenty-five years, recently transferred to Southview Hospital.

Leaving Englewood, we turn left onto Union Road and travel through town to SR 49 where we turn right and head north soon merging onto IR-70 west toward Indiana. As the sun rises higher in the clear sky, the fog begins to dissipate. Passing Brookville, our view is still limited. Continuing west through farmland, we drive under the beautiful Ohio Archway entering Indiana. After traveling a short distance, we take the first exit making a huge curve to the right and while on the exit ramp we enter Ohio and continue to National Road (U.S. 40). We follow U.S. 40 east to SR-320 where we turn left and drop back into the fog as we wind through some wooded terrain and continue to New Paris, home of Rodney Griffin.

Rodney was born in Newport News, Virginia, on December 16, 1966. When his father was saved in 1970, they moved west to Somerset, Kentucky. His dad started attending Cedar Creek Bible School in Pineville, Kentucky. They later moved to New Paris where his father became pastor of the First Baptist Church. Rodney lived in New Paris from the fourth grade through the ninth grade where he spent a lot of time playing football with his friends. Growing up in church, he developed a love for southern gospel music. He started attending National Trail High School, but at the end of his freshman year, the family returned to Kentucky where he lived until he left to attend Berea College in Berea, Kentucky.

After graduating in 1988 with a degree in biology, Rodney moved back east to Newport News, Virginia. He took a job working on aircraft carriers and submarines for the navy at the Newport News Ship Building in their Nuclear Quality Department. Shortly after arriving in Newport News, he started attending a great church, and having a heart for southern gospel music, he was soon singing with the Galileans, a local group in Chesapeake, Virginia. Soon Rodney had left his good job and returned to Ohio to pursue a full-time singing career.

Moving in with his parents, Rodney took a part-time job at the Pizza Hut and started singing with a local group in Hamilton called Higher Dedication. The group only lasted for a couple of months until they disbanded, and he was able to go full-time with a group from Russellville, Arkansas, called the Brashears.

Rodney enjoyed traveling with the Brashears, but after just six months, he attended the 1991 NQC and was offered a position with the Dixie Melody Boys. He moved to Kinston, North Carolina, and remained with the group for two years. In the fall of 1993, he joined the group Greater Vision, singing with Gerald Wolfe, former member of the Cathedrals. Rodney has been with Greater Vision for almost fifteen years and is really enjoying this ministry.

He says, "The group enjoys singing in Ohio. Those folks continue to come out in good numbers, and our music is well received."

One night while traveling along Interstate 75 near Valdosta, Georgia, Greater Vision was pulling a trailer behind their bus when a tire went flat, causing the wheel to come off the trailer. They quickly pulled off to the side of the road and called AAA. They were assured someone would be there as soon as possible. It was very late, and after a while, they were getting sleepy. Soon Rodney had waited long enough and headed to the back of the bus to get some sleep. This left Gerald Wolfe, who was sitting in the driver's seat, and Jason, their new eighteen-year old tenor, who was sitting in the front of the bus about half asleep.

They sat for a little while until Gerald went to the back of the bus to use the restroom. While Gerald was still in back, Jason Waldroup heard someone knock and opened the bus door. There stood a deputy sheriff who said, "Hey, can I help you, guys?"

All they needed was a tire tool, and they could change the damaged tire. Not thinking, Jason quickly responded, "No, we're fine, somebody's coming to help us."

The sheriff went on his way. Returning to the front of the bus, Jason shared what had just took place as Gerald watched the rear lights of the patrol car, their only source of help, fade away into the darkness. Apparently, the next morning was "as soon as possible," and the man from AAA finally showed up. Yes, Jason is still alive!

Rodney continues to travel with Greater Vision and has written over three hundred songs producing such well-known tunes as, "My Name is Lazarus," "He'd Still Been God," and "Just One More Soul." He considers in a real honor and a true blessing to have been named Favorite Songwriter of the Year by the Singing News Fan Awards for nine years in a row. In 2008, Ivan Parker topped the charts with another song written by Rodney simply entitled, "I Choose."

Leaving New Paris, we look for SR-121 and turn around twice before we realized we were already on the route. New Paris is still mostly asleep, and they remain peacefully unaware but would have laughed to know we almost got lost in their little town. Continuing on, we pass through the town of Braffetsville and drive out of the fog. Entering New Madison, we note the American Legion Chicken Dinner that we're going to miss. We then turn left onto Hollansburg-Arcanum Road only to quickly turn around and head east to Arcanum, home of the famous Brumbaugh Fruit Farm. Arcanum is also home to the Gospel Ambassadors, a group of young men who attended the same church and joined to form a quartet from 1971 to 1977. In the later part of their existence, the quartet became a trio and traveled throughout the Midwest, singing with some of the nation's top groups. One of their recordings was made at the Cathedral of Tomorrow in Akron.

They were at an event one evening with the Blackwood Brothers when John Means, a member of the group, was talking with a man named Jimmy and asked if he drove the bus for the Blackwood Brothers. That Jimmy was actually Jimmy Blackwood!

Leaving Arcanum, we turn left onto Main Street and drive a short distance to SR-49 where we turn left and travel north through some windy farmland. We pass through Abbottsville and drive by the church where they hold the annual Midwest Gospel Singing Convention and make our way to Greenville, home of the famous Wall of Gum located on the sides of the Maid Rite Sandwich Shop where customers can pull up to the drive-through window and stick their wads of gum on the adjacent brick wall. Every square inch of the building's exterior is covered with used gum including the windowsills, doorframes, and entire street-side facade. Greenville was also the home of a young girl named Annie Oakley who at age seventeen had become such a good shot that she traveled to Cincinnati to take part in a shooting match. She won the match by defeating the world's best shot, Frank Butler, by one shot. Greenville later became home to four little girls who came to be known as the singing Kuhn Sisters.

Before becoming a Christian, their father played country music and entered his little girls into a number of contests, several of which they won. Their father later played for several different groups in Dayton and for the Apostles in Arcanum. The Kuhn Sisters were born in a time when most people held high moral values, yet many times Christ wasn't a part of their lives. The Lord led an older couple in the community to invite the girls to church, and they learned about Christ. Soon they became Christians, and eventually, their parents became Christians as well. When they were younger, they sang in the youth group and the choir at their local church. As they grew from youth into young adulthood, they remained involved in singing. In 1973, while working with a woman who was a pianist in their church, they were asked to sing at a local community gospel singing and made their first appearance as a group called the Kuhn Sisters.

In all the years of their ministering, they never once asked to sing at any church—they simply traveled singing wherever the Lord would lead. Many times they were asked to sing for specific programs within their own community. They always made it known that their goal was to sing gospel music and that they would only sing if allowed to give a word of testimony as to why they were singing. Through the years they had the opportunity to do many things that were very enjoyable, and the Lord was able to use them within their community.

Traveling by car, they sang mostly throughout Ohio and Indiana. About two years after they started singing, their pianist read an article, a little blurb in their local paper, about the Ohio State Fair holding a gospel singing contest. Entering the contest, they came in second place to a group of men from Columbus who were very professional and did an excellent job.

The Kuhn Sisters recorded four albums, two of which were recorded in the Gaither Studio in Alexandria, Indiana. Over the years, they were able to sing with some great groups and were privileged to meet some very talented people. As their ministry began to grow, their families were growing also, and soon their primary goal was caring for their families. Believing that taking their children to a different church every week would make it difficult for them to establish roots within the church, they were soon forced to make a decision. As a result, they determined to only be gone one Sunday morning each month. They continued to travel almost every Sunday evening, their children and their husbands traveling with them.

Leora says, "We could never have done it without our husbands. They are the ones who did all the work. We just got to sing. They set up the sound equipment, and they supported us. It was really neat ministering together as couples. We were also thankful that our children could be a part as well."

The group had a fantastic pianist named Janet Weimer who could play by sight-reading music but was also gifted at playing by ear. In addition, she possessed a lovely voice, and through the years as the sisters started having children, they would just switch parts and Janet was able to sing the missing part allowing them to continue. Janet had previously played for her brother's group, and after the Kuhn Sisters stopped singing, she continues to play for a local funeral home.

As they were singing one Sunday evening in a very small church, Leora felt impressed that they sing a particular song. It was an old, old hymn entitled "He Hideth My Soul." After the service was over, a man came up to Leora and shared with her that he had a very serious health problem and was dying. He then shared that he had been feeling discouraged and had told the Lord he would really like for someone to sing that old hymn "He Hideth My Soul" that day for him. What a blessing to be used by the Lord in that way!

Even though one of the sisters moved away, they remained close, and the other sisters continued to sing until 2004 when Leora moved away from the area. Leora (Lee) Minnich says of their ministry, "Looking back, even though we were sisters, I think it was because we were together so much traveling and singing that we remained really, really close through the years. So I just thank the Lord for all of the opportunities He provided."

* * *

Gaylen Blosser was born on May 21, 1949 in Bellefontaine, on the same day as Atlanta Braves manager Bobby Cox. He grew up in West Liberty, attending a Mennonite church. When he was a young boy, his parents used to take him to Memorial Hall in Dayton to watch the big-name quartets sing at Lloyd Orrell's all-night singings, so his southern gospel influence came early. He remembers that Lloyd Orrell held an all-night singing in Dayton the day President John F. Kennedy was assassinated, featuring several groups including the Blackwood Brothers. A few years before James Blackwood, passed away, Gaylen asked James if he knew where he was the day President John Kennedy was killed.

James said, "Yes, sir, Memorial Hall in Dayton."

In 1968, Gaylen was drafted into the army and sent to Vietnam. He was in the infantry for a year. In 1998, Gaylen started singing with the Chordsmen in Union City, Indiana, and in January 2000, he helped form the Promised Heirs with a group of guys from Darke County.

After doing a recording at Charles Novell's studio, Charles recommended a bass singer named Noah Wilson and a tenor named Dave Oglesby who were both taking voice lessons from him. One year, Ryan Berry came to the Midwest Gospel Singing Convention as a newspaper reporter. Gaylen had him sing one song, and he "knocked it out of the park." Needing a lead singer, the group quickly hired him.

While working with Capital Artists in Colorado Springs, Colorado, they were told that it was very difficult to book them because of the similarity of their name to other groups of the same name. Many groups use the same ending, some spelling it "heirs" and some "aires." Some people were confused and actually came expecting to hear the Kingdomaires. Their agency pressed them to change their, name and on January 1, 2005, they changed their name to Acclaim, which means "praise."

Gaylen had seen many of the great artists while growing up. So when his group, Acclaim, began working with Angelic Talent Agency, the same agency as the Blackwood Brothers', frequently singing with them was a dream come true! In 2007, Mark Crary, a young man from southern Ohio, who operated Daystar Promotions for over fifteen years, was named executive director of Angelic Talent Agency. That same year, the Angelic Talent Agency sent out a single by Acclaim to one thousand radio stations. The song was entitled, "Good Old Fashion Way" and was written by Jonathan Stone, from the Lebanon area. The group Lighthouse had previously recorded the song, but as it had never been released to the radio, their song was considered an original. Their first song with such radio play was a real breakthrough for the group.

Acclaim's producer is John Daren Rowsey. He sang with Karen Peck and New River and wrote two of the title songs on Gaither videos. They recorded at Harvest Studio with Mark Hale.

Gaylen's all-time favorite song is one that J.D. Sumner sang as a solo. It was written by Steve Adams, a distant relative of Gaylen and Bill Gaither's first keyboard player. In 2003, they collaborated on a project named *Steve Adams Writes . . . The Promised Heirs Sing* featuring "All Because of God's Amazing Grace."

Gaylen and Noah are both Vietnam veterans, and both were awarded the Bronze Star. Gaylen has a Combat Infantryman Badge, and Noah has a Combat Medical Badge. They meet many Vietnam veterans who enjoy talking with them. In 2007, they were at the First Baptist Church in Denton, Maryland. During the Sunday morning service, they were told that three of their church members just got called up to Iraq and would be gone for over a year. One was the chairman of the deacon's board, and they were older gentlemen with families and grandchildren. The men were encouraged to talk with Gaylen and Noah as they could grasp the seriousness of their upcoming experience.

The group had a number of personnel changes when they were called the Promised Heirs. At one time Matt Felts, who now sings with the Monument Quartet, sang tenor for the group. Dave Falenous also sang tenor for a while. Dave previously sang with Ed Crawford and Mystery Men and went on to sing with the Worleys. Chris Horn went on to sing with a group from Kentucky and later sang with the Skyline Boys.

In 2006, they held 220 concerts. They are on the road every weekend, so they consider themselves a full-time group. They travel to Texas every year and have been as far east as Maine. They have performed on cruises to the Bahamas, traveled throughout the southern states, and sung frequently in Nebraska and Iowa.

Gaylen believes there's no better music than southern gospel. He shares concern as to the future of the ministry because traveling on the road can be a financial struggle, and sometimes, they have to borrow money to keep going. Gaylen believes that to keep a quartet on the road today, you almost have to have some financial backing. He also feels it is becoming more difficult to draw a crowd, and many churches today are no longer having Sunday evening services.

They travel in a thirty-five-foot RV pulling a twelve-foot trailer. They enjoy traveling together, and they often eat and sleep in the RV. They have spent many nights in Wal-Mart parking lots, a favorite resting place for many groups on the road. The group truly appreciates this blessing. Some of the major groups are struggling to the point where they are getting rid of their buses and traveling in vans. Gaylen recalls seventy-two-year-old Doug Oldham telling him that if it hadn't been for his bus, he would be a millionaire.

In 2002, Gaylen started the Midwest Gospel Singing Convention, now an annual three-day event. Charles Novell emceed the event for the first four years, and now Gary Shepherd, former tenor for the Kingsmen, is the emcee. They bring in some top talent and groups come in from all over the United States, and among the notables, Buddy Liles attends every year. In 2006, Joyce Martin of the Martins dropped by, and although she didn't come to sing, they had her sing a few. Held at the Lighthouse Christian Center in Greenville, the event is like a family reunion, and the groups love it. Gaylen says, "I don't like competition in the industry. I think southern gospel groups have to stick together. To me, it's not a competition. It's about fellowship and sharing of the gospel."

Driving through Greenville, we pass the Darke County Fairgrounds and a statue of Annie Oakley. Turning onto Broadway, we stop at Broadway Joe's Coffee Shop, where the pounded metal ceiling and the pull-handle toilet are evidence of a place that cares about history. After a delicious muffin and a cup of great coffee, we head back to the circle and, making our best guess, travel SR-121 to Krucksburg Road where we turn right and find SR-127. Traveling north along 127, we cross over the upper portion of the Stillwater River, swollen with the recent rains. Passing through North Star, an early home of Annie Oakley, we continue north and looking to the east as we enter Celina our eyes catch a great view of Lake St. Mary's. Celina, founded in 1834, is home to the largest gathering of Amphicars. These 1960s era amphibious cars are a huge attraction for area residents and visitors during the annual Lake Festival.

On January 6, 1887, long before the Amphicars were around, a young man named Virgil Brock was born into a very devout Quaker family living somewhere near Celina. An ordained minister at the tender age of nineteen, he became pastor of the Christian Church in Green Forks, Indiana, where he met Blanche Kerr. They were married in 1914 and began traveling and ministering as the Singing Brocks. They traveled within their home state of Indiana from 1922 to 1936. In 1936, while attending the Winona Lake Bible Conference, Virgil penned the words to a popular song entitled, "Beyond the Sunset." Virgil's final days were spent working at the Youth Haven Ranch in Rivers Junction, Michigan.

Leaving Celina, we drive by a number of historic buildings including a church with a green copper dome. Turning right on SR-29 and traveling east, we cross over the Saint Mary's River and exit onto SR-66 (not the famous Route 66). We follow the Miami and Erie Canal and pass through Spencerville, a town originally powered by canal water, and soon arrive in Delphos. In 1987, a trio called the Denominations formed in Delphos. The name seemed appropriate as each member of the group was from a different denomination. Wetcel, father of one of the members, sang with Wendell Adams (father of Gary Adams) in a group called the Ambassadors. Donna Kiehl sang with the Denominations and then went on to sing with the Heavenaires.

Before leaving Delphos, we stop to fill the gas tank. We head north on SR-66 where we shortly take SR-30 west and cross over the Auglaize River. We exit onto SR-127 taking it to Sycamore Street, ignoring the insistent instructions of the GPS that is trying to get us to turn off the highway where there is no ramp—you've got to love technology. Entering Van Wert, we pass by the Trinity Friends Church where the Gospel Music Expo is held annually. Driving into town, we stop at Balyeat's Coffee Shop to sample some local cuisine. At one time, Van Wert was the only place in the world producing Liederkranz cheese. This pungent dairy product was made at the local borden plant. On November 10, 2002, an F4 tornado ripped through the town killing two people.

In 1975, Dane Bailey started doing solo and duet work. He began singing bass for the Evangels from Van Wert in 1987, remaining with the group for four years. Then in 1999, after winning a recording contract from a contest held in Bedford, Indiana, he started a full-time solo ministry, and today, he is known across America as the Singing Auctioneer.

* * *

Gary Adams was born on December 13, 1936, in northwest Van Wert County in the "big" town of Wetzel, about fifty people. His mother was quite an accomplished pianist and was the accompanist for his dad, Wendell Adams, who sang with Gary's uncle Carl Miller, Howard Dunlap and Paul Swartz in the Ambassador Quartet. Growing up in this environment was the start of Gary's music career as he often traveled with the group and has slept on many church pews. Later when Uncle Carl and Howard were called to serve the Lord as full-time pastors, the group disbanded.

Gary began singing in high school, and after marrying a young girl named Barbara in 1957, he began a new group called the Zionaires singing with his mother and his mother-in-law. They sang throughout Ohio for many years until Gary's mother, Nellie Adams, and his mother-in-law, Lorene Unland, decided to retire to warmer weather. Gary says, "I always kid about how difficult it was singing with two older women, but it really was very nice. My mother always prayed that I would continue to sing with a new group. She said, 'You don't want to be singing with old people.' So now the old man is singing with two young girls."

In 1982, Gary put together a trio called Trinity singing with Terry Amstutz and Steve Placke. When Steve later left to answer his call as a full-time minister, Scott Fleming and Chuck Dunham joined the group. Both Scott and Chuck had grown up singing in family groups, and for a short stint, Trinity was a male quartet. Soon the Lord was working again as Scott felt the call to change his ministry and also became a full-time pastor. It was at that time that Trinity added the first female singer to the group as Betty Dunno, who had previously sung with Terry Amstutz, joined the mix. The group was referred to as the Trinity Quartet at this time. As often happens in gospel groups, people come and go, and as Terry Amstutz was led to step down from the group, Kyan Rinner joined for a new mixed quartet sound. Within a few years, Betty also decided to follow a solo ministry, and she was replaced with Pam Smith. It was during this time that the group recorded their first Roger Talley—produced project entitled, "He is the Reason We Sing." Soon after the release of this project, Kyan decided to step down as she was pursuing her doctorate degree in psychology. Then in 1994, Kim Mason was asked to take Kyan's place. Kim's father had been Gary's pastor, and she was a friend of his children. She had sung as a soloist for many years, had been a member of the Youth for Christ Contemporaries in high school, and majored in vocal music at Defiance College. In 1995, when Chuck decided to step down to spend more time with his family, Trinity decided to remain a trio.

In 1999, Cheryl Burk joined Trinity and this mix of Gary, Kim, and Cheryl has been together almost ten years. Cheryl had previously sung with her family known as the Hunters of Glenmore. She later had a duet ministry with her sister Pam Peters. They initiated Cheryl quickly as her first performance with the group was a live television program. Cheryl's next concert was also very eventful. Pam Smith was still traveling with the group to give Cheryl a chance to learn all of the music. The group was in the basement of a small church before the concert, and going to the restroom, Pam became stuck in the ladies' restroom and couldn't get out. The pastor had given Gary the signal that they were ready to start, and there was no Pam.

Then Cheryl heard Pam pounding on the restroom door and let the group know that she thought Pam was stuck. When Pam tried to pull on the door, the doorknob came off in her hand. Gary and several men from the church were working on the door and telling her to kick it, not thinking that she was in high heels and a dress! The sanctuary was full of people, and soon you could hear the laughter floating down into the basement. Finally, some old farmer who had came to church in his pickup said, "I will get a crowbar, sir, and we'll get that door off of there."

Eventually they ripped the hinges right off the door, and Pam was able to make her exit. The crowd continued to laugh for about fifteen minutes as Trinity tried to change the mood of the service.

Life on the road is never dull for Trinity. The group became lost in northern Ohio one morning. The church was a country church, and the directions were not clear. After driving around for quite a while and running the risk at missing the concert, they finally stopped at a local church they had driven by several times to ask them for directions. Mark Hartman, one of the soundmen, ran to the front door to ask for help. As Gary pulled around the church to pick Mark up, their prayers were answered. The billboard at the church said, "Concert today with Trinity." They had accidentally found the right church!

Humor comes in all forms. Gary was singing his signature song, "The Lighthouse" at a Methodist church in Columbus. As he moved back into position after his solo, he fell through a trapdoor in the floor. He finished the song with just his feet and head showing! The sound man was laughing so hard he had to leave the room.

In 2001, Trinity began the Southern Gospel Music Expo now held annually in the Family Life Center at Trinity Friends Church. Each year, approximately thirty to forty groups come to Van Wert from across the country for four nights of southern gospel music. The Expo Finale has been blessed by such national groups as the Talley Trio, the Booth Brothers, Greater Vision, and Young Harmony. The 2008 Expo saw the largest Sunday night crowd as the Booth Brothers sang and blessed over a thousand gospel fans. Trinity has also had the opportunity to open for the Hoppers and the Pfeifers.

In November 2007, Trinity released their newest project, "Welcome Home" written by Cheryl Burk and dedicated to Gary's brother-in-law, Jerry Stemen. Jerry went home to be with the Lord in the fall of 2005. The morning of his passing, Cheryl awoke with a special song in her heart and on her mind. Trinity is excited about their opportunity to sign with Willowood Productions. God continues to open many doors for their ministry, and they are letting him guide them through each one.

Gary, a retired farmer, refereed high school and college basketball for thirty years and has served Van Wert as county commissioner for twenty years. Concerning the current group, Gary says, "The group I am singing with now, these girls are such a great bunch to sing with, and I think the growth I have seen out of our group, our ministry, is very solid and we praise the Lord for that. My wife always says, 'Keep these girls as they're the best of the best.' So when your wife tells you that, that means something, doesn't it?"

Leaving Van Wert, we take U.S. 30 (Abraham Lincoln Memorial Highway) west to SR-49. Turning right onto SR-49 we continue north passing a small herd of ten deer in the middle of a field. We cross over Flat Rock Creek, which has overflowed its banks. Passing through Antwerp, we cross the Maumee Scenic River and find ourselves in Hicksville, where Daeida Hartell attended private school before moving to Canton.

In 1883, Daeida married H. H. Wilcox, and traveling by train, they moved west, settling in Los Angeles where they purchased 120 acres of apricot and fig groves for $150 per acre. This property later became the Wilcox Subdivision, and in 1887, the subdivision name was officially changed to Hollywood, California, with street names including Sunset Boulevard. According to the Ohio Women's Hall of Fame, many of the streets and location names within this new subdivision were created using the names of friends and places from Daeida's hometown.

Randy Long was born in Hicksville in 1957. Growing up in northwest Ohio, Randy started singing at his grandma's house when he was a little boy. After church on Sunday morning, they would all go to grandma's house for dinner. When dinner was over, they would gather around the piano and sing just as loud as they could while grandma or Aunt Minnie played. Young Randy would get up at 6:30 AM on Saturday morning to watch *The Gospel Jubilee* on TV with his father.

Randy recalls, "I would listen to Dad sing every song and watch him come alive with the music of southern gospel."

After leaving home, Randy left his religious roots singing secular music for about forty years. Randy came back to Christ and, with the help of his good friend Gary Adams of Trinity, began singing for the Lord in May 2004. Since that time, he has traveled across the country from New York to Texas singing everywhere from private living rooms to state fairs. Randy has also appeared on the *Gospel Hour* and *Livewire* television programs. He has even sung on a Bahamas gospel cruise.

Leaving Hicksville, we head northeast on SR-2 passing through the town of Farmer. Immediately after driving through Williams Center, we turn right onto U.S. 6 and head east to SR-66. Turning north on SR-66 we travel to SR-2 and, in Archbold, we stop for a brief tour of Sauder Farm and Craft Village where you can often hear some good southern gospel music. Leaving Sauder Farm, we continue along SR-2 until we reach the town of Wauseon where we finally realize we missed Pettisville. Backtracking and with a couple of good guesses, we find the very small town of Pettisville, home of LaMar Yoder who sang in a gospel quartet in high school. In 1971, through the efforts of Roger Rupp, also a member of the high school group, the Messengers Quartet was formed using some of the members from his high school group. The group sang at the 1975 NQC in Nashville, Tennessee, and in 1981, they completed a cross-country tour traveling as far west as Iowa. They continued to minister as a part time group until 1985.

Back to Wauseon, we turn left on SR-108 taking it north to IR-80. Taking IR-80 east, we travel about thirty miles crossing the Maumee River. Traveling along IR-80, I'm reminded of a young lady named Carolyn Connor who, at the young age of four, traveled throughout the northern part of Ohio singing spiritual songs such as "Mansion Over the Hilltop." After paying the toll, we enter IR-75 and head north to Toledo, home of Tony Packo's and the Bun Museum where more than a thousand autographed (Styrofoam) buns line the walls. Tony Packo's has served Hungarian-style dogs since 1932, smoked sausage split down the middle with onion and chili over the top. They are also known for their deep-fried pickles and chili sundaes.

Adopted in 1946, Gary Herren was raised in Toledo and began studying classical piano when he was six years old. Shortly after beginning piano, he started learning the clarinet, and eight years later, he began playing the alto saxophone. In 1989, he asked Jesus into his life, and since that time, he now proclaims the gospel through his gift of music. Playing a medley of meditative and inspirational music, Gary has touched the hearts of many during his presentations at churches, fairs, and a variety of musical events.

* * *

The Soul Seekers were based in Toledo and started traveling full-time in 1984. One of the founders of the group, Wardell Langston, was born in 1926 and had previously sung with another Toledo group, the Pilgrim Wonders, for twenty-five years. Singing primarily in churches, the Soul Seekers traveled across America in their limousine until they came off the road in 2005.

* * *

Larry Orrell was born on January 27, 1944, right after World War II, in the Cherry Street Hospital in Toledo. His dad, Lloyd Orrell, a native of Weakley County, was born in 1907 and was in charge of OPA rationing in Toledo. Six months after Larry was born, the family moved to Detroit. His father was working for the National Life Insurance Company of Nashville, Tennessee, and later managed an automobile dealership for Chrysler/Plymouth. Many southerners had moved to Detroit to find work on the assembly lines of General Motors and Chrysler, and they would have gospel sings in local churches on the weekends.

Soon some of them got together and formed the Greater Detroit Gospel Singing Association, with Lloyd as president. Lloyd questioned why they couldn't bring groups like the Blackwood Brothers and the Statesmen up to Detroit for a concert. So he contacted James Blackwood and Hovie Lister, and they set a date. Lloyd rented the Masonic Temple Auditorium, which seats 4,678 people. The cost to rent that auditorium was steep, and the association backed out. They believed it was too much money to risk. So with their permission, Lloyd put himself on the line for all the expenditures and, on October 15, 1955, brought in the Blackwoods and the Statesmen. It was a huge success, the building was packed, and the police reported that another two thousand people were turned away. This event launched Lloyd Orrell's career as a gospel promoter.

Soon people were coming from Chicago, Indianapolis, and Dayton to attend the concerts in Detroit, and they began to ask why these concerts couldn't be held in their cities. It wasn't long before Lloyd was packing houses everywhere he promoted gospel music. When J. G. Whitfield was introducing the now-famous *Singing News Magazine*, he recruited the help of Lloyd Orrell and WB Nowlin. They agreed to mail copies of their concert lists in return for advertising.

At one Orrell production booked in Dayton's Memorial Hall, a new group named the Oak Ridge Quartet called James Blackwood and asked if he would convince Lloyd Orrell to let them sing a couple songs on the program that night. He said they would sing for free, and of course, the rest is history.

Larry was raised in this era when the Blackwood Brothers, the Statesmen, the Speer Family, and the Oak Ridge Quartet were booming. Growing up in that environment, Larry soon wanted to be a part of gospel music, and two days after he graduated, his dad put him on a plane to the Stamps School of Music down in Dallas, Texas. Also attending the school was Tony Brown, who is now the president of MCA Records. Two of the Blackwood boys, Terry Blackwood and Jimmy Blackwood, were there along with several other gospel music notables. Returning home, Larry put together a quartet called the Orrell Quartet. That quartet was comprised of Jim Murray, Walter "Buddy" Liles, John Marine, and Chuck Ramsey. They had been together for four years when Jake Hess asked Jim Murray if he would like to be part of the Imperials. Jim Murray joined the Imperials, and the Orrell Quartet broke up. Chuck Ramsey joined the Stamps Quartet, and Walter "Buddy" Liles went to sing for the Florida Boys, and John Marine became the pastor of Auburn Hills Baptist Church in Pontiac, Michigan.

Despite the Orrell Quartet breaking up, Larry believed God had given him a vision and decided he couldn't quit. He met a young man by the name of Gordon Jenson at Brightmoor Tabernacle where he worshipped. Gordon was fifteen years old and just starting to write songs, and Larry talked to him about his vision of gospel music. They soon found a guy by the name of Wayne Hilton who was just graduating from North Central Bible College in Minneapolis, Minnesota, and the three of them launched out singing Gordon's songs such as, "I Should Have Been Crucified," "Redemption Draweth Nigh," and "Tears are a Language that God Understands." These were significant songs, and because of the uniqueness of this fresh material, the Benson Company, Heartwarming, in Nashville, signed them to a contract, and soon the Don Light Talent Agency was contacting them. Gordon had three songs on the top ten airing on many of the southern gospel stations. Pretty soon, their little trio was in the forefront, and the Don Light Talent Agency began to book them, opening at times for the Goodman Family and at other times for the Oak Ridge Boys. A very interesting time for the group, they traveled for seven years until Gordon accepted a pastorate at the Bridemoor Tabernacle in Detroit, Michigan, and the group broke up.

Sometime later, Gordon moved to Nashville, Tennessee, and called Larry to see if he would be interested in moving to Nashville and reforming the group. Larry agreed and moved to Nashville, where he continued to live for twenty-eight years. Because of his father's influence, Larry took the spot opened by Lloyd Orrell's resignation from the Board of the Gospel Music Association and served five terms as a board member. The group disbanded when Larry joined the Gospel Music Association. Larry later worked with Dr. Paul Olson and with the Billy Graham Crusade as a soloist.

When Jake Hess left the Statesmen, Rosie Rozell talked to Larry about putting together another super group with Roger McDuff and the great bass singer London Paris. He had even talked with several piano players about playing for the group. He wanted Larry to manage that group as it would take somebody strong to keep a humble perspective with the kind of egos these stars could possess.

Larry still promoted gospel music and has actually promoted gospel music longer than his father. When he first started promoting, Larry had no interest in promotions as he was busy with evangelism and the ministry. However, there were two guys that wouldn't let it rest convincing him he needed to be promoting. Those two guys were none other than Eldridge Fox and Glen Payne. Stepping into his father's shoes was a big task, but they told him that if he would be willing to try, they would help him fill the auditoriums. At the time, there seemed to be a lull in southern gospel music, but he believed Glen Payne and trusted Eldridge Fox. These were two men of great integrity, and what they said tended to be the way it was. So a joint tour of the Kingsmen and the Cathedrals soon built interest back up in Indiana, Michigan, and Ohio.

After they had filled numerous auditoriums, Larry suggested separating the two headlining groups putting the Talleys with the Cathedrals and putting the Hinsons and Gold City with the Kingsmen. The Cathedrals began to grow in stature, and by the end, he was featuring them alone.

Larry says, "The gospel music industry needs to retain the kind of character that people like Glen Payne and George Younce maintained."

One day, Larry was sitting in Eddie Crooks's office in Hendersonville, Tennessee, and Eddie said to him, "Larry, if there's one thing you could do that is a dream of yours, what would it be?"

And he said, "Put together a super group. I would like to have a group that could just sing and not try to be funny, not try to work the people, and just sing great music and have great arrangements."

After tossing around some names, the idea sounded good, so Larry went to work making some contacts. He talked with some pretty big names like Larry

Goss who had picked an unknown singer named Michael English, a song "I Bowed On My Knees And Cried Holy,", and a slow tempo that turned it into a ballad and one of the epic songs of gospel music. Finally, a group evolved with Terry Blackwood, Chuck Sullivan, Big John Hall, and Larry called the Friends Four. Their first project was called "An Offering." Soon the Southern Baptist Convention opened the door for them to sing at Music California, and they became very popular in the California market. They sang at all of the big churches in California including Dr. David Jeremiah's church, and it wasn't long before doors were opening up in other big Southern Baptist churches. The group remained together for five years.

Reminiscing, Larry says, "Dayton will always hold a special place in my heart, and every group I have ever talked to says if they could sing anywhere, they would want to sing in Dayton at Memorial Hall auditorium."

Larry remembers the Speer Family singing at Memorial Hall, and the Nazarenes would gather in and shout and praise the Lord.

Larry says, "Probably two of the greatest influences in Christian music were Jake Hess and Hovie Lister. When the Statesmen hit the stage, they were a pretty classy bunch. When Rosie came in and started singing 'O What a Savior,' the Lord would often come down and bless the concert."

Larry remembers the first time Rosie Rozell sang with the Statesmen. It was in Dayton's Memorial Hall auditorium. His father was over on the wings watching Rosie sing, "Oh What a Savior," and Larry remembers tears streaming down his dad's face.

As of 2008, Larry is involved in ministry in Italy and Switzerland and Sicily. He and his wife, Ruth, live on a farm in Minerva along with his wife's eighty-five-year-old mother. They watch over her mom as she manages a farm that milks four hundred cows every day. Larry has even had the privilege of birthing some of the calves.

Larry says, "When I look back on my life, I see the hand of God. I have been through some storms, I have been through some battles, but I am like David—I was once young, now I am old, and I have never seen the righteous forsaken or His seed begging bread."

* * *

Henry Newsome was born in Sunflower County, Mississippi. Henry started singing with the Groover Harmonizers of Mississippi in 1946 and was with them for eight years. Moving from Mississippi to Memphis, Tennessee, he joined the Sunset Travelers in 1958 and stayed with them until 1962. While Henry was with the Sunset Travelers, his brother-in-law, wife, and daughter sang together in a group called the Zionettes in Mississippi.

While on their way to a concert in Durham, North Carolina, the Sunset Travelers were pulled over by the highway patrol. When the officer discovered the driver did not have a driver's license, he allowed them to continue on to their destination subject to one small requirement—he confiscated all of their instruments and amplifiers. They made it to the concert but had to sing without the use of instruments. They continued for almost a month, doing their engagements without any instruments until the equipment was returned.

Henry later moved to Toledo where he sang with the Pilgrim Wonders for a year. The Pilgrim Wonders started in Arkansas and moved to Toledo in the 1940s. After Henry's stint with the Pilgrim Wonders, he sang with his wife for five years in a duet called the Wheeler Singers until she passed away.

After the passing of his wife, Henry formed a family group called the Newsome Singers. The group consisted of seven members.

Henry says, "There be one who is not family, but all the rest of them is my kids."

The "kids" to whom he refers are his daughter, his two sons, a granddaughter, and a grandson. The group has traveled over thirty-one years singing in such places as Mississippi, California, Chicago, and New York.

The year 2007 was an exciting year for the Newsome Singers as they took third place in a singing competition held in Jackson, Mississippi, and had the new Swan Silvertones out of Pittsburgh, Pennsylvania, sing at their anniversary celebration. Henry is a great witness for Christ because, despite having only one leg, he lets other see that he can still do something for Christ even with a handicap.

Turning onto SR-25, we drive through downtown Toledo, passing the Hamilton Hotel and several historical buildings as we make our way to IR-280 where we travel south to IR-80. Great, another toll road! We continue in a southeast direction, crossing the Portage River to SR-53 where we exit the turnpike and travel south to U.S. 20. We cross the Sandusky River and soon reach Clyde, the home of Sherwood Anderson who, in 1919, wrote a collection of short stories called Winesburg, Ohio, a sarcastic telling of life in small-town America. Clyde is also the home of the Fisherman Quartet.

Larry Kessler has been in gospel music all his life. When he was just a little child, his dad included Larry, his brother, and two sisters on his radio broadcast until they were about the age of eleven. As Larry got older, he thought he knew a better way. He always tried to do things his own way, and that never did work.

When he was thirty-three, Larry again had a desire to sing gospel music, so he and his brother Jim Kessler, got together, and they started singing with the pastor's wife. Soon they decided they wanted to sing more and, as the pastor's wife couldn't leave the church, Larry approached Max Wright and talked to him about traveling with them. After Max accepted the position, they got together with Larry's daughter, Yvonne Kessler. She was eleven or twelve at the time and was going to play piano for the group. So the Fisherman Quartet was formed in 1973 and, soon after, added a bass singer—Ed Conrad, Jim's stepson. They continued with this lineup for a while, and then Larry's brother, Jim, replaced Yvonne, playing the piano for four or five years.

Their intention was to be fishers of men, and that's actually how they come up with the Fisherman Quartet as the name of the group. As they were always on the road, they didn't get to be in their home church, so Larry had a habit of studying his Bible through the week to have something to share with all the men as they traveled.

They started out traveling in a little van that soon got too crowded, so they started pulling a trailer. They traveled in this manner until 1978 when they met a boy in Kentucky who was selling a 4104 bus. It was a big dream of theirs to own a bus, but they could not afford it. So they started praying, and God provided. When they went to get the bus, everything worked out, and they were able to buy the bus, making payments to the owner. Having the bus helped out tremendously. They proceeded that way until 1983 when they updated to a Silver Eagle bus.

Larry says, "The group travels for nothing other than the Glory of God and to present gospel music to God's people, that all hearts would be blessed."

Years earlier, when they first started producing their tapes and records, they had gotten their bus, and the future was looking bright for the Fisherman Quartet, and Larry's dad sat him down and told him, "Now, son, the next thing you've got to look for and the next thing you've always got to keep in mind is pride because pride is going to hit you. Pride escapes no one. It hits every individual that's ever come or ever will come, and you be aware of that."

Larry left the group in 1987, and the group fully disbanded in 1990. Larry had never worked overtime on his job, but God had always provided.

But when he left the Fisherman, he started working a second job. Larry began running an auto repair shop out of his home while he continued to work at Ford Motor Company, a job he held almost forty years. He was working both day and night, and it wasn't long before he again developed a hunger for gospel music and started looking around for someone to sing.

In 1994, Larry went with a group called the Crimson River Boys in Alyria a good but short-lived group. In 1995, three of the original quartet members, Larry, Max, and Jim, started the Fisherman Quartet all over again. Soon after they reorganized, Jim decided to move back to North Carolina. Larry had a small recording studio in his home, and determined to continue for the cause of Christ, they chose to record both the bass and tenor parts on a track. Using the tracks, they went out singing four-part harmony with Larry singing the lead and Max singing the baritone. In their home church was a young singer named Larry Chumley whom they approached about singing tenor for the group. He was thrilled to death and was a terrific tenor singer until the Lord called him home.

They had been singing somewhere in West Virginia, and when they got ready to leave, the bus was sitting on ice and would not move. The wheels just kept spinning, and it would not move at all. Finally Larry said, "Fellas, we only have one choice. We'll have to push the bus."

The guys started laughing and said, "We can't push this bus."

Larry told them they didn't have any choice, so even though it sounded ridiculous, they agreed to give it a try. After a short prayer, the guys went out, got behind the bus, and pushed it off the ice. After moving the bus, they began to laugh in amazement. Returning to the bus, Larry reminded them, "The Lord always goes before every move we make, and there are a lot of things we won't understand. We simply have to believe."

Several of the group members went on to further their careers. Rusty VanSicle from Martin went on to sing country music. Doug Anderson now travels with Ernie Haase & Signature Sound. Michael Allen, who started singing with the Fisherman Quartet in 1983, left the group after about a year.

Born Michael Allen Hofacker to Norma Jeanne Hofacker, in Port Clinton on August 3, 1962, he learned about Jesus from his grandmother. Mike's grandmother volunteered him at age five to sing "Away in a Manger" at church. Mike later learned to read music while singing in the high school choir. Some time later, a trio was singing at his church, and he asked if they were interested in a bass singer. They liked the idea, and soon he was singing with the Melody Boys of North Ridgeville, home of the annual Buckeye State

Singing Convention. After singing with them for over three years, he joined the Fisherman Quartet. At the age of twenty-two, he joined the United States Marines, and while in the marines, he called a radio station looking for a group. Soon he connected with John Jarman who sang with the Dixie Melody Boys for a number of years. They formed a trio called Spiritwind.

Seven years after Mike came home from military duty, John Jarman's son Tony contacted him, and in 1995, he started singing with Phil Cross and Poet Voices. For the next few years they participated in all of the Gaither Homecomings. Because of the difficulty of pronouncing his name, Mike decided to simply use his first and his middle name when joining Poet Voices, and is known to most people simply as Mike Allen.

After Mike left Poet Voices, Bill Gaither invited him to remain, and in early 2000, while the Homecoming group was in London, England, bass singer Rex Nelon passed away. Mike sang bass on the video, and after he returned home, Guy Penrod contacted Mike asking him to be part of the Homecoming tour family.

Once Mike asked George Younce where he purchased the cologne he was wearing. George told him it was no longer available, but as he liked it so well, before they discontinued the product, George purchased several cases of the cologne. It wasn't long before Mike received a bottle of the cologne in the mail.

Mike was always available to fill in and provide the bass part but hardly ever sang any solos. He has been labeled by some as the only Stunt Singer in gospel music. After doing around a hundred videos, he stopped traveling with them in late 2006.

Since that time, he has sung with Ed Hill and the Prophets. He is also singing a part of an unnamed quartet featuring Johnny Minnick, Johnny's wife and son, along with Allison Speer. He has done some special projects with some of the other Homecoming members, and his first solo project entitled "Way Down Deep" was released on Crossbridge Records.

In 2006, Larry Chumley went to be with the Lord at the age of fifty after having a massive stroke. Jim Kessler, who had left the group in 1985, came back to be their tenor singer. Jim stayed until May 2007 when he again returned to be with his family. He was replaced by Brenda Babb. She and her husband, Dave, previously had their own little ministry going by the name, the Babbs. She now plays the piano and sings the alto part. She fits in well as a female vocalist even though they had always determined to be an all-male quartet.

In 2007, averaging fifty-two weekends a year, they decided to slow down and only did forty-nine weekends. They still possess the same attitude today singing for the glory of God, and they try to be a blessing everywhere they sing. They sang a song entitled, "Just Ask," and it talks about the old pilgrims. Larry says, "We can learn from our old pilgrims and from our old mentors. I am thankful for the men of old that have served God, and I'm thankful for them being a part of my life."

Passing the Whirlpool Corporate Training Center, we resist the urge to stop at the Twistee Treat (shaped like a giant soft serve ice cream cone) and leave the small town of Clyde. We miss our turn for SR-101, and after turning around, we take SR-101 south passing the boyhood home of General McPherson. Passing through Tiffin, we turn on SR-18 where we travel west and pass Heidelberg College, stopping at the BP for fuel and a restroom break. Back on the road, we continue through town a short distance to U.S. 224 where we travel west to the town of Findlay where in 1908, shoe salesman Tell Taylor sat on the banks of the Blanchard River fishing and wrote the song, "Down by the Old Mill Stream." The mill in the song was the Masamore Mill that once stood near his family's farm. The song sold more than a million copies after it was published in 1910. Several quartets were also formed in Findlay.

The Gospel Messengers, a male quartet, was organized in 1962 and traveled throughout the local area singing in churches, school auditoriums, and for civic organizations. Reverend Daniel Eshleman says of this group, "I have personally witnessed the change brought about in men's lives as a result of their honest, forthright presentation of the Gospel through singing and personal testimony backed up by a life that shows the change that only Christ can make."

* * *

The Evangels, got their start accidentally one evening when Ed Green, who was born in Middletown, joined a group of men at church to sing around the piano. They sang their first appointment on Palm Sunday of 1969. In 1970, one of the original members, Charles Rosson, was called to pastor a church and was replaced by Glenn Sprang who was born in Kenton.

* * *

In May 1998, Russ and Betty Brauneller put together a duet called Jericho Road. Before coming together, both of them had traveled through much of northwest Ohio singing with other gospel groups. They were a unique combination with Russ playing the bass guitar and the harmonica while Betty played the piano. In November 2000, Jesse Davila, a dedicated Christian with a Hispanic background, joined the group making it a trio. A couple years later, Joy Walker joined the group making it a quartet. Joy and her husband, Daryl, who ran sound for the group, later stepped down from the group to raise their family. They later started traveling together under the name Heartfelt Ministries.

In 2005, a young man who won a talent search at the Hancock County Fair caught the attention of the group. Soon this young man, Ernie Pagal, was singing with the group. Ernie was born in the Philippine Islands and grew up singing while riding his water buffalo on the way to the family farm. He moved to America in 1976 settling down in Findlay. Shortly after Ernie joined the group, they did a concert for TV 39 in Marion.

While working on their sixth project, the group was devastated when Betty Brauneller suddenly went home to be with the Lord. Her position was temporarily filled until October 2006 when Dan Clark joined the group making them, once again, a quartet. Dan grew up just outside of Carey and started singing at age three. Growing up Catholic, he sang in the church choir before joining the group. He also sang with a group called Living Branches.

Russ retired from the group in 2007, leaving ownership to Jesse and making it, once again, a trio.

* * *

The Sojourners started their group in 1991 as a contemporary Christian trio recording their first project of original music in 1992. As their popularity spread they began to sing at churches and festivals throughout northwest Ohio and Michigan. After a short breakup, the group was soon back on the road again, and in 1993, the group became a quartet. When Jim Baney left the group, he was replaced by Michael Bohn, who had previously traveled with Word of Life Ministries. By 1997, they were doing over eighty appointments a year, and after doing a project at the Gaither Studio, Bill Gaither invited the group to the *Back Home in Indiana* taping. It was apparent the focus of their ministry was beginning to change, and in 1998, the group became totally southern gospel.

Since then, the group has performed at several of the NQC Regional Artist Showcases, has been on several radio and television programs, and they had a number one song in Europe on the Internet radio. They once sang on a cruise ship as part of the Matt Hunt Gospelfest. Mark May, a good friend of the Booth Brothers, enjoys traveling with them from time to time as they tour the local area. In 2006, several of the members left to form a new group called Exodus based in McComb. Despite several personnel changes, the group continues to minister completely devoted to Jesus Christ not only through their ministry but through their personal lives as well.

OHIO 14

While in Findlay, we stop at the Tokyo Steak House for some great salmon and duck. Leaving Findlay, we follow SR-224 to SR-12 and head west. Entering IR-75, we travel south to SR-15 where we exit and travel east. After several miles, the route changes to SR-23. The sun is setting as we reach Upper Sandusky, home of Nancy Keeton.

Nancy was born in Upper Sandusky on June 5, 1969, and when she was about six months old, she became infected with a terrible disease. After being in the hospital for a while, the doctors soon informed her non-Christian parents that there was no hope.

In the meantime, God had impressed upon the heart of a local minister to go to the hospital and visit the family. Upon arriving at the hospital, the minister was informed that Nancy had just been pronounced dead by the doctor. Praying with her grieving parents, they both accepted Christ as Lord and Savior, and then while praying for Nancy, her life was miraculously restored.

Growing up, Nancy remembers, "Every Sunday morning, Dad would load all six kids in the station wagon, and we were soon off to church."

At age seven, Nancy started singing in church with her sisters in a family group called the Nunley Sisters.

At fifteen, she joined the King's Heirs from Ashland, Kentucky, and sang with them for three years. Then on June 10, 1989, she married Dan Keeton and sang with him in a trio called the Keetons before Dan joined the Dixie Melody Boys.

When he was sixteen, Dan Keeton joined the Veterans Quartet, from Leitchfield, Kentucky. Later he was awarded the opportunity to perform for two weeks with the Speer Family and the Singing Americans before moving to Branson, Missouri, where he joined the Blackwood Quartet and won first place in the Campbell's Ozark Country Jubilee Talent Competition. He also performed with a group from Louisville, Kentucky, called the Impacts for two years. He has filled in with Gold City, and in July 2004, he moved to Kinston, North Carolina. He joined the Dixie Melody Boys and was nominated as one of the top ten Horizon individuals of 2005.

Now living in Rush, Kentucky, Dan and Nancy recently formed a new group called the Dan Keeton Quartet. Singing with the group is Rick Grey of Morristown, Tennessee, who was formerly with Divine Purpose in Tennessee. When you hear him talk with that deep voice, you will know what part he sings. Also with the group is Chris Little of Baltimore, Maryland, who started playing piano at age four and, at age eleven, sang in a duet called Born Again Children. He later traveled with Squire Parsons's brother in a group called New Creations from Tennessee. He also traveled with the Faithful Quartet of Ansted, West Virginia, and the Prophets in Nitro, West Virginia.

Leaving Upper Sandusky, we travel southwest on SR-67 through farmland, passing through the town of Mareilles. Continuing along SR-67, we cross Tymochtee Creek and continue to Kenton, home of Jacob Wilson Parrot**,** the first recipient of the Medal of Honor. This award was presented to several soldiers for their participation in the Great Locomotive Chase, a military raid that occurred in northern Georgia on April 12, 1862. Volunteers from the Union Army stole a train in an effort to disrupt the vital Western & Atlantic Railroad, which ran from Atlanta, Georgia to Chattanooga, Tennessee. Also from Kenton is a man named Bud Motter. Before becoming a Christian, Bud Motter performed as a country artist. In 1995, Bud started singing in a gospel trio called Living Proof. In 1997, he left the group and continues today as a soloist.

* * *

Lillie Mae (Haney) Whitaker was born in Roundhead in 1940 and started singing with her dad and her sister when she was eight years old. Her dad wasn't always a Christian, and he used to play for square dances and other type events. After he got saved, he wouldn't do anything but gospel. So ever since Lillie was born, it's been gospel.

They were called the Haney Family. Her dad was a wonderful musician, and they were on the radio two times a week and were singing at all the local churches. Her dad taught her to play the straight guitar, and he played the electric. Her sister, Wilma, played the mandolin. Lillie met Molly O'Day when she was thirteen and started writing to her weekly. Molly encouraged her to continue singing, telling her she had a good strong voice. Lillie just adored her and thought she was the greatest singer and even tried to imitate her at first.

When Lillie was fourteen, Charles Whitaker, who was a talented mandolin player, joined the group. When Charles started with the group, they did a radio program every Sunday morning in Bellefontaine that was sponsored by the church and had a great following. They received almost three hundred letters a week! Lillie's dad wasn't comfortable doing the emcee work, so Lillie did all the advertising and the talking, trying to get people to come to church. Charles stayed with them, and they would practice all week getting ready for the broadcast.

Charles was twenty and Lillie was fifteen, and soon her mom was saying, "I think Lillie's struck on that mandolin player."

But her dad said, "No, she's just a baby to him. He wouldn't go with a little girl of fifteen."

Then, at fifteen and a half, she ran off to Kentucky and married him. Her dad was very upset. He quit playing with them and told them, "You'ns won't stay together six months."

For a long time, he didn't play with them, but eventually, he come back because he liked Charles quite a bit.

They had an old 1947 Greyhound, and it was a junker. Once while traveling down the road, the engine stopped running. They simply pulled off to the side of the road and parked the bus. It had a mind of its own, and it would start when it had cooled down a bit. They waited patiently, but it wouldn't start. Finally, Lily told the boys, "Boys, I believe if you would give it a little nudge down the hill, it would start rolling." So they all three got, out and going to the back of the bus, they gave it a push. About that time, along came an old truck driver just a flying down the road. Soon he was on the CB calling out for anyone to quickly confirm that he had just saw three guys pushing a Greyhound bus along IR-70.

Once they were scheduled to play for a New Year's Eve service in Steubenville. They had an old Silverside bus, but it wouldn't make the trip, so they had to travel by car. As the bass fiddle was too big to fit in the car, part of it was sticking out of the trunk. On the way to the church, it started pouring rain, so they had to cover the fiddle with plastic. When they got to the church, it was still raining so they had to back the car up to the door of the church to keep the fiddle from getting wet. After watching their struggle to keep that fiddle dry, the pastor took up a special offering to help them buy a bus. They soon purchased a bus from the Rhythm Masters. It was a good bus, and they drove it for about twelve years.

Lillie's dad had quit, but they were still doing the broadcast, and they weren't going to be defeated. Hiring several new members, they were soon on their way. When Lillie's dad was with the group, he played the electric guitar, and they sang southern gospel, but after her dad left the group, they switched to bluegrass because all Charles knew was bluegrass as he had patterned his playing after Bill Monroe. They started out calling themselves the Southern Gospel Singers but soon changed the name to the Dixie Gospelaires.

The Dixie Gospelaires kept going, playing primarily in Ohio and doing local events. Then they started booking in Indiana, Michigan, Kentucky, and soon they were traveling to places like Alabama and Georgia. They were playing every weekend, and after having three boys, it became somewhat difficult to travel. So when they got their big beautiful Silver Eagle bus, they put beds in the back. Then the wife of one of the group members would travel with them, and she would watch the boys while the group performed. As a result, the boys grew up on the bus listening to, and playing, gospel music, and they have become terrific musicians. These multitalented boys now travel on their own as the Whitaker Brothers. They sing some beautiful harmony patterned after Monroe and John Duffy. They sing gospel, but they sing life songs like railroad songs, flood songs, and songs that tell a story.

They had parked the bus one evening, and George was in the back almost asleep. Suddenly, he heard this little voice, "George, George, where am I George?" He quickly jumped up and whipped on the lights, and Jimmy Dutton was having a nightmare about being crushed. He had gotten clear out of the bunk and was hanging on the closet door swinging back and forth. It took a while, but they finally managed to get him awake and settled down.

In 1974, the Dixie Gospelaires received a call from Washington DC asking if they would represent bluegrass gospel for the entire United States. Lillie thought it was a joke, and thinking it was a Baptist preacher they knew, she said, "Okay, Doug, you quit joking."

The man said, "Beg your pardon? I'm from the White House in Washington DC. and we are having a special event. There will be many different types of music including Diana Ross and the Supremes."

She quickly acknowledged her error and agreed to sing for the event. It was a wonderful experience; they had people from all walks of life set up in tents between the Washington Monument and the Lincoln Monument. They received the key to the city and Lillie said, "Our eats were furnished. We were taken anywhere we wanted to go and nothing cost us. It was a trip we will always remember. Some of them people acted like they never heard of bluegrass, and we sold tapes galore."

While in Washington DC, Lillie went to the Smithsonian Institute and gave a talk explaining that bluegrass was the oldest music in the United States and that the banjo was the first instrument brought over to America. She also explained that gospel music was sung in the fields by African-Americans while they were working. She then told them that a man named Bill Monroe came along and put five instruments together and called it bluegrass. They made a film of that presentation and put it in the Smithsonian for schools to rent.

Once at a singing in Lake Placid, New York, the group was up on the stage doing an a cappella rendition of that great song "Precious Memories." While they were singing, a sweet spirit came over the place, and the lead singer began crying and moving around. With his eyes closed, he did not realize he had moved to the edge of the platform, and he fell off the stage. Unable to control themselves, the group burst into laughter to the point where they couldn't finish the song.

In 1975, they started booking with Monroe Talent Agency doing the big bluegrass shows, with people like Lester Flatt and Bill Monroe covering the gospel portion of the program. They played a number of big festivals like Berryville Festival, and they played one of the biggest bluegrass festivals in the United States, the Bean Blossom, held in Indiana, for twelve years. Lillie says, "I always tried to say something about the Lord when I was up there."

Once they told her, "Now you know we got people here from all faiths."

She responded, "I'll just talk about Jesus Christ and that He is a wonderful person to know and that we like singing about Him."

They developed quite a following, and their recordings began to be in high demand. They have been featured in the *Bluegrass Unlimited* magazine several times.

In 1981, Bill Monroe contacted them requesting they come off the road so Charles could drive his bus and sing bass in his quartet when he did a gospel number. Bill was Charles's idol since he was a little boy, so they moved to Nashville. After moving to Nashville, they were no longer doing gospel music, and after only one year, Lillie got very homesick and became tired of that life. They were also drifting farther and farther away from God, so after about two years, they moved back to Ohio and put their group back together with their son Jeff taking over the lead part.

Thanks to Bill Monroe, they've been on the *Grand Ole Opry* five times, and Lillie has written hundreds of songs. During a show in Canada in 2005, she was so surprised to hear her songs being sung over the radio. She enjoyed listening and was pleased with the way they had been arranged.

Lillie has always been dedicated to gospel music. She felt she had a great life and enjoyed it immensely. In January 2007, she had a heart attack. As a result, she was in the hospital four months and was laid up all summer recuperating. She hopes her lungs would come back to full capacity because she had a very strong voice prior to having health problems. She believes God has brought her this far, and He will bring her through. She says, "If it's His will for me to sing again, I will. If it's not, I'll just thank Him for all that He has allowed me to do and for letting me live."

The Dixie Gospelaires partake in an annual bluegrass festival held in Rosine, Kentucky. People come from all over the United States and the world for this event, and while there, they visit the restored homestead of Bill Monroe. On Sunday, they go out to his gravesite, and singing some of those old Monroe songs, they have a special church service that is televised locally.

Down through the years, they've worked hard traveling all over the country, and they even went to Athens, Greece, and Egypt. They all held jobs, so they took the money they received at the concerts and purchased a bus. Then Charles and Lillie would pay their musicians but put their share of the money into the bus. And it turns out that Lillie's dad's prediction seems miscalculated. During 2007, Charles and Lillie celebrated their fiftieth wedding anniversary.

Regarding the effect of their ministry, Charles said, "When people come up and tell you that a song changed their life, that's your reward."

Leaving Kenton, we head south on SR-31 crossing Painter Creek, which I'm sure is lovely in the daylight. To us, it is just a sign on a bridge. Shortly we pass through Mount Victory, and Byhalia welcomes us a few miles down the road. Then we pass through Somerville, a blur of darkness with a flashing yellow light. We make a pit stop in Marysville and then turn right onto U.S. 36. Merging onto SR-4, we pass the Ohio Reformation for Women Facility and continue to Irvin where we merge onto SR-161 and travel to Mechanicsburg, the home of Berry Maust.

Berry was born on May 27, 1968, and moved to Ohio at age seventeen. He started singing gospel music in 1987 with the Crestmen from Mount Crawford, Virginia. He later sang with the Gospel Echoes Prison Ministry from Goshen, Indiana. Barry now lives in Mechanicsburg and has been traveling full time with the Calvarymen Quartet in Flint, Michigan, since 1993. Nominated Michigan's Ambassadors of Good Will in 1976, the Calvarymen have been together since 1956.

Leaving Mechanicsburg, we head west on SR-29, passing through Mutual. We turn onto U.S. 36 and pass by the Johnny Appleseed Museum and arrive in Urbana where the movies, *Little Giants* and *Toy Soldiers* were both filmed. While living in Urbana, concert pianist Steve Adams worked in Xenia, and after the 1974 tornado, he wrote the song, "Peace in the Midst of the Storm." Steve also traveled with Doug Oldham as pianist for about six years and assisted Bill Gaither in the early years of the Gaither ministry. Steve has traveled for over twenty years performing piano concerts and choir arrangements. He has played for two presidents and has performed at the White House. Steve has been guest of such well-known evangelists as Billy Graham, Charles Stanley, and Jerry Falwell and has been on CBN, Trinity Broadcasting, Canadian, Dutch, and Swedish television. Steve is currently part of the Steve Adams Trio traveling with his wife, Jan, and his brother Nate.

* * *

Marion Monroe, known to all as Sis, sang with New Beginnings in Fairborn for eleven years, and one of the women in the group was totally blind. Leaving the group, she sang solo for about six months before joining Eastern Sky. One of the members of Eastern Sky, Larry Counterman, later joined the

Songsters in Akron. Another member, Matt Henry, now sings with a group called His Way2. Marion remained with Eastern Sky until 2004 when she left the group to form a new group with her husband, Bill Monroe, called His Call. Marion writes most of their songs, and One Accord has recorded some of her songs. The group was privileged to sing on a 2007 cruise tour with the Songsters and others.

Marion's son, Tim Monroe, sang with the Calvary Mountain Boys in Dayton for six years. He then sang with a group called Canaan's Creek in Urbana for another two years. He also sang with the Beacons for three years, and in 2005, he started a bluegrass group with his three children called the Monroes.

Leaving Urbana, we take U.S. 36 west traveling through Westville. We then pass through Saint Paris turning right onto SR-235. Heading north, we pass by Kiser Lake, but the view is limited because of the darkness. Turning left on SR-29, we pass through Pasco. Making another left onto SR-706 we cross over the Great Miami River and arrive in Sidney, home of the Spot Restaurant and the beautiful historic Shelby County Courthouse located in the center of the square. Materials for the courthouse construction, consisting of limestone, sandstone, and marble, were brought in on a canal boat. The 170-foot center tower is constructed with galvanized iron and features four clocks.

Allen Law started playing piano for Charles Feltner at age eighteen. Donna, Randy Miller's sister-in-law, started singing with them in 1980. Traveling together, Donna and Allen fell in love, and after getting married in 1982, they left the group. From 1985 to 1989, Allen and Donna traveled with the Crusaders of Columbus. In 1983, they formed a trio based in Sidney named Higher Calling. As a result of a name conflict, the group's name was changed to First Born in 1996.

Attending the same church, Wendall Davis, who had played bass for the Dayton Ambassadors for a number of years, agreed to play bass for the group. In 1997, they released their last project. Terry Knasel was with the group for a while, and when he left, Allen's daughter took his place.

Once they were singing in a little country church using an old upright piano when a mouse came out of the piano, causing Donna to stop singing. She screamed, "It's a mouse!"

Frightened by her scream, the mouse quickly ran away, and the singing continued.

Using much of their own material, they remained a family group until 2003. Allen has done some fill-in work with the Southern-Aires and took part in their fiftieth Anniversary celebration. Allen wrote the song, "It Won't Be Long" as recorded by the Down East Boys, and Allen's son Travis is working hard to carry on his heritage of gospel music.

* * *

Ralph Royse started singing in 1975 with an a cappella group in Sidney called the Masters Singers. The group traveled extensively singing many of those old songs we love so dear. While singing in Canada at an International Religious event, they stopped in Montreal and purchased some cheese at the request of someone back in Greenville. It didn't take long to realize that there wasn't room enough in their fifteen-passenger van for both them and the cheese. It might have been good cheese, but because of its horrible smell, the cheese was privileged to travel to its destination on the outside of the van.

In 1981, Ralph left the Masters Singers to form the Joy Quartet. They traveled together until 1988.

OHIO 19

Leaving Sidney, we follow SR-47 back to IR-75. We take IR-75 south to U.S. 36 where we exit to Piqua, home of Luther McCarty, the 1913 Heavyweight Boxing Champion. The Mills Brothers (John, Herbert, Harry and Donald) were all born in Piqua in the early 1900s. As the boys grew older, they began to sing in the choir, and after school, they would gather in front of their father's barbershop to sing and play the kazoo. Entering a contest at Piqua's Mays Opera House, and realizing he had lost his kazoo, Harry simply cupped his hands to his mouth and imitated the playing of a trumpet, thus the beginning of their unique sound. They had been called the "Four Boys and a Guitar," but on Sundays, they went by the name, the Mills Brothers. They signed a contract with CBS, making them the first African-American group to have a network show on radio.

OHIO 20

Leaving Piqua, we continue west on U.S. 36 to Covington where we turn left and travel south on S.R. 48. We pass a unique restaurant called Buffalo Jack's where you can get anything from a buffalo burger to turtle soup. Continuing along S.R. 48, we reach Ludlow Falls where for years the falls, covered in Christmas lights, provided entertainment to those who would travel long distances just to view the Ludlow Falls Christmas Display. From Ludlow Falls we continue south on S.R. 48 passing through Pleasant Hill to the Village of West Milton, where in 1927, *Songs of the Blessed Hope: A Collection of Standard Church Hymns* was published by one of the nation's best-known gospel composers and publishers—John Henry Showalter.

* * *

Sheri Ann LaFontaine was born in Tucson, Arizona on October 25, 1979. Her parents, John and Loretta LaFontaine started traveling as a duet in 1964. As their four children became actively involved in their ministry, they became known as the LaFontaine Family. Traveling throughout the country, the family would minister in song, and John would preach the Word.

Sheri's childhood dream was to be a gospel singer, and using her bed as a stage, she would often sing her little heart out. One time, she would be Karen Peck, and the next time Candy Hemphill. In 1994, Sheri set out to become a solo gospel artist, but when the Ruppes recorded her song "My Want's Been Changed," her plans began to change.

With a little help from Jeff Easter, Sheri was singing on the road full time with the Arnolds. Her dream had come true. While traveling with the Arnolds, they appeared on the Gaither video *Freedom Band,* singing "I Shall Not Be Moved" along with the Nelons, Jeff & Sheri Easter, and Jake Hess. Sheri also sang "I'm Glad" during a Gaither Homecoming concert. She remained with the Arnolds almost four years, and in 2003, she became a solo artist holding concerts as far away as the Philippines. Possessing excellent songwriting skills, her songs have been recorded by Kim Hopper, Lordsong, Sue Dodge, Brian Free & Assurance, and the Hoskins Family.

Leaving West Milton, we take SR-571 east crossing the Scenic Stillwater River and passing an elk reserve on the right. We continue east crossing over IR-75 and reach Tipp City, where the historical site of Snowball Flour is presently occupied by the Tipp Roller Mill & Theater.

For about fifteen years, the Jones Family Trio had a radio program on WQRP radio called *Keeping Up With The Jones.* The family generation before the Jones Family also had a group called the Roundtree Sisters, and they remained together for about four years.

* * *

Almost fifty years ago, a family group was formed calling themselves the Christian Pilgrim Quartet. The group was named after the church they attended and consisted of Jessie and Anna Tipton, Anna's sister Jewell Hall and their best friend Virgie Thacker. They sang mostly in the home church that Jessie pastored located in west Dayton. Their music was provided by Jessie playing an old Gibson electric guitar and their son, David, playing the accordion.

The group evolved into the Tiptons and their children over the years. Jessie and Anne Tipton raised their children singing southern gospel music around the dinner table. In the early days, they styled themselves after the Rambos and the Chuck Wagon Gang. Over the years, the group's style has evolved, and today, they play and sing mostly southern gospel.

In 1995, during a watch-night service, Greg Tipton asked his grandpa if he could sing bass with the group. After Jessie, his grandpa, told him he didn't think he could carry a tune in a bucket, he agreed to give him a try. Now the group consisted of family members from three generations, and they changed their name to the Kingsway Quartet.

After mom and dad decided to stop singing and Willena left the group, their sons Mark and Eric, along with two of their children Greg and Erica continued singing under the name Kingsway. Although Greg only remained with the group for about six years, Erica continues to sing, and along with Mark, Eric, and pianist Joan Billheimer, they make up the current version of Kingsway. In addition to Eric, Erica writes some of the group's music, including one of their current favorites, and the title of their latest project, "A Crown of Life."

Leaving Tipp City, we continue east on SR-571, crossing the Great Miami River. We wind through some hilly farmland to New Carlisle, where on June 10, 1933, the infamous John Dillinger committed his first bank robbery, taking $10,000 from a bank that occupied the building on the southeast corner of Main Street and Jefferson Street.

In 1936, Roy J. Plunkett left New Carlisle to become a research chemist at a company in Deepwater, New Jersey. Then on April 6, 1938, Plunkett was checking a frozen container of tetrafluoroethylene, a chemical used in refrigerant production. When he opened the container to remove some material for chlorination, nothing came out. He discovered that a white powder had formed that did not adhere to the container. The tetrafluoroethylene in the container had polymerized into a waxy solid with amazing properties such as resistance to corrosion, low surface friction, and high heat resistance. Roy had discovered the material we now refer to as Teflon.

Also from New Carlisle, the Burress family has carried the gospel of Jesus Christ to many people through their music ministry for over thirty years. As a child, Tom Burress learned to play several instruments, and by age nine, he was both singing and writing songs. His songs have been recorded by several artists including the Cooke Brothers. Vonda Burress started singing and playing the organ at age six and picked up the piano five years later. In April 2005, their daughter Amber started singing with the family. They have been privileged to sing with several of the nation's finest groups.

Returning Home

Leaving New Carlisle, we take SR-235 south to Medway where we enjoy dining at the Melody Restaurant, a great place to get some delicious broasted chicken and a dish of their famous coleslaw. Leaving the restaurant we head north on SR 235 to U.S. 40 where we turn left and travel west crossing Taylorsville Dam. We enter Vandalia and the end of Tour No. 1.

BLUE GRASS GOSPEL AIRES

CHRISTIAN FAMILY SINGERS

GIBBONS FAMILY

* Rodney Griffin

* Rodney Griffin with
GREATER VISION

APOSTLES

PROMISED HEIRS

PROMISED HEIRS

ACCLAIM

TRINITY

MESSENGERS

Lloyd Orrell

Larry & Ruth Orrell

ORRELLS

PILGRIM WONDERS

FISHERMEN

* Mike Allen

Mike Allen with PROPHETS

JERICHO ROAD

SOJOURNERS

Nancy Keeton with
DAN KEETON QUARTET

DIXIE GOSPELAIRES

Barry Maust with CALVARYMEN

JOY

MILLS BROTHERS

LAFONTAINE FAMILY

JONES FAMILY

KINGSWAY

Chapter II

Monroe Tour

From the Depths of My Heart

It hasn't been a bed of roses since I started on my way
And Lord you know I'm not complaining,
there's just something I should say
For I've reached desperation and I've stumbled since my start
I've grown weary thru the years now I'm crying
bitter tears, from the depths of my heart

It's not a prayer from my lips, it goes much deeper than words
It's not a worthless expression I just need to be heard
For Lord I need to reach Your throne I know exactly what I'll do
I'll just fall down on my knees I know you will hear
the pleas from the depths of my heart

From the depths of my heart, Lord, I'm calling out to you
For I need you to lead me, I've done all I can do
Lord I'm trying to do my part to see that others make it through
And I know I don't deserve You, still I'm trying hard
to serve you from the depths of my heart

—Sonya and Ben Isaacs
(Used with Permission)

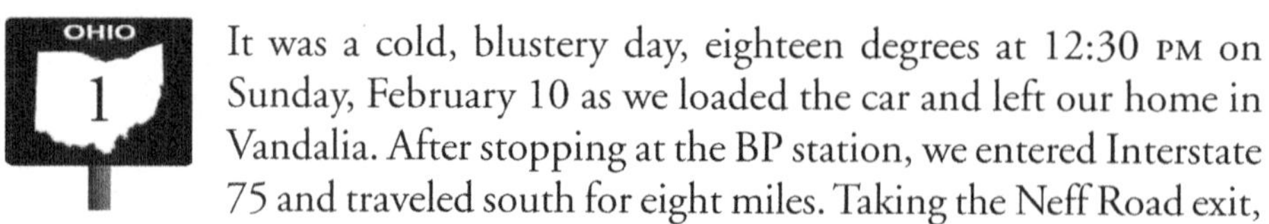

It was a cold, blustery day, eighteen degrees at 12:30 PM on Sunday, February 10 as we loaded the car and left our home in Vandalia. After stopping at the BP station, we entered Interstate 75 and traveled south for eight miles. Taking the Neff Road exit, we followed Neff to Dixie Avenue, turned left, and stopped at Marion's Pizza for lunch. Started in 1965, Marion's is famous for their wonderful pizza and numerous photographs of famous actors and actresses who visited Marion's while performing at Memorial Hall. After a delicious pizza, we head south on Dixie to IR-75. Turning left on Stanley Avenue, we discovered the ramp was closed and had to turn around driving all the way back to Marion's to take another ramp. Finally back on IR-75 we head south to Dayton where we continue through major construction another eight miles to the Dryden Road exit where making a huge loop we turn onto Dryden Road and enter Moraine. Sometime in the early 1960s, a levee was constructed by the Miami Conservancy District providing protection to a portion of Moraine from potential flooding of the Great Miami River.

Moraine was the home of John Burke and the Layman Trio, a bluegrass group that formed in 1971. The group received a four-star rating by the *Bluegrass Unlimited Magazine*. John Burke is a former alcoholic who gave his heart to Jesus and dedicated himself to serving others. John loved to cook, and he always took good care of his fellow group members. It is said that he rarely slept in his own bed as he was always taking someone in for the evening.

On one occasion, the group was trying to drive their bus up Barnes Mountain located just south of Irwin, Kentucky. The bus wouldn't make it, so they had to back the bus down the hill. They put cardboard in front of the radiator and made their way slowly to the top of the mountain—about ten feet at a time. Once at the top, they sang at a little church for about fifteen people. But the trip was well worth the effort as one young girl gave her heart to Jesus during the service. After the service, the group was invited to the pastor's small log home. The cabin was so small that Larry Polley couldn't stand up straight inside, but that did not stop them from sharing a wonderful time of fellowship.

Larry Polley was with the group for thirteen years altogether. He was also with the Faithful Travelers from Xenia for five years and then sang with the Wilson Brothers for three years. Most recently, Larry has enjoyed ten years with Dayton's Grace Brothers.

Leaving Moraine, we continue south on Dryden Road and crossing Sellars Road we are reminded of a local group from the village of Miami Shores, located just across the Great Miami River. The group was called New Life Trio and they started singing in 1968. Traveling in a van and later using a sound system the purchased from Rick Doran, they continued singing for about 21 years. Reaching Central Avenue we turn right and drive through West Carrollton, home of the Appleton Paper Mill where millions of gallons of water flow through the plant daily. West Carrollton was also home of the Glorylanders Quartet who formed in 1971 and enjoyed eleven years of ministry.

* * *

Steve Ladd was born in Dayton's Miami Valley Hospital on June 10, 1976, and grew up in West Carrollton. His father had moved up from Tennessee looking for work and settled in the area taking a job with General Motors. His father quit the job at GM to become an evangelist, and when Steve was seven, the family moved to Greenfield for two years and then moved to Hillsboro, remaining there until they moved out of state. Growing up, Steve's brothers and sisters all learned to play instruments, and the family traveled as the Ladds until 1995. After singing in the family group, Steve sang with Southern Heritage from Apex, North Carolina, for six months.

One day while working in a music store, Steve encountered Duane West. Duane was a good friend of Terry Carter, a member of the Anchormen Quartet, and he agreed to put in a good word for Steve. Soon Steve was singing tenor for the Anchormen of North Carolina, and he remained with them for about eight years.

Once while traveling with the Anchormen, they were at a concert, and thinking he had plenty of time before he had to sing, Steve went to the restroom. Just as he had made final preparations to use the restroom, he heard someone announce, "And here are the Anchormen."

So much for "rest."

Growing up, Steve attended many of the events held at Dayton's Memorial Hall, and one of his favorite groups was Gaston, Alabama's, Gold City. He had purchased all of their recordings and had learned most of their songs. While still singing with the Anchormen, he was offered a position with Gold City. This was a dream come true, and soon he was singing the tenor part for Gold City, becoming the first Yankee to join the group. Steve struggled at first trying to be someone he was not but soon realized the importance of being himself, and now he sings with a newfound freedom.

Gold City sang for Reverend Jerry Falwell shortly before he passed away. The event left an impression on Steve as he clearly remembers the excitement expressed by Reverend Falwell as they sang.

In 2001, while living in North Carolina, Steve married a young lady named Dayna. After becoming a member of Gold City, he and his family moved to a small town in Alabama. The town they live in is so small it only has one stoplight, but it is home, and on those rare Sundays when Steve is not on the road, he enjoys going to church with his family.

Although Steve no longer lives in Ohio, when passing through the area, he loves to stop at the White Castle Restaurant for some of those delicious little hamburgers.

Leaving West Carrollton, we continue south on Central Avenue following the Great Miami River to Miamisburg. In 1986, Miamisburg was the scene of a serious train accident when several freight cars derailed while passing through town along the west side of the Great Miami River. Miamisburg holds claim to one of the largest conical Indian mounds east of the Mississippi River and is also home to three talented groups.

The Kegley Sisters (Hester, Edith and Mary) began singing as young ladies. They previously sang with Mildred (Brown) Patrick and Emily Wells in Morehead, Kentucky. Hester got married and moved to Dayton. Edith moved to Garden City, Kansas, after she got married. In 1958, Mary went to live with her sister Hester and was married in 1959, after which she moved to Garden City, Kansas, as well.

Mary moved back to Dayton in 1961 and began attending church. She soon gave her heart to the Lord and began singing with her sister Hester and Hester's husband, Carl T. Hall. In 1964, Edith and her husband, Earl, moved to Dayton, and the three sisters started singing together as the Kegley Sisters. They were soon traveling all over Ohio, Kentucky, Tennessee, and Indiana.

Their first long-play album came by the generosity of two members of the Miamisburg Freewill Baptist Church, Carl and Dottie Smith, who provided funding that allowed the group to record. Carl Smith also made contact with the people who operated the *Midwestern Hayride* program, and the Kegley Sisters were scheduled to sing, but the program was discontinued before the group's appearance. The group made a second recording at Rose's Recording Studio in

Vandalia owned by Paul Mullins. They continued to sing until 1971, traveling by car and using whatever sound equipment was available at the churches where they sang. The Kegley Sisters sang beautiful harmony, and they possessed a wonderful blending of voices reminiscent of the McGuire Sisters.

Mary's husband, Roger Ready, and Lawrence Bishop were very good friends. When Lawrence was about fifteen years old, he played on a long-play album with Roger. They remained very good friends, and when Roger and Mary took the pastorate at a church in Richmond, Kentucky, Lawrence agreed to place them under the direction of the Solid Rock Church.

In 1972, Mary began singing with her daughter Sue and Glenda Elam. They called themselves the Melodyettes and frequently sang with the Marlow Brothers throughout the 1980s. They also frequently sang at the CB Coffee Breaks. One evening, after singing in Dayton at a church on Mia Avenue, one of the group members was nearly run over by two girls in a car. The reasons remain unknown, and the group was not deterred. The Melodyettes continued singing until 1982.

* * *

The Parks Quartet formed in 1969 with Clyde Parks singing bass, Mary Parks singing alto, Lucille Peters singing tenor, and Linda Vorhis, daughter of Mary and Clyde, singing lead. They traveled and sang throughout the Midwestern states. They were once privileged to do the gospel portion for the Country Music Show in New Castle, Indiana featuring Hank Snow and Ernest Tubb.

One evening while traveling home from Indiana, the group was caught in a major snowstorm. They were forced to spend the evening at a nearby motel and the entire group, including Linda Vorhis's two children, had to share one room. As there was no place to eat, they had to eat peanut butter and crackers out of the motel vending machine. Snow continued to fall through the night, and the next morning, it was so deep it almost reached the door handles on the van. Eventually, no doubt with help from local snow removal services and the sun's warmth, they were free to return home.

Both Francis Chamberlain and his son, Mike Chamberlain, were with the group at one time. Francis later played steel guitar for the Crusaders and the Dayton Ambassadors. The Parks Quartet continued singing together until 1976.

* * *

The United Gospel Singers started singing in the early 1960s when two sisters along with their husband and one other person began traveling around with the sisters' evangelist father. At first, they were a female trio with the men playing the instruments. The group maintained a low level of promotions, singing primarily in churches when invited. Money was never an issue, and they could often be found along the side of the road eating bologna sandwiches on the way to their next concert. The group continues to sing today as a female quartet.

Leaving Miamisburg, we turn right onto SR-725, cross the river, and drive up the big hill. Topping the hill, we continue west, passing by the Dayton Ambassadors' bus, to SR-4 where we turn left and travel south. Continuing to where SR-725 leaves SR-4, we turn right on SR-725 and drive a short distance to Germantown, settled in 1804 by German-speaking settlers and home to the Wright Family.

The children of Nathan and Willa Wright started their musical heritage back in the 1920s when three little boys, Dale, William, and Paul Wright sang together on radio station WSMK as the Three *W*s. The Wright family moved to Germantown in 1936, and in the early 1940s, with only a guitar accompaniment, they created the Wright Family Ensemble made up of family members and their spouses. They traveled for a number of years and even sang on the *Arthur Godfrey Show*. In 1953, the family retired from the active concert circuit after the untimely death of oldest brother, Dale Wright.

After some time passed, three of the Wright sisters formed a trio and, wanting to retain the family name, called the group the Blendwright Trio. They soon became regulars on the weekly WHIO TV program *At Home with Brother James* that lasted for nine years. The group, traveling in an old airport limousine, ministered throughout the world singing primarily in African-American churches.

Eleanor Wright played piano for the group and has written a number of songs, one of which was recorded by the Talley Trio. Alice Thomas took over on piano and became a mainstay for the next twenty years. Alice grew up both watching and listening to the piano playing of Eleanor Wright and the famous Harmoneers, a secular group. Residing in West Carrollton, she currently plays piano for solo artist Maxine Jones.

During those years when the Blendwright Trio was traveling, there was still some cultural unrest. Truly a blended group, the Blendwrights were a mix of black and white singers and so had to use discretion when choosing their stops along the road. Once, while touring in New York City, a church deacon questioned whether they really got along while traveling on the road together.

Larry Blackwell developed a close relationship with the Blendwrights, and the trio backed him up on some of his solo performances. Larry was born on July 1, 1938, and his family moved to Ohio while Larry was a child. Starting his music career at a young age, Larry could be found in church at age six standing on a stool singing "Amazing Grace." Larry developed his musical ability during high school by singing with a gospel quartet. From 1959 to 1961, while attending the Southern Missionary College in Collegedale, Tennessee, he sang with a group called the Southernaires. Larry continued his education at the Cincinnati Conservatory of Music.

While working with the Blendwrights, Larry maintained a solo ministry on a weekly TV show in Dayton for seven years. Leaving the Blendwrights, he continued in active solo ministry and later established a couple record labels known as Black Label in Lexington, Kentucky and Black Pearl. In conjunction with Jimmy Rhodes, Larry has developed a musical therapy program, which he presents all over the country at retirement homes, assisted living facilities, and nursing homes. His son now carries on the legacy as vice president of EMI Gospel, Black Gospel Division, in Nashville, Tennessee.

* * *

Ernest Carter and the Hymn Trio started in 1962 and continued until 1970 when the group disbanded. Ernest later relocated to Kentucky and formed a group called Ernest Carter and the Bluegrass Hymn Trio. They are still traveling occasionally. Ricky Todd began singing with the group when he was only eleven years old.

Ricky later played steel guitar for the Southern-Aires of Dayton and the Singing North Family in Mount Orab. Ricky also played with Loretta Carter and the Sounds of Praise and was with Lawrence Bishop for four years.

Loretta Carter sang with her sisters as the Vaughn Sisters of Franklin before forming the Sounds of Praise. The Sounds of Praise started in Germantown as a trio with a live band in 1972. They began traveling in a van, and the last couple years, they traveled in a Silver Eagle bus. They performed several concerts at Memorial Hall in Dayton but sang primarily at churches covering twenty-six states and parts of Canada. They traveled part-time until 1982 when they relocated to Orlando, Florida, and became a full-time group.

Once while the group was traveling south on IR-75 on their way to Florida, they were crossing the Jellico Mountain, and one of the engine injectors stuck. They pulled the bus over and were forced to leave it along the side of the road until the next morning when it could be towed to a local garage.

While living in Florida, their piano player, Stanley "Junior" Chism, went to a local mall one evening and never came home. His car was found, and although his body was never found, police reports indicate he was murdered. The group came off the road in 1988 shortly after this tragic event.

Another member of the group, Kelly Back, traveled with the Hinsons for a while. He now does studio work in Nashville, Tennessee.

Leaving Germantown, we turn left onto Cherry Street, cross Twin Creek, and continue to Sugar Street where we turn left toward SR-123. Turning left onto SR 123, we continue east, passing through the village of Carlisle on our way to Dayton Oxford Road. Before leaving Carlisle, we hear the sound of a train whistle, and just ahead, the gate starts dropping across the road. We sit watching as sixty-eight train cars pass by. Soon we're on our way and crossing the Great Miami River again, we turn right onto Dayton Oxford Road and head south where turning onto River Road, we arrive in Franklin. The famous race horse Belmont was born and bred in Franklin and was taken to California in 1853. Talk about fast-moving, the Hoskins Family came on the scene and climbed to the top very quickly.

God, who is the giver of all gifts and abilities, equips individuals with talent and places within them the desire to use that talent for Him. Through prayer, trust in God, and obedience to His will, those desires are fulfilled and the results are immeasurable. Rick Hoskins, his wife Reva, his daughter Angie (Hoskins) Aldridge, collectively known as the Hoskins Family, saw those results as God took their ministry to new heights over and over again. Rick is carrying the torch as his father was a member of a bluegrass group known as the Country Gospel-Aires.

The Hoskins Family's first top 40 song, "Mission Of Love" was written by Angie for her grandfather, who is also her pastor.

Their ministry was solely committed to their home church until the retirement of Reva's father from the pastoral ministry in 1998. It was then that God began to call the Hoskins Family into a different venture. Their next single "Help Me Stand" became their first top 20 hit, reassuring them that they were headed in the right direction. Within eighteen months, the Hoskins Family had a top 5 hit with "Joyful Morning." Danny Jones, editor of the *Singing News Magazine*, described their *Jaywind* project "Safe Thus Far" as the definitive recording to which all their others will be compared and it reached number one on the charts.

The Hoskins Family has recorded some of the most memorable songs in recent years including another number one hit entitled "When the Savior Wipes the Tears." Promoters and pastors all across the country have quickly recognized the Hoskins Family's potential. They appeared in a number of major events including the NQC, Dollywood, Branson's *Silver Dollar City*, Gaither Homecoming Tours, ISPN and TBN. Angie (Hoskins) Aldridge, born in Middletown on May 17, 1973, possesses a rare voice. In 2006, Angie busted a vocal chord and had to stop singing for a while.

Around that same time, Reva's father passed away. He was a pillar of strength to the family, and soon the Hoskins Family, after having nine Dove Award nominations, decided to come off the road. Angie remains active through her work through Angie Hoskins Promotions promoting such artists as Gerald Crabb, Crabb Revival, the Benge Family, and the Maharreys.

After singing at a church in Castalia, a lady came up to Angie and shared her story. She told Angie that recently her life was falling apart. Experiencing a divorce and losing her family, she had no desire to live. So she decided it was time to end the misery. She was in her car and had the pistol in her hand. She confessed that she had never been fond of gospel music, but for some reason, when she turned the radio on that day, it was on a gospel station. The song that was playing was "Safe Thus Far." As she listened to the words of the song, her attitude began to change, and right there in her car she gave her life to Jesus.

* * *

Ken Ankney was born in February18, 1955, in a house somewhere in Kettering because his mom and dad said he was going to be born in a house, so the doctor made a house call.

His first exposure to southern gospel music came in 1966 when they moved to Michigan, and his father became pastor of a local church in Crump, Michigan. A singing family named Abilious was previously scheduled to perform at the church, so his father allowed them to sing, and they sang quite a few Gaither songs including that great old song "He Touched Me."

In 1970 in Lebanon, Ken took a group of guys that had never sung before, and one who had just returned from the army, and formed a group called the Ambassadors. The group stayed together about two years.

He then did a small stint for a year with a local church group called Third Generation in Trenton, and in 1972, Ken joined Paul Roark and the Maranathas, a mixed group from Carlisle. The group moved to Tennessee and started traveling full-time as the Roarks. In 1977, he joined the Blessings Unlimited and was with them for five years, leaving just before their tragic bus accident.

In the early 1980s, Ken joined the Apostles of Columbus along with Maurice Frump on piano, lead singer J.R. McNeil, baritone Jim Black, and bass Dale Murphy.

In 1983, while singing with the Apostles, Ken was working as a painter for Koogler Painting in Centerville and wasn't making much money. They took a Sunday evening appointment to sing at Grace Memorial Church in Columbus. They had a wonderful time, and before the service was over, revival was in the air. During the service, Ken shared that his son Bradley was just born, and for some reason unknown to the doctors, Bradley's body had turned blue from his head to his waist. They were fearful they were going to lose him.

After the service the pastor, desiring to keep the revival spirit going, told Ken, "I will pay your salary so you can spend every day at the hospital with your wife if you will come up every night to do a revival with us."

This situation suited everyone as Ken would spend the day at the hospital with Bradley, and then go straight to revival every night. The revival lasted two weeks and was an unbelievable event. People were being drawn in off the streets. Individuals passing by in their cars would pull over, come into the church, and end up getting saved. Amazingly, the pastor never preached one sermon during the two-week revival—all they did was sing. Ken believes the sacrifices that were made allowed the Holy Spirit to work freely.

Ken took a break from singing until Charlie Feltner called him indicating the Crownsmen were in need of a tenor singer. He deliberated for a month and then agreed to fill the position. In 1986, he went back on the road singing with the Crownsmen, and he stayed with them until 1991.

After singing with the Crownsmen, Ken helped form the Blessings Quartet along with his brother Michael and Jerry Coulter. They group lasted less than a year.

Later Jim Roundtree, who had played piano for the Blessings, called Ken requesting he come over to Towne Boulevard Church as they were putting together another group. Ken agreed to join them. With the addition of baritone Dale Hausman, the Townsmen Quartet was formed. Bill Phelps later replaced Roundtree at the piano. Wendell Dennis, bass singer for the Townsmen attended church with Jim Hill, who was at that time the music director of Towne Boulevard Church of God.

The Townsmen were in Ashland, Kentucky, at a Baptist church, and while preparing the song list, a disagreement arose as to which songs they should sing. Suddenly, Dale Hausman spoke up telling them they would simply choose songs as the Holy Spirit lead. As they made their way to the platform, there still seemed to be a little unrest, but when they stepped out onto the platform, it was as though a curtain opened and a new day had dawned. The service was unbelievable, the singing went smoothly, and one entire family got saved—mom, dad, and all three kids gave their heart to the Lord.

In 1999, his son Bradley Ankney told Ken, "Dad, I want to sing."

That's all it took, and Ken left the Townsmen to form a new group called Touch of Grace with Bradley singing lead, Mike Miller singing baritone, and Jerry Coulter singing bass. Because of health problems, Jerry was later replaced by Dale Hausman.

After singing for a while Touch of Grace came off the road because of conflicting work schedules. About a year later, as work and school schedules eased up, Bradley suggested, "Why don't we just go ahead and pick up."

So they found a lead singer whose name was Ben Liston, and with Dale Hausman singing bass, they formed the Keystones. Now with Justin Sayger singing bass they continue to travel under the name of SonShip Quartet.

* * *

Doug Oldham was born on November 30, 1930, in Akron, Indiana. When he was three years old, the family moved to Dayton where they attended the West Third Street Church of God. While in Dayton, Doug sang for the Inland Manufacturing Choir. He ventured out in a solo ministry in 1945 while singing with the Roosevelt High School Choral Club. Later that same year, the family moved to Anderson, Indiana. In Anderson, he arranged the Christian Brotherhood Hour program and began a four-year stint traveling with the Christian Brotherhood Quartet.

Doug later moved back to Middletown to work in the music department at Pastor Cliff Hutchinson's church. Moving to Franklin, he lived for five years in a big white mansion built in 1848 and located along the Great Miami

River. He moved back to Anderson, Indiana, where he worked with both Bill Gaither and the Slaughters. Before going on the road as the Gaither Trio, Bill Gaither played piano for Doug Oldham. Concert Pianist Steve Adams also traveled with Doug Oldham for about six years.

Doug has won GMA awards and was inducted into the Gospel Music Hall of Fame. Doug Oldham introduced that beautiful song "He Touched Me" as written by Bill Gaither but is perhaps best known for his rendition of the great song "The King Is Coming." He is presently on staff at the Thomas Road Baptist Church, which was established by Reverend Jerry Falwell.

* * *

Martin Neal was born on May 7, 1938, in a little town called Hawk's Nest, West Virginia. The house where he was born was located between the railroad and the river. If you went out the front door of the house and took about three steps off of the porch, you were on the railroad track. If you went out the back door and went down the steps, you were on the boat dock. One winter, Martin was traveling to town with his family when a wreck occurred. Both his mother and his younger brother were killed. His father received multiple injuries, and Martin received one small cut on his head.

Martin's father later remarried, and he was forced to go live with his grandmother on a little hillside farm in West Virginia on a total income of $60 a month. Over the years, he loved to listen to music, probably because his aunt Anna had a great voice and absolutely loved to sing those old gospel songs. His aunt Anna didn't like to drive, so they would get in the old truck, and Martin, age thirteen, would drive them to church. While riding along in that old truck, they would sing their hearts out.

Somewhere along the line, Elvis came on the scene and later the Crew-cuts. Martin began singing more and more of their music since it was the contemporary sound of the era. He still continued to sing those gospel songs, and one day, his grandmother heard him singing a gospel song. It was not her kind of music, and she said something to his aunt Anna.

Aunt Anna said, "Listen, Mother, he could be singing that other stuff that Elvis and all those pop groups are singing."

With this in mind, his grandmother never again complained about him singing those southern gospel songs.

While singing in a high school chorus, they performed at an Easter sunrise service held at a state park called Hawk's Nest. In high school, he sang with a quartet called the Lost Chords. None of them were Christians, but the churches allowed them to sing with the prayer that they might eventually bring those young boys to the Lord. At age twenty-nine, Martin accepted Christ as Savior, and looking back, Martin simply says, "Bless those churches that believed."

He began singing with a quartet in the church where he was saved. They didn't have a name, but they sang every opportunity they received. He later directed music at a start-up church, and once they could hire their own music director, he moved on to a church located in Carlisle. He immediately got back into singing with three other guys that loved music, and they sang together for a number of years, again, without a name.

Sometime later, while talking with Gary Bates, Martin indicated they ought to try singing together. Gary Bates was the son of a minister who for thirty-five years had a southern gospel radio program in Rushville, Indiana. His father won an award from Daywind for successfully keeping the program on the air so many years. Gary grew up singing with his family in the church and, at age fourteen, started singing with the Chapel Keys from Andersonville, Indiana. He was drafted to Vietnam in 1968, and shortly after returning from Vietnam, he was married. In 1969, he started singing with a group called New Happiness, a mixed quartet based in Dayton.

In 1996, Martin and Gary, along with Lucy Boyer and Ken Wagner, formed the Waymakers. During one of their community concerts at a church in East Dayton, they got up to sing and discovered they were having major problems with the sound system. But good news is good news, and five decisions were made for the Lord that day despite the technical difficulties. Another time, at one of the Waymakers' more memorable concerts, they sang to a crowd of only twelve people. After singing for at least forty-five minutes, those twelve people loved it, wanting them to keep singing. Yet another time, Gary showed up for an event, and as he went to change clothes, he found he had left both his tie and his socks at home. Gary realized he would be dressing in a more contemporary style that day. The Waymakers stayed together for nine years, and as the group's priorities began to change, the group fell apart.

Gary's next opportunity came when Mike Miller, who previously sang with Touch of Grace, called wanting to start a new quartet. Working together, they formed an all-male quartet called Higher Ground. They were privileged to open for the Blackwood Brothers at a concert held in 2006. When the concert was over, the tenor singer, who had previously sung with the New Happiness Quartet, didn't speak to anyone. He headed straight for the door, got into his car, and left for home. When Gary called to find out what had happened, he informed Gary that he couldn't handle the pressure and would no longer be singing with the group. Needing another voice, they contacted Diane Woods, and although she was actively singing solo, she accepted their offer and joined the group.

Leaving Franklin, we continue along River Street passing by the house where Doug Oldham once lived. Just around the corner from Doug's old house is the famous Pizzanillos Pizza House where gospel concerts are routinely held in the upper level ballroom while enjoying some delicious pizza. Turning right onto Verity Parkway, we travel south along the Great Miami River to Middletown, host of the Midfirst Ohio Challenge hot air balloon festival and home to the McGuire Sisters.

As part of their forty-six-year career, the McGuire Sisters—Christine, Dorothy, and Phyllis—touched generations across America and around the world. They performed in the White House for five presidents and also performed for the Queen of England. The McGuire Sisters had a blend that was hard to match. They began singing in a church in Middletown where their mother was an ordained minister and were soon performing at military bases and numerous church functions.

In 1949, the McGuire Sisters attended a concert held in Dayton featuring the famous Blackwood Brothers. Then in 1954, they did the *Arthur Godfrey Show* with the Blackwood Brothers in New York City. A lasting friendship developed, and one evening, the Blackwood Brothers were invited for dinner. It was a memorable evening as they gathered around the piano to practice for the next morning radio program singing "Lead Me To That Rock." After appearing on the *Arthur Godfrey's Talent Scouts* show, their popularity expanded rapidly. Signing a contract with Coca-Cola, they appeared on some major TV shows, and played a variety of venues from Las Vegas to New York's Waldorf-Astoria.

In the highlight of their career, the McGuire Sisters were again featured on the *Arthur Godfrey Show* with the Statesmen. After performing at a gospel concert in Calgary, Alberta, Canada, the Statesmen Quartet were guests of Dorothy (McGuire) and her husband, Lowell Williamson, at Hy's Restaurant. During dinner, Dorothy and Jim Hill shared memories of those days when they sang together for the Hamilton County Singing Convention in Cincinnati. At the peak of their popularity, in 1968, the McGuire Sisters decided to step out of the spotlight. Over the next seventeen years, their singing activity was limited to a few family functions. Phyllis continued doing solo work while Dorothy and Christine devoted much of their time to raising families.

One day, Christine and Dorothy were visiting Phyllis in New York City. While shopping, they were repeatedly stopped by fans asking for autographs and questioning where they would be appearing. This spurred new life into the group, and after six months of rigorous rehearsals, they were back on the road again making international headlines. They found longtime fans waiting in lines along with some new ones. Their music quickly bridged the generation gap and the McGuire Sisters were a hit once again. Although their singing career drifted from the church, there's no question that these three voices created a smooth blend, and their vocal style was natural and very real. The McGuire Sisters were one of the best-known and best-loved sister groups of the 1940s and 1950s.

* * *

Ronnie Merrill was born on June 3, 1963. He grew up in the Middletown area before moving to Campton, Kentucky, for his freshmen year in high school. In high school, he started singing with the Entertainers. This group was formed by the high school music director, and they performed throughout the state. During his high school years, he also performed with the Pine Ridge Boys from Campton, Kentucky that included his younger brother and his cousin. He later started performing with the Kentucky Echoes who performed at the 1982 World's Fair.

In 1986, he started singing with the Silver Creek Quartet out of South Lebanon. He was with them for about three years. Then in 1989, he joined Eastbound out of Lexington, Kentucky. He remained with them for a period of twelve years. Also singing with EastBound was Rob Morgan, a native of Cincinnati, born on January 29, 1962. Before joining EastBound, Rob sang with the White Oak Valley Boys of Batavia and later formed Rob Morgan & Company also based out of Ohio.

In 2002, both Ronnie and Rob left Eastbound to form their current group Higher Vision, a bluegrass gospel group, from Boonesville, Kentucky. Higher Vision was privileged to play at Carnegie Hall in NYC, and they also took part in a special presentation entitled, "Appalachian Christmas."

* * *

Warren and Betty Proffit, were from Kentucky but later moved north and settled in Middletown where their son, Jim Proffit, was born on October 3, 1957. In 1961, his parents were saved, and they immediately began singing country gospel music as a duet. It wasn't long before young Jim was singing with them.

On May 5, 1978, Jim was joined by his wife, Shirley. Shirley was born in Hamilton on June 4, 1959, and soon after her birth, the family moved to Middletown where she has lived most of her life. Shirley got saved at age ten, and although she had sung in several choirs, she had never sung by herself as she was too nervous. When she married into the family, Jim handed her some words to a song and said, "Here, we are going to do this."

"Where is the music?" she asked him.

"We are not using music, we're just going to sing," he answered.

Soon after she started singing with the group, they became a mixed trio with a five-piece band. Jim and Betty would sing, and then Jim and Shirley and Warren would sing.

Back in the early 1980s, they had a 1959 Model-4104 bus. The only way you could start that old bus was by spraying some starter fluid on the engine. So one morning, after priming the engine, Jim pulled the bus out onto the road. It was a four-speed, and the transmission wasn't synchronized. So he was double-clutching to shift gears. All at once, he felt a nudge. He knew something didn't feel right, so he shifted up into third gear. Then looking in the rearview mirror, he saw a Ford LTD and a woman standing in the middle of the road. The bumper was lying on the road, the grill was busted off, the hood was crumpled up, and steam was shooting out of the radiator. Wondering what had happened, he immediately pulled over to the side of the road and ran back to see if she was okay. As he approached her, she said, "Please don't tell my husband, please don't tell my husband."

"Tell your husband what?" he questioned.

"That I hit you," she said.

He then looked at the back of the bus, and all he could see on the back of the bus was where something very small had dented the bumper.

"How in the world, I mean how did you hit me?" he asked.

"Because I didn't see you," she replied.

Jim and Shirley continued to sing even after Jim's mother and father stopped singing with them. For a while, they traveled as the Proffit Trio, singing mostly southern gospel, but after Tony Bostic left the group to further his education, they gravitated back more toward country gospel and became known simply as the Proffits.

Tony began singing with a Cedarville College choral group to help pay his tuition. He traveled with the Gibbons of Englewood for a little while because their schedule was more flexible.

Since 2001, the Proffits have been traveling full—time, preaching and singing in churches across America. Over the past six years, they have seen hundreds of people give their hearts to Christ and as Jim says, "That is what it is all about anyway."

Jim Compton sang with the Proffits for a brief time but had to quit because they were on the road too much. He had previously traveled with a group called Joyful Noise, and he also sang with the Townsmen.

Jim recalled that a lady gave them a motor home so they went to Texas to pick it up. They arrived just before Christmas. When they got there, they were informed the motor home had previously been caught in a hurricane and sustained numerous problems. As a result, they ended up staying in Texas for twelve days and missed spending Christmas with their families.

After being in Texas a couple days, Shirley was beginning to question why things had to be so difficult. Jeanette Lundsford, a promoter, approached them expressing a desire to take them around to some places and have them sing. They agreed, and soon the woman was on the phone contacting people. The weather might have been warm, but it was still Christmas, and she was unable to find a place for them to sing. Refusing to give up, she started inviting people to her own house telling them she was having cookies and punch for Christmas. After the people arrived, she would introduce the Proffits and have them sing. She would put their CDs on the table and tell the people, "You need to buy them, or they can't get home."

In 2007, they received nominations from the Southern Gospel Music Fanfair, Diamond Awards, and the West Georgia Gospel Music Convention for Duet of the Year. They recently completed three projects with Chapel Valley Studios and have another one coming out very soon.

It's been twenty-two years since Jim Proffit wrote the song entitled, "I'm Not a Poor Man," but he believes the words are still true today, and he says, "It is amazing how God just supplies those needs, whatever they are. You know, you are rich in the Lord if you just hang in there and go on."

* * *

The Revelers, traveling in a fifteen-passenger van, starting singing in 1955 and continued into the 1980s. Their versatility, wide range, and smooth harmony ranked them high on the charts of gospel artists. Group member Don Hall, pianist and arranger, was a member of the Dixie Melody Boys and the Jubilaires shortly after attending the Stamps Quartet School of Music in Houston, Texas. After his time with the group, Wendell Dennis sang with the Townsmen Quartet for eight years in the 1990s.

* * *

Roy Parks organized the Victors Quartet in 1966. At the beginning, the members included Roy, Howard Sears, Bill Jordan, Herb Hays, and Roy's brother Ronnie Parks. Keith Chapman came to sing the tenor part and stabilized the lineup for quite some time. Herb Hays eventually left the group to be a missionary in the Philippines.

When they first started traveling, they had a Cadillac limousine they had purchased from a funeral home and a trailer for their equipment. Once as they were going along the highway, they had a flat tire on the trailer. Pulling over, they unhooked the trailer, took the tire off, and took it to a nearby service station to have it repaired. Ronnie and Howard stayed with the trailer, and while they were waiting, the Southern-Aires came by. Dall Miller pulled their bus up behind the trailer and wanted to know what was going on. Ronnie said, "We're just taking a break, I pulled the trailer this far, and Howard is going to pull it the rest of the way."

During the 1970s, they purchased a 4104 Greyhound bus and traveled quite a bit, mostly in Ohio, Kentucky, Indiana, and Michigan. On one trip, the bus engine quit running, so they had the bus towed home to the local GM dealer. He told them the engine repair cost was going to be around $10,000. As funds were limited, they didn't know how they were going to fix the bus.

One evening, soon after that, Roy and his wife had taken their grandchildren to the *Holiday on Ice* at the Cincinnati Gardens. During the intermission, he was talking with the gentlemen sitting beside them about quartets and their different situations and mentioned their current bus problem. The gentlemen suggested they get acquainted with Jerry Robbins who owns and operates the Price Hill Coach Company located in Cincinnati as he did some bus repair and might be interested in looking at theirs. The next Monday morning, Roy went to see Jerry. Having just taken out of service a bus with a good strong 671 GM diesel engine, Jerry agreed to trade engines for $1,000. The engine wasn't new, but it was in very good condition. There was only one catch—they had to remove the old bus from his property. They agreed, and Jerry exchanged the engines. When the repair was finished, they found a wrecking company in Middletown that was willing to take the bus off their hands. So they drove their bus away with the new engine, and the old bus was hauled away for scrap.

On another trip, an operating lever broke off the air ride that controlled the air, causing one side of the bus to continue pumping up after the other side had stopped. It looked like the bus was ready to fall over as the one side just kept rising. There was a man in the church where they were singing that evening that assured them he could fix the problem. He told them to go ahead and sing, and he would have it fixed when they come back. Sure enough, he fixed the bus while they were singing and did not charge for his work.

Then one Sunday afternoon, they broke down right in front of a welding shop, and of course, the shop was closed. The owner lived right next door and agreed to open the shop. He welded the part back on, and once again, they were on their way in only a couple of hours. Roy says, "When things happen like that, it restores your faith that God's looking over you and taking care of you after all."

The Victors once opened for the Blackwood Brothers at Memorial Hall, and Roy believes this was one of the highlights of their ministry. The group sang together until the mid-1980s when they decided to stop singing because of age and health issues.

Howard Sears, another longtime group member, reorganized the group one year later. Because of some changes in their voice range, some of the members had to switch parts. The reorganized group was only together for a couple years.

Retiring from AK Steel in 1992, Roy still had a strong desire for gospel music, so he organized the Victors once again. All of the group members returned except Howard Sears, who had passed away because of cancer. Duane Early, who had previously sung with several groups, joined to sing Howard's part. Duane wanted to do more singing than he could with the Victors, so he soon left to join the Southern-Aires. He was replaced by Gary Crowley. Gary had sung with the Gospel Mariners for several years on the TV show *Good Ship Zion.* He had also sung with a group called Compassion and the Ohio Valley Boys.

Keith developed some voice problems and dropped out, and Gary Coffey came in to sing first tenor. As of 2008, they continued to sing with Gary Coffey on first tenor, Gary Crowley on lead, Bill Jordan on baritone, Ron Parks on bass, and Roy Parks playing the piano. Although they still possess a great desire to sing gospel music, they have lost their taste for the road and now stay pretty close to home.

OHIO 7

Leaving Middletown, we continue along Verity Parkway south to SR-73. Missing the exit, we are forced to continue south to Hamilton-Middletown Road where we turn right. Passing the historic Excello Locks, part of the Miami & Erie Canal system, we enter the town of Excello. Now back on path, we turn left onto SR-73, cross the Great Miami River once again, and enter the village of Trenton, a small town with a big heart. Trenton is home of Shelly's Ice Cream and the McCrarys.

Howard McCrary of the McCrarys has written a number of songs for the Mighty Clouds of Joy including "The World Is Not My Home." The McCrarys, a sibling quintet from a family of twelve, cut their first album in 1972 while some members were still teenagers. In the '80s, after working in the secular field backing up Cat Stevens and Stevie Wonder and a few others, they returned to the gospel arena appearing on albums with, among other artists, Andre Crouch. Howard later toured as Reverend Winter in the sold-out London production of *Mama, I Want to Sing*. The McCrarys continue to do such TBN programs as *Praise the Lord*.

OHIO 8

Leaving Trenton, we turn left onto Hamilton-Trenton Road. Approaching some farm fields, we watch as the brisk wind moving across the field creates little dust twisters. Then passing through the little community of Overpeck, and seeing the Redeemer Baptist Church, I'm reminded of that great song, "I Know My Redeemer Lives." We continue on Hamilton-Trenton Road for a couple miles to SR 127. Taking 127, we pass through New Miami and enter the city of Hamilton, the birthplace of Joe Nuxall, star pitcher and longtime announcer for the Cincinnati Reds. Singer and movie star Doris Day broke her leg when riding in an automobile that was struck by a train in Hamilton. In the 1920s, many Chicago gangsters had a second home in Hamilton giving it the nickname Little Chicago, and John Dillinger is documented to have visited Hamilton. Along with these famous people, there are a number of gospel artists from Hamilton.

In 2002, as a result of some songs provided for an Easter service, the group Four for One (441) was formed. They all attend the Green Hills Baptist Church in Williamsdale. Traveling with a live band, they feel that God has truly blessed them. Although some would call their style of singing southern gospel, they haven't quite figured out what to call it. They enjoy their ministry, and it shows in their performance. Lead singer, Joe Ramsey, started out singing secular music and has been singing for many years. Terry Abrams sang with Psalms of Praise before singing with 441. Eddie Hall, inspired at the age of fourteen after hearing George Younce sing, started practicing right away to develop a smooth bass sound. Before singing with 441, he sang with a group called In Him for one year. In 1993, Eddie announced his calling to preach the gospel.

* * *

Donald Edward Baldwin was born in Hamilton on November 30, 1931, but the family soon moved to Chicago where Don grew up. Don developed an interest in gospel music during his teen years. During the Korean War, he was stationed near Las Vegas and would frequently listen to the Blackwood Brothers on the radio during his drives back and forth to Chicago. Don's interest in quartet music continued to grow, and in 1954, he decided to form a quartet. Joining with Lem Boyles and a tall young man named Dave Kyllonen, they were on their way. In 1956, they acquired the services of a young tenor from Iowa named Duane Nicholson and a first-rate pianist from Memphis named Eddie Reece who had been with the Songfellows Quartet. In 1957, with their new lead singer from Illinois, Neil Enloe and Don singing baritone, they were soon on the road as the Couriers, and their reputation grew rapidly.

In 1958, Don formed Hymntone Records in Harrisburg, Pennsylvania, and in 1965, he stopped traveling with a group to focus on the record company. This is when Don began his solo ministry. Don filled in for a while with the Vicounts, a group owned by the Couriers. Don hired a young man named Nick Bruno to supervise the activities in the recording studio. Nick remained with Don until 1970 when he moved south to join the Kingsmen.

Don was master of ceremony for the NQC during the mid-1970s. In 1986, he sold the studio and relocated to Florida. In 2002, Don was named to the Pennsylvania Gospel Hall of Fame, and in 2006, he was presented with the Living Legend award at the Grand Ole Gospel Reunion (GOGR) held in Knoxville, Tennessee.

* * *

Ernest Benge has been a pastor for over forty years. Ernest and his wife had six children and could not afford to send them for music lessons, so they simply trusted God. As the children grew, they developed a love for music and seemingly a natural ability to minister musically. The Benge Family started singing as a trio in 1997, and their ministry grew as God opened the doors. The group now consists of five vocalist and a live band offering a progressive sound that is rapidly becoming popular in today's gospel circle. Jeff is recognized as an accomplished musician, and his goal is to make the Word of God come alive through their songs. Kathy has been singing since age four and brings to the stage a great big voice that has found its way in to the hearts of many. Jeff and Julene have both written several songs that have charted on the *Singing News* charts.

* * *

The Burton Family started singing in the early 1960s. Grady Burton and his wife both came from musically oriented families. Before singing with the family group, Grady's father, also named Grady, sang with the Elmwood Quartet in Cincinnati. Younger Grady sang with the Fellowship Christianaires before forming the Burton Family.

The Burton Family traveled extensively, making a number of recordings and going through three buses. Although they stopped touring in 1971, the family has remained active in the music field throughout the years, even operating a recording studio for a while. Two of the songs written by the group were recently featured on a Nashville Showcase and made the charts. The songs were, "The Storms May Come" and "Memorial Day." Although the group is no longer together, they occasionally hold special events where the group comes together for some singing. Grady is currently working on the development of a program allowing him to promote southern gospel music by holding scheduled singings similar to the Gaither Homecoming events.

* * *

The Chancellor Gospel Quartet started in 1958 under the management of Floyd Arthur. With a deep compassion for a lost and dying humanity, they traveled approximately forty thousand miles each year in their little blue and white Corvair bus.

* * *

John Dill "JD" Jarvis was born on April 21, 1924, and grew up in the mountains of Kentucky. After suffering serious combat wounds in the U.S. Army, he moved north and settled in Hamilton operating a paint contracting business. After devoting his early adulthood to a rowdy lifestyle, Jarvis converted to Christianity and began focusing his energy on sacred music. He sang in churches for years and began a recording career in the 1960s.

* * *

The Thompsons, a family group, were together for about thirty years. At age thirteen, Anna Thompson started singing with the Sunnyside Trio in Covington, Kentucky. She remained with them for about five years.

While in Hamilton, we stop at McDonalds for a very much-needed restroom break and an ice cream cone. Leaving Hamilton, we continue south on SR-127 for about five miles, passing some beautiful homes, to Fairfield, home of the famous Jungle Jim's International Market. Inside you'll find a lion with a pompadour crooning Elvis songs, a General Mills Big G Cereal band serenading shoppers, and a full-size 1952 fire engine marking the thousand-variety hot sauce shelves.

In 1998, after years of singing in their home church, Jason Allen Begley and Kimberly Renee (Hall) Romine along with some cousins officially started the group Arise. In 2003, they were semifinalists in *Exalting Him* a national talent search. As of 2007, the group is no longer together.

* * *

Undivided Hearts, a male quartet, started in 1995 and ministered for about eleven years singing with several of the nation's top groups. Once while Undivided Hearts were on their way to sing in Anderson, Indiana, they were pulling off the freeway exit ramp when their van stopped running and would not start. To add to the trauma, their cell phone would not work. Nonetheless, they were able to get a tow truck to the scene. As the tow truck could not hold everyone, Greg and a young boy who was traveling with them remained behind to be picked up when someone could return. As he and the young boy started walking along Indiana Route 9, a sheriff car pulled over to check them out. While explaining what had happened, they saw a vehicle drive by carrying the guys that were coming back to pick them up. The officer told them to get in the car. He rapidly spun away traveling up the road at about eighty miles per hour to catch the car and pulled them over so they could get back together. It took three trips to get everything to their destination, but despite all the problems, they made it to the church and had a wonderful service. During the service, a lady in the church had her husband work on their van to get them back on the road.

Greg Dungan had previously earned a degree in music composition from Miami University where he studied trumpet throughout college. After Undivided Hearts divided, Greg formed a solo ministry called the Sound of the Trumpet Ministries in which he continues to minister using his musical abilities.

Leaving Fairfield, we continued south on SR-127 ending up in the turning lane where we had to sit until there was a break in the traffic. Soon we were moving again, and traveling about four miles, we arrived at IR-275. Turning left, we head east crossing over IR-75 and dodge barrels for about nine miles to U.S. 42. Turning left on U.S. 42 we pass the Runyan Pioneer Cemetery, home of some really old grave markers, on our way to Pisgah—home of the Eastmen Trio, who started singing in 1961.

Dave Liles the younger brother to Buddy Liles sang lead for the group. Dave came from another group from Newport, Kentucky. Their first tenor was Pisgah's own Doug Crowley.

Leaving Pisgah, we continue north along U.S. 42 to West Chester Road. Turning left onto West Chester Road, we soon come to a sharp curve leading to a small tunnel. Coming out of the tunnel, the road winds like a snake—a difficult passage for a tour bus. Continuing along West Chester Road, we soon cross over IR-75 and turn right onto Union Center Road, then taking a left onto Beckett

Road, we continue to Princeton-Glendale Road (SR-747). Taking SR-747 we continue northwest to SR-4 where we turn right and enter Monroe enter Monroe, home to the Murphy's, a family group that is all about ministry.

The group consists of Danny Murphy, his wife Max Murphy and their two daughters Rikki and Barb. Max does most of the lead vocals while writing some of their music. Her gospel heritage runs deep as her grandmother and her aunts sang and preached revivals together for years known as the Parker Sisters. Being raised in the hills of Kentucky, Danny possesses more of a country singing style and adds variety to their ministry. Their ultimate goal is to be a blessing to others, to help make people's hearts a little lighter and to lead others to Jesus Christ.

The King of Kings statue outside the Solid Rock Church facing IR-75 is reportedly the largest sculpture of Christ in the United States. It is sixty-two feet high and weighs about sixteen thousand pounds. Because of its posture, arms raised skyward and parallel to one another, it is sometimes referred to by locals as "Touchdown Jesus." Those more familiar with scripture will see that he is not indicating a football score, but is gesturing toward heaven—home of the Savior depicted in the statue and our eventual home.

Pastor of the Solid Rock Church and sister church Solid Rock South, Lawrence Bishop, was born in 1942 at Zag, Kentucky, and learned to play the guitar during evenings when the family would gather around the porch. He started playing the guitar in church at age ten.

Moving to Ohio with his family at the tender age of twelve, Lawrence soon discovered a talent for trading horses. He purchased his first horse for $25 and after bringing it home. His father informed him the horse was blind. Lawrence washed, groomed, and trimmed the horse until his dad didn't recognize it. He later sold the horse for $250. Thus, his horse-dealing career had begun. Since that first transaction, he has built one of the most successful quarter horse ranches in the nation. Horse traders come from across the United States and all over the world to buy quality horses from the LB Ranch.

In 1975, Lawrence reached a desperate point in his life. He knew his priorities had to change. Then one night, after much prodding by his wife, he attended a local church service. During that meeting, he felt as if the preacher were speaking directly to him. Lawrence recommitted his life to Christ and, a short time later, surrendered to the call of ministry. This calling culminated in the founding of the Solid Rock Church located along IR-75 in Monroe.

In recent years, he felt a calling to start a bluegrass ministry at Solid Rock. He formed a band called Lawrence Bishop and the Circuit Riders. He later had to change the name to avoid conflict with another group. Lawrence and his group have made numerous appearances at concerts and festivals in Ohio, Kentucky, and Indiana. He has also become a successful bluegrass promoter, staging concerts at Solid Rock, featuring such top-level performers as Ralph Stanley, Doyle Lawson, and Ricky Skaggs. Lawrence has written over fifty songs, and four of them became number one hits. He was voted Music Evangelist of the Year at the Ryman Auditorium and has held concerts in Paris, France, with some of his music reaching the top of the European charts. He performed in the movie called *Segregated Sunday* and is presently working on another film he coproduced entitled *Animals in Paradise.*

* * *

Lily Fishman was born on September 20, 1947 in Munich, Germany, an immigrant daughter of Oscar and Faye Fishman, Jewish Holocaust survivors from Poland. Her mother, Faye (Jakobi) Fishman, was eighteen years old that dreadful day in 1939 when the alert came that the Nazis were headed into the town. Faye's mother had sent Faye and the other children into town to buy groceries, and that was the last day Faye saw her mother. Later that same day, Faye and her future husband, Oscar, were taken captive by the Nazis. In 1945, after years of imprisonment, hard labor, and many near-death events, Oscar and Faye were finally liberated from Nazi imprisonment. Lily's father passed away in 1980, but her mother, Fay (Jakobi) Fishman Blauschild, surviving her second husband, Irving Blauschild, still lives in New York City enjoying good health at the age of eighty-eight.

While she was still a child, Lily's parents moved to New York City, earning their American citizenship in 1956. Growing up in New York City, Lily developed an interest in theatre arts and appeared in several of Manhattan's Off-Broadway plays and musical productions. In 1967, she had a contract with Columbia Records working with Maria Newmound and singing folk rock. They even reached number one status in Wichita, Kansas, for several weeks. They performed at a party before such actors as Steve Lawrence, Eydie Gorme and Bobby Vinton.

In 1968, she met Joe Isaacs while his group from Kentucky, the Green Briar Boys, was working in New York. Joe Isaacs was born in Jackson County,

Kentucky, the youngest of seventeen children and the son of a preacher. He grew up listening to a few country records on the family's old crank-up Victrola. He moved to Lebanon at age seventeen and soon became a bluegrass artist. He started playing banjo with Larry Sparks. While he was still with Larry, Ralph Stanley offered him a job, but he chose to remain with Larry.

Joe and Lily were married in 1970. Later that same year, Joe's older brother was killed in an automobile accident. This event ultimately led to both Joe and Lily giving their hearts to the Lord. After becoming Christians, they started singing in local churches on the weekends as Joe Isaacs and the Calvary Mountain Boys.

Around 1974, as Lily became more involved in the group, they changed their name to Joe Isaacs and the Sacred Bluegrass. This mixture of bluegrass and Lily's folk style of singing created a unique sound. Their children, Becky, Ben and Sonya, started singing harmony at around age five and soon became an active part of the group. They were asked to let the children sing everywhere they would go. Along the way, the children acquired such nicknames as the Little Gospel Chipmunks, the Briarhopper Hebrews, and the Little Jewbillies.

Their son, Ben Isaacs, was born on July 25, 1972, in Middletown. He later became a part of the family group playing the standup bass, and he has written several songs. Making his proposal while sailing through the glaciers of Alaska, Ben later took Mindy to be his wife during a beautiful private ceremony held in Monroe in 2006.

Sonya Isaacs was born on July 22, 1974, and was raised in Morrow. Sonya wrote her first song at age seven and graduated an honor student from Little Miami High School in Morrow. The first event that helped Sonya Isaacs open the door to a country-recording career occurred in 1994. Artist, manager, and publisher Mark Ketchem heard her voice on the radio while driving through Nashville. She was singing a gospel hit called "I Have a Father Who Can," and the power and purity of her a cappella vocal delivery grabbed Ketchem's attention. Possibly the best sound he'd ever heard, he had to find out who this young lady was. It was her emotionally charged vocals on the gospel hit "From the Depths of My Heart" that helped turn the Isaacs into a top gospel act.

Rebecca (Isaacs) Bowman was born on August 2, 1975, in Morrow where she lived until 1993 when she relocated to Lafollette, Tennessee. An award-winning songwriter, Becky has written over forty songs including "Stand Still." In her spare time, Becky loves woodworking and has built several pieces of furniture.

In 1981, Joe had tragic accident at work requiring three major back surgeries and could no longer remain employed. At this time, they started taking more appointments. Those early days on the road consisted of traveling in a station wagon carrying a cooler of sandwiches. In 1985, they became a full-time family band, and in 1988, changing their name to simply the Isaacs Family, they purchased a 1960 4104 GMC bus and hit the road. Their first weekend on the road after purchasing their new bus, they were scheduled to sing somewhere in Alabama. Excitement was high as they headed down the road in their new vehicle even though they had no restroom and had to sleep on the floor with the windows open as there was no air conditioning. They later purchased a 1970 MCI bus, making their long hours on the road much more comfortable. Lily says, "It's work to have a bus, but you can't work without the bus."

In 1989, after continually being referred to as the Isaacs, they decided to change their name once again. They are now simply called the Isaacs. The year 1993 created another turning point in their career when the group became popular on the *Grand Ole Opry.* It was there that another of Sonya's dreams was realized—she met a man that had made a similar journey from bluegrass to country years earlier—Vince Gill. He would call her out on the Opry stage to sing with him on "Go Rest High on that Mountain" and "Real Ladies Man." She didn't know it at the time, but she had just met one of the producers of her first country album. Dolly Parton also contacted Sonya and Becky requesting they sing harmony on her acoustic album. Sonya was excited when Dolly sang on her album, but she was elated when asked to sing on *Dolly's.*

On June 4, 1994, Becky married John Bowman. John was born in Mount Airy, North Carolina, but was raised in Virginia. Growing up, John learned to play several instruments, and in 1988, he started traveling with the Appalachian Trail band. He remained with them until 1990 when he took a full-time position with Doyle Lawson & Quicksilver.

Before Becky was married, the Isaacs were singing at an Amish Mennonite event in Lancaster, Pennsylvania. Becky had been playing baseball, and after taking a shower, she was walking toward their bus with a towel wrapped around her head. Meanwhile, Doyle Lawson & Quicksilver had arrived. She really didn't know John Bowman at this time because he had just recently joined the group. As she came near, John and Doyle were tossing a softball. She stopped to talk with some people she knew, and John, hearing them talking, looked over at Becky. As he did, Doyle threw the ball hitting John square in the head.

In 1997, John surrendered to God's call to become an ordained minister. John and Becky now have two children who often join the Isaacs on stage to sing special songs. Becky remains a woman of great courage as she continues to raise her family while traveling on the road and managing a difficult personal struggle. For six years, Becky has been battling Crohn's disease, an inflammatory condition that can severely damage various parts of the human body.

The Isaacs now appear regularly at the Gaither Homecoming gatherings and continue to reach hearts wherever they sing. The heart of their ministry is reaching souls for Christ, and their music is even being heard in special ways. Let me explain. Around 2002, Lily received a letter from a man named Butch. He was homeless and was living on the streets of Atlanta, Georgia. Lily had written an article about the Holocaust in the *Singing News Magazine*, and while digging through the trash in search of food, Butch had found a copy of the magazine and read the article. He had been alone on the streets for seventeen years, but her article reached his heart. After receiving the letter, Lily sent him a Bible, and through continued correspondence, two years later, Butch gave his heart to the Lord. Butch still lives in an old abandoned car, but he has since made contact with some of his family, and one of his grandchildren has even been named after Lily. This fascinating story has another twist. Butch, the man brought to Christ through the ministry of a musician, is deaf. He would have never heard the sound of their voices in song, but the message of Jesus still shone brightly through their lives.

Tim Surrett, sang with the Isaacs for a while and now sings with Balsam Range in Haywood County, North Carolina.

Leaving Monroe, we take Hamilton Lebanon Road (SR-63) east passing by the Lebanon Correctional Institute where the Dayton Ambassadors once did a program in conjunction with the Athletes in Action team witnessing around thirty inmates give their hearts to Christ. We continue eight more miles to Lebanon, home of the Golden Lamb, a unique restaurant built in 1803. The Golden Lamb has eighteen rooms each named after famous people who stayed there. These include Charles Dickens and Samuel Clemens. In addition to the Golden Lamb, Lebanon was the hometown of another lamb.

In October 1960, following a terrible automobile accident near Berea, Kentucky, on Red Lick Road, a four-year-old boy was rushed to Central Baptist Hospital in Lexington, Kentucky. The doctors informed Reverend Emery Lamb and his wife, Dorothy that their son only had thirty minutes to live because of massive brain damage and injuries incurred during the accident. Christians in several states began to pray for healing for the little boy. Another day passed, and the doctors told the family that even if the child survived, he would be an invalid. They were told the damage to his brain would leave him both blind and deaf, and they indicated he would never speak again. Both his parents and the many prayer warriors believed otherwise, trusting God to restore the young boy to complete recovery.

One the fourth day, the doctors were astonished at the boy's recovery and shared with the parents that this was the most unusual and miraculous thing they had ever witnessed. The X-rays revealed that the boy's brain was now completely normal, with no scar tissue. As the boy gained strength, plastic surgeons were called in reconstruct the damaged areas to his face. The young boy was Denver Lamb.

Before long, Denver was singing at church meetings where his family was invited to share their miraculous testimony. His mother would tell the details of the accident, and after sharing the story of God's healing touch, they would sit Denver on a Bible stand so the audience could see him, and he would sing a song.

Denver wrote his first song at the age of six, and by 1972, though Denver was still in high school, he recorded an album with his sister Brenda entitled "I Won't Have To Worry Anymore." He worked with Joe and Lily Isaacs, back when they were called Joe Isaacs and the Sacred Bluegrass, on an album called *The Family Circle*. In the early 1980s, he also worked with the Dalton Gang on their first album, which was recorded in Clinton, Tennessee, with the McKamey's.

In 1984, Denver went to the Hilltop Recording Studio in Nashville, Tennessee, to make his first professionally produced solo album titled *The Trumpet Sound*. Coming from a small town in Ohio, he had no idea what would come of this recording. The song entitled "Go Down to the Pool" was pulled from the album and mailed to radio stations by the producer Eddie Crook and was soon hitting the charts making it all the way to number sixty-nine. It wasn't long before the phone was ringing, and he was receiving requests to sing for churches and special events.

At the same time, he was hosting a TV show entitled *Living Waters* on a cable network based in Hamilton. By November 1984, he had completed the TV contract and decided to form a gospel group. Denver called his cousin Thelma Peyton, and they discussed the possibility of forming a group. Confirming God's leading in this matter, she agreed to get in touch with a friend named Jerry Hopkins. She also recommended another cousin, Bryan Hisle, to play piano. After Denver contacted Gary Hymer, who had played bass with him on the TV program, they all came together for a special meeting.

They opened with prayer and then sang a few old hymns. When the evening was over, everyone felt confident that God had brought them together, and these five people formed the Denver Lamb Singers. They made their first appearance on January 6, 1985, and were received very well. They were soon invited to several major concerts to work with some well-known promoters in Ohio, Kentucky, and Tennessee. In their first year, they sang with some of the nations finest groups.

Denver has written over three hundred songs including the number one hit favorite "It'll Be Worth It After All," which was nominated for southern gospel Song of the Year in 1990. In addition to his singing ministry, Denver Lamb worked for several years as a DJ on a local radio station in Middletown hosting a six-hour show called *The Midnight Express.*

After the Denver Lamb Singers stopped singing, Denver joined the Dalton Gang again and traveled with them for a while. In 2003, Denver started a solo ministry. His first solo album, entitled *Reflection*, is a reflection of his life, highlighting his most requested songs. There was also a new song on the album called "Red Lick Road," which tells of the accident and the miracle he experienced as a young child.

As of 2008, Denver was still traveling around sharing the message of Christ through his songs and testimony. Denver often says, "He writes the song, I hold the pencil.

"I'm just a vessel He chose to use. I could never repay Him for what He has brought me through, and my heart's desire is to do everything I can to reach as many people as I can, to let them know what a great friend we have in Jesus! Reminding them He's still in the saving, delivering, and healing business."

* * *

Bonnie Smitty and her husband formed the Masters Quartet. In 1976, with the addition of David Griffith, they formed the Miami Valley Quartet. Not too long after that, they became an all-male quartet and changed their name to the Miami Valley Boys. The quartet continued together until about 1990. After his time with the Miami Valley Boys, David formed the Lighthouse Quartet. This group remained together until 2003 when David became the bus driver for Signature Sound. He has since become the production manager for the group.

* * *

At age nine, Paul Joseph "PJ" Clouse was instrumental in getting his mother, Mary Jo Clause, and his grandmother Penny Cavanaugh in church. Then in 1993, the Skyward Bound Trio, a family group, was formed by Penny Cavanaugh. They have traveled throughout the Midwest and sung at numerous churches. They also sang for the NQC Regional Artist Showcase, the Ohio State Fair, the Tri-State Singing Convention held in Big Stone Gap, Virginia, and the Chicken Festival in London, Kentucky.

On one trip they were passing near Walden, Kentucky, when the axle on their bus suddenly broke. The broken axle also damaged the air line to the brakes. Having no brakes, they quickly let off the gas, keeping the bus on the road as it coasted to a stop and praise the Lord nothing came into their path before they stopped.

Leaving Lebanon, we take a quick turn to the south and travel along SR-48 for five miles to South Lebanon home of the famous Cash D. Ambergy Bargain Barn. South Lebanon is also home of the Bowman family.

A very busy gospel band from southwest Ohio is Blaine Bowman & HIS Good Time Band. The capital letters in *HIS* is for Jesus. Known for many years as Them Bowmans, this family band performs about 250 times a year from coast to coast.

Christine Maxon started playing the piano and singing with her two sisters in a family trio called the Maxon Sisters. In her teens, she started playing for the Roger Noble Singers and later the Southern-Aires Quartet. In 1975, while playing for the Southern-Aires, she met a young man named Blaine Bowman.

Blaine began traveling in 1972 with a band called the One Way Express as guitarist. In 1973, he and his sister Diana formed a group called Blaine Bowman & the Children of Light, which continued until 1980.

In 1977, Blaine and Christine were married. Their daughter, Tiffany, was born in 1984, and their son, Luke, was born in 1985. The children have traveled, sang, and played in the band since they were little children. The group does a variety of music styles including country, blues, gospel parodics, jazz/fusion, western swing, southern, and bluegrass. They do comedy, and Blaine preaches the word in most of their meetings. They have won many awards including Band of the Year, Comedian of the Year, and Trio of the Year as well as receiving much airplay nationally and internationally. They are known as "God's Idea of a Good Time"!

Leaving South Lebanon, we head north on U.S. 42 passing the Red Stewart Airfield on the left and a green building with a purple roof on the right known as Doggy DayCare Center. After traveling ten miles, we reach Waynesville. On April 7, 1900, the village was ravaged by a tragic fire that destroyed all but the two buildings along the west side of Main Street between North Street and Chapman Street. Since the village offices were located within this section, all village records were destroyed. The annual Sauerkraut Festival has been held in Waynesville since 1970. Over eleven thousand pounds of sauerkraut is used to make ice cream, donuts, brownies, and pizza. If you don't like sauerkraut, you may just want to stop in to hear Eva Brock sing.

Eva Brock had been part of a ladies trio within her local church for many years. In 1982, because of some personnel changes, Eva started singing with her husband and her two daughters, Donna and Brenda Brock. They continued to sing together as a family until 2001, but in 1982, they became known as the Gospel Foundation.

In 1997, during a service in Springboro, a teen came into the church after the service had started. After listening to the singing, he came to the altar and gave his heart to the Lord. When he gave his testimony, he shared that before coming to church, he had given up and was planning to commit suicide.

Eva possessed a fun-loving spirit and carried the nickname Ms. Grace as she was always falling. She has fallen while carrying equipment, while leaving a restaurant, and once, she fell stepping off the sidewalk and sprained her ankle. One evening, while carrying water to the stage, she fell over a monitor, dumping water into the soundboard and requiring the group to finish singing without microphones. But one thing is certain, her falling down never kept her from lifting up others.

In 2001, when their mother eventually stepped down from the stage (no, she didn't fall), Donna and Brenda continued singing as a duet and, in 2004, picked up the name the *Hearts of Faith*. Since that time, they have received special recognition for their singing and performed at the 2006 NQC Regional Artist Showcase.

Leaving Waynesville, we continue north along U.S. 42 passing the Der Dutchman Restaurant where, for several years, Norm Livingston has been holding Gospel Dinner Concerts with some of the area's finest groups. Traveling about fifteen miles, we come to Xenia, where you'll be taken back in time as you watch the famous *Blue Jacket*, an outdoor drama portraying the struggle between the Shawnee Indians and the frontiersmen.

Not quite as far back in time, Gary Cohn played banjo for John Burke and the Layman Trio and for a while he was also with the Charles Feltner Singers. He was a favorite DJ for a local radio station (WBZI) and later became editor for *Gospel Voice Magazine* and the host of *Inside Gospel*. In 1972, Gary joined George Kidd and Jamie "Ben" Holiday, a local police officer, to form the Gary Cohn Trio. The trio traveled together for four years.

On one occasion, they were working on an old bus they had acquired and became frustrated as they were unable to get it to start. The bus was a standard transmission, and someone suggested they jump-start the engine by pushing the bus across the parking lot. Everyone except the designated driver gathered behind the bus, and as they began to push, the bus started rolling. They had made several attempts to jump-start when suddenly they realized the bus was headed straight for the road. The bus was equipped with air breaks, but as the engine had not started, there was not enough air pressure to stop the bus. Standing in the parking lot, they watched helplessly as the bus rolled across the road and ended its journey in a ditch on the other side of the road. Except for a little damaged pride, the designated driver was unharmed.

In the early 1970s, George Kidd played for his wife's group, a group of female cousins called the Singing Gospel Jewels. George's son Tim Kidd began playing the drums in his grandfather's church at age seven. Being influenced by such artist as Tony Rice and Ben Isaacs, Tim later learned to play the upright bass playing for the Hoskins Family and for the Beacons from Carlisle. He presently plays for a bluegrass group called Joe Mullins and the Radio Ramblers.

* * *

Before creating the group New Generation, Jimmy and David Haney were part of the Hanings Family singing group. The group New Generation was started in 1989. Before marrying Jim, Crystal (Arp) Hanings sang with the Tru-Lite Gospel Singers from the early 1960s until about 2003.

In 2004, the group name was changed to True to the Call. Traveling with a live band, the group encompasses six families and spans three generations. David Hanings writes some of the music for the group and has written a number one song entitled "Jesus Signed My Pardon." In 2008, the group decided to go back to their roots and perform under the name of the Hanings. Although they're still using a live band, they have downsized the number of families traveling together.

Driving through Xenia, we pass the Stelton Road Church of God, home church for the Southern-Aires Quartet. Making a right turn in town, we view a beautiful courthouse clock covered with construction scaffolding. Leaving Xenia, we continue east on Martin Luther King Parkway (U.S. 42) for four miles to the small town of Wilberforce. Tucked away in central Ohio, far away from the hustle and bustle of the big city, Wilberforce has a little post office, a museum, and miles of farmland. This is a little town with no mail delivery, no shops and no restaurants, has two universities and a big heart, and is full of history. It is home to Wilberforce University, the country's first private historically African-American college located directly across the road from Central State University. In 1930, Howard Daniels, a teacher at Wilberforce University formed a group called the Harmony Four, which later became the Charioteers, taking their new name from the song "Swing Low Sweet Chariot." Winning an Ohio State Quartet Contest, they landed a recording contract with Decca Records and a radio spot on WLW in Cincinnati for two years. They later had a radio show in New York, and they were also long-term guests on the *Bing Crosby* radio show. Although none of their songs made it to the top of the charts, they became popular because of their radio programs and personal appearances. After taking a contract with Columbia Records, they soon converted to a pop group, and the group disbanded in 1957.

Leaving Wilberforce, we continue east along U.S. 42 for five miles, passing the Indian Mound Reserve on the left, to Cedarville, home of Cedarville University where groups such as the Gaither Vocal Band and the Cathedrals could often be heard singing in the beautiful campus chapel. Cedarville is also home to the Cedarville Opera House, a renovated opera house from the late 1800s presenting a variety of programs including drama, comedy, and music.

Born in Ohio, Phil Brower attended Cedarville College, and after graduating, both Phil and his wife, Lynne, were in a group called the Spurrlows. Having handled the programming for several cruises and working with Maurice Templeton, Phil was given the challenge of coordinating all of the musical elements of the NQC. He also does the production work for the Gaither *Homecoming* radio program.

In 1966, another group of students from Cedarville College formed a quartet called the Travelers. In their first year together, they traveled almost five thousand miles including a nine-week, fifteen-state tour during the summer of 1967. As representatives of the college, their theme was "Traveling for the word of God and the testimony of Jesus Christ."

Returning Home

Leaving Cedarville, we take SR-72 north to the quaint village of Clifton where, turning into town, we drive by the historic Clifton Mill and Opera House. It is only a little disappointing that it is not near Christmastime when the mill is annually lit with one of the country's largest and most beautiful Christmas light displays. Returning to SR-72, we turn left and travel about eleven miles to IR-70. We enter IR-70 west and, as the sun sets in the west, head home traveling about twenty miles to IR-75 where we head north to Vandalia ending Tour No. 2.

GOSPEL BOYS

LAYMEN TRIO

GLORYLANDERS

Steve Ladd

* Steve Ladd with GOLD CITY

KEGLEY SISTERS

PARKS

WRIGHT FAMILY

HYMN TRIO

HOSKINS FAMILY

TOUCH OF GRACE

SONSHIP

Doug Oldham

HIGHER GROUND

MCQUIRE SISTERS

Ronnie Merrill with HIGHER VISION

PROFITTS

REVELERS

VICTORS

Don Baldwin & JD Sumner

Don Baldwin & Jim Hamil

Don Baldwin & David Young with COURIERS

BENGE FAMILY

BURTONS

CHANCELORS

EASTMEN TRIO

MURPHY'S

Lawrence Bishop

SACRED BLUEGRASS

* ISAACS

ISAACS

* ISAACS

Denver Lamb

MIAMI VALLEY QUARTET

HANINGS

CHARIOTEERS

TRAVELERS

Chapter III

Akron Tour

It Will Be Worth It After All

We need our Spirit-filled preachers to teach us right from wrong
We need our old-fashioned seekers who'll pray all night long
We need some good Gospel singing to help us go another mile
The church will triumph, Oh Lord, and go home in a little while

When you're down in the valley, prayer is all I can do
Then the Lord sends deliverance and strengthens you
And when you're up on your mountain and you see me struggling along
Lift my name up to Jesus, let's help each other make it home

It'll be worth it after all, child. It'll be worth it after all
After all of these trials, we'll hear Jesus call
It'll be worth it after all, child, it'll be worth it after all
After all of this climbing, it'll be worth it after all

—Denver Lamb
(Used with permission)

OHIO 1

Leaving Vandalia, we head north on IR-75 to IR-70. Taking IR-70 east, we start out on a road made bumpy by the winter weather. Reaching Columbus, we make a slight left onto IR-670 where we watch a car spin around and crash into the wall. It appears the driver is okay, so we continue along IR-270 taking it to SR-62. Shortly leaving SR-62, we merge onto SR-317 and cross the Big Walnut Creek. We notice swans swimming in the creek as we enter Gahanna, a small town founded by John Clark in 1849 and designated by *Money Magazine* as "one of the top 100 best places to live." The name *Gahanna* is derived from a Native American word for three creeks joining into one.

The God's Ambassadors Quartet started in 1990. Singing primarily in churches, they continue today as a dedicated family group. They have shared the stage with such groups as the Perrys, the Hoskins, and the Crabb Family.

Violet Maynard started singing in 1981 when she played piano for a group from Louisa, Kentucky, called the Bradley Gap Trio. She moved to Ohio in 1988, and in 1992, she started traveling with the God's Ambassadors Quartet. She also played the piano and sometimes the bass guitar, remaining with the group until 2004. In 2005, she started a solo ministry.

* * *

The Hamilton Road Gospel Quartet, a male quartet, started singing in 2003. Their regional ministry developed from a local church group in Gahanna. Rick Hinkle, the group's manager, was exposed to southern gospel as a child when his pastor was actively involved in the promotion of gospel concerts. Rick did some singing in high school but was not involved in anything major until the Hamilton Road Gospel Quartet. He loves southern gospel music and enjoys meeting new people as they travel throughout the country. They counted it a special honor when the group was given the opportunity to open at a recent concert in their community featuring the Imperials. Shannon Smith of the Imperials says, "I thoroughly enjoyed Hamilton Road's performance. Tight harmonies, great personalities, good hearts! Even better then what they do on stage is that they are *real* around the dinner table as well."

Leaving Gahanna, we take SR-317 south, and as we cross Rocky Fort Creek, we watch an airplane come in for a landing, and it looks as if it is flying right across the road. Turning right onto IR-270 we travel to SR-3 were we exit and travel north to Westerville, home of Otterbein University established in 1847 by the United Brethren Church. Otterbein was the first institution of higher learning in the United States to admit women without restrictions.

Speaking of higher learning, Reverend Dennis Hager was introduced to southern gospel music as a Nebraska high schooler. In 1982, he had the opportunity to hear the Cathedrals. After graduating from the seminary, he asked his brother, Virgil Hager, to help him start a quartet. They formed several groups, but as a result of his ministry obligations, he has relocated several times and has had to restructure the group each time. Their present group, the New Presence Quartet, is based in Westerville and has been together since 2002. They sing at a number of nursing homes, and Virgil says, "What hits home for me is going to a care center and seeing some of these people start singing that haven't spoken or can't remember their name."

Before leaving Westerville, we make a quick stop at McDonalds then get back on the road, heading south on SR-3 to IR-270. We take IR-270 to SR-161 where we travel east crossing over Rocky Fork Creek again. Captivated by the white farm fence lining the side of the road, we are able to keep our mind off the heavy construction along the way. Traveling through fertile farmland, we watch someone riding their horse and spot some llamas on the left. Turning left onto SR-539A, we cross the creek and arrive in Granville, a historic village established in 1805 by New Englanders from Granville, Massachusetts, who were in search for fertile farmland. A mural in the Granville Post Office, as painted in 1938 by Wendell Jones, depicts the first Sabbath service held by those 1805 settlers. In 2001, with perhaps some of the same ambitions as those earlier settlers, a group called Freedom Voice was formed by three young men who were dedicated to introducing the Master to everyone.

Ron Roesink had been raised on southern gospel music, and when he was seventeen, he started singing with the Sons of Harmony in Flint, Michigan, and they were national champs at the NQC held in Memphis, Tennessee, in

1962. They were awarded recording contracts and their own television show. They sang together for ten years.

In April 2002, Ron discussed singing together with Jamie Caldwell, who had sung professionally and toured with Ed O'Neal and the Dixie Melody Boys. After tossing the idea around for several months, Ron finally called his good friend Sam VanHorn who had sung for a short time in a Columbus group called the Associates. Nephew to Jim Hill, Sam had been raised on gospel music. Jim and Ron shared the stage frequently when Ron was singing with the Sons of Harmony. And Jim was singing with both the Golden Keys and the Stamps. They put together a recording session, and soon Freedom Voice was started.

On May 6, 2005, while in Columbus, they launched their Freedom Fest Extravaganza program, which became a huge success everywhere they ministered. What an incredible night it was as fifty-two people accepted Christ and another fifty recommitted their lives to Christ.

Freedom Voice recorded a live video in September 2005 at the Genoa Baptist Church in Westerville. Powerfully illustrating our Lord, Justin Wells sang "Champion of Love." Then Sam Van Horn reminded the crowd of how sweet it is "since Jesus came into my heart." And finally Ron Roesink confirmed our American freedom as he sang, "This Piece of Cloth."

After one fabulous weekend in Michigan and Toledo, they were returning home and were just praying and thanking the Lord for a great weekend. They had been out for about four nights and had seen many people come to the Lord. It was an incredible time. Right there on the coach, they started praying, and God's Spirit came on that place and they kept praying and praying. One guy would pray, and then the next guy would pray and then the next until all had prayed, and then they would start all over again. It was just an incredible forty-five minutes coming out of Toledo. God's Spirit came on that coach, and there is not a soul in Freedom Voice that will ever forget that night. They arrived home that night, and the next day, they had a writing session planned, and the song "Sweeter" came from that night on that coach. The first verse asks, "Have you ever felt the awesome presence of God in your prayer?" and describes the feelings they had that night on that coach.

Freedom Voice did several tours in Great Britain, the last one in November of 2006, and they had fabulous thirteen nights over there with packed houses every single night. They did the Glasgow Amphitheatre on Saturday night, and they also performed in Belfast. They witnessed hundreds of people come to know the Lord, and it was an incredible experience.

Freedom Voice toured Georgia and Florida every year. After making several trips across the ocean, the group was deeply humbled to sing in Brookville, Florida, for a huge crowd of senior adults. These were people who had fought the fight and remained faithful through the years and, in spite of life's trials, stayed close to the Father's hand. Another great confirmation that even in this crazy world . . . *we can make it*!

They traveled in a beautiful H345 Prevo coach, and one New Year's weekend in Florida, they had an electrical fire in one of the back compartments. They usually let the coach run to keep it cool during their concerts, particularly when they were in Florida. For some reason, they had decided to shut it down. The Lord was watching over them because when they came out to start the coach, they actually saw smoke coming out of the back compartment. The Prevo Company provided excellent service and immediately sent a tech crew down to check out the problem. Finding a malfunction in the electronic system that had happened on some other Prevos, the crew fixed the problem, and soon they were on their way. The next day, they discovered they didn't have any lights, a result of the way things had been put back together. When they contacted Prevo, the company requested they drive the bus to Jacksonville. Having no headlights, they had to wait until the next day before everything was straightened out, and they were once again on their way.

They performed in Silver Dollar City in Branson, Missouri, every year and were always a hit down there. They did several events with Gary McSpadden and actually did a DVD with Gary in Branson at the Americana Theatre. Andrew Polson, a great talent in England, Scotland, and Ireland, came over to the United States and did a short stint with them while he was visiting. Jamie actually ended up moving to Dallas, Texas, taking a position with Southwest Seminary and was in charge of their musical groups that went on the road. Scott Mullen later sang for a few months with the Gospel Harmony Boys from Charleston, West Virginia.

Passing Dennison University on the left, we leave Granville, taking SR-661 north. The area becomes wooded and very hilly as we pass through Fredonia, and it starts raining hard. Reaching U.S. 62, we notice about five turkey vultures along the side of the road enjoying an unidentified feast. Turning right onto U.S. 62, we enter an area of large farms with gas wells scattered throughout the area. We stop for gas in Utica and, back on the road, we pass through Martinsburg, Artanna, and Millwood. We cross the Kokoshing Scenic River and pass an

Amish buggy riding along the left side of the road. Passing through Danville, we pick up SR-205 and continue north to Wooster Road (SR-3) where we drive through some scenic rock and beautiful forested areas as we approach the Mohican State Scenic River. Soon we pass through Loudonville, prior home of Charles Kettering. Continuing along SR-3, we pass through Craigton and Springville, enjoying a great view of the rolling hills across the valley. Merging onto U.S. 250 and then U.S. 30 we continue east to SR-57. Turning left onto SR-57, we travel north, passing the Smucker's Store and Café, and soon arrive at Orrville, home of the Toy and Hobby Museum. Over ten thousand pencils, four thousand five hundred toy trucks, and one thousand unique salt-and-pepper shakers are on display at the museum. Orrville is also home of the Cogar's Singing Jubilee, promoting southern gospel music locally for over twenty-four years.

Driving through Orrville, we travel south on SR-57, driving past Smith's Dairy where there is a giant cow on top of the silo, to U.S. 30 where we turn left and travel east passing through Dalton, pronounced *Dal-ton* as in *Dallas* not *Doll-ton*. Dalton was home of the Slabach Sisters who sang together most of their life as a female quartet. Beginning in 1958, they combined moving spirituals with a smooth rhythm to create a great gospel sound. They were alike in many ways, and when dressed alike, it was difficult to tell them apart. Their friendly personalities allowed them to develop friendships with thousands of people as they worked their way from high school auditoriums to television shows.

Continuing east on U.S. 30, we merge onto SR-172 and pass through East Greenville. Soon we arrive at Massillon, home of the Massillon Museum, which includes the Immel Circus display, a hundred-square foot hand-carved replica of a circus consisting of 2,620 pieces. As the Glick Family traveled along in their converted bus with their nine children, it probably seemed like a circus at times.

In 1998, the Glick family started singing, and they have been traveling full-time for about five years. John Glick, the father, sang with his cousins in the Glick Quartet before he was married. To add to the confusion, the mom, Lanette Glick, married her adopted cousin, so she was a Glick both before and after marriage. Using all live instruments, they maintain an active prison ministry throughout the USA, Canada, and Mexico. Traveling with nine children has its challenges. Once when returning from a two-week tour in Mexico, they stopped at a local laundry somewhere in Texas, and it took forty-eight wash loads to get them back on the road.

One of the Glick sisters now travels with a gospel group in Cody, Wyoming, called the Gospel Messengers. Lanette's brother, Loren Glick, also sings with his family in Wooster.

* * *

LaVerne Lois Williamson was born on July 9, 1923, in McVeigh, Kentucky. LaVerne started her radio career in 1939 as Mountain Fern and later as Dixie Lee. In 1942, she adopted the stage name of Molly O'Day. Married in 1941 to Lynn Davis, they soon became legendary figures in the fields of country and gospel music. Lynn Davis was born in Johnson County, Kentucky, on December 15, 1914.

In 1950, both Molly and Lynn joined the church and devoted their talents to the Lord. The intense feeling and sincerity that Molly put into her songs allowed her to reach many people's hearts. It was also in 1950 that Molly recorded her version of "Don't Sell Daddy Any More Whiskey," which had a major impact on the southern culture.

Stricken with tuberculosis in 1952, Molly had to have part of her lung removed. Then from 1952 until her passing on December 5, 1987, Molly became known as, "the girl with a million friends." She devoted her life to God, hosting a radio program on WEMM in Huntington, Washington, called *Hymns from the Hills*.

At various times, Lynn held the pastorate at three churches in Massilon. Also it is reported that sometime in the mid-1960s Molly's song "King Jesus Will Roll All Burdens Away" was played over the loud speaker in a Woolworth store in downtown Columbus.

Before leaving Massillon we stop along Lincolnway at the Top of the Viaduct restaurant for a wonderful lunch, including sweet potato fries. Leaving Massillon, we take SR-21 north traveling along the viaduct and through more road construction. Turning left onto Clinton Road, we travel to Hametown Road where we are stopped by a Road Closed sign and are forced to take a detour. Following the detour, we enter an area of houses but no city. Turning around, we take SR-585 west and turn left on Gates Street finally reaching Doylestown. The town's landmark, a doughboy statute located in the center of the village, was erected in 1920 to honor those who served in World War I.

Back in the 1950s, leaving the northern part of Georgia, J. D. Cole headed to Ohio in search of a job.

Faran was a young boy, about six years old, when he started playing the guitar and singing on radio WOIO in Canton before his father would preach. His uncle played guitar and also sang with them. They started as a group named the Calvary Gospelaires in 1968. After a few years with this arrangement, Faran started playing piano and his sister, Brenda, started singing and playing the bass guitar with the group. At that time, they decided to change the name from the Calvary Gospelaires to the Cole Family Gospel Singers.

They cut their first album in a town called Blacksburg, South Carolina, at Cherokee Sounds recording studio. They did another two albums at Echo Sound recording studio in Pensacola, Florida, which is owned and operated by Randy Shelnut of the Dixie Echoes. The late Kenny Hinson, of the Hinson family, at one point also helped them produce several recordings.

In 2008, the Cole Family Gospel Singers celebrated forty years of ministry. They have traveled in everything from motor homes to a Silver Eagle bus and covered about fourteen states. Although Faran became a pastor in 1999, they continue to do about forty engagements a year, mostly through the week so he can get back in time for the four services held on Sunday at their home church.

When they purchased their new Silver Eagle bus, the group held a meeting to decide who was going to be responsible for keeping the port-a-pot clean and emptied out. Unable to come to an agreement, they decided the group members would just have to use the rest areas as they had done in prior years.

One day, they were traveling through Virginia headed up a big mountain when Faran and another guy had to go to the rest room. J. D. agreed to stop but, after traveling quite a while without seeing a public restroom, they talked the driver into pulling over along the side of the road near the top of the mountain. They quickly ran up into a wooded area, and while they were using the restroom, Faran heard a rattlesnake. He told the other musician they needed to hurry. As they were working their way back to the bus, they heard the noise again. Turning around, there it was curled up, ready to strike.

Faran screamed, "Rattlesnake!" and they ran as fast as they could. Arriving at the bus, they banged on the side of the bus door until the driver opened the door. Once on the bus and no longer shaking, Faran soon realized it wasn't a rattlesnake he had seen. His tie had simply flown up, and there it was about three inches from his face, starring him right in the eyes. They laughed about that one for years. Wendy Bagwell, plenty familiar with rattlesnake stories, would appreciate this story.

When Faran was about nineteen years old, shortly after he had been called to preach, they were doing a service in Cleveland when a man came in toward the end of the service. It was apparent he had been riding a motorcycle; he was dressed in leather, had long hair, and looked really rough. At the end of the message when the altar call was given, the man came forward. Faran was fearful and was thinking, *Is he going to attack me or pray?* As he knelt down, Faran didn't see one tear in his eyes. The man mumbled the sinner's prayer along with Faran, got up, walked out the back door, and was gone.

About ten years later, Faran's brother was having a kidney transplant, so the Cole Family had canceled everything for about three months. During this same time, the piano player for the Paynes had left to join the Bishops. In anticipation that the Paynes were disbanding, they asked Faran to come and play piano for their last three months of tour. Their last concert was a New Year's Eve gospel sing held at the local high school in Elyria. And there on the front row that evening sat the guy who had came to the altar ten years earlier.

While Faran played the piano, the man was smiling and waving at Faran. After the concert was over, the guy hurriedly came up to him and questioned if he recognized him. The guy was neatly dressed, his hair was neatly combed, and he said, "Ten years ago, I came to one of your revival services and walked forward. I looked like a motorcycle rough rider because I was, and I was hanging with a motorcycle gang. And that night I came up there, gave my heart to the Lord."

Faran acknowledged the event as the guy continued, "I had to hurry out that night as it was about ten minutes until 8:00 PM, and my wife had told me if I wasn't home by eight o'clock, she was going to quickly pack her bags and be gone. She was tired of the drinking, tired of the drugs, simply tired of everything. After giving my heart to the Lord, the very next week, we went to another church where I grew up as a kid, and my wife gave her heart to the Lord."

He then started introducing his family and said, "About three years ago, I was called to preach, and I am helping at a Baptist church down in Wellington."

Every June, for the past twenty-five years, the group has returned home to Blue Ridge, Georgia, where part of the Atlanta Olympics was held, to hold a gospel music convention at Bullen Gap Gospel Park. They have also been doing an annual tour to Jamaica for about sixteen years.

In 2008, traveling in a thirty-one-foot motor home, they continue to sing as a three-generation group consisting of Faran, his wife, Diana, and their two sons, Faran and Jonathan, along with George Langley and Brenda (Cole) Langley and their son Brian, and of course, mom and dad—J. T. and Kathleen Cole. Brian was nominated in the Top 10 Male Vocalists of the year the last two years in a row for the Diamond Award. They recently opened up a small twenty-four-track digital recording studio.

Departing Doylestown to the north, we turn right onto SR-585 to Wooster Road. Merging onto Wooster Road we continue east to Barberton, established in 1891. In 1894, Barberton became home for the Diamond Match Company.

Barberton is also home to a group called Christ Unlimited who was formed in 1975 during a youth rally. Once after singing at a nursing home in Kenton, they were talking with an elderly woman and had the privilege to lead her to Christ. Wanting to be baptized as soon as possible, she was baptized that evening in a physical therapy tub. She passed away the next week.

They traveled throughout the Midwest, and in the 1980s, they did a two-week tour in Florida. Starting out as a quartet, the remaining sisters became a trio in 2002. Although the third sister no longer sings, the other two sisters still do some singing together, adding the third part by soundtrack.

* * *

Shannan Parker was born in Barberton on October 9, 1975. Shannan's father, before giving his life to the Lord, sang country music in bars. When Shannan was two years old, her father accepted Christ and began singing for the Lord. He sang with several part-time gospel groups.

Shannan grew up in the Canton area, and when she was around fifteen years old, she sang with Richard Reese Ministries any time they were in the Ohio area. When Richard Reese passed away suddenly, Shannan recalled of him, "He allowed us to get our feet wet and gave us the push we needed to continue on the path God placed before us."

In 1993, Shannan started traveling with the Overcomers of Akron. She had only sung with the Overcomers for about two years when Steve Miller, the owner of the group, was diagnosed and died from cancer.

Warren Parker was playing piano for SonShine City, a part-time southern gospel group from Southern Ontario, Canada, when he first met Shannan at a truck stop of all places. The Overcomers were on their way to the NQC and had stopped to fuel their bus. Warren's group had also stopped for fuel. Warren was playing for the Merediths from South Carolina when he finally connected with Shannan.

Warren and Shannan were married in 1996 and soon formed the Parker Trio, also known as P3. Their album *Live in Havana* was voted Album of the Year by the Canadian Gospel Music Association in 2005. As their range of engagements throughout the United States continued to expand, the Parker Trio relocated to Nashville, Tennessee.

On January 8, 2006, the group had just arrived at Calvary Church of the Nazarene in Goose Creek, South Carolina, where they planned to take part in the morning worship service. Brandt was maneuvering their bus into the church parking lot, and to prevent damage to the bus, Warren was standing on the highway checking for clearance and directing traffic. Suddenly, a pickup truck crashed into the side of the huge bus with Warren in its path. Emergency crews rushed Warren to the nearest hospital where he passed away as a result of massive body trauma. He was only thirty-four.

Canadian soloist artist Andrew Martin, remembering the joyful heart of his friend, commented, "Warren used to run across the room and jump at me, and I would catch him every time. I just wish that could happen right now."

Warren was never afraid to show his human side. One time, when he was dumping their bus sewage at a campground in Huntsville, Alabama, where they were singing, someone came around the corner while he was dumping and yelled, "Excuse me, I hope that's not sewage you're putting in the fresh water tank!"

Leaving Barberton, we head east on Wooster Road to IR-76 toward Akron exiting onto SR-59 in downtown Akron, the rubber capital of the world. Among the factory workers of the early 1920s was the young Clark Gable. Akron is also home of the Crowne Plaza, a mall made out of the old Quaker Oats factory. The oat silos have been transformed into hotel rooms, providing a unique experience to guests. The round rooms are each about twenty-four feet in diameter. The Rambos would often sing at the Cathedral of Tomorrow located in Akron. Reba remembers the fun she had on that big stage that came up out of the floor. But during one of their New Year's Eve visits, things were not pleasant as young Reba was very sick. Maude Aimee had to bath her with cool rags and alcohol to get her fever down as Rex continually prayed over her.

* * *

Eddie Hawks started singing in a family group with his sister Dana Hawks and his uncle Paul Furrow. The group was called the Hawks Trio, and they were from West Virginia. They sang with such groups as the Rebels, the Harvesters, and the Chuck Wagon Gang. They also did a concert with Johnny Cash. Eddie also played piano for the Couriers for a couple years. After leaving the Couriers, he reformed the Hawks Trio with the help of his wife, Sharon, and another young lady named Helen Foley. When he graduated from college, they moved to Akron where he took a position as a school teacher. In 1969, soon after moving to Akron, Eddie, his wife Sharon, Phil Enloe and his wife formed another group called the Embers.

Phil was just sixteen when he began traveling full-time with the Marks Quartet of Portland, Oregon. When that group disbanded, he joined the Junior Blackwood Brothers in Memphis, Tennessee. After a couple years, he left the group to take a position with the Couriers replacing Don Baldwin. Phil stepped down from the group in 1968. After leaving the Embers, he flew to Las Vegas to join the Imperials but only remained with them a short while. He and his wife later started their own family group.

David Hamilton joined the Embers at a young age recording his first album at age fifteen. Dave was with the group just a few years until he joined the Abraham Brothers of Youngstown. Dave stayed with them until they stopped singing sometime in the mid-1970s.

In 1972, Paul Furrow joined the Embers singing with Eddie and Sharon along with their bass player, Ron Anderson. The group had a regular spot on WJAN TV, Channel 17 in Canton. The group continued to sing with groups such as the Downings and the Cathedrals. They also put together a concert program called the *Good News Company* consisting of the Embers, the Campmeeting Singers, and a group from Indiana called the Good Time

Singers. They stopped singing in 1976 but continued singing in their church and around the Akron area.

Eddie took a position as minister of music at Ravenna Assembly of God Church in Ravenna. The Embers relocated to South Bend, Indiana. Paul and Eddie were pastors at Calvary Temple, and most of their singing was at that church and on the TV programs from the church. Today Eddie Hawks is the minister of music for Victory Church in Lakeland, Florida. Paul Furrow pastors a church in Colonial Heights, Virginia. After the group relocated to Indiana, Ron Anderson played with two other groups, the Privetts and Beulah Land.

* * *

Joe Knight was born in Akron in 1957. He began taking piano lessons at age eight and became the church pianist at age twelve. His first job was music director for a small church in Stow, making a weekly salary of $25. In 1975, while still in his teens, he helped form the Emmanuels Quartet. In the late 1970s, they won the heart of Lou Wills Hildreth, president of New Direction Artist Guild in Nashville, Tennessee. Both Lou and her husband, Howard, were impressed with these young men, and she became their agent. Lou recognized the super talent and devotion of Joe Knight, and as the relationship grew, the group was invited to stay at her home many times. Sending a letter to Larry Orrell, Lou told him, "We must take time to invest in young talent to insure the future of gospel music as you and I know and love it. I believe the Emmanuels Quartet is worthy of our encouragement. Please consider them."

They sang throughout the United States for a period of five years traveling full-time for one year. While on the road, the group was privileged to spend a night in a home previously owned by Johnny Cash.

Joe Knight wrote one song that charted. It was titled "He Never Once Gave Up on Me." Joe was offered the piano position with the Cathedrals when several of their members left to form the Brothers Quartet. Joe told Glen Payne if he could wait until Monday, he would give him his decision. Glen told him this would be okay unless someone else accepted the position before Monday. Come Monday, Joe was informed they had hired Roger Bennett to play piano.

In 1982, Joe performed at the World's Fair held in Knoxville, Tennessee. He later put together a project for Former U.S. Attorney General John Ashcroft and handled production of the *Sunday Gospel Jubilee* a variety show in Branson, Missouri. He presently lives in Greenville, Texas, and has been music pastor at the Family Fellowship Church since 1995. One of the other members of the Emmanuels Quartet, Mark Flakey, sang with both the Florida Boys and the Kingdom-Heirs after leaving the group.

* * *

Jim Buckner was born on November 6, 1923, in Johnson City, Tennessee. His family moved to Ohio during World War II looking for employment. Jim started singing in the Akron Baptist Temple Choir and, around 1950, helped organize the Gospelaires Quartet. He remained with them for 15 years. Leaving the Gospelaires, he joined the Gospel Tones from Akron. After singing with the Gospel Tones, he joined the Evangelaires and remained with them until they broke up. After the Evangelaires disbanded, Jim sang with the Songsters for one year. He then sang with Jordan River from Massillon and later with Ransomed from Rittman for several years. He now sings with the Gospel Reunion Quartet from Akron Baptist Temple and has also been singing with the Gloryway Quartet for about five years.

On one occasion, the Evangelaires were singing in a large auditorium somewhere in West Virginia. The promoter wanted to do things right, so the stage and decorations were immaculate. He even waxed the piano bench. When the group was announced, they all ran onto the stage, including JoAnne, their piano player. She slid onto the piano bench, and much to her surprise, she continued sliding clear across the bench and off onto the floor. Nothing was hurt but her pride.

Another original member of the Evangelaires, Sammy Capps, started singing in a quartet at age thirteen. He sang throughout his teenage years at church and school events. During his service in the army, he became a member of the Fort Bliss Army Chorus. Returning from military duty, he sang with the Spiritualaires, and soon he was singing with the Dixie Knights, a very popular group in the 1950s. They became regulars on the *Archie Campbell Show*, the Mull Singing Convention, and the *Grand Ole Opry*. They went on the road full-time and became one of the featured groups at the first NQC.

In the late 1950s, Sammy had an opportunity to sing with Lee Roy Abernathy and the Miracle Men. In 1967, he began singing at the Cathedral of Tomorrow in an eight-man chorus with George Younce, Glen Payne, Danny Koker, Joe Parker, Mack Taunton, Johnny Hope, and Bob Shumate. He remained with the choir until the formation of the Evangelaires. While with the group, he kept a very unique daily diary documenting every event that took place. The Evangelaires sang at Jim Jones's church and had a good service. They were shocked when Jim Jones later formed the cult that followed him to their death during the terrible Jonestown Massacre.

The Evangelaires became good friends with the Prophets Quartet as they often traveled to Ohio. Shortly after moving to Stow, the Prophets were singing in the area. Sam had agreed to take them to the church where they were scheduled to sing. As Lou Garrison weighed almost five hundred pounds, Sammy did not have room in his car to take all of the members at one time, so he had to make two trips. When he returned, Lou was standing on the curb talking with George Younce, who was living in the same neighborhood. Sam was not aware the George lived nearby, but George and Sam soon became very good friends.

After leaving the group, Sam moved to North Carolina where he sang for two years in a group called the Trailways Quartet in Boone, North Carolina, with Bud Younce, a cousin of George Younce. He had a brief stint with the Harvesters Quartet in Greensboro, North Carolina. In 1981, he moved to Chattanooga, Tennessee, and joined the Noblemen with whom he continues to sing today after twenty-seven years.

Gary "Teddy Bear" Herron sang with the Evangelaires in 1974 and later sang with Jerry and the Singing Goffs. After one event in the winter of 1974, they were traveling home to Ohio when, just outside of Jellico, they encountered a snowstorm. The further north they drove, the heavier the snow fell. Gary was driving the bus for his first time in the snow. Sammy looked over, and Gary was singing "Just as I Am." At that point, Sammy thought it best to take over, and Gary was very appreciative.

In 1973, the Evangelaires became a full-time group, but this only lasted for about eighteen months because of financial difficulties. The Evangelaires later reunited as the Spokesmen for several years.

* * *

A group was formed in Detroit in the late 1920s as the Masonic Glee Club. Their early success can be attributed to their great bass singer, Jimmy Bryant. In 1933, an Akron minister changed their name to the Heavenly Gospel Singers, and they became a semiprofessional group traveling throughout Michigan and Ohio. Their home base shifted several times from Akron to Charlotte, North Carolina. After moving to Charlotte, they developed a close association with the Golden Gate Quartet, and as a result, the group's popularity continued to grow.

In 1938, Jimmy Bryant left the group. Bryant later sang with the Gospel Light Jubilee Singers and the Detroiters.

Jimmy was replaced with another fine bass singer, Willie Bobo. Willie left the group after three years to sing with the Dixie Hummingbirds.

After the end of World War II, the group reformed under the leadership of Henderson Massey, but they never regained the popularity previously attained. One of their members, Bob Beatty, went on to sing with the Sensational Nightingales, the Violinaires, the Gospel Knights, and the Soul Lifters.

* * *

Martha Bell (Childers) Humbard played and sang during her husband's services, and along with their son Alpha Rex Emmanuel Humbard and two of their other children, they formed the musical Humbard Family. During the late 1930s, they were regulars on KTHS out of Hot Springs, Arkansas. They turned down an offer to become regulars at the *National Barn Dance* in Chicago, refusing to add secular songs to their sacred repertoire. In 1939, Virgil O. Stamps put them on a program at the Dallas State Fair Auditorium, and they later made several commercials.

On August 2, 1942, Rex married Maude Aimee Jones, and she soon became an active part of popular Humbard Family. By 1950, the family was holding three-week-long crusades across America. In 1953, Rex decided to settle down in Akron where he began a radio broadcast and started a church called Calvary Temple.

In 1958, the great Cathedral of Tomorrow was built, having a seating capacity of 5,400. The services were televised on national network, and the cathedral had a platform that could be lowered or raised during the services. One Sunday, as Rex stepped out on the platform, it began to lower. When it reached the bottom, it started back up. While the platform continued to rise and fall, the choir and the congregation began to laugh hysterically. Rex began to adlib, saying things like "In life, one can go up and down" and "heaven is high and hell is low," which only added to the laughter. Finally, at one point when the platform had moved to the upper position, Rex stepped off the platform to an area near the altar.

Singing continued to be a tradition with the family, but by the 1960s, the Cathedrals Quartet became regulars on the broadcast.

The famous Elvis Presley routinely watched Rex Humbard on TV, and when Elvis was on tour in Las Vegas, someone sent a message back to J. D. Sumner that Rex and Maud Aimee were in the audience. They were on vacation and wanted to stop by and visit with Elvis. When Rex arrived backstage, he and Elvis went into a private room. They remained in the room for almost an hour while Elvis questioned Rex about the Bible and prayed. Then on August 18, 1977, standing in the living room of the Graceland Mansion, Rex paid tribute to his close friend while J. D. Sumner and the Stamps along with the Statesmen Quartet and Kathy Westmoreland performed some of Elvis's favorite hymns.

Rex Humbard passed away in 2007 at the age of eighty-eight, and in honor of this great evangelist, many wonderful comments were expressed at his funeral by Bill Gaither, Richard Roberts, and others. The hearts of those present were also touched as a special group featuring the Gatlin Brothers with Bill Gaither singing bass and Ernie Haase on the tenor sang several wonderful songs.

* * *

Dorothy Davis, known to all as "Dot," was born in Repton, Alabama, and moved to Akron where she began singing at age two. She was once asked to tour with the late Mahalia Jackson, but her mother decided Dorothy was too young to leave home. Dorothy was a gospel warrior and a phenomenal singer. Rev. Melford Elliott said, "She sang with such vigor and boldness, with a flavor like Albertina Walker, Shirley Cesar, and even a little bit of Aretha Franklin."

Dorothy sang lead for the Royal Angelettes, a gospel quartet in Akron, for over forty-five years. Dorothy loved music, the church, and she truly believed in praising the Lord. She felt convinced that if she could just touch one person with her singing, she had done her job. Singing with several gospel groups, Dorothy continued to sing across America until she passed away at age sixty-two.

* * *

Sharon (Leek) Miller was born on October 10, 1948, in West Virginia. She started singing in a family group called the Heaven-Aires at age eight. The group was based in Canton and traveled from place to place in an old station wagon. They also sang as regulars on a local radio program for a period of nine years.

Later, after the family group stopped singing, Sharon joined the Pathfinders in Akron where she remained for sixteen years. The Pathfinders were involved in radio work for six years and also made a few television appearances. When Sharon's sister joined the group, the name was changed to the Overcomers. The group remained active for several years, appearing a number of times on a television program in Lewisville.

When her husband's health began to decline, the group continued for another seven years until he passed away. As her husband's poor health created financial difficulties, their good friend Kevin Spencer held a benefit sing to assist them with some of the expenses. After the passing of her husband, Sharon did solo work for almost four years until she joined the Jordan River Trio of Canton. Her sister started another group based in Canton called Crossways that stayed together for three years.

Sharon left Jordan River after one year and joined Master's Voice in Akron where she remained for four years. During Sharon's time with Master's Voice, they hosted the *Down Home Gospel* radio program on WHLO and did several live broadcasts on a local TV program. Bruce Wells of Master's Voice later went on to sing with a group from Akron called Restored.

Sharon eventually remarried and became Sharon Tawney, and in 2002, she created His Servants, a group that is at times a duet and other times a trio.

* * *

In 1979, Roy Tremble, George Amon Webster and Lorne Matthews left the Cathedrals Quartet to start a group of their own called the Brothers. The Brothers started out traveling in a van pulling a trailer. When they later purchased a bus, Roy and George Amon did most of the driving.

Once after singing in Florida, they were headed to Nashville, Tennessee, to complete a record contract. They were supposed to be there on Monday morning, and on Sunday evening, they were still in Florida. From Florida to Nashville overnight would be a long stretch to make, but they decided to try. Lorne, who very seldom did the driving, told the guys it was going to be a long trip. He said, "You guys get some rest, and I will get us there." This was a bit unusual to say the least, but needing some rest, they agreed to let Lorne drive. Sometime during the night, even George Amon fell asleep.

George woke up around 4:00 AM and realized the bus was not moving. Looking out the window, he noticed they were in a rest area and were still in Florida. He got out of bed and hurried up where Lorne was, finding him sound asleep. Knowing they were supposed to be in Nashville in a few hours, George woke him up to find out where they were, but Lorne had no idea. George Amon took over the driving and soon realized there were no more than sixty miles down the road from where Lorne had started driving. They did make their appointment, but perhaps we should not discuss how fast they traveled that morning on their way to Nashville.

Roy Tremble was born in Joplin, Missouri, and growing up in Galena, Kansas, he developed a love for gospel music. In 1965, he attended the Stamps Quartet School of Music in Dallas, Texas. While attending the quartet school, he won a talent contest, and shortly after returning home, he received a call from some of guys that were in the old Junior Blackwood Brothers. They were starting a new group and wanted to know if he was interested in traveling with them.

Soon, at the age of eighteen, he was off to join a trio called the Lancers in Memphis, Tennessee. In 1969, after singing with the Lancers for a while, he left to travel with Whitey Gleason's group. Leaving this group, Roy traveled with the Weatherfords.

Traveling with the Weatherfords, they often worked concerts with the Cathedrals. One day, Glen Payne called him asking if he would consider moving to Akron and joining the Cathedrals. In the spring of 1971, Roy moved to Ohio. He stayed with the Cathedrals until the end of 1979. Roy still holds fond memories of the night the Cathedrals were given a chance to sing for the Dove Awards in Nashville with the Ralph Carmichael Orchestra. And perhaps one of the greatest experiences was the night of that big Cathedrals Quartet reunion, when all of the past members got together and did a live video recording in Nashville.

Roy later went on to sing with the Blackwood Quartet working the theatres in Branson, Missouri. He left the Blackwood Quartet to help Amon Webster form a group called the Heartland Boys. Since leaving the Heartland Boys, Roy has maintained a solo ministry for the last twelve years in Chesterfield, Indiana. Roy still visits Ohio often as his two children and four grandchildren still live in the Akron area.

The second member of the Brothers, George Amon Webster was born in Arkansas on December 10, 1945, the youngest of ten children. He grew up in a musical atmosphere as three of his brothers played the piano. After moving to Flint, Michigan, he formed a local group called the Templeaires, which included his brother and a guy named Mack Taunton. While yet teenagers, they were singing every weekend and traveling throughout country. In 1961, they won the NQC talent contest in Memphis, Tennessee, adding to their popularity. Traveling with the Templeaires, George was exposed to a number of people like George Younce, who at the time was singing with the Blue Ridge Quartet, and Glen Payne who was singing with the Weatherfords.

A few months later, when Danny Koker left the Cathedrals, they called George Amon. This was while they were still with Rex Humbard at the Cathedral of Tomorrow. George went down to Akron, and taking the position, he stayed with them almost three years. He moved back to Michigan but, soon after, received a call from Glen and returned to the group for another eight years. George Amon says of his experience with the Cathedrals, "I had a great, great time and worked with some of the best guys and greatest talent in gospel music. I have truly been a blessed man."

George Amon went on to sing with the Blackwood Quartet in Branson, Missouri. He left the Blackwood Quartet to form a group called the Heartland Boys with Roy Tremble. George Amon remained with the Heartland Boys until 2003 when he had a stroke that seriously affected his left side, leaving him partially handicapped. Sometime later when his wife also had a stroke, they determined it was time for them to retire and move to Florida. After moving to Florida, they never felt peace regarding this decision, and George became convinced that God was not through with him yet. While in Florida, George Amon formed a quartet called the Brothers, which included his two brothers Danny and Larry and his son Tim.

In May 2007, Terry Toney of the Toney Brothers called George Amon asking him if he knew of a baritone singer. At sixty-one years of age, George Amon, somewhat jokingly told Terry, "I'm a pretty good baritone singer." Terry indicated they needed some help over the next couple of weeks to do some dates. George accepted the challenge, and they flew him down to meet with them. It only took a couple of singing dates to cement the arrangement. George Amon believes God has been gracious to him as his health is now much better, and his voice is stronger than ever before. He still can't play the piano because of problems with his left hand, but he thoroughly enjoys singing.

The Brothers third member, Lorne Matthews, was born on June 20, 1941, in Toronto, Canada. Lorne was raised in the church, and when he was just a teenager, he and a close friend went to their first gospel event at Massey Hall in Toronto, Canada. They had seats way up in the top looking down at the Blackwood Brothers, the Speer Family, and the Statesmen as they sang. Sometime during the evening, Lorne turned to his friend and said, "Someday I will be down there on that stage playing the piano for a quartet."

He started playing piano when he was ten years old, and as a boy in Canada, he played for a number of local groups. One of the first groups he played for was a girl's trio called the Batten Sisters during the Youth for Christ days. In the 1950s, he started playing with a group called the Sons of Praise, a quartet with the two Benson brothers and two other guys. He was educated at the Toronto Conservatory of Music and at London Bible College. In 1959, he auditioned for a group called the Kings Men who had established a ministry in Australia and recently came back needing a piano player. So Lorne started traveling with them, and it was during that summer that he met his future wife, Jimmie Ruth Rutledge.

Lorne states that when he saw her, he instantly fell in love with her. Talking to some people, he found out that she was a graduate of Moody Bible College. She was from Tennessee and had just auditioned with the Speer Family. She was a quite a pianist and singer herself. Dad Speers wanted to hire her, but the other members of the group thought she was too young. They got married six months later on December 28, 1962.

In 1963, Lorne was hired by a quartet in Canada called the Saltan Brothers and started traveling with them. His wife also traveled with them until she became pregnant. They were the first full-time group in Canada and had the first television show of any gospel group, a thirteen-week series broadcast in London, Ontario. He traveled with the Saltans for two years until they disbanded.

Believing there would be more opportunities in America and wanting to get away from the cold, they moved with a dream down to Tennessee. While Lorne was doing work as an accompanist, Jerry Goff, who was pastor of a church in Glen Burnie, Maryland, hired him as music director.

Later, they moved to Baltimore, and one night, a concert was held at their church featuring the Stamps Quartet, who at that time consisted of such greats as Jim Hill, Roger McDuff, and Big John Hall. Sometime during the evening, Lorne was talking with Big John Hall and asked him to step down into the basement with him. Down in the basement of the church, Lorne sat down at the piano and played some Jackie Marshall licks and a few other melodies for him. He told Big John if he heard of a quartet needing a piano player, to keep him in mind. That night when Big John got on the bus, and knowing that Roger was incubating the thought of forming a trio with his two evangelist brothers, he told Roger McDuff, "I heard your piano player tonight." He told him when they were ready to form the trio, they needed to call Lorne Matthews.

So about six months later, he did. Lorne went down to Memphis, Tennessee, and Roger took him over to Jackie Marshall's house. Lorne was somewhat nervous but figured he would simply play some of that old Blackwood Brothers—style playing. After playing for about five minutes, Jackie stopped him and said, "Roger, hire the guy right now."

So in 1967, Roger hired him, and as a new group, they made quite a splash in gospel music. They did a lot of work at the NQC and were staged with the Statesmen and the Blackwoods. After two years, they decided to go back to preaching, and the trio would no longer be a full-time job. So once again, Lorne was looking for work.

Leaving the McDuff Brothers in 1969, he put together a family group called the Lorne Matthews Family. He was then hired by Dr. John Rawlings and did a short stint with the Landmark Quartet in Cincinnati. He traveled with them for a few years, and then he started traveling with his wife and family. It was during that time that he stopped by the Cathedral of Tomorrow and talked to Glen Payne who was traveling with George Younce in a quartet for the Cathedral of Tomorrow. They were the most televised quartet in America at that time. They had heard Lorne with the McDuffs and, having developed a friendship, he was just stopping by to say hello. Then after traveling a few years with his family, they moved to Indiana to be music directors at the Calvary Temple in South Bend.

It was at that time that Glen and George went through the transition of leaving Rex Humbard, and their piano player had decided to stay at the Cathedral of Tomorrow. While Lorne was still at the church in South Bend, the Cathedrals came for a concert, and Glen indicated they needed a piano player. The next week, they were going to be traveling up in Michigan and asked if Lorne would come up and talk with them. He went up, and soon he was moving from South Bend, Indiana, to Stow.

The first date he did with them, they picked him up on the bus and went to Halifax, Nova Scotia, in 1970. They were very hot in Canada at the time. It was a very interesting tour, back to his home country of Canada, and the first few days he was with them, they sold so many records he couldn't believe it.

He traveled for two years with the Cathedrals and then felt led to go back with his family and did another few years as the Lorne Matthews Family. Then one day, Glen called him and told him the guy that had replaced him, Haskell Cooley, had just left the group. He wanted to know if he had any interest in rejoining the group. As some of the family group was ready to stop singing, Lorne said, "When do you want me to come?" Glen told him they had a date the next night in Atlanta, Georgia, and asked if he could fly into Atlanta. He returned to the Cathedrals in 1979 for another two years and enjoyed being with the guys very much.

The second time Lorne joined the quartet, they had a date booked at Landmark Baptist Temple. There were three thousand people in the church that evening, and the event was broadcast all over the nation. Lorne was sitting there, having been with the group only a couple of weeks. Then George, forgetting that Haskell, the man who had traveled with them for two years, was gone, called out a song Lorne didn't know. Not knowing what to do, Lorne quickly said, "Well, George, why don't you hum a little bit of that, I might know it if you hum it, but I've never heard that song." The people started laughing.

The members of the Cathedral Quartet loved to bowl, so George Younce, Glen Payne, and Bud Seeker, the bus driver, formed a team of the old—timers, and Roy Tremble and George Amon Webster and Lorne Matthews formed another team. They would be fanatically bowling every evening after their concerts. Even if the concert was not over until midnight, they would find a bowling alley and bowl at least two games. They got serious about it once to the point of getting matching shirts, and they had a lot of fun. The group also loved to play golf, and the orders to Bud Seeker were, "When you drive out of a town headed to the next appointment, don't go to a hotel, go to the golf course. When we wake up, we'll play golf, and then we will go to the hotel and clean up for the next program."

When Lorne returned to the Cathedrals, Roy Tremble was singing tenor and George Amon was singing baritone and playing bass. They came to him after a few months of being with them and mentioned to him they would like to form a trio, and he just laughed it off. Two years passed by, and they kept talking to him about the idea, and soon he began to realize they were very serious. So they agreed to start practicing and see how it sounded. Determining it was something they could do, they began to make plans. They started thinking about making a recording, and of course, George and Glen didn't know anything about their plans. They started talking to a man that produced records, and as soon as they let the cat out of the bag, the man went and told Glen and George.

Then one weekend on their way to Indiana for a concert, George came to them wanting to know about the recording they were preparing to make. When they confirmed that they were in fact making a recording, George informed them this would be their last trip as part of the Cathedrals. Lorne immediately contacted his wife telling her they were going to need her help with the bookings as she had always done the booking for the family ministry. She got on the horn and started booking their new group called the Brothers.

Soon Roy left the group and was replaced with a guy from the Blackwoods named John Cox, a California kid that sang tenor and played the trumpet. They sang together for two years, making three recordings and even had a contract with the Benson Company. The group experienced some hard times, including some marital issues, and soon the group was dissolved, and they went their separate ways.

After the Brothers separated, Lorne continued to travel quite a while with his family and got involved in different ministries. One day, his wife expressed concern that although he had been involved in several different ministries, he had let his piano playing go by the way side. So in 2000, he started doing piano concerts developing the "Keyboards for the King" ministry, touring with his wife, Jimmie Ruth Matthews. In 2003, he was inducted into the Piano Roll of Honor Hall of Fame and received the Living Legend Award for over forty-five years in gospel music. He also played "The Battle Hymn of the Republic" for President Ronald Reagan's First Congressional Prayer Breakfast.

Before George Younce passed away, Lorne went by his home and had prayer with him. As he was leaving, he said, "George, you are the greatest bass singer I have ever heard and just a great emcee, but there's another thing you did well, and that was your recitations. I remember night after night at the concerts playing different songs behind you as you did your recitations. Whether it was 'Forgive Me when I Whine,' 'The Old Violin,' or 'Suppertime.' When you were finished, there wasn't a dry eye in the place. You really have a gift at that, how about putting a CD out of all your recitations?"

He indicated that because of his current health problems, he didn't have the strength. Lorne told him, "George, you can get Ernie to take you to your garage. You have a great studio back there, you can record your voice, and then later on, they can put music to it."

So a few months later, Lorne was going to Florida for the winter, so he stopped by and said good-bye to George. While visiting, he asked George about the project they had discussed. George smiled and said, "I just finished it yesterday—it's called *Poetic Reflections*."

It's the last thing George recorded before passing on.

Lorne was greatly shocked when Anthony Berger passed away. When Lorne was with the Cathedrals and Anthony was still with the Kingsmen, they did a piano duet. In fact, they were the ones who came up with the arrangement for "Firing Line" and they tore the crowd up—people loved it.

Lorne says, "Anthony was a very gifted and wonderful guy."

He has performed in several countries, and in 2006, at a concert in Nigeria, over eight million people listened as Lorne Matthews and the McDuff Brothers performed. In 2007, Lorne and his wife flew to Mexico City for three days, and arriving back in Ohio, they went directly to a camp meeting where they ministered to all of Ohio's seniors for the Assembly of God. Then they headed down to the NQC to be with all of their old friends. In October, it was back to Florida where, as permanent residents, they minister to millions of seniors, "snow birds" they call them, who come down to Florida for the winter months.

* * *

On December 28, 1896, a baby boy came into the world. His family named him Vandall, the same name as one of the uncivilized tribes that ravaged Europe during the Middle Ages. They had such a reputation for viciousness and destruction that their name gives our language today the verb *vandalize*. To go with his savage surname, his parents named him Napoleon B. Vandall, after probably the most indomitable French general of all times. Shying away from such a double-barreled connotation of fierceness, he always went by simply N. B. Vandall.

In 1920, Vandall was spiritually born during a Methodist camp meeting held in Sebring. He later became a gospel songwriter and song evangelist, assisting in revival meetings throughout the country. The song entitled "My Sins Are Gone" is perhaps one of the most popular songs written by N. B. Vandall.

In 1934, while living in Akron, Vandall's son Paul was nearly killed after being hit by a car. As a result of this tragic event, he wrote the words to a song, which he simply titled, "After." The song reminds us that after the heat of the day and all our troubles have passed, we will see Jesus at last. His son survived the accident and lived to the age of seventy-five.

* * *

Earl Weatherford was born on October 10, 1922 in Pauls Valley, Oklahoma. He would often hurry home from school to listen to the Frank Stamps Quartet on the radio. During World Was II, Earl moved to California where he worked in the shipyard. Young Earl attended many singing conventions in the Southwest. In 1943, Earl Weatherford, while living in Long Beach, California, sang with a male quartet called the Gospel Harmony Boys. Shortly thereafter, he met a beautiful sixteen-year-old lady named Lily Fern Goble. They fell in love and were married in 1945.

Lily was born in Bethany, Oklahoma, on November 25, 1928, and was raised in California. She could sing harmony and maintain pitch before she was old enough to talk. Before meeting Earl and singing with the Weatherfords, Lily sang in a ladies trio with Martha Brown and Dorothy Bright. They were featured on a radio program in Long Beach, California. Earl's sister Bette Jo Weatherford later joined that group, making it a female quartet. Lily then filled in with the Gospel Harmony Boys for a while until another tenor came along, and then she was out.

Earl started his own group in 1944 calling them the Weatherford Quartet and started making plans to travel full-time. Now ready to hit the road, they left California in 1949 touring the country in their 1948 Buick, which pulled a one-wheel trailer. After traveling for a while, they finally settled down in Fort Wayne, Indiana, where they were on the radio station WOWO for two years. At the same time, Raye Roberson became pregnant and decided to retire from traveling and was replaced by Danny Koker. Shortly before leaving California, they hired a sixteen-year-old youngster from nearby South Gate named Armon Morales.

Armon Morales was born in Los Angeles, California. He met Earl Weatherford and Lily Fern when they were living in Lynwood, California. They had a part-time singing group, and the baritone singer was attending Armon's church. In 1949, he told Armon they needed somebody to sing the low end. He didn't have any experience but Armon agreed to go over and try out. Accepting the position, he remained with them until he was drafted and went to Korea for two years. Near the end of his Korean tour, he received a letter requesting he join the Oak Ridge Boys. He accepted their offer, but when he got out of the service, he found they had disbanded. The Weatherfords had replaced Morales with George Younce.

In 1953, when the station stopped using live music, the Weatherfords went over to Akron and started working with Rex Humbard at the Cathedral of Tomorrow where they remained until around 1963. It wasn't long until Earl called Armon and wanted to know if he would consider moving to Ohio as they were working at the Cathedral of Tomorrow with Rex Humbard. Armon agreed, and moving to Ohio, he stayed with them until 1963 when he left to join Jake Hess in forming the Imperials.

The group was still going through occasional personnel changes, and a young man named Jim Hamill joined the group for a while.

While they were in Akron, the group that everybody remembers was Earl Weatherford, Lily Weatherford, Armon Morales singing the bass, Glen Payne on the lead, and Henry Slaughter, who had taken Danny Koker's place, was playing the piano.

Henry Slaughter was born on January 9, 1927 in Roxboro, North Carolina. He acquired his education from regular music teachers, gospel music, public radio, and the church. When he graduated from high school, he went away to the Stamps-Baxter School of Music in Chattanooga, Tennessee, for a couple of weeks. He stayed for three months and took private lessons. He entered the military for eighteen months until 1947 when he went to work with a gospel quartet out of Siloam Springs, Arkansas, called the Ozark Quartet. Henry remained with them until 1951. On December 20, 1952, he married Hazel Myers who was born in Meridian, Mississippi, on May 29, 1935. Hazel sang in local churches with Henry for about eight years.

In 1956, he started playing for the Tulsa Trumpeteers, and in 1958, he joined the Weatherford Quartet and played with them during their ministry at the Cathedral of Tomorrow in Akron until 1963. When Henry got to the Cathedral of Tomorrow, in 1958 they were moving into the nearly completed building, and there was so much excitement about doing the television program. They were all riding high in expectancy, and it had to be one of the most exciting times in their life, but the real excitement was what was going on spiritually at the Cathedral of Tomorrow.

At the time, Henry was living in Cuyahoga Fall, and he made an album with the Weatherfords called *In the Garden*. It was considered one of the great gospel albums of all times, spotlighting the smooth, close harmony of the group and was distributed all over the United States. While at the cathedral, they traveled to a number of states because of television work, and he wrote a number of songs. He was also music director for a while at the Cathedral of Tomorrow, and in 1959, he started his own publishing company, Harvest Time Publishing.

In 1963, he joined the Imperials and was with them three years. Leaving the Imperials, Henry and Hazel traveled together for a while until they became a part of the Gaither team, who began traveling nationally. They were with the Gaithers for seven years and then continued traveling another ten years as husband and wife.

Since 1966, they have been living in Nashville, Tennessee. In 1969, Henry developed the famous Henry Slaughter Piano Course and started traveling with the Bill Gaither Trio. Henry and his wife, Hazel, traveled with the Gaither Trio until 1976. They completed twenty-four recordings and received five Dove Awards. Henry owned a studio for a while, has written numerous songs, has published music, and has played sessions as a studio musician. The Slaughters traveled the nation until the mid-1990s when they began to wind down—considering themselves semiretired.

Henry says, "I suppose when it comes really down to it, of all the things we have done, playing the piano is probably my favorite."

Henry won his five Dove Awards for Best Instrumentalist of the Year and was nominated several other times. He was placed on the southern gospel Piano Roll of Honor by the Grand Ole Gospel Reunion.

Henry and Hazel still do some singing together, and they have done some breakfast clubs. In fact, one of the last dates they did in the summer of 2007 was with the Weatherfords just south of Canton at the Sugarcreek Breakfast Club. Their daughter Amanda Joy continues to manage Harvest Time Publishing from her home in Bryan.

The Weatherfords sang in almost every town in Ohio because Earl booked everything he could. Then they would show up on Wednesday and Sunday to do the TV show for Rex Humbard. They became one of the smoothest-sounding gospel quartets of all times. Lily had taken time away from the group in the early 1960s to spend time with a new son. Earl hired Bobby Clark to take her place. Koker returned to the group as pianist after Slaughter resigned to lead the choir at the Cathedral of Tomorrow in early 1963.

When Earl and Lily Weatherford decided to leave Akron, Glen Payne, Danny Koker, and Bobby Clark opted to stay with Humbard forming the Cathedral Trio. George Younce left the Blue Ridge Quartet and joined them shortly afterward, and they stayed with Humbard until 1969. This is the group that later became the Cathedral Quartet.

Earl and Lily went back on the road with Armon Morales singing bass and Mack Evans singing the baritone part. Also with the group was a little piano player named Jerry Evans, and Vic Clay played the bass. They traveled that way until 1964. Armon was mainly in charge of the bus and was working on the bus all of the time. Once they were traveling on the turnpike in Ohio and had an oil leak. As he couldn't figure out where the oil leak was coming from, he crawled under the bus back to the engine with a flashlight in his hand while they were traveling down the road.

In 1963, Jake Hess left the Statesmen Quartet wanting to put together a quartet of the highest quality. He contacted Armon Morales and Henry Slaughter and requested they join this new group to be called the Imperials Quartet. Henry spent several months preparing the music for this new venture. Because of the unique sound of the Imperials, they were soon hired to sing backup for Elvis Presley. After a couple years, Henry left the group and was replaced by Joe Moscheo. Armon also left the Weatherfords to sing with the Imperials who at that time consisted of Jake Hess, Cheryl Nielson, Henry Slaughter, and Gary McSpadden.

After two and a half years, Jake felt his health declining and decided to move on and do other things. Later, when Roger Wiles and Terry Blackwood came to the group, they formed a whole new style of music averaging about 280 dates a year. Things were a little rocky for a while because neither the southern gospel market nor the church markets were interested in contemporary music because of the drums and other instruments. However, knowing Chet Adkins, they were able to do some work in the studio, along with the Jordanaires, backing several country artists. After doing an album with Jimmy Dean, he asked them to be a part of his team. They joined him, and this launched them into the secular field. Their first appearance was in California at the Circle Star Theater with the Lennon Sisters. This opened a whole new door, and they ended up doing a record with Elvis Presley and becoming a part of his team also. They did this for seven years until they were strong enough and felt the Lord really wanted them to go back singing gospel.

Starting part-time, they began doing gospel when they didn't work with Elvis or Jimmy Dean. They moved back to Nashville, Tennessee, and their gospel career blossomed from there. In the 1980s, the Imperials were singing in Dayton at Memorial Hall. Rick Doran was helping work their record table, and shortly after the concert was over, Rick was walking around and looking into the empty auditorium. He noticed Armon Morales standing near the stage presenting the Gospel and leading someone to Christ.

Armon says, "I went to Bible school in Southern California and witnessing was our main focus, especially in the church work we did outside of the concert work. We always gave altar calls, things like that, and we still do!"

In 2005, Armon went to Hawaii for a couple of years and formed a group called the Classic Imperials, which now works in Tennessee. They have a new album coming out, and it looks like God has opened a door to a whole new thing for guys his age. Armon's son wanted to keep the group going here, so he let him carry on the Imperials name.

While in Akron, the Weatherfords had a phenomenal ministry and were on television sometimes three times a day. People came from everywhere to see the Humbards and the Weatherfords as a result of their television ministry. Many evangelists came in, and during the ten years that the group ministered there, they saw some phenomenal meetings at the Cathedral. Many times, Rex wouldn't even get to preach. He would simply give an altar call, and people would start coming to the altar. Rex was a faith-believing man, he had a great ministry, and Armon confirms that it ministered to him. Lily believes she learned more about faith in God, exercising her faith and believing in what God can do for her, at the Cathedral than she would have learned in a lifetime anywhere else.

She says, "It was a wonderful experience. I have been a Christian all my life. My dad was a Nazarene preacher, but I never really understood what real faith was until spending time at the Cathedral of Tomorrow."

Since that time, with the present group, they have had bus breakdowns and other problems that they could not possibly handle on their own. But in each case, God would perform a miracle, and it would be taken care of. This has happened three times in the last year and a half, absolute miracles all because they placed their faith in God. Lily calls all of those things that come along in life, all the problems they faced, "faith builders" because they work to build our faith in Christ and in God and in what God can do.

Lily is almost eighty, and she says, "The longer I live, the more I realize there is just nothing worth worrying about when you have Jesus Christ. He is a firm foundation to base your life on. It is the only way to live. Put Christ first and you will always make it."

When they left Akron, they established a new home base in Johnstown, Pennsylvania. After a couple years, they moved back to California where they stayed for a couple more years. Finally, they moved back to Oklahoma, their home for the last thirty-seven years.

More singers would come and go as the years went on, including Dave Rowland, Dallas Holms, Mike Allen, Bob Thacker, Fulton Nash, and Roy Tremble. Despite all the changes, the one constant that always remained was the smooth harmony that Earl was ever the stickler for, and the marvelous alto of, Lily Fern who remains a great singer and trooper today, after all these years.

Earl passed away on June 19, 1992, but his memory lingers on. Lily and her son Steve still travel carrying on an old tradition. Traveling with her son Steve and a young man named Cody Boyer from Oklahoma City, they still go by the name *the Weatherfords*.

Armon says, "Lily still sounds good and still does well, and I have to honor them because they brought me into the singing business. I was real sorry when Earl got so sick and his arthritis bothered him all like that. That was pretty sad for me."

Lily considers Armon Morales to be the smoothest bass singer of all time. Lily says, "Glen Payne was the best all-around lead singer to ever sing Gospel music."

Leaving Akron, we take SR-8 south to IR-76 where we head east, passing thc Goodyear World Headquarters on the left, and continue to SR 532. Traveling south on SR-532, we pass through Tallmadge and arrive at the small town of Mogadore, which was named after an Arabic word meaning *beautiful* and is the home of the Songsters.

Jerry Waldrop II was born on January 25, 1958, in Akron. His grandfather taught music and was also a music director in Alabama. His grandmother was also involved in music, playing the old pump organ. The family moved up from Alabama to Akron looking for work during the Depression, bringing with them the knowledge of reading shaped notes and the experience of singing quartet music. Jerry grew up in a house where they routinely had quartet practice every Tuesday and Thursday. Jerry started singing when he was two years old, and when he was old enough, they allowed him to carry the microphone stands.

When Jerry was young, his dad made sure he attended singing school. Bill Echols had a group called the Echols Brothers at the Country Baptist

Church. Every year, he held a class that taught shaped notes. He also taught singing skills and taught people how to direct music. You would learn your "do-mi-so-dos" and develop good timing. Jerry was only eight or nine when he first had to stand and direct music. Jerry still has his old textbook entitled *The Rudiments of Music*. His Dad worked second shift and would get home from work around 7:00 PM just as quartet practice was suppose to start. He would come home, and moving as quickly as possible, he would set up the equipment and try to eat a little bit before everybody started showing for practice. Before long, Jerry was setting up the equipment before dad got home. Both literally and figuratively, Jerry cut his teeth listening to quartet music.

While Jerry was growing up, large gospel events were held in downtown Akron at the Goodyear Auditorium. Different church choirs would come bringing their shaped-note songbooks, and people would fill the auditorium to hear these choirs directed by different music directors. At home, his dad would play songs by such groups as the Statesmen, the Blackwoods, the Prophets, or the Rebels. Sometimes, after they had picked beans from the garden, they would gather around and sing while snapping the beans. They'd be snapping those beans and singing away, but soon dad would say, "No, no, no, you're not staying on your part. This is your part." His dad was very good to help young singers and people who had some talent but needed development or needed to learn how to sing harmony.

Jerry Waldrop I and Maynard Leatherwood were the founding members of the group at the Akron Baptist Temple. The Songsters started in 1960 and there were fifty-six people that passed through the group over the years.

Joe Knight helped start the Singing Emmanuels when he left the Songsters. They were a group of people in their late teens or early twenties that were going to Bible College. They made a mark because Bruce Cummings really loved them and provided them a letter of recommendation that opened the door to a large number of independent fundamental Baptist churches across the country. They traveled for about two years based in Massillon.

When Mark Flakey came to the group, he had a nice high voice but needed some direction. Jerry Waldrop I taught him how to stay on his part. He later auditioned with the Singing Emmanuels and traveled with them a little while. He then joined the Florida Boys for a while and later traveled with the Bible Tones.

After leaving the Songsters in the late 1960s, Joe Grosso sang with the Southland Boys.

The Songsters got to know Mack Taunton and others when passing through the Cathedral of Tomorrow as they sang over there quite a bit. Bobby Clark, the Cathedrals' first tenor, lived at Bill Echols's house for a long time. He was with Bill Echols for a long time before he went over to be with Glen Payne.

When Jerry Waldrop II was fourteen he started playing bass guitar. Brother Harold Hays—a great pastor and preacher—taught him how to play the bass and showed him much about music. He told him most southern gospel music is based on a one-four-and-five chord pattern and showed him how to use the numbering system. Soon he was teaching him when to move to the sixth chord, and that when you hear the seventh tone on your dominate chord, you know you will be moving to the fourth chord. Then a young pianist named Joe Knight, sixteen years old, joined the group. He was amazingly talented and really knew how to play the piano. Playing with Joe actually helped Jerry significantly improve his skills on the bass guitar.

However, it was a while before Jerry was able to travel and play for the group as back in the 1970s, even though many groups started out using guitars, there were still many churches that didn't want instruments, especially electric instruments, used in their services. As a matter of fact, when Jerry first started, they actually received several phone calls from pastors questioning if they had a bass guitar in the group. When Jerry's dad would say, "Yes we do, it's my son," they would tell him the group wouldn't be able to come and cancel the appointment.

Later when Jerry's brother-in-law Allen, a great drummer, got saved and wanted to serve the Lord, they went through the same process concerning the use of the drums. Before Allan was saved, when the drummer for one of the nation's top rock groups, Three Dog Night, had resigned, the rest of the group flew into Akron and tried to convince Allen to come on the road and play the drums for them. The Songsters almost lost out on that one!

Jerry Waldrop I was interested in having a group that didn't just sing, but made a difference. That was the main focus of the Songsters through the years. The reason why so many pastors have come out of the group is because, using the group as a training ground, they learned how to minister for the Lord. Jerry's dad taught that singing is a tool to be used of the Lord.

Jerry says, "It all boils down to one thing, the most important thing, the altar call."

At one time, they had a big bass singer in the group named Dan Flynn and a guitarist named Jeff Castle. The other members were Jerry, his wife Sharon, and Jerry's dad. In his later years, Jerry's dad had heart problems and would become shaky and nervous around large crowds. So the doctor prescribed some nerve pills, but believing them to be a little too strong, his dad would cut them in half and only take a half dosage.

Once they were singing somewhere up in the hills of West Virginia. It was the second weekend of August. It was hot. And although there were only a few houses around, when it came time for the singing, people came out of the woodwork with their lawn chairs, blocks, and boards to sit on. There were around a thousand people there before the singing was over. It was crowded, and at that time, they had a 1955 Via 100 Flex bus so there was little privacy as the windshield was low and people walking in front of the bus could look right in. As a result of all the activity, dad had taken a nerve pill. It seemed to help, but to be safe, he took another pill.

After the concert was over, they put the equipment in the bay and loaded the bus. Soon they were winding along old Route 33 headed toward home. As they traveled down those country roads, it felt like they could read the license plate on the back of their own bus as they took those hairpin curves, winding up and down the mountains. Trying to make good time, they would speed up on the straight portions and slow down when they came to a curve. As they continued down the road, dad said, "Let me drive."

Dad loved chocolate, and Sharon had made chocolate no-bake cookies. So they were headed down the road in the middle of the night eating chocolate no-bake cookies, and dad was driving. Normally, dad was a very cautious driver. But this night, possibly because of the mixture of medication and chocolate, dad's driving was rather fast. They were all sitting near the front of the bus as they traveled through those West Virginia hills. Soon Dan—with those great big old hands—reached over, tapped Jerry on the shoulder, and said, "Jerry, it's about time for you to drive, isn't it?"

Trying to give dad a hint, Jerry simply responded, "No, no, no it's not time for me to drive." He didn't want to offend or upset his father.

After hitting another curve, the bass singer once again commented, "It's about time for you to drive, isn't it, Jerry!"

By this time, Sharon had her hands on his other shoulder, and she squeezed his shoulder and whispered, "Jerry, tell your dad you want to drive."

Finally he agreed, "Okay, I will, I will."

At this point, they were flying down a straight portion of the road. Suddenly, they spotted a big sign ahead warning them to get over. While Jerry was realizing it was too late to hit the brakes, dad turned around from the wheel and said, "Give me another cookie." Suddenly, everyone was screaming. Jerry hit the floor, and Sharon landed on top of him. Dan fell on top of Jeff as someone was throwing up. Dad quickly turned around and, as they hit the gravel on the side of the road, he turned the wheel, and the Lord reached down, turned the bus, and guided it safely through. After the bus had come to a stop, dad calmly said, "You know, I think you should drive, Jerry."

Jerry's dad, Jerry Waldrop I, was promoted to Glory on January 12, 1996. The group traveled many miles and sang with many big name groups. It is good to see their ministries go on, but Jerry says it has been a roller-coaster ride. The group is currently working through Representing Christian Artists and Capitol Artists and hosts a yearly gospel cruise to the Bahamas or Western Caribbean. They held a drawing for a free cruise at the 2007 NQC.

Pastor Carl Leipold says of the Songsters, "Their desire is not to entertain but to minister to people's needs and to reach lost souls for Christ. They have a real heart for Christ and a real desire to serve."

* * *

At the age of fifteen, Bob Christy started playing bass for the Way Maker Trio, a southern gospel trio in Ellet. Then he played with the Ron Warren Singers from Akron for two years doing a lot of traveling. At age eighteen, he did some work with the Melody Boys, and then at age nineteen, Bob started playing at a church in Akron where Dave Lemon attended. David had previously attended the Stamps-Baxter School of Music. Together, Dave and Bob formed the Gospel Echoes and have been singing on and off for twenty-two years. They also sang for a while with an Akron group called Four by Grace.

Group member Wes Kretzer started playing a Magnus Chord Organ when he was very young and eventually found his home at the piano. He played for a quartet during his teen years and started singing solo in his church at age nineteen.

Another member of the group, Bill Wiczen, started singing at a very young age. He sang "Jingle Bells" for his father's Christmas party at the age of three. He credits his ability to hear and sing harmonies to his mother who sat patiently at the piano and taught him to sing. He started traveling with a group from eastern Ohio called the Gospel Heirs in 1972, remaining with them until he joined the navy in 1974. During his navy tour, he performed with the U.S. Navy Blue Jacket Choir.

As a member of the Ohio Valley Christian Music Association, the Gospel Echoes continue to sing. Whether at the Atmosphere Cafe in Niles, or in Cambridge at the Spring Valley Gospel Jubilee, their mission is the same—to spread the great message of Jesus Christ in song.

We continue south on SR-532 to U.S. 224 where we turn left and continue east to SR-43. Turning right onto SR-43, we pass through Suffield where we're confronted with a unique lineup of cows at a feeding trough with their tails facing the road. Continuing south, we soon arrive at Hartville, home of the Hartville Market Place and Flea Market, one of Ohio's largest flea market attractions.

Hartville is also home to Reverend Mike Abernathy Sr., founder of the Solid Foundation Ministries. Mike has performed gospel music for over twenty-five years, singing with such groups as the Richmond Quartet, the Gospel Conquerors, and the Solid Foundation Ministries. During his ministry, he has shared the stage with some of the nation's top artists.

For three years, serious illness forced Mike to stop traveling with a group. But for the past eight years, he has been doing solo ministry and he states, "My goal is not to be an entertainer, but to be a blessing to all."

Leaving Hartville, we follow SR-43 north to U.S. 224. Turning right onto U.S. 224, we pass through Randolph to Atwater. *North by Night: A Story of the Underground Railroad*, written by Katherine Ayres, is the story of Will Spencer who, at the age of sixteen, leaves his family's farm in Atwater to become a peddler and plays a significant role in the freeing of slaves. The Singing Weavers, also from Atwater, play an important role in leading the lost from their slavery to sin.

Linda and Verlin Weaver are originally from Jellico, Tennessee, and were married in 1957. As their family developed, they maintained musical positions in their home church and were frequently asked to sing at other churches. When they started out, Linda and Verlin were joined by their fourteen-year-old son, Dennis, and two daughters. Dennis played the bass guitar, mom played the piano, his other sister played the organ, and dad played the tambourine. They lived with that tambourine until about five years ago.

One day, Verlin fell off a building and lay paralyzed from the waist down. They just let him lay there in the hallway because they thought he was going to die. But Linda got on the phone and began to call everybody she knew. God healed Verlon, and it wasn't long before he was walking out of the hospital. As a result of this event, they made a strong commitment to do whatever they could for the Lord.

They were known simply as the Weaver Family for years. One evening, they were singing at a church near Mentor and Painesville when the man introducing the group said, "Now, I'm going to bring to you the Singing Weavers." They liked it, and they told him he had just named the group. Although they continued to provide music within their home church, by 1971 they were receiving so many calls asking them to come sing that in 1972, they officially became the Singing Weavers—a full-time gospel group.

They started out traveling by car, buying equipment that would fit inside the trunk. In 1977, they started using a passenger van and added to that an old boat trailer chassis was converted into a trailer—quite an undertaking! In 1981, they purchased their first motor home and, in 1982, acquired a 1964 Model 4106 Greyhound bus right off the bus lines, and they did the conversion themselves. When they purchased the bus, Dennis had never driven a bus in his life. So they hopped in and said, "Okay, we're going," and grinding a few pounds off of the gears, they kept on going.

One time, they were in Mentor and lost their air brakes. Someone in the congregation went home, got some tools, and temporarily fixed the brakes by putting a pair of vice grips on the air line to stop the loss of air. They traveled all the way home with vice grips hanging from one air line and only three brakes.

They were privileged to sing at Watermelon Park with the Hoppers, and they did a showcase at NQC in 1983. They also sang at two Ohio state fairs and have sung at the Summit County Fair for ten years. They even sang in a barn one time in the Canton area. The cows were right underneath them, and as they sang, you could hear the continual mooing of the cows. They have been fortunate to travel to a lot of the southern gospel fanfares like Southern Gospel Music Fanfair in Chattanooga, Tennessee, and the Cave City Fanfare, which is a gospel music tour. In 2003, their daughter Alyssia received a three year scholarship to attend the Stamps-Baxter School of Music. She attended the school from 2004 through 2006. This launched the Singing Weavers in a whole new direction.

When they were traveling in the bus, even though there were bunk beds on the bus, they would carry a little Longenberger laundry basket with a pillow in it, similar to Moses in the bullrushes, for their daughter Alyssia to sleep in. They would carry it right in the room and set it down on the floor. As she grew, she was often found behind them, sitting on a preacher's knee, as they sang. Alyssia was six when she sang for the first time. That same year she had her tonsils removed but was singing again just three weeks later!

Selling their bus to a group of singers from Denver, Colorado, they purchased a motor home, and in 2003, they purchased their current motor home.

One of the most difficult times for the group came five years after Dennis married his wife, Chris. They had just built a new house, and the bus needed some repairs. It was going to cost around $10,000 to fix the bus, but their money was tied up in building the house. When it became clear they would have to go to the bank and borrow money, they stepped out on faith, and God allowed them to pay the loan off in one year.

Dennis and Chris have been married for over twenty years, and over time, the group has transitioned. When Chris was needed, she stepped right in. She's been by his side, his helpmate, and just kept growing with the family. Two thousand and one brought a shortage of bookings, and it appeared that their ministry was coming to a close.

God had a different idea, and in 2002, their daughter, Alyssia, expressed a strong desire to start singing. So they restructured the group, creating a trio consisting of Dennis, his wife, Chris, and their daughter, Alyssia. Dennis's mom and dad still travel with the group, and they have remained a local gospel group. Their preference is to sing in churches because they feel led to have a ministry in song rather than to just perform.

Three different songwriters—one from Mississippi, one from Florida, and another from South Carolina—all came to them about the same time feeding them a tremendous amount of songs. They were able to record six CDs in four years because of these writers. That has helped to keep them a little different from the average group because they don't get up and sing all of the same songs that are normally heard on the radio. They provide fresh songs the people haven't heard, and they believe this keeps them a little unique from everyone else.

In 2006, they sang in Boonville, Mississippi, at the national rally for Life Cancer Society. This large fundraiser had about six thousand people in attendance. In September 2007, they had a song written by Ray Holliday that was released nationally by Lo Records titled "When I Depart." The song has charted on four major southern gospel charts.

They have traveled throughout most of the northeast United States. The group has always been a mixed quartet, and they've always held full-time jobs, so they had to be able to get to work even if they got home at five in the morning. Continuing to the third generation, the ministry has remained a family group. They always try to coordinate to have some of the same color throughout their outfit. And when you see those ladies in their red dresses together with those men with the red shirt and tie, you will be reminded of the importance this group places on coordination.

Grandma (Linda) says, "It's amazing the people God keeps bringing into their life. You can see it fitting together like a puzzle. Grandpa and I are too old now but the second and third generation desires to go professional."

She believes God is going to use them and commends Dennis's family for standing with him. She points out that God doesn't call just one. He calls everybody—just like He called their whole family in 1972.

Following his heritage, Dennis expresses, "And as long as we are faithful, God's always going to take care of us and always provide for us. And He's just so good. If we could get that message to a lost and dying world or to those who are suffering or need encouragement, then I feel like we've done our job in serving our God."

Leaving Atwater, we head north on SR-183 to SR-4 where we turn left and cross under IR-76. Then turning left onto SR-59, we drive to Ravenna, founded in 1799. Ravenna is the home of Tappan Glass and the home of Duane Frame who was born in Charleston, West Virginia, and remained actively involved in music throughout his younger years.

When Duane Frame was thirteen, his family moved to Akron where he continued to sing with his mother and his brother in a group known as the Frame Family. He now maintains a solo ministry from Ravenna where he lives with his wife.

Driving through Ravenna, we travel west on SR-59. Passing Brady Lake along the way, we travel about 6 miles to Kent, home of Kent State University where more than three thousand models of hearing aids, the largest collection in the world, are on display at the Kenneth W. Berger Hearing Aid Museum and Archives. A hearing aid wasn't necessary when taught to sing the way Valerie Mayfield learned to sing.

Valerie Faye Mayfield was born in Blackhorse after her parents moved up from Kentucky to escape the culture of the coalmines. Surrounded by many albums in a house filled with instruments, bluegrass was always a big part of her life. While sitting on the front porch in her old rocking chair, and brushing her hair that hung all the way to the floor, Grandma Augusta Sergeant would rare back and break into a song, teaching Valerie to sing the "Old Time Baptist" way. Valerie started playing bass with her father at the age of eight. They performed mostly in churches, but they also sang in grange halls and even some bars. After twenty-six years of marriage, her parents divorced, and her idyllic life was suddenly filled with mishaps and disappointments.

Then in 1981, at a bluegrass festival in Mantua, she met and eventually married David Mayfield. David Lee Mayfield started playing with his family at a young age. After high school, he helped start a group called the Bluegrass Gentleman. In the early 1980s, he helped form another group called the Bottom Line. David also did some recording session work with Seana McDowell, a female vocalist from Australia.

David and Valerie now travel with their children under the name of the One Way Rider, a family band performing a unique combination of bluegrass, newgrass, country, gospel, a cappella, and progressive appalachian music. Although not strictly gospel, they present an entertaining and comedic stage show that appeals to the entire family.

They purchased an old 1956 Flex tour bus and used it for six years before finding out that it previously was owned by Bill Monroe and was called "the Bluegrass Breakdown." It wasn't long before they understood how the bus inherited its name. The good news is that everywhere it broke down, God would send someone along to help.

Once, they broke down somewhere in Pennsylvania, and not having enough money to pay for the repairs, they set up outside the repair shop and started playing. After hearing them playing for tips, the repairman agreed to waive the bill and sent them on our way commenting, "You guys are the real thing!"

Leaving Kent, we follow SR-59 west five miles to Stow, where the Catch the Healthy Bug exercise program was initiated as a fun way for Stow residents to commit to regular exercise and track their way to health and wellness. I'm certain George Younce would approve.

In 1963, when the Weatherfords decided to take their ministry to California, the remaining members of the group—Bobby Clark, Glen Payne and Danny Koker—formed the Cathedral Trio.

Bobby Clark started singing with the Deep South Quartet in 1955. He also sang with the Oak Ridge Quartet and the Rangers Quartet. In 1961, he joined the Weatherfords and was with them until their move to California.

Glen Payne was born on October 20, 1926, in Royce City, Texas. As a young boy, barefooted and dressed in overalls, he was growing up in the midst of poverty, but he had a dream to sing in a quartet some day. In 1938, his grandfather scraped together fifty cents so he and Glen could go to Josephine, Texas, to hear the Stamps Quartet perform live at a school. At age twelve, Glen took a trip to Dallas with his father to pick up some new songbooks for the church from the Stamps-Baxter Music Company. Upon arrival, they met with V. O. Stamps, and Glen was overwhelmed as he stood in the presence of, and shook hands with, one of his heroes.

In 1939, unable to find the funds for Glen to attend the singing school, his grandmother wrote V. O. Stamps to tell him of her grandson's great love for gospel music and desire to attend the school. Stamps was moved, and as a result, Glen attended the school from 1939-1942, and it didn't cost anything. During his years at the singing school, Glen would work so hard to raise money for the next trip that his friends thought it a little strange. One year while attending the school, Glen was privileged to sing in a choir directed by the famous Albert E. Brumley. Glen remained connected with and even taught at the school.

While still in high school, Glen started singing baritone for the original Stamps Quartet along with Hovie Lister. By 1948, he was singing with the Stamps All Star Quartet, and in 1951, he joined the Stamps-Ozark Quartet. Later, Glen moved to Akron to sing with the Weatherfords. In Akron, Glen met his future wife, Van Lua Harris, whom he married on November 30, 1958. Rex Humbard performed the ceremony, and Maude Aimee Humbard, dressed in a beautiful red velvet gown, sang "Wherever Thou Goest." Earl Weatherford was one of the groomsmen, and Lily Fern Weatherford was a bridesmaid. This was the first televised wedding to take place at the Cathedral of Tomorrow.

Since he was born on February 22, 1930 (George Washington's birthday) in Lenoir, North Carolina, his father thought it fitting to name their newborn George Wilson Younce. From his younger years, when he listened for the sound of his father's Model A Ford coming down the road, George has always been an entertaining individual. In the sixth grade, he was the highest voice in the class, showing promise as a tenor singer, and even made an appearance on the *Little Rascals* television program. In 1945, George experienced his first live gospel concert featuring the Harmoneers Quartet. By 1946, he and his friends had put together a group called the Spiritualaires and they attended the Stamps-Baxter School of Gospel Music in 1947.

In 1950, George answered the call to military duty, serving in the Army's Eighty-second Airborne Division. While in the army, he became a popular entertainer at the NCO club, allowing him to spend a large portion of his military tour at Fort Bragg. After leaving the military, he took a job in the mines of Alaska. He went from jumping out of airplanes to digging in the depths of the earth.

In 1953, he joined the Watchmen from West Virginia. Later he left the Watchmen to take a position with the Weatherfords. He enjoyed being with the group and Earl always called him "Country Boy." On April 27, 1955, George and Clara, the love of his life, traveled to Raven Cliff, West Virginia. They purchased a marriage license for three dollars and were married.

The Weatherfords soon moved to Ohio to become worship singers at Calvary Temple in Akron for Rex Humbard. George left the Weatherfords for a short stint in Milwaukee, but things didn't work out, and soon George and his new bride were packing their bags and heading home. Through the connection of an old friend, Ace Richman, George landed a position with the Blue Ridge Quartet in Spartanburg, South Carolina. Singing with the Blue Ridge Quartet, he emerged from poverty to middle class. One day, the Blue Ridge Quartet was traveling down the road when along came George Younce riding with a carload of drunks, his head hanging out the window, and he was frantically waving his arms as though he had been taken captive. It seems the quartet had left George at a little restaurant after singing in Thomasville, Georgia. The drunks were the only ones willing to accept the challenge of trying to catch the group's bus.

During an NQC held at Memphis, Tennessee, in the late 1950s, George was privileged to sing backstage with a young rock star named Elvis Presley. During the concert, George received a personal invitation from Elvis to join some of the other singers at Graceland later that evening to sing around the piano. This sounded great, but after hours of driving around Memphis, George was unable to find Graceland and headed back to the hotel.

In 1958, he left the Blue Ridge Quartet to take a position with the Florida Boys only to return to the Blue Ridge Quartet within three months. One evening, while traveling with the Blue Ridge Quartet, Elmo Fagg encouraged a West Virginia crowd to stop by their table and pick up an album or two on their way out. When the Blue Ridge Quartet finally made their way to the table, there were only a few albums left. Responding to Elmo's request, the people had picked up an album on their way home—without paying, of course.

In 1964, Rex Humbard was seeking a bass singer to transform the Cathedral Trio into a quartet. He contacted George and offered him the position. George accepted, and the Cathedral Quartet was formed. At that time, their following was limited, but there was one young man who would drive miles to hear this new group sing. He first heard the Cathedral Quartet when he was seventeen years old. It was a rainy Friday afternoon in 1967 when the young man loaded up his 1959 Chevy Impala with snacks and Pepsi and headed off to York, Pennsylvania. It was a three-hour drive, but he had a great love for gospel quartet music. As he drove along the turnpike, the passing trucks and the rain made driving difficult. Finally, he arrived at the York High School auditorium at around 8:30 PM. Hurrying across the parking lot, he bought a ticket and quickly sat down in the back of the packed auditorium just as the local part-time group had finished singing.

As the emcee was making the introduction, the Cathedrals entered the stage wearing bright green sport coats and white pants. Danny Koker sat down at the piano, adjusted the microphone stand, and turned and greeted the audience. After a first-class piano intro, the four men began to sing the song "Since Jesus Passed By." Mack Taunton was singing tenor, and Koker sang the baritone part while he played the piano. The smooth lead singer was Glen Payne, and the extraordinary bass singer was George Younce. The young man drove home to Philadelphia that night believing in his heart he had just heard the greatest gospel group of all time.

About a year later, the young man had put together a little part-time singing group called the Faith Four, and they were hosting the Cathedrals in Pennsauken, New Jersey. He rented a church, paid the guys their flat rate fee of $400, and after the concert, he invited them to his home in Philadelphia for dinner. Accepting his invitation, they drove their bus right down the street to his house where they enjoyed his mother's meatballs. Before leaving, they sang a few songs for his disabled father. He couldn't believe it—the mighty Cathedral Quartet was actually singing in his little Philadelphia living room. Just eighteen at the time, these men helped set a course for his life, drawing him closer to God not only through their music, but also by the example they set before him.

Within a year, he was struggling along singing full-time with the Keystone Quartet. The Keystone Quartet was privileged to work with the Cathedrals many times over the next several years. He would sometimes ride on their bus and sit up late at night talking with George about the art of singing. George shared his testimony with him and became the single biggest influence of his early twenties. The young man, Joe Bonsall, remained with the Keystones until 1973 when he joined the Oak Ridge Boys. He credits George Younce with making him a better singer.

Bobby Clark was with the group until 1968. After leaving the Cathedrals, Bobby sang with the Dixie Echoes for a brief period, and in 1995, he started singing with the Men of Music. He remained with them for three years. He continues singing today, working as a soloist in Texas. Mack Taunton replaced Bobby Clark. A year later, Danny Koker also left the group and was replaced by George Amon Webster.

Although performing at the Cathedral of Tomorrow, having a permanent base of operation and steady income, would be considered a dream job for any quartet, they knew it would not last. Although they continued their association with the Cathedral of Tomorrow for several more years, in 1969, George and Glen decided they should go out on their own.

It was a risky move with no guarantee of a paycheck as they started singing throughout the eastern United States, traveling in a station wagon and pulling a little trailer. Their lack of name recognition and the fact that many considered them simply a church quartet made it difficult to establish a solid audience base. The early group embodied a unique sound, and Marvin Norcross from Canaan Records had faith in them. His willingness to keep them on, even when their sales were not great, gave them time to develop their sound. Then Les Beasley featured them on the Gospel Singing Jubilee. This was a great help to them in establishing a following. There were some lean times in those first few years, and they tried many things to enhance their popularity including wearing some strange-looking suits.

Once while singing in southern Ohio, they were given a pumpkin pie. Glen took the pie to their station wagon and placed it on the front seat. That evening when the singing was over, it was dark, and Glen had forgotten about the pie. As they loaded the station wagon, Danny Koker sat right down on that fresh pumpkin pie, making a terrible mess of his trousers. Of course, George began laughing vigorously, and not having a change of clothes, Danny had to wear those messy trousers all the way home.

The Cathedrals were scheduled to do a special performance in Miami, Florida, with the Statesmen called "Moon Over Miami." The show was a flop from the start, and they spent more money on their airplane tickets than they earned that night.

Changes in personnel continued to take place except for the two pillars of the group, Glen Payne and George Younce. Both Roy Tremble and Bill Dykes served short stints with the group filling the baritone position. Once, while Roy Tremble was driving the bus somewhere in Virginia, he was involved in a wreck. The group was terrified as the bus slid 125 yards down the side of a mountain.

Haskell Cooley joined the group as piano player. Haskell was born in a little community in southeastern Oklahoma called Buffalo Valley, which is near Talihina, Oklahoma. He grew up in church listening to church music and southern gospel music. When Haskell was nine, his parents purchased a piano, and he started pounding away on it. He started playing for the Travelers Quartet from Poteau, Oklahoma, at the age of thirteen. Beginning at age fourteen, he attended two summer sessions of the Stamps Quartet School of Music in Dallas, Texas. His piano teacher was Easmon Napier, pianist for the Stamps Quartet. They formed the Cooley Brothers and kept them together for several years.

After completing college, he taught piano at a music school in Wichita, Kansas. Onc of his students was a young lady named JoLee. In 1966, after two years in the army, Haskell married JoLee. In 1972, Haskell became piano player for the Weatherford Quartet and remained with them for two years. While with the Weatherfords, he met the Cathedrals. Two months after leaving the Weatherfords, the Cathedrals offered him a position playing piano. Accepting the position, Haskell and JoLee left their home in Ada, Oklahoma, and moved to Stow. Haskell was pianist for the Cathedrals for five years.

Being a country boy from Oklahoma, Haskell said, "The most special place I played the piano while with the Cathedrals was on the campus of Columbia University in downtown Manhattan, New York."

Leaving the Cathedrals, Haskell moved to Wichita, Kansas where he and his wife later started singing as a duet called simply the Cooleys. When their two children started singing with them, they changed their name to the Haskell Cooley Family. The family had their share of adventures. On more than one occasion, the piano's sustain pedal would stop working, and Haskell would stop the singing, fix the pedal, and continue with the program.

One time in Alabama, they had to sing outside, and the only piano was a big old upright that had been stored in a little shed. The piano was covered with so much dust it looked like dirt. Haskell's wife got a pail of water and a cloth and washed it off. As they began to sing, the piano was so out of tune it was difficult for them to find the pitch.

Traveling in a motor home, they have been ministering for almost twenty-eight years. In October, 2005, JoLee and Haskell attended the concert in McPherson, Kansas, to hear one of their favorite groups, the Booth Brothers. During the second half of the program, they invited Haskell to play for them. Ronnie Booth wanted to have some fun, so a big, long, grand piano was pushed out onto stage from behind the curtains. The Booth Brothers gathered around the piano, and Haskell suggested they do "I'll Fly Away" and "What a Day That Will Be." They finished to a well-deserved standing ovation.

The song "Gonna Shout All Over Heaven," written by Haskell and JoLee, was recorded twice by the Cathedrals. The Cathedrals's recording of their song "I'll Sail Away Home" was on the nation's top ten for almost a year. The Kingsmen recorded a song written by Haskell titled "I'll Sail Away Home." Another song, "Someone Like You" was recorded by the Inspirations. In 2008, after twety-nine years, the Haskell Cooley Family is still traveling in a full-time gospel music ministry. Haskell says, "Arthritis doesn't have my fingers, yet."

By 1974, the Cathedrals had established a lineup that would last for several years. With their new hit single, "The Last Sunday," they finally started getting airplay and winning some awards. During the late 1970s, the group gained additional recognition when they made an appearance at a Bill Gaither Praise Gathering held in Indianapolis, Indiana. Shortly afterward, they were inundated with requests for appearances.

The group annually traveled to a little place in Oklahoma where they would participate in what was called an "all-night singing." It is just a little spot in the road, but the singing would start in the afternoon and continue until the sun came up the next morning. When they first started singing at this event, the Cathedrals didn't know anyone. But over the years, they became acquainted with some wonderful people. Local people would bring picnic baskets full of chicken and other dishes to feed the singers and help the groups sell items at their tables.

Another evening, they were singing in a Pennsylvania church, and George was doing the emcee work. He introduced a song that featured him singing the lead, and so they kicked it off and started singing. When it came to the verse, he forgot the words. So George started making up words, and then he forgot that he was singing the lead. He was up there singing crazy words and singing the bass part instead of the melody. It was all Lorne could do to keep playing. Finally, Glen lost it and started falling on the floor laughing. Soon Roy and the other guys were also laughing. So old George, when he knew the trick was up, stopped singing and said, "Ladies and gentlemen, I forgot the words." He said, "Start that up again, Lorne, maybe we will remember it this time."

In 1979, the group suffered a severe blow when three of the members—Roy Tremble, George Amon Webster, and Lorne Matthews—left the group to form a group called the Brothers. Later that year, Haskell Cooley also left the Cathedrals as his wife had just given birth to their first child, and he wanted to spend more time with the family. This was a hard decision for Haskell as he believed they were a good group of Christians. Haskell said, "George Younce was one of the kindest men I have ever met in my life. The enjoyment we had traveling together was special."

The loss of these group members was a terrific setback, but George and Glen were not defeated and soon began to reform the group. They enlisted the help of Kirk Talley, previously with the Hoppers, along with a young man named Steve Lee who could sing baritone and play piano. It was Steve and Kirk who happened to hear someone playing piano for a local group that was opening for the Cathedrals. They urged George and Glen to get off the bus and listen. After listening, they were all blown away by the talents of this young man, and Roger Bennett was soon added to their ranks. The first song Roger played for the Cathedrals was "Holy Is Thy Name." While these great music masters vocalized to unbelievable depths and heights, he stopped playing several times in awe. Steve Lee was later replaced by Kingsmen member Mark Trammell.

Timothy Mark Trammell born May 11, 1959, in Searcy, Arkansas, was the youngest of four boys. Growing up a preacher's son, he was always in church and was exposed to gospel music at a young age. In 1974, at age fifteen, he joined a regional group called the Senators. He remained with them several years taking a Continental Trailways bus every weekend to meet with the group before they would head out to sing. In 1977, Mark joined the Kingsmen Quartet, sharing the stage with one of southern gospel music's best-loved tenor singers, Ernie Phillips. Today, Ernie's son Eric Phillips sings tenor for the Mark Trammell Trio.

Mark remained with the Kingsmen until 1980 when he became the new baritone for the Cathedrals. While singing with the Cathedrals, he lived in Stow three doors down from George Younce. Mark considered George a true mentor, and George's humor helped the group cope with those little problems along the way. He remembers that George would often step off the bus during cold weather, turn right around, get back on the bus and holler, "This is not funny, God!"

In January 1987, the group was traveling through Kansas. They were somewhere near Topeka, and the weather was terrible with blowing and drifting snow, and George could only travel about ten miles per hour. Sitting there on the bus in the midst of the storm, Mark wrote the song, "He's My Lord." When he had completed the song, he took it to the back of the bus and shared it with Danny Funderburg and Roger Bennett. After working it out they headed back to the front, and standing in the stairwell of the bus, they started singing the new song to George. While they were singing, George got happy, and one minute he was crying and the next he was laughing.

Mark sang with the Cathedrals for eleven years until he left to help Gerald Wolfe form the group called Greater Vision. In 1994, he moved to Gadsden, Alabama, and took a position with Gold City.

While doing a tour on the Isle of Patmos, Mark began to understand God's call of evangelism, and although he enjoyed singing with Gold City, he left the group in 2002 to start evangelistic work. He formed the Mark Trammell Trio, and they sang their first concert in August 2002. From time to time, the masterful piano playing and vocal sounds of Steve Hurst are added to the group.

Throughout his career, Mark has been privileged to perform in some very prestigious venues including Radio City Music Hall, Brooklyn Tabernacle, and the South Lawn of the White House. He performed for President Jimmy Carter and noted pastors and evangelists such as the venerable Dr. W. A. Criswell, Dr. Charles Stanley, and others.

In 1978, Mark married a young lady named LaResa, and their son Nicholas Mark "Nick" Trammell was born on May 18, 1984, in Akron. Growing up around gospel music, Nick presently sings with the Perrys. Nick is soon to be married to Jessica Brown, member of the Browns a family group from Lemars, Iowa.

The combination of George, Glen, and Mark lasted for a while with several tenors, and they became a very successful group with songs like "Step into the Water," "Moving up to Gloryland," and "I Know a Man Who Can." They recorded Glen's signature song "We Shall See Jesus." Kirk Talley left the group in 1983 to form a group with his brother Roger Talley and Roger's wife, Debra, called the Talleys. He was replaced by Danny Funderburg, a young man from the Singing Americans. His unique and powerful voice was used to good effect on songs such as "I Just Started Living" and "Somebody Touched Me."

In 1986, Roger Bennett left the group to head up Christian label Journey Records in Cincinnati. During this period, with Gerald Wolfe playing the piano and doing some singing, the group continued to improve, even recording half of an album with the London Philharmonic Orchestra. This period produced another popular song for the group entitled "Champion of Love" as led by Gerald Wolfe. In 1988, when Gerald decided to leave the group to pursue a solo career, he suggested they call Roger Bennett again. Returning to the group, Roger stayed with the Cathedrals until the group retired.

The Cathedrals had become popular with crowds everywhere because of their superior singing and their entertaining stage presence. In 1987, George had a heart attack, but after a slow and difficult recovery, he was able to return to the road. George was an excellent emcee with a humble demeanor and a terrific sense of humor. George would often make fun of Glen's age, calling him "the Old Man" followed by his jab, "I love old people."

In 1990, Danny Funderburg left the group to start a solo career. Later, he put together a group called Perfect Heart. The tenor position was filled by a young man named Ernie Haase.

Ernie was born on December 12, 1964, in Evansville, Indiana. While in school, he maintained an unusual combination of singing in the choir and playing football. Then while attending college, Ernie sang with the Nobleman Quartet from Indiana for three years. After leaving the Nobleman, he sang in an ensemble called Earthlight. It was while singing in this ensemble that he first met Scott Fowler. Shortly after turning twenty-one, Ernie did a very brief stint with the Dixie Melody Boys, and in 1986, Ernie sang with Squire Parsons and the Redeemed. While traveling with Squire, he kept a poster of his dream quartet, the Cathedrals, hanging on his bunk wall.

In 1990, he opened for the Cathedrals at an event held at his old college in Oakland City, Indiana. The next week, he received a call from George Younce telling him he had knocked his hat in the creek, which meant he had done a really great job. Within a week, he was headed for Stow to fulfill his dream. About eight months after joining the group, Ernie married Lisa, the daughter of George Younce. Shortly after this, Mark Trammell left the group to become one of the founding members of a group called Greater Vision along with former member Gerald Wolfe. Upon the recommendation of Ernie Haase, they hired Scott Fowler to sing the baritone part.

Scott Fowler was born July 9, 1966, in St. Louis, Missouri. His father was an evangelist, and as he traveled from place to place, Scott and his mother would provide the singing prior to the message. This pattern continued throughout most of Scott's childhood, but after high school, Scott, planning to establish a career in the medical field, entered a nursing school in St Louis, Missouri. During his second year of nursing school, he was given an opportunity to sing with a group from Houston, Texas, called the Sound. While traveling with the Sound, he sang alongside Terry Davis, former member of the Florida Boys, for several years, and then in 1989, at a concert in Flint, Michigan, the group was privileged to open the program for the Cathedrals. A few months later, when Mark Trammell announced his resignation from the Cathedral Quartet, Glen and George had remembered Scott from that concert in Michigan.

Early one morning, Scott received a phone call at his apartment in Houston, Texas. Answering the phone, Scott heard a voice ask, "Is this Scott Fowler?" After confirming that he was speaking to Scott Fowler, the voice on the other end of the line said, "Scott, this is Glen Payne with the Cathedrals." Scott, in disbelief, was certain someone was playing a joke on him. After confirming that he was in fact Glen Payne, he then shared with Scott that Mark Trammell had just announced his resignation and would be leaving the group within a couple of months. Glen further indicated they would love to set up a meeting with Scott next week as they passed through Texas on tour.

He agreed to meet with them, and one week later, arriving at a Hyatt Hotel in Odessa, Texas, he walked into the little hotel room, and there were Roger Bennett, Glen Payne, George Younce, and Ernie Haase. They had a little electric piano set up, and soon they were singing around the piano. Scott sang some stuff with the group and did a couple of songs by himself. That night, Scott rode with them to a concert there in Odessa, Texas, where they sang at the First Baptist Church. On the way to the concert, no one shared any comments, and although it was an enjoyable evening, he still had no idea what they thought of his singing. After the concert, Glen took him out to the bus to tell him that all of the guys were in agreement, and that if he would like to join the Cathedrals, the position was his. Scott replied, "Let me pray about it. Okay, I prayed about it." It took him about thirty seconds to say that little prayer and accept the offer. It was a dream come true. When Scott joined the group, he moved to Stow where he lived with Roger Bennett for about six months until he got settled.

George Younce was famous for his sense of humor. On one occasion, they were traveling down the road in the bus late at night. Everybody had a bed on the bus, and they are stacked up like bunk beds three high from the floor to the ceiling. Roger was on the bottom bunk, George was on the middle bunk, and Scott was on the very top bunk, where he slept right above George for ten years. They had just gone to bed and were pulling together the little curtains on their bunk. They turned off all the lights for some quiet rest. After about five or six minutes of total silence, George, without any prompting, starts laughing. As George continued to laugh, Scott pulled his curtain back and, looking down at George, asked why he was so frantically laughing. While laying there in his bunk, George had thought of a joke he had heard years ago, and remembering it made him to burst into laughter. He was unable to stop the laughter until he got out of bed and told the joke to everyone.

Scott lived in Stow for seven years. Then the last three years they were together, after they cut their dates back to a hundred a year, they told the group members they could live anywhere they wanted to live as long as they showed up for their appointments. It was then that Roger Bennett and Scott moved to Nashville, Tennessee.

Looking back, Scott commented, "What a great ten years of my life. I owe everything I have, in an earthly sense, to George and Glen. They were legends, and they were men of character, men of integrity, and as I always used to say, 'If George or Glen told you that it was Easter, you'd start hunting eggs.' What a great opportunity to get to know those guys. Working and traveling with them, they were like family. We miss George and Glen, and I will never forget them and the great legacy, if you will, of the Cathedral Quartet."

This lineup lasted throughout their remaining years. Around this time, they became regulars on the Gaither Homecoming videos and took on a whole new fan base. Ernie Haase continued to thrill crowds everywhere with his rendition of that Rosie Rozell classic, "Oh What a Savior." George was bringing people to tears with one of his favorite songs "Suppertime," and the "laughing" song was a true expression of George's personality; he loved to make people laugh. George Younce kept everything on the light side, and they had a great time. Nevertheless, he took his work seriously as he could often be found in the front of the bus vocalizing as they traveled down the road in their Silver Eagle.

Things were going great, and the group was at the top of their career. Health problems forced them to begin cutting back on their scheduling. By 1999, George was suffering from kidney failure, and his heart was too weak for a kidney transplant. They decided it was time for the Cathedrals to end their ministry.

Bill Gaither put together a *Cathedrals Farewell Celebration* video. The video, recorded live on May 18, 1999, is a great example of the Cathedrals' stage presence and will remain a treasure highlighted by George's hilarious emcee work. The Statler Brothers, the Oak Ridge Boys, Sandi Patty, Guy Penrod, and Bill Gaither joined them for this special occasion. During the celebration, Oak Ridge member, Duane Allen, related a story of a night years ago when he was asked to roast Glen Payne at a banquet. Duane recalls stammering around behind the podium and finally admitting to the audience, "I cannot think of a bad word to say about this man. He is simply the best singer in the world."

Several months later, Glen Payne was diagnosed with liver cancer. Later that same year, Glen sang that great song "I Won't Have to Cross Jordan Alone" over the phone from the Vanderbilt University Hospital in Nashville, Tennessee, to a very attentive crowd at the 1999 NCQ. This was his last performance as he prematurely passed away on October 15, 1999. You can rest assured that when Glen stepped off that ole ship of Zion he was doing one of his little glory dances. Roger Bennett sang the lead part for their remaining concerts, and their final concert was held in Akron where it all started many years ago.

When the group disbanded, Ernie Haase started a solo ministry. He also sang with George and the famous Jake Hess in a short-lived group called Old Friends. He later formed the group Signature Sound. Roger Bennett and Scott Fowler formed the group Legacy Five where Scott continues today, ministering throughout the world. In 2005, Roger's son, Jordan Bennett, became a part of Legacy Five. Scott is also on the board of directors for the NQC, yet he still finds time to spend at home with his wife and their two children.

George made his last public appearance at a Gaither Homecoming concert where he sang "Suppertime." Then on April 11, 2005, George passed away just sixteen days prior to the celebration of his fiftieth wedding anniversary with his wife Clara. George Younce was honored in style with a home-going celebration held on Tuesday, April 20, at Akron Baptist Temple in Akron. In front of the church stood a casket surrounded by hundreds of flowers. Standing next to the casket was a portrait of George Younce and a stand holding his famous cowboy boots. The home-going celebration began with a welcome from Dr. Arnold Fleagle, followed by Jeff Easter on the harmonica playing "Amazing Grace." The Homecoming Choir joined in with Bill Gaither leading the congregation. Hearts were blessed as the choir and the congregation joined in on "I'll Meet You in the Morning," "Canaan Land Is Just in Sight," and "What a Meeting" (in the air). The Gaither Vocal Band performed "I Believe in a Hill Called Mt. Calvary" followed by Ben Speer singing the lead on one of George's favorite songs "Suppertime" with the late Jimmy Jones doing the recitation. Family member Ernie Haase, along with Signature Sound, sang that wonderful song "Oh What a Savior" and, following a wonderful video presentation, Gloria Gaither described George as only she can. Later, while reminiscing, Bill Gaither shared how George would buy him new tennis shoes and send them to him in the mail. The service ended with the song "Because He Lives," and as the pallbearers carried the casket down the aisle, the choir sang "Oh Come, Angel Band." Such a celebration could only be commended in the words of George Younce, "Well Glory!"

When the Cathedral Quartet needed a bus driver, Bud Seeker was the man for the job. Seeker spent twenty-seven years not only driving the Cathedrals' bus but also making thousands of friends across the country. Bud passed away January 23, 2006 at the age of eighty-two.

Roger Bennett, who had been previously diagnosed with leukemia, passed away on March 17, 2007. Scott Fowler says of his close friend Roger, "The day before he died, with ventilator tubes, feeding tubes, and everything else they could put in him, he rallied for a few hours and even made his nurse laugh . . . He spent his life trying to ensure the happiness of others."

* * *

In 2003, having the blessings of his father-in-law, George Younce, Ernie Haase left the solo field to form a quartet called Ernie Haase & Signature Sound. The first year on road, they received the Singing News Fan Award for Horizon Group. One of their first singles was a song by Rodney Griffin called

"Do You Want to Be Forgiven." The original members were Ernie Haase, Ryan Seaton, Doug Anderson, Tim Duncan and Roy Webb.

Ryan Seaton was a quiet child, and his mother, who had sung in country gospel groups and as a soloist most of her life, expressed concern that he was too shy to ever sing in public. Ryan performed in a barbershop quartet in high school and later sang with the Melody Boys Quartet. In 2004, he married Krista, his girlfriend since the seventh-grade.

Doug Anderson, after thrilling high school basketball fans during the late 1980s, was enshrined in the High School Hall of Fame for his basketball achievements. He later began a walk down the path of his dreams singing with Lighthouse before joining Signature Sound. A small-town boy at heart, he married his high school sweetheart in August, 1998. They continue to live in his hometown of Lapel, Indiana.

Tim Duncan had a great desire to sing that fantastic tenor part, but the natural tones coming from this young man were much lower than the tenor part. He later learned to sing bass under the direction of legendary bass singer, London Paris. Tim previously sang with both Master's Voice and Poet Voices. Moving from Alabama, Tim and his family now make their home in Columbus.

Roy Webb was born October 21, 1970, in Dayton and grew up in Huber Heights graduating from Wayne High School—home of the Warriors. His piano teacher Leeann Murphy gave him six lessons and, after the sixth lesson, told his grandma, "He doesn't need lessons, he's got it." His grandpa Pastor Roy Gibbs was a popular minister in the Dayton area, and he was always having groups like the McKameys at his church to sing. Roy acquired a love for gospel music at a young age and would often attend the concerts held in Dayton at Memorial Hall, listening to such groups as the Kingsmen, the Cathedrals, Gold City, the Hinsons, and the Paynes. He loved their music and bought all their recordings.

In 1992, Roy started playing for Lighthouse and stayed with them for eight years. Dave Griffith, one of the founders of the group had previously sung with the Miami Valley Boys. David later started driving the bus for Signature Sound and became their sound engineer. Doug Anderson, who also sang in Lighthouse, was now singing baritone for Signature Sound. With the recommendation of these guys, it wasn't long until Ernie Haase was asking Roy to consider playing for the group. Roy, having just built a new house in West Chester and having a good job, didn't seem to have any interest in traveling with the group. Then in 2003, believing that God was leading in this direction, he agreed to take the position and started playing with Ernie Haase & Signature Sound.

One of the first weekends Roy went out with Signature Sound, they were traveling in the old Cathedrals' bus, and Roy was sleeping in George Younce's bunk. He remembers thinking, *Wow! Here I am sleeping in George's bunk and riding on the Cathedrals bus.* This brought to mind that evening when he and his wife were out on a date, and the Cathedrals were singing at Landmark Baptist Temple. They drove to the church, and not having tickets to the concert, they simply passed through the parking lot allowing Roy to get a close-up view of that big beautiful bus.

Leaving Signature Sound in May 2007, he continues to study music at the Conservatory of Music at the University of Cincinnati and is presently working as a piano soloist. With those magic fingers and his quick humor, he continues to be a blessing wherever he performs. He enhanced the sound of the Booth Brothers as he accompanied them during their performance at the fiftieth NQC held in Louisville, Kentucky.

Signature Sound has sung the national anthem for several NBA events. They have performed before President Bush during the National Day of Prayer events, and they've even been to Africa. When Roy told his grandmother that Signature Sound was doing another tour in Africa, she commented, out of fear for her grandson's safety, "Aren't there any churches left in America where you can sing?"

With upbeat suits, shortened ties, and spiky hair, Signature Sound is causing people of all ages to sit up and notice. When they first step out on stage, there'll be some young people on the edge of their seats with excitement, and possibly, a few of the elderly will be headed out the door. But with their mixture of choreography and those golden-age songs, they are captivating both the old and the new.

Ron McNeal of the Crusaders says, "There is a group right now called Signature Sound, and some people don't like what they are doing—all the choreography, the dancing, and carrying on as they sing. Personally it's not my taste, but they have an outstanding sound—a terrific southern gospel sound. And I have to believe that it is going to be a means to pull more young people into southern gospel as they see what can be done with southern gospel music. So my hat's off to them even though it's not my flavor when they do that kind of thing."

Although they continue to present private concerts, they have also teamed up with the Gaither Vocal Band and are having great success. The first weekend, their fall Give It Away tour was presented to sold-out crowds in both Maryland and Virginia. The events featured The Gaither Vocal Band and Ernie Haase & Signature Sound along with other special guests. The concerts were enhanced by an innovative set design. Thrilled at their debut success of "Get Away, Jordan," Joe Bonsall, long-time tenor for the Oak Ridge Boys, comments, "They can also take classic old songs like 'Get Away Jordan' and make them sound new and fresh . . . I really appreciate the boys because they're doing something the Oak Ridge Boys tried to do back in the middle '70s without as much success, and that's try to take southern-style gospel to the masses."

Leaving Stow, we take Fishburg Road to SR-91 north, where we pass through Hudson, home of JoAnn Stores Inc. Passing through Twinsburg, we take IR-480 west merging onto IR-271 where we continue north, and for the first time today, the sun is brightly shining, and the rain is gone. As IR-271 ends, we merge onto IR-90. We take IR-90 to SR-615 and continue north to U.S. 20. Turning right onto U.S. 20 we pass through Mentor, and more road construction, to Painesville, where Joseph David Edward Habedank was born on December 16, 1985.

Soon after Joseph was born, the family relocated to Sturgess, Michigan, where he lived until he was four years old. Leaving Michigan, they moved to Xenia where he spent the remaining years of his childhood.

When Joseph was about four years old, he started singing with his family in a group called the Sanlins. As the family would travel, he would sing with his two younger brothers doing songs like "He's Still Workin' on Me." Everybody loved to watch these little boys sing.

When Joseph was five or six, he and his brothers had an imaginary friend named George who traveled with them everywhere they sang. One Sunday morning, they had left home early, about 6:00 AM, and were traveling in their van to Indianapolis, Indiana where they were scheduled to sing at the Faith Baptist Church. Suddenly, Joseph questioned his grandpa, "Where's George? He's not in here!"

Grandpa responded, "He's running alongside of the van." Then grandpa, quickly opening the door to the van, told George to jump in and then shut the door. It was a close call, but they got him in the van, and their imaginary friend, George, made the appointment.

When Joseph was ten years old, both his aunt Charity and his uncle Josh got married and, along with Grandma Salle Sanlin they came off the road. Joseph and his brothers were older now, and they started singing with their mom, and the Sanlins continued as a family ministry for another six years.

At age sixteen, Joseph ventured out singing solo. He won a Crabb Family talent contest, and they helped him make his first solo album. After hearing a song off his solo album, the Perrys contacted Joseph, and although Tracy was a little skeptical at first because of Joseph's age, they offered him their baritone position. Accepting the position, seventeen-year-old Joseph was soon traveling on the road full-time. About three years later, their lead singer left, and although he was hesitant at first, after much prayer, he agreed to become the lead singer for the Perrys.

After Joseph joined the Perrys, his mother, Leah Sanlin, started singing in a new group based in Anderson, Indiana, called Common Ground. The group was formed by Phil Sowders, but after traveling for a couple of years, the group decided to quit singing.

Phil was raised in a Christian home and, at the age of seven, gave his life to Christ. Besides his own godly father, the two men who had the greatest spiritual impact on his life were Pastor Travis Hudson and his current pastor, Pastor Jerry Siler. Married twenty-six years, he considers his wife Barb Sowders a true blessing from the Lord. Phil spent twelve years singing with a Dayton group called New Life and also sang for a while with the Toney Brothers of Nashville, Tennessee.

The soundman for Common Ground was Robert Dixon. Growing up in Miami Township, just south of Dayton, Robert vividly recalls his salvation experience at his Christian school. On that particular day, Mrs. Fugate had presented a flannel graph story during the Bible class. The Lord convicted his young heart, and he stayed inside during recess to ask the Lord to save him. He was privileged to work with several gospel groups before joining Common Ground, and he now travels with the Pfeifers from Washington Court House.

Joseph has written several songs. One song entitled "He Forgot" actually went to number three on the national charts. He later coauthored a song called

"The Grip of Grace" with his mom. He acknowledges not only inheriting his singing ability but also his writing ability from his mother.

Before leaving Painesville, we take a drive to Lake Metro Park where we enjoy a beautiful view of the sun setting over Lake Erie. Heading back to U.S. 20, we pass a deer standing along the road that seemed to be saying, "Thanks for stopping by." Continuing northeast on U.S. 20, we pass by Perry, home to the Circle of Friends, a group formed in July 2002. The unique arrangements created by Lisa Pierce and Debbie Ashburn give the mixed group a special blend, which repeatedly captivates their audience. Their southern gospel harmonies have been heard in churches and gospel events throughout the state.

They were invited to sing at a Sunday morning worship service at Wildwood Acres Campground in Andover. They were told it was to be a drive-in service. Since it was located next to a drive-in theater, they didn't give this matter a second thought. However, they were somewhat surprised when the cars started gathering in and parking in drive-in theater format along the front of the stage. Instead of applause, their appreciation came in the form of honking horns. Although they didn't see any faces, when the people really felt the Spirit, they rolled down their windows so their raised hands could be seen.

Group member Bobby Greener says, "Our primary purpose is to give glory to God through our songs, to encourage people and to win the lost to Christ and have fun while doing it!"

Through the efforts of bass singer Brad Ashburn, an annual event called The Gospel Trail evolved in Perry and is hosted by the Circle of Friends. The group is going strong today.

Continuing north on U.S. 20 (Coastal Trail) we pass a huge nuclear plant along the lakeshore. Passing through several lakeside towns, we reach Ashtabula, which was once a major location on the Underground Railroad. Poet Carl Sandburg wrote a poem titled "Crossing Ohio when Poppies Bloom in Ashtabula."

Philip P. Bliss was born in Rome, Pennsylvania on July 9, 1938. He was raised in a simple log cabin in a mountainous region of Pennsylvania, and the prayers of his father were ingrained into his future. Hearing the sound of a piano at age ten, he developed a strong desire to become a musician. Leaving home at age eleven, he spent the next five years working in a lumber camp where, in 1850, he accepted Christ as Lord and Savior. In 1851, he became assistant cook at the camp, making $9 per month.

In 1859, he married a young lady named Lucy and worked on her father's farm for a monthly income of $13 while continuing to study music. Moving to Chicago in 1864, he soon connected with the famous D. L. Moody. In 1873, Moody asked Bliss to be his director of music. Surrendering to evangelistic work, his life was about to change forever. Bliss compiled a songbook for use in their revival campaigns and received royalties in excess of $30,000.

On December 29, 1876, just as things were beginning to look up for this gifted songwriter, he boarded a train in Rome, Pennsylvania, the Pacific Express, headed for Chicago. The train was pushing its way through a blinding snowstorm, and as they approached Ashtabula, the train was passing over a trestle bridge. Suddenly, as the first engine reached the other side, the bridge, weakened by floodwaters, collapsed plunging the remaining portion of the train seventy-five feet down the ravine into the icy water.

A fire broke out, and fanned by the winds of the ravine, the flames were rapidly moving through the coaches. Bliss, crawling through a window, managed to escape the fire, but realizing his wife was pinned under a seat, he returned to her assistance. Soon, overtaken by the flames, they, along with almost a hundred others, lost their lives. Philip P. Bliss left behind numerous songbooks and perhaps some of the world's greatest hymns such as "Almost Persuaded," "Jesus Loves Even Me," and "Let the Lower Lights Be Burning."

Leaving Ashtabula, we take IR-84 west to SR-45 where we turn left onto SR-45 and drive to Austinburg where we spend the night at the Comfort Inn. After a continental breakfast, we're on the road again. Turning left onto SR-45, we head south leaving Austinburg. Turning left on SR-307, we travel east, passing through Jefferson, to SR-46. Turning right onto SR-46, we travel south, passing through Rays Corner, Colebrook, and Mecca where we drive around the roundabout and continue south. Reaching Cortland, we turn right taking a short drive down to view Mosquito Creek Lake. Leaving Cortland, we turn right taking an S-curve across some railroad tracks. At SR-5 we stop for fuel. Back on the road again, we travel to Warren, home of the Hot Dog Shoppe. People from neighboring cities and states come to Warren just to eat at this booming small-town restaurant.

People also came from miles around to hear Everlasting Hope, an all-female quartet comprised of two sets of sisters who created a unique blend of harmony. Both of their fathers previously sang in a quartet in Warren called the Sentenials. The girls got their start singing together for the National Fine Arts competition, and by 1985, they were actively singing together in their church. Soon they were singing in other churches, and in 1990, they officially started traveling on the road part-time. In 2003, with the help of Wesley Pritchard, they produced their first recording. They have sung at several local conventions, including a Southern Gospel Convention held in Pennsylvania. They sang the national anthem several times before Cleveland Indians baseball games. In late 2005, they determined it would be best to stop singing and came off the road.

* * *

The Stevens Family has been traveling since 1985 singing in thirty-five different states. In addition to their musical abilities, they have written some great songs recorded by such artists as Greater Vision and Phil Enloe. Rich Stevens was greatly involved in music in his home church from a very early age. His abilities range from talented singer to gifted arranger and producer. His wife, Tami, a gifted vocalist, speaker, and songwriter, began taking piano and voice at the age of six and continued her training through college. Tami was soloist for two years with *Revivaltime*, an international radio broadcast. Their multiple talents have begun to exhibit themselves in their daughter Erin, who possesses a strong voice and a sweet spirit to round out this Christ-centered family ministry that continues to sing in harmony and share a heritage.

OHIO 19

Leaving Warren, we take SR-169 south approximately five miles to Niles. Taking SR-46 we pass the, passing the beautiful William McKinley Library. Born in Niles on January 29, 1843, William McKinley Jr. became president of the United States in 1897. During his years in Washington, he regularly attended church and often entertained guests with Sunday evening hymn sings in the executive mansion. McKinley was also the son of an ironmaster and driving by the Niles Recycling Center, we notice a huge statue of a man made out of scrap metal. Turning left on Salt Springs—Youngstown Road, we drive to CR-1239 where a helicopter appears to be flying right at us. Shortly we arrive in Youngstown, a hilly city and the birthplace of the Good Humor brand of ice cream novelties. In 1964, the fast-food chain, Arby's, opened the first of its restaurants in the Youngstown suburb of Boardman. Then in the late 1980s, the Avanti, an automobile with a fiberglass body (originally designed by Studebaker to compete with the Corvette), was manufactured in an industrial complex located on Youngstown's Albert Street. The Warner Brothers were also from Youngstown, and a beautiful theatre was constructed in honor of a brother.

Another set of brothers from Youngstown started singing as a duet in their Sunday school class at age four. They loved to sing, and both Don and Gary Abraham played the guitar. They both attended the Stamps Conservatory of Music in Texas for two summers when they were teens and recorded their first album in Youngstown at just thirteen years old! Deciding to expand their ministry and calling themselves the Abraham Brothers, they first hired Johnny Porrazzo to sing tenor and play piano. Johnny received many other offers, however, and soon moved on. Howard McCrary played with the group, but his time was also short lived as he had a group of his own called the McCrary Five.

Once while the Abraham Brothers were touring with the Keystones (whose members later became part of the Imperials and the Oak Ridge Boys), the Keystones wrecked their bus. The two full groups, with equipment, albums, and personal belongings, were loaded on one bus and continued traveling down the road. Needless to say, this period of time generated quite a set of stories.

Mark Maynard, previously with the Chords also of Youngstown, later joined the group.

In 1973, after traveling with the Embers, David Hamilton joined the Abraham Brothers, staying with them until they stopped singing. After leaving the group, Dave returned to western Pennsylvania and married Deb, his teenage sweetheart. Since 1997, he has been part of an award-winning bluegrass band named Church Street Blues. Recording solo projects and regularly performing with CSB, he's become quite a busy "part-time" musician.

Finally, the Finnie brothers joined the group. Ed Finnie sang tenor and Bob Finnie played piano and sang as needed. They traveled extensively throughout the United States and Canada.

The Abraham Brothers disbanded in 1975. Mark Maynard and his wife, Cindy, have been ministering together for about thirty-three years and are actively doing some recording projects. Cindy started singing at the age of four when she was so small she had to stand on the platform railing to be seen. At a very early age, she appeared on a television show along with the Three Stooges singing "If You'll Take My Jesus." She continued singing throughout her childhood and later sang with a trio traveling to various churches.

Piano player Bill Dunbar went on to have a successful ministry with Jerry Falwell, and drummer John Foster is now a *scientist*!

* * *

George Bennard was born in Youngstown on February 4, 1873. His family moved to Albia, Iowa, where George met and accepted Christ as his personal Savior. Losing his father at age sixteen, he joined the ranks of the Salvation Army. He was ordained in the Methodist Episcopal Church after which he conducted revival services throughout New York and Michigan. Convinced the cross was more then merely a religious symbol, he became inspired to pen the words to perhaps one of the greatest hymns "The Old Rugged Cross." After the writing of this great song, he continued his evangelistic ministries for another forty years. George passed away on October 9, 1958, at the age of eighty-five.

* * *

When she was just four, Linda McCrary started singing around the kitchen sink with her nine siblings. Her father, Charles McCrary, had traveled and sung with his brothers and provided musical training to all his children. They were exposed to large audiences at a young age while singing for evangelist Katherine Kuhlman during her visits to Youngstown. By age eleven, Linda and some of her siblings were singing on weekends as far away as Canada. Just a year later, they sang on the Ted Mack *Amateur Hour* program taking second place, and they soon had their own television show.

As a result of this exposure, they relocated to California where Linda began doing backup work for such secular artists as Elton John and Diana Ross. Linda started traveling down the wrong path, and soon she was into drugs and living on the street. Then in 1989, after a visit from an old friend, she found her way back to Christ. God began to give her songs, and she now travels doing solo concerts singing and sharing her testimony.

* * *

Lynn (Royce) Taylor was born on October 21, 1951, in Murphysboro, Tennessee, while his father was stationed at Stewart Air Force Base. His mother and father were both from the northeast Ohio area, and once his dad had finished his time as an officer in the air force, they hurried back to Ohio to raise Royce. His dad was a singer of sorts, and his mother was the church organist for years. The unusual side of his mother, unknown to most people, is that she was raised in the Mennonite Church. She loved what she labeled "hillbilly music" and would often listen to it on the radio. She grew up with a radio in the home listening to country music on WWVA from Wheeling, West Virginia. She liked it so well she started playing the guitar, which was very strange for a Mennonite girl.

As a young boy, Royce would see that little guitar propped up in the corner, and every now and then, his mother would play it. His dad later bought his mother a fabulous Gibson guitar in exchange for a 1947 Harley Davidson motorcycle for himself. One day, Royse decided he would like to play the guitar, so he got her old one out and began strumming away, but the neck was warped, making it very hard to play. After his mother agreed to let him use the good guitar, he would sit for hours in his room teaching himself to play.

In 1967, Royce Taylor and David Musselman put together a little duet called the Gospel Chords. They sang at the Youth for Christ camp, and before they knew it, they were invited to sing a couple songs at their church. After they sang a couple of songs at church, someone invited them to sing at the Mahoning County Fair. From there, it escalated rather quickly, and it wasn't long before they were doing the entire service at some of the churches. Over the course of about two years, they were being invited to sing at rallies and started traveling throughout the Midwest.

Royce says, "We were too young to know any better, and we didn't sing all that well. So it had to be something bigger than the both of us to propel us forward that rapidly."

Lynn Deeter joined the group for a while, making it a trio. He was replaced by Steve Biffle of Boardman, who played piano and sang baritone. In 1970, Mark Maynard of Ravenna joined the group at age fourteen, making it a quartet. Their first album was nothing to brag about, just some young boys who didn't know any better going in to make a recording. They gleaned what knowledge they could from the folks that were obviously the professionals in the business like the Blackwood Brothers, the Statesmen, and the Stamps.

The Imperials had the most profound effect on them because of their fresh, contemporary sound. They eventually moved in that direction, reducing their name to simply the Chords. This opened the door for them to sing in more secular venues, like county fairs and corporate events. This also took them out of mainstream gospel music and propelled them in a little different direction than some of the other groups were going. Their staple was still very much singing in the churches and church-related venues, coffee houses, and other youth rallies.

They were driving through St. Louis, Missouri, one morning when they heard that sound that nobody ever wants to hear, and all of a sudden, the bus just stopped moving. It rolled to a halt, and they discovered the engine had blown and there was oil dripping all over the ground. At the time, St. Louis actually had tow trucks that would run along during rush hour traffic, and if a breakdown occurred, it would come over and hook you up and tow you off the pavement to prevent the traffic from backing up. They were blessed as a wrecker came by within minutes, and the bus was towed to a diesel garage just a couple of exits down the road. They arrived at the garage, and the mechanic opened up the back of the bus. After looking at the engine, he called his manager to come out and look. The manager looked at the engine, made a phone call, and the next thing they knew, they were receiving a new engine. Apparently, a problem with the original installation caused the engine to blow.

Various members came and went but the group continued to grow. Perhaps the best known roster of members was together in the mid-1970s. This lineup was made up of David Musselman, Lynn Royce Taylor, Scott Cole, Tom Fowler, and Gary Vogel. In 1979, the members wanted to go in different directions, and the group decided to disband.

After the Chords disbanded, Tom Fowler and his wife, Millie, moved to Sharon, Pennsylvania. As his wife is a marvelous vocalist, they have done some duets together and have become very much involved in their church. Scott Cole went to the little town of Saxonburg, Pennsylvania, where he was invited to become the music director for a local church.

Mark Maynard joined the Abraham Brothers from Youngstown. Steve Biffle was a pianist early on with the group, and he is now a pastor in the Columbus area. Steve Bowden, another pianist for the group, and his wife, Laurie, are music directors at a church in Fort Worth, Texas. Gary Vogel, the last pianist for the group, lives somewhere in Arizona where he and his wife Debbie are worship leaders in a local church.

Royce continued doing some part-time solo work throughout the 1980s but was off the road working jobs to raise his three boys. In 1991, he joined a group called the Vogues. They were an oldies group in Pittsburgh, Pennsylvania. They had a number of regular popular rock-n-roll hits including

"Turn Around, Look at Me" and "You are my Special Angel." Chuck Blascoe still maintains a group of Vogues that works around the Pittsburgh area. With the revival of oldies radio, they began getting requests to do some touring again. So until 1997, Royce toured the country singing tenor for the Vogues. He enjoyed it quite a bit. They did some great shows, and it reminded him of some of the secular shows the Chords had done. In the fall of 1996, he became very concerned. He acknowledged that his calling was gospel music and traveling with the Vogues was not where he should be, so he chose to resign.

Once again, he planned to embark on a solo career but, after doing a few concerts, ended up having to go back to work in order to pay the bills.

In 2002, he went on the road singing tenor with Ed Enoch and the Stamps, staying with the Stamps for four years. From there, he joined the Blackwood Singers singing with Ron Blackwood, R. W. Blackwood, and Paul Hyde in Pigeon Forge, Tennessee, at their *Blackbear Jamboree Theatre* show. He remained with them until September 2006 when John Rulapaugh accepted the position and became the new tenor for the group. Shortly thereafter, Terry Toney gave him a call, and once again, figuring he would only be singing for a few weeks, he stepped aboard to fill a temporary position. Royce did the 2006 NQC with the Toney Brothers and remains with them today.

Royce, with his weaving on and off the road, reminds us, "The road is difficult, and it's far from a glamorous life. It may look glamorous, but even on a big beautiful bus, the inside of that bus starts getting pretty ordinary after a while."

Yet even Royce would agree, the following story makes it all worthwhile.

One day, Royce received a call from a young man named Randy. The young man began to share how that, at the age of twelve, he had gone to hear the Chords when they were scheduled to sing at the high school in his little town of Golden City, Missouri. Arriving at the concert with his family, he remembered waiting with great anticipation for this group to show. When they came driving into the parking lot, their big bus really impressed him. The concert was terrific, and Royce and some of the other guys even talked with him afterwards.

Randy told Royce that the effect of that experience was so strong it led to him giving his heart to the Lord. Randy is now married and a deacon in his church. He was excited as he and his wife, Carla, had just adopted four of the cutest little girls. Coming out of an abusive home, the girls' and their family were going to be broken. The courts were sending these little girls in different directions until Randy and Carla came along.

Royse says, "This is just one of those stories that you just scratch your head and say, 'Wow!'"

Leaving Youngstown, we get on IR-680, take one last look at Youngstown, and head south. Taking the last exit before paying toll, we turn right onto Western Reserve Road. Turning right on South Avenue, we follow SR-164 to Woodworth Road (SR-626). Continuing east, we pass through New Springfield and leave the city area driving back into the country, and the road becomes like a roller coaster. Passing through Unity, we turn left onto SR-165 and enter East Palestine, where songwriter Dr. Judson W. Van DeVenter, while visiting the home of George Sebring, wrote the words to the beautiful song often sung in church "I Surrender All."

Driving through East Palestine, we are stopped by a train. After the train has passed, we continue through town passing a beautiful Methodist church with an old church bell. We also drove past the Boatman Cemetery, a historical site. To enter the cemetery, you have to pick up the key to the gate at the police station. The cemetery is named after Boatman, a veteran of the American Revolution. Taking SR-46, we follow alongside another train on the right to Columbiana where we lose SR-46 and continue along SR-14. Continuing west, we pass through Washingtonville, and after crossing Bear Creek, we drive up a big hill and reach Salem. Leaving Salem, we continue to SR-62 where we travel west, passing through Damascus, Westville, Sebring, and Alliance, home of Mount Union College. We finally reach Canton, home to the Professional Football Hall of Fame, the Hoover (vacuum) Company, and the beautiful Canton Palace, where local residents have listened to some of the finest southern gospel music including the hometown voice of Matt Felts.

Matt Felts was born in St. Louis, Missouri, on December 11, 1977, and grew up attending the Merrimac Cavern singing events. He was a big fan of the Lesters since they are also from St. Louis. He developed a love for gospel music at an early age as the sound of the Blackwoods, the Goodmans, the Statesmen, or the Cathedrals could be heard any day at his house. During high school, he drifted away from southern gospel and started listening to more contemporary Christian. He had been involved in music in high school, and he was actually offered a music scholarship to the Julliard School in New

York City. At the time, he was teetering between music and baseball. Taking a baseball scholarship, he set his musical desires aside and completed college.

Shortly after college, he spent some time playing Minor League baseball before moving to Canton, where he started working for Babies R Us as an HR director. While in Canton, he got involved in a local church, and the Lord began to deal with his heart about singing. The fire was soon rekindled, and he now had a desire to sing in full-time gospel music. Not having any idea how to get started, he remembered meeting George Younce when he was eighteen and George telling him, "The only advice I will give you is to sing every chance you get, every opportunity you can, just sing, and God will open the doors." So taking that advice, he began singing with a local group from his church. He also helped lead the praise and worship and would sometimes sing solos.

One day while his pastor was eating at a Denny's Restaurant, someone from a local gospel group based in Mansfield stopped by to post a flyer for an upcoming concert. The pastor started talking with them, and during the conversation, they commented, "We are looking for a tenor singer. You don't know any singers, do you?"

To this, he responded, "Actually, we have a great tenor singer at our church. We would hate to lose him, but we know he's looking."

Matt agreed to meet with them, and when he went for the audition, it was an instant match. The Gloryway Quartet had found a tenor, and Matt had found a gospel group. He enjoyed singing with them, but as they all had full-time jobs, they wanted to stay local.

After being with the group for little over a year, he received a call from the Skyline Boys in Manassas, Virginia, offering him a job. Believing God had given him a higher calling, he accepted the position and was soon on his way. While singing with the Skyline Boys, the group was nominated twice for Horizon Group of the Year. Matt was also named Tenor of the Year and New Voice of the Year by the Buckeye Southern Gospel Association. He also won several awards from the Gateway Gospel Music Association including Favorite Tenor. All this recognition was very exciting, but he didn't believe he was home yet. He continued to ask God, "Where are you calling me to?"

While with the Skyline Boys, he continued to live in Canton, simply driving back and forth to Virginia. As Stow was only about ten minutes from Canton, he soon developed a really close friendship with Ernie Haase. Ernie took on the role of mentoring Matt, not just about music, but more about just how to live on the road, how to balance having a family, what things to avoid, and how to really stay close to God and to His calling.

In June 2006, after much prayer, Matt decided to leave the Skyline Boys and move to Nashville, Tennessee. As Matt was married now, this was a nerve-wracking transition as they had no idea where to go or what to do when they arrived. Matt shared with his wife that Johnny Minnick had a church in Smyrna, Tennessee. As he had heard many good things about him, perhaps they should start attending his church and trust God to open the next door. Then before they could even make the move, Matt received a phone call from Marshall Pugh of the Monument Quartet. Matt had previously sung with the Blackwood Gospel Quartet for a short period, and his friend Brad Smith of the *Blackwoods* had called Marshall telling him that if they were looking for a tenor singer, they could quit looking as he had found their guy. Matt asked Marshall where the group was based, and when Marshall said, "Smyrna, Tennessee," Matt began to get nervous. Still somewhat shaken by the oddity of this event, Matt continued his questioning, and upon finding out the group was based in Johnny Minnick's church, Matt responded, "I will be there in two days." With great excitement, he shared this information with his wife, but she still had reservations, reminding him the group had not even heard him yet.

Soon Matt was on his way to Tennessee, and when he arrived at the church, he found himself sitting around the piano singing with the group and listening to Johnny Minnick play. Minnick had traveled with Howard and Vestal Goodman, so this sing-along was a great honor for Matt, a longtime fan of the Happy Goodman's. After about five minutes, Johnny shut the piano lid, looked at Marshall, and confirmed his approval. After Marshall offered him the position, Matt called his wife, and she responded, "I'm already packing the house."

Matt accepted the position, and it wasn't long before he was traveling with the Monument Quartet. With their new tenor, the group continued singing in churches across America, and their tribute to the Happy Goodman Family was well received by crowds everywhere.

Recently, they began to feel the Lord leading them in a different direction. Believing they had been called to the secular market of country music, they crossed over and are singing mostly at fairs, festivals, and corporate events. A portion of their program remains gospel, and excitement is high as they believe God is opening doors where gospel groups have never been allowed to go. When they sang in Canton before a crowd of around six hundred people, the mayor presented Matt with the key to the city. This was an exciting event because these were people, neighbors, coworkers, from his community, and many were not saved. Matt believes they are now reaching people that would never have entered through the door of a church. Their somewhat different approach is still seeing people get saved and lives being changed and reminds him of the words of that great song by Kenny Hinson, "Ain't That What It's All About."

Looking back over the path, he has traveled, Matt gives all the glory to God as he shares, "I never would have dreamed four years ago, while working at Babies R Us, that I would be singing in the NQC, sitting on Bill Gaither's bus, and developing friendships with people I grew up listening to. I told my dad, 'Sometimes I have to pinch myself, it's just amazing.' A kid from Missouri and Ohio, you just never would have dreamed it would turn out like this. But God's good, God's good."

Returning Home

Leaving Canton, we take SR-62 west. We pass through Navarre, and nearing Brewster, we almost miss a sharp curve to the left. Turning left onto SR-93 we travel south through some sheep country. Passing through Beach City, we continue to Sugarcreek and enter Holmes County, home to a large population of Amish. The lifestyle around us is changing rapidly as we began to notice clothes hanging on lines and repeatedly pass Amish buggies along the road. Arriving at Sugarcreek, we turn right onto SR-39 and head west to Berlin. Stopping in Berlin, we have dinner at the Boyd & Wurthmann Restaurant, a quaint little Amish restaurant established in 1938 that serves some really great food. After a little shopping, we take a scenic drive south through Amish farm country. Winding through the hill country, we pass farm after farm and even drive through an active sawmill. Finally back onto SR-36 we head west, passing through Nellie, and work our way back onto SR-62. Taking SR-62 west, we turn right onto SR-161 and travel to Columbus taking IR-270 to IR-670 west. Reaching IR-70, we travel west to IR-75 where we turn north to Vandalia and end Tour 3.

GOD'S AMBASSADORS

HAMILTON ROAD

NEW PRESENCE

FREEDOM VOICE

SLABACH SISTERS

COLE FAMILY

PARKER TRIO

EMBERS

EMBERS

EVANGELAIRES

EVANGELAIRES

Lorne Matthews

Lorne Matthews with
MCDUFF BROTHERS

Roy Tremble

WEATHERFORDS

John & Lily Weatherford

Armon Morales with IMPERIALS

Henry & Hazel Slaughter

SONGSTERS

SINGING WEAVERS

ONE WAY RIDER

CATHEDRALS

CATHEDRALS

* George Younce

George Younce with
BLUE RIDGE

* George Younce & Ernie Haase with
OLD FRIENDS

Gerald Wolfe & Mark Trammell

* Gerald Wolfe with
GREATER VISION

MARK TRAMMELL TRIO

Mosie Lister & Roger Bennett

Scott Fowler & Roger Bennett with
LEGACY FIVE

* Roy Webb

* Roy Webb with
SIGNATURE SOUND

* Ernie Haase

* SIGNATURE SOUND

Joseph Habedank

Joseph Habadank & Nick Trammell

* Joseph Habedank with PERRYS

CIRCLE OF FRIENDS

STEVENS FAMILY

ABRAHAM BROTHERS

ABRAHAM BROTHERS

ABRAHAM BROTHERS

CHORDS

CHORDS

CHORDS

Royce Taylor with STAMPS

Royce Taylor & Amon Webster with
TONEY BROTHERS

Matt Felts with
MONUMENT QUARTET

CHAPTER IV

Portsmouth Tour

What a Day That Will Be

There is coming a day when no heartaches shall come.
No more clouds in the sky, no more tears to dim the eye;
All is peace forevermore on that happy golden shore.
What a day, glorious day that will be.

There'll be no sorrow there, no more burdens to bear,
No more sickness, no pain, no more parting over there;
And forever I will be with the One who died for me.
What a day, glorious day that will be.

What a day that will be when my Jesus I shall see.
And to look upon His Face, the One who saved me by His grace;
When He takes me by the hand and leads me through the promise land.
What a day, glorious day that will be!

—Jim Hill
(Used with Permission)

Leaving Vandalia, we head south on IR-75 to Dayton. Driving through Dayton, we see road construction all around, including the present demolition of the Monument Avenue Bridge. Exiting onto U.S. 35, we travel east and cross over IR-71. My wife is saddened as we drive past the Ohio Factory Outlets without stopping. Finally, we exit onto SR-22, and crossing Paint Creek, we enter Washington Court House. Driving through town, we view the giant eight-day Seth Thomas clock, the second largest in America at the time of installation, on top of the Fayette County Courthouse. Inside the courthouse murals painted by Archibald M. Willard, painter of *Spirit of '76,* adorn the wall of the second-floor corridor. Speaking of higher things, there is a gospel group in town called Higher Call.

Growing up in a rural area of Fayette County, Randy Woods started singing with his siblings in their home church while their mother accompanied on the piano. In 1976, he met his future wife Debbie, and they sang together in a group called Heritage Trio. Debbie stopped singing when they adopted a beautiful baby girl named Alexa Rose from Bolivia. Before putting together the group Higher Call, Scott Maddon had also traveled with several groups. In 1997, they formed the group Higher Call, and in May 2001 while flying to Brooklyn, New York, for a singing engagement, they were able to view from the air, for the last time, the famous World Trade Center shortly before its tragic destruction on September 11, 2001.

* * *

Another group from Washington Court House, the Pfeifers, continues to lift spirits across America. John Pfeifer was born in Nipgen on June 17, 1951, back in the days when babies were being born in the home. John's family lived in Ohio at the time, and that Sunday morning his mother was in hard labor and Doctor Hass had already arrived at the house. John's father, a young preacher, had gotten dressed and was planning to go to church when the doctor said, "Young man, your wife is about to have a baby, you are going to stay here." So Mr. Pfeifer missed Sunday school that day to be present for the birth of his son.

John grew up like most kids in the 1950s and had a wonderful childhood. Grandpa Pfeifer started singing on ABC Radio in Columbus in 1935. Both grandfathers sang gospel music, and there was a unique anointing on these two men. God richly blessed each time these two men stood to sing with guitar and mandolin in hands as well as their trusted songbook, which contained more than a hundred songs written by them.

His father was a very successful pastor, and growing up, John lived on a farm with ponies and just about everything a child could ever want. When John was old enough to start thinking about college, he received an offer for a full-paid scholarship to Ohio State University to play his trumpet. He also had a letter of invitation from West Point Military Academy.

Despite all the good things in John's upbringing, he started dabbling in drugs and alcohol and really made a mess of his life. By the time John was twenty-nine years old, he had been in Alcoholics Anonymous for five years and had been in jail in every town where he had lived. In the mid-1970s, John's dad started fasting and praying. At one point, he even fasted forty days and forty nights. Believing in the power of intercessory prayer, he continued requesting others to pray for his son, John.

Then one hot summer night in 1980, while John was sitting in a bar, the power of conviction came over him, and turning to the man sitting next to him, John said, "I am leaving here and never coming back." The man had no idea what he was talking about, but John got up and left the bar. Walking out onto the sidewalk, he asked Jesus into his life, and right then and there, things began to change.

John's sister, Candy Pfeifer, was born in Waverly on March 24, 1959, and grew up under the watchful eyes of three older brothers. In high school, Candy was a successful basketball player, and she was named a high school All-American and received a basketball scholarship. In 1979, Candy moved to Roanoke, Virginia, to attend college, but after two years of college, she chose to leave school and pursue her first love. She started a little gospel group named the Believers, and as her father was doing evangelistic work at the time, he would take the Believers with him to sing wherever he would preach. Candy recently authored a devotional book, and continuing to perfect her God-given songwriting ability, she has penned several popular songs including "This Same Jesus," "Jumpin' In," and "When Desperation Meets Faith."

After John got saved, he started setting up interdenominational crusades for his father's ministry. With dad preaching, Candy's group, the Believers, singing, and John directing the crusades, they ministered for about three years and saw many people come to the Lord.

Later when their grandfather became ill and their father had to slow down, John took leadership of the group. In 1984, they changed their name to the Pfeifers. The group is now based in Washington Court House where they also have a studio called Court Street Studio where Candy, when she isn't traveling on the road, spends much of her time doing production work for various groups and soloists. Since 1985, the core of the group had been John, Candy, and Mary Jane as the Lord continues to open doors to their ministry.

Mary Jane Carter was born in Greenfield on September 25, 1949, and began singing on stage at the age of nine. Mary has many years of voice lessons to her credit as both a student and teacher. Her voice continues to move people to their feet, night after night, as she shares songs like "Further Still" and "This Same Jesus." Her on-stage charisma is fresh and exciting and has made her a favorite among audiences nationwide. Mary has been twice nominated for Female Vocalist of the Year.

Turnover within the group has been limited. Two past members moved on to become pastors. Two are now worship leaders within large churches, and the other one is very much involved in his home church in Roanoke, Virginia, and owns a couple restaurants. They had a sound engineer, Rob Snyder, who traveled with them for about twelve years. He is a now a contract engineer and has been honored to set up sound for the NQC.

Over the years, the group has worn out three buses. Their first bus, an old 4104, was inherited from the Believers. When they put this bus to rest, it had traveled over three million miles. In 1983, they were able to purchase a newer bus, a 1982 Model 10 Eagle, and they were excited as this bus was only one-year-old. They customized the interior, and it was a beautiful bus. They kept this bus for seventeen years, putting a million miles on it before it was sold. Their last bus, an H3 Provo, was big and beautiful. When they sold this bus in 2005, they had already put eight hundred fifty thousand miles on it. As they began thinking about purchasing a new bus, they realized a suitable bus would cost around $700,000. John, the principle driver, began to question if buying another bus was the best thing for the group. John was a pilot and never really wanted to be a bus driver. He concluded, "We can fly!"

So they purchased a Kenworth truck to haul their equipment, and while the guys travel ahead getting everything set up, the group, rested and full of energy, flies, sings, gets a good night's rest at a local motel and flies home or on to the next appointment. John says, "It may not work for everybody, but for us, it is working rather well."

Audiences across the country stand to their feet as this talented trumpet musician plays such great songs as "How Great Thou Art" and "We Shall Behold Him." With their radiant personalities and dynamic testimony, the

Pfeifers are making a difference in the lives of people all across the country. John began playing trumpet at a very young age and today is recognized as one of gospel music's most talented instrumentalists. He was nominated as one of the 2006 Top 5 Favorite Musicians by the subscribers of the *Singing News Magazine*, and in 2007, at the fiftieth anniversary of the NQC, the crowd rose to their feet with a thunderous applause as he played the final notes to that old Dottie Rambo favorite, "He Looked Beyond My Faults."

In October 2007, Justin Hill of Dayton joined the Pfeifers as keyboard player. Justin has been playing the piano since age ten. The son of a pastor, he has been involved in music most of his life. He lives in Dayton with his wife, Elizabeth.

As part of their ministry, the Pfeifers very intensely desire to see people saved and to see God's children uplifted, encouraged, healed, and set free. For five years now, they have been holding a community Bible study called "The Gathering Place" in Washington Court House, and John was privileged to lead the morning Bible study at the 2007 NQC. They are excited about their future and have developed a new program called "The Most Wanted Gathering." It will be an evangelical music event geared toward soul winning and personal evangelism.

John says, "Sometimes the church almost appears as if it has its chin on its chest. I want to see the things of the Lord edified and people really stepping up to the inheritance that we have as children of the King."

Leaving Washington Court House, we take SR-41 south, crossing over U.S. 35, and as we drive along the rolling hills, we are blessed with a beautiful panoramic view of the southern hills just prior to arriving in Greenfield, birthplace of General John Hull. A small town where you can often hear some good southern gospel music, Greenfield is home to the Singing Disciples.

The group was formed in 1981 through the effort of Lanny Bryant. Before forming the Singing Disciples, Lanny sang with the Royalaires in Columbus. Over time, the ministry of the Singing Disciples began to grow. They took part in several of the annual Westfall Singings, and their songs have been played on radio stations throughout America.

One time while returning from Kentucky in their 4104 bus, they were crossing the big double bridge over the Ohio River. Suddenly the throttle line, which runs from the front to the back of the bus, came loose. Traffic on the bridge began to quickly back up when a man from two cars back came running to the bus. He indicated he owned a bus company and agreed to help them work out a plan. Taking a rope out of his car, he hooked it to the throttle. Then running the rope through the little side door in the back of the bus, they tied the rope around Jim Barrett's waist. He then told them when they wanted to go forward Jim Barrett would have to run toward the front of the bus and pull hard. If they needed to back off, he had to run the other direction. Soon they were once again headed north, and for the next thirty miles, Jim continued to run back and forth inside that old bus until they could reach the bus company where the throttle was repaired.

Another time, while traveling down the road in their bus, they had a very frightening experience. It was winter and, although it was cold and cloudy, upon arrival at the church there was no snow on the ground. About ninety minutes later, when the service was over, they came outside to find snow everywhere. Shortly after leaving the church, they started down a big hill. Looking down the hill, they saw two cars coming up the hill directly in their path. Just as they reached the cars, somehow they miraculously parted, and the bus drove right between the cars. The next day, they received a call from a minister who said he was driving one of the cars they passed through during the snow storm. He expressed to them that he was unable to move the car out of their way and still couldn't explain how the car moved.

In 2005, after the group stopped singing, Lanny started singing with his family under the name, the Homeward Bound Quartet. At one point, both Cliff Chablin and Dennis Glascok became members of the group.

In 1960, prior to singing with the Homeward Bound Quartet, Cliff Chablin started singing with the Southern-Aires. He remained with them for ten years. Once while the Southern-Aires were on a Holy land tour, they were traveling from Jerusalem, and when they passed by the gates to Golgotha, Cliff looked at Charles Feltner and suggested he write a song about their experience. The song that Charles was inspired to pen was one of his greatest entitled "I'll Never Be the Same Anymore." Cliff also sang with the Campmeeting Singers for two years and later started a Dayton based group called the Viceroys. The group remained together for five years.

Before Dennis Glascok sang with Homeward Bound, he sang with a number of groups, including the Revelations for about four years, the Gospel Echoes in Manchester for one year, and the New Pilgrims Quartet in West Union for eight years. Once while traveling with the New Pilgrims, Dennis had just been laid off from his job at General Motors, and they were singing at a small church in Michigan. After the service, a gentleman approached Dennis, sharing his enjoyment of the service. Before walking away, the man slipped a fifty-dollar bill into hand. He said it was just for Dennis as the Lord had directed him to do so. There was no way the man could have known about the layoff. Isn't God great? Dennis also sang for the Royal Descendants in Sardinia for three years, the Apostles in Georgetown for two years, and the Southern-Aires for four years.

Jim Barrett's son Dusty Barrett acquired a love for gospel music after attending a concert featuring the Gold City Quartet and listening to Jay Parrack. Dusty had a smooth tenor voice and felt God calling him to sing gospel music. He soon became a part of the group Crystal River. In 2008, he left Crystal River to start singing with Soul'd Out from Georgetown.

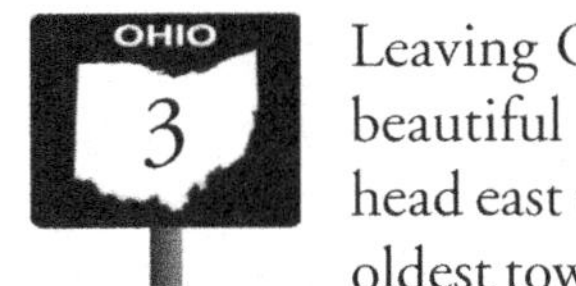

Leaving Greenfield, we travel east along SR-28 through some beautiful hill country. Eventually, we turn onto U.S. 50 and head east to Chillicothe, once the capital of Ohio and one of the oldest towns in the state. While driving through downtown, we are captivated by the many murals painted on the town's structures. We stop at the historic Majestic Theatre home to the Gospel Music Opry where you can hear some of the nation's top groups perform. Speaking of historic, some of the members of the Guardians have been around for quite some time.

Dale Uhrig was born in Chillicothe on July 16, 1927. The Uhrig Brothers started singing at their local church around 1947. The group was made up of two brothers from one family and three of another, and their dads were brothers, so they were first cousins. The first time they sang, they were called the Beulah Chapel Boys because they were singing at their home church, Beulah Chapel, which is also where the Pfeifers originally attended. But we'll get to that. This name remained with them for several years until they were billed as the Uhrig Brothers for a concert at a rather large tabernacle. They liked the name and kept it until forming the Guardians.

People started calling them for revivals, and before they knew it, they were becoming very busy. They all had families and worked full-time jobs, so they traveled mainly on the weekends, doing some two week revivals along the way. The only music they had was a guitar that Dale played, an old Gibson. They traveled about thirty or thirty-five years, and the very first record they made was an old 45 rpm with four songs in 1965.

Finally, some of the brothers wanted to branch out and start their own groups, and it wasn't long until one of the brothers decided he was going to retire. After a few years, another member resigned, and one of Dale's brothers passed away, but the singing never stopped. Eventually, all of the family members were gone except Dale. In 1967, Dale's son Neil started singing with them on weekends during his senior year of college. They did fairs and concerts and continued to do plenty of church work. For a while, some of their children came along and formed a band. At one point, they had a bass guitar, lead guitar, some rhythm guitars, drums, and a trombone. Some of the young band members would occasionally sing.

In the late 1970s, the Uhrig Brothers sang at the Kentucky Homecoming in London, Kentucky. Governor Combs was there and introduced the group, and out of thirty groups, they won the trophy as the most popular group.

They were very busy taking all the bookings they could handle. They traveled in a Silver Eagle bus, and it had private bunks, recliners, a stereo system, and even two TVs (one in the front and one in the rear). Everybody had their own closet, and they later took on a bus driver who also ran the sound. Doing a lot of concerts in schools, fairs, and churches, they had a wonderful time traveling together, but their main goal was to spread the Word to those who are in need.

Once, the Guardians put on a gospel event with Lloyd Orrell, and later sang for the all-night concert at Busch Stadium in Indianapolis, Indiana, for his son Larry Orrell. After hearing them sing, Larry wanted to take the group to Nashville for two weeks and promote an album, but they were unable to take the time off from their jobs.

Down through the years, they have had several members come and go. Dale's cousin Larry Reaster sang tenor with them for a while. He left to join the Journeymen and was replaced by Dean Hickman. Dean was previously with the Sentries, and he also sang with the Golden Keys Quartet for a while when Jim Hill left to sing with the Stamps Quartet. He traveled with the group for about five years.

Danny Gaither and Dean Hickman, just young guys, would paint houses during the day time to make a living. Danny was singing with the Golden Keys at that time, and they would travel on the weekend singing Bill Gaither's songs, and soon many of the songs became popular.

The Guardians have had several piano players, and one of their latest was Harold Patrick, who was previously with the Golden Keys Quartet. Another member, Homer Fry, used to be with the Gospel Harmony Boys in Charleston, West Virginia, and has been involved in gospel music for over sixty years.

One of the highlights each year is going to Hillsdale, Michigan, to sing at what is called the Gospel Barn. The barn has three balconies, and of course, the walls are covered with farm equipment like collars, harnesses, and buggy wheels. Many of the professional groups have sung there, and people gather in from two or three different states, filling the place up every Saturday night to listen to nothing but gospel.

The Guardians were traveling through Texas on their way back to Ohio after a weeklong tour. They were almost to the Arkansas border when all of a sudden the bus engine started heating up. Driving around, they finally found a garage, and going ten miles per hour, they begged the bus to make it to the garage. The mechanic checked it over and said he couldn't get any parts that day, so they would have to find another way home. He agreed to get the bus up and running, and someone could either come after it, or they could bring it home. The only thing they could do was rent three cars, leaving the PA system locked up on the bus along with their other equipment and recordings. They made it home in the rental cars, and later, the garage called telling them it was going to cost about $20,000 to put another engine in the bus. Believing they could get the work done cheaper, they hired a guy to go down with a great big wrecker. They payed $3,000 to have the bus towed to a mechanic near McArthur, where the Pfeifers have their bus worked on all of the time.

Dale had this connection from Don Pfeifer, who played his first horn solo in the church choir at Beulah Chapel, where Dale was the song leader. Don's dad was pastor of the church, and they lived about half a mile down the road. Candy and all of kids grew up at Dale's house while his wife regularly babysat.

So they got the bus down to McArthur, and the bus was soon back on the road. They managed to save some money, even with a $3,000 tow bill. Sometime later, they had a differential drop out while they were down in Charleston, West Virginia, but overall, they haven't had many breakdowns along the road.

One of their piano players went on to play for the Kingdomaires. He was a very good piano player and worked with a number of groups including the Singing Americans. Once he and another guy from the Nashville area were considering putting a group together, so as Dale had a bus and a PA system, they called him requesting he join them to form this new group. Dale wasn't anxious to leave the Guardians but told them he would consider it. The group never got off the ground, and they ended up going their separate ways.

The Guardians witnessed many conversions during their services, but one particular event involving a young girl stands out in Dale's mind. The group was singing in Waverly at the old Canal Days show. This is an annual event, and they put up a big tent. It was Saturday evening, and there was a really big crowd. It was a fairly routine event, not a very spiritual type of atmosphere; and after singing their portion of the program, they exited the platform. While they were tearing down their equipment and making preparations to leave, a young lady walked up to Dale. She was crying and asked him, "Could you please take time to pray with me?" She said, "I need to be saved."

The group stopped what they were doing and gathered around her for prayer. The young lady found the Lord, and the crowd was totally unaware of what happened.

Dale recently celebrated his eightieth birthday. He worked during the day time at Mead Research, Mead Paper Company, retiring about fifteen years ago after almost forty-two years of service. Dale has about three thousand songs in sheet music or on tape, and when not on the road, he often sings at his home church especially on Sunday morning.

* * *

Joe "Broadway" Diehls started singing gospel music with his brother in a local group. He sang with the Christian Aires in Ross County for eighteen years. The Christian Aires were together from 1973 to 1998. He also sang with the Spirit of Praise in Pike County for three years. Mark Depugh, another member of the Christian Aires, also sang with the Spirit of Praise. The Spirit of Praise started singing as a trio in 1984, and in 1985, they became an extended group.

The Spirit of Praise was preparing to sing at the Oswaego Baptist Church, a little country church in Otway. While they were unloading their equipment, a small billy goat started running after Jamie Bakenhaster, chasing her right into the church. Mark Depugh had to grab the little goat by the horns and lead him out of the church.

In 1998, starting the Singing Diehls, Joe sang duet with his wife, Kaye, for one year. In 1999, Lula Varney joined them, forming a trio. Lula started singing at a young age with her family traveling as the Varneys.

Once while the Singing Diehls were still a trio, they were scheduled to sing in Chillicothe for the Farmers Fall Festival. When it came time to sing, Lula wasn't there, so they had to start singing without her. She finally arrived just in time to help them sing their last song. Turned out she had gotten confused and ended up in Bambridge at the Festival of Leaves.

Sometime later, Dennis Jolly, a man who actually lives on Easy Street in Manchester, joined the group as their new bass singer, making them a mixed quartet. The group continues to bless souls as they travel throughout Ohio singing that music they love so well.

* * *

The Sounds of Latter Reign started out in 1981 with five vocalists. They later dropped to a quartet, and when Paul Minney left the group, they remained a ladies' trio. The group was very jovial and could be disturbing in a restaurant as a result of their jokes and laughter. The group did a lot of benefit-type programs and stopped singing in 2006. After leaving the group, Paul Minney sang with a group called the Goshen Run Bluegrass, also based in Chillicothe, for two years, and he now continues singing solo.

Leaving Chillicothe, we take U.S. 23 south. As we leave town, we can see the smoke flowing from the big paper mill, and we're glad the wind is blowing the other direction. Along the east side of the road are huge stacks of logs and several train cars full of logs. Continuing along U.S. 23, we soon arrive at Waverly, home of a two-hundred-year-old hard maple referred to as Ohio's Perfect Tree. Waverly was also home to the Gospel Tones.

The Gospel Tones started singing in 1960, traveling mostly on weekends. Once, while singing at the Beulah Chapel Revival, they continued to sing the song "Sweet Jesus" for about one hour as people repeatedly came forward to the altar. The group continued to sing until around 1967. Before joining the group, Clarence Felty played for the Sego Brothers.

Also from Waverly, Verlin "Cookie" Kritzwiser, uncle to John and Candy Pfeifer, and Morse Noel joined the Fisherman Quartet in Chillicothe. Morse now sings with a group based in North Carolina. Verlin's son Todd presently sings with a Batavia group named Trinity.

Leaving Waverly, we continue south along U.S. 23 for another six miles to SR-32 where we turn right, and cross the Scioto River heading east. In the bright spring sunlight, we can see the red glow of buds sprouting on the trees along the way to Peebles. Many people visit the Peebles area to view Serpent Mound, one of the largest and by far the most unique Native American effigies and burial grounds. Nearly a quarter mile long, it represents a giant serpent partially coiled up and apparently swallowing an egg of some kind. Information is limited, but historians believe the mound was built by the Adena Indians. Peebles is also home of Jim Daulton who in 1967, with the help of his wife Ann, Clyde Brewer from Miamisburg, Denny Yearly from Lebanon and Olin Flowers from Red Lion, formed the Atonement Quartet based out of Miamisburg.

Traveling throughout the mid-west they sang with some of the nation's top gospel groups making several appearances on "The Good Ship of Zion" program.

The Atonements took first place in a singing contest called "Star Trails". They were the first gospel group to win the contest three weeks in a row making them Grand Champions of the contest.

Clyde left the group around 1970 and was replaced by Mike Cleghorn from Dayton. The Quartet disbanded in 1979. Denny Yearly went on to join the Blackwood Singers as bass singer and Mike continues to minister in Texas.

The Daulton family continued singing as the Atonement Trio and in 1984 they moved to southeast Ohio where Jim Daulton remained pastor for over twenty years. Shortly after relocating Jim's brother, Ray Daulton, joined the group making the Atonements a quartet once again. Ray passed away a few years ago but the Atonements are still singing and doing God's work within the church.

Continuing along SR-32, we pass through Locust Grove and turn right onto SR-73. Following the creek, we wind through the hills, passing several lumber yards. The creek is overflowing its banks, and at several places, it is quite close to the road. We continue along SR-73, through Brush Creek State Forest, to Otway. At Otway we turn left onto SR-348 and head uphill along another creek and pass several beautiful little waterfalls along the way. We crest the hill and are provided a great view of the countryside. We pass through Crabtree, spot a couple of deer, cross the Scioto River, and turn right onto U.S. 23. After a quick stop for fuel, we continue to Lucasville, native home of the Trace Family Trio.

The family started singing in 1945 and was comprised of Sylvia Trace and her two daughters. Their style of singing, with smooth high quality harmony and the use of only a guitar, produced a sound similar to that of the Carter Family. They would later add piano accompaniment. They frequently sang on WPAY in Portsmouth, and in 1952, they signed with King Records in Cincinnati and released a total of sixteen recordings over the next six years. They ministered at churches and songfests throughout Ohio until 1962 when Sylvia was injured from a backward fall down a flight of stairs, and they were forced to retire. Their songs have been recorded by such artists as Eva Mae LeFevre, the Happy Goodmans, and the Stanley Brothers.

Leaving Lucasville, we continue along U.S. 23 following the Scioto River, which is also out of its banks at several locations, until we reach Portsmouth, where in 1897 the Enos Reed Pharmacy was the first business in the town to sell Coca-Cola. In 1900, Buffalo Bill Cody's Wild West and Congress of Rough Riders visited the community. The Great Flood of 1937 left thirty-five thousand residents homeless. It was a difficult time, but the community survived to produce some of the nation's finest southern gospel artists. One of these artists was the famous Jim Hill.

The night Jim was born, his family was gathered around the piano singing out of an old James D. Vaughn songbook. Wondering what they were going to name their new family member, someone suggested they call him James Vaughn Hill after James D. Vaughn. Being named after Vaughn, it seemed inevitable that he would become a gospel singer.

While living in Portsmouth, Jim became the tenor soloist in the Portsmouth Male Chorus sponsored by the Detroit Steel Corporation. Their two biggest concerts were an Easter concert and a Christmas concert. While singing for the choir, he took private vocal lessons from Portsmouth voice teacher Mildred Deering. Also a talent scout for the Cincinnati Conservatory of Music, Mildred influenced Jim to study opera. One of Mildred's other students was a soprano named Kathleen Battles who today is known around the world as one of the greatest Metropolitan Opera singers.

At age seventeen, Jim attended a Baptist camp meeting in Wheelersburg along with a close friend named Harold Patrick. Harold was a piano player, well-known in the area as a great musician. Harold was going to sing that night in a trio with John Conley, another school friend, and Willis Baldridge. Willis was a very big tenor who was attending Olivette Nazarene College and who later became Patrick's brother-in-law. While the group was preparing to sing, Jim happened by, and someone joked that they needed a bass singer and suggested Jim join the group. Jim laughed at their offer and, not believing they would call him up to sing during the service, agreed to sing a song with them. But that evening during the service, Jim was wrong, and they called his bluff. After singing, he went back to his seat. Later, they were giving the invitation, and as he started to leave, an elderly lady that he knew from his church stopped him. She asked if Jim would like to join his friends at the altar and give his heart to Jesus. At that moment, Jim realized his need for salvation and headed straight for the altar. Now the wheels of God's plan were beginning to roll.

Going back to his vocal teacher, he soon realized his heart was no longer in the opera. In response to his teacher's concern, he said, "I accepted Christ last night as my personal Savior, and I am singing a different song today." She acknowledged his experience, yet she expressed concern that he no longer desired to move forward with his training. Jim then told her, "I want to sing gospel music." He sang for her the song entitled "The Stranger of Galilee." As she listened, the song must have touched her heart because from that time forward, she never questioned him again about the opera.

In 1945, Jim Hill, Harold Patrick, and John Conley formed a trio called the Campmeeting Boys. They began singing in their local church and at some of the singing conventions. In 1947, a fourth member was added to the group, and they became known as the Golden Keys Quartet. The quartet was a very popular group in the Ohio area for many years. Later Pat Duncan, from Waverly, and Clarence Claxon, from Vanceburg, Kentucky, also joined the group. Harold Patrick sang and played piano for the quartet as he had played since he was eleven years old.

When Jim was nineteen, he married Ruth Baldridge, daughter of Rev. A. L. Baldridge, a very popular evangelist. Her brother was also a gospel soloist and possessed a terrific tenor voice. Shortly after getting married, Jim got called to the army and was shipped to Korea.

When he arrived in Korea, our soldiers had just suffered a defeat in a battle on one of the mountains, and Jim's group was headed for the front line. They were given their ammunition and were loading the trucks to be shipped out when over the public address system, he heard the following message, "Jim Hill, please report to the Company Headquarters." It seems that when reviewing his papers, they noticed he was a graduate of Ohio Business College and had taken both typing and shorthand. Short on male stenographers, they immediately pulled him out, and he was transferred to the Eighth Army Headquarters back in Seoul, Korea, where he became personal stenographer for General Maxwell D. Taylor.

In 1953, Jim had eight months left in the service, and the area where he was stationed experienced nightly plane attacks. Jim ran into a group of Christian soldiers. They formed a little group that met regularly for prayer and worship. Having a southern background, soon four of the boys got together and formed a little quartet. On Sundays, a captain with a jeep at his disposal, who was also the son of a First Presbyterian pastor in Hollywood, California, would take them out into the woods, actually off-limits, to hold services for those bombed-out Korean civilians who were still living in the area. They would simply get out of the jeep and start singing, and the people would gather around.

The officer also had access to bombers that were flying over North Korea, and he worked it out that when they were dropping bombs, they would fly a little further and then drop a sack of gospel tracts written in Korean language. The tract told a story about a GI who, in his last letter to his mother, shared a premonition that he was going to die, and during the very next battle, he was killed. The GI was a Christian, and through his experience, he presented a very touching plan of salvation. Jim considered it a blessing to be part of this exciting ministry as thousands of tracts were dropped over Korea.

The Koreans had little planes that could fly under the radar, and when the bombing would start, Jim and his fellow soldiers would have to hurry to a big bomb shelter located just outside of their headquarters. One night in the shelter, they were talking to each other when one of the guys created a little game for them to play. He requested everybody to think about what they would like to do when they got back home. Jim's little Pentecostal friend was such a great Christian, and he said, "You know, I would rather write a gospel song that would help people get saved than be president." Jim held these words deep within his heart.

In 1956, a while after Jim had returned home from the army, his mother-in-law had a stroke. She became paralyzed and had to be cared for like a baby for three years. Just before she died, they had gone to see her and came home that Monday morning feeling different and so quiet. After a time of meditation, walking in the yard, Jim went back in the house and began to pray. Questioning the Lord as to why this should happen, he began to think,

There will be no sorrow there. No burdens to bear. Jim grabbed an envelope and an old ballpoint pen on the kitchen table, and began to write down the words as God laid them on his heart, creating that wonderful song, "What a Day That Will Be." The song was first presented by the Golden Keys and first recorded by the Homeland Harmony Quartet. It became one of the most requested songs by the Golden Keys, and the Speer Family touched crowds everywhere with their arrangement of the song. The Stamps' first Skylite recording, with Jim Hill singing "What a Day That Will Be," was one of the biggest selling albums at the 1963 NQC.

Jim continued his position with the Golden Keys and for a number of years, interrupted by a short stint with the Ambassadors Quartet. The Golden Keys soon grew from a local part-time group to one that became quite active in the gospel music field. They were one of few part-time groups invited to perform at the NQC. Their vocal arrangements were not extremely challenging, but the emotion with which they presented their songs made them a very exciting group. The Golden Keys maintained an outstanding vocal blend and a great working relationship. Their programs often showcased the exciting tenor vocals of Jim Hill on sacred classics such as "I Walked Today Where Jesus Walked" and "The Stranger of Galilee." The group performed many top gospel songs of the day, but their real forte was performing the new compositions of Jim Hill. The Golden Keys not only furthered the writing career of Jim Hill but they also often performed in concert with the early version of the Gaither Trio. They were also responsible for bringing some of the songs of fledgling songwriter Bill Gaither to the gospel music community.

Daniel Joseph Gaither was born on November 20, 1938, in Alexandria, Indiana. He first sang with his brother Bill Gaither in a group called the Log Cabin Four. After Danny graduated from Ball State University, he moved to the Portsmouth area to begin his teaching career. Recognizing this nearby talent, Harold Patrick relinquished his role as lead singer for the Golden Keys, and Danny Gaither moved into this position and stayed until 1966. Danny was inducted into the Gospel Music Hall of Fame, and a terminal illness took this great singer on April 6, 2001.

With Patrick now able to concentrate on the piano, the Golden Keys continued to polish their sound and continued as a popular element in the gospel quartet circuit. Along the way, the Golden Keys Quartet introduced several Gaither songs to the gospel singing world including "I've Been to Calvary" and "Lovest Thou Me." Bill Gaither credits the Golden Keys Quartet for bringing many of his songs to the gospel music forefront. One of the first

Gaither songs ever produced on sheet music featured a picture of the Golden Keys Quartet.

The Southern-Aires, based in Dayton, started about the same time as the Golden Keys and was one of the first quartets they were privileged to work with.

The popularity of the Golden Keys Quartet may have eventually led to their disbandment as all of the members had full-time jobs, and the requests for bookings was rapidly increasing. The Golden Keys Quartet should be remembered as a group of weekend warriors who proved that hard work and dedication can make for an outstanding career. This fine quartet helped chart the course for several elite gospel music artists, creating a great beginning point for several that have affected the gospel music industry in an important way. Although the Golden Keys were in great demand, it still wasn't enough for the group to become a full-time quartet.

In 1962, Jim Hill felt the call to full-time gospel music and accepted the offer from Doyle Blackwood to join the "New" Stamps Quartet along with Roger McDuff, "Big" John Hall, one of Jim's favorite bass singers, "Smilin'" Joe Roper, and Terrell Blackwood. Jim's position with the Golden Keys was filled by Al Harkins and later by Dean Hickman.

In 1966, when Danny Gaither left the group, Harold Patrick again resumed double duty as pianist and lead vocalist until the Golden Keys retired their name. After the Golden Keys disbanded, Harold Patrick joined the Gospel Harmony Boys as pianist and played for them for several years. He also was a member of other groups including the Sentries in Portsmouth and the Guardians.

With his dynamic vocal ability, Jim led the Stamps to even greater heights in the gospel music community. After two years, J. D. Sumner decided to take over management of the quartet, trading his partnership with the Blackwood Brothers in exchange for the Stamps Quartet. Shortly before the group was to start traveling with Elvis, Jim decided it would be best for him to leave the Stamps, J. D. asked Jim to remain with the group, but Jim declined and started traveling with Hovie Lister and the Statesmen Quartet as their new lead singer.

Jim considered it a real pleasure working with such professional men as the Statesmen were his idols growing up, and it was always his dream to sing with Hovie Lister, Big Chief, and the rest. Jim brought several of his top songs to the Statesmen Quartet, and they soon became some of the most requested songs in the Statesmen programs.

Jim recalls one night while singing at a concert in Long Beach, California, Elvis Presley was sitting backstage listening to the group sing. Yelling out to the group, Elvis requested they sing "For God So Loved." As Jim was leaving the stage, he stopped to shake hands with Elvis only to find him in tears, and he later learned that this was one of Elvis's favorite songs.

One Sunday evening, Don Butler had scheduled them to sing at Bostick Street Baptist Church in Chicago. That afternoon, they were driving their bus around Chicago looking for the church. Everyone they asked simply glanced at their big bus and said, "You're going where?" Finally, they had found the church, a little storefront building located in one of the roughest neighborhoods in the city. There were dirty children playing ball and kicking cans in the street, and from the outside, the church didn't look like it would hold a hundred people. As they parked the bus in front of the church, Hovie commented, "For goodness sake! What has Don Butler gotten us into?" They were just about ready to leave when they noticed an elderly guy in a black suit with a red tie hurrying up the street to greet them. Introducing himself as the pastor, he was thrilled to see them and invited them to come upstairs to a small apartment over the church with the words, "Mamma's been waiting."

Inside, the apartment was very clean, and a saintly little lady came out to meet them with cake in her hands. After an enjoyable visit, they set up their equipment, and when the service started, the little church was packed. They sang and Hovie preached, and before long, the altar was full and people were getting saved. What a blessing! After the service was over, they loaded their equipment and climbed aboard the bus. Still experiencing an emotional blessing from the service, Hovie shared with the group, "This is one of the greatest experiences I've ever had."

Jim's song "For God So Loved" is a tremendous song, and that classic "What a Day That Will Be" remains one of the most popular songs in the history of gospel music. In 1969, Jim was nominated for a Dove Award, and the mayor of Portsmouth designated May 22, 1969, as Jim Hill Day.

In the early 1970s, Jim had flown back home to Portsmouth after the passing of his mother. During the funeral services, Jim talked with an old friend who had become vice president of the Williams Shoe Manufacturing Company in Portsmouth. The next January, they were on tour in California, staying at the Hollywood Roosevelt Hotel, when Jim received a phone call from the sales manager of Williams Shoe Manufacturing Company. He asked if Jim was interested in a job. Jim accepted the position and was to report to Portsmouth on February 22. Jim shared with the group that this would be his final tour. So on their way home from their Chicago concert, they dropped him off at an Indianapolis bus station. He caught a Greyhound bus traveling directly to the shoe company. Jim was soon living in Dayton and working as an account executive (traveling salesman) for the Williams Shoe Manufacturing Company, and in two years, he was promoted to national sales manager.

He took a part-time position as minister of music for the Towne Boulevard Church of God in Middletown where he worked with the choir and led their worship for almost sixteen years. Jim continues today doing solo work and taking part in the Gaither Homecoming series. Jim enjoys spending time with his buddy Bill Gaither. Sometimes Bill calls wanting him to go to a Pacers game in Indiana, and when Bill does a concert in the area, Jim always tries to spend some time with him helping Bill to relax. Jim speaks well of Bill Gaither confirming, "Bill Gaither has never forgotten his past and is quick to give credit to everybody who has been in his past."

One Sunday morning, Bill Gaither and his father came to speak at the Towne Boulevard Church of God. After lunch, Bill came to the house to spend some time visiting with Jim. While watching television, Bill mentioned he was planning on getting some old friends like the Goodmans and Jake Hess together to do the backup on that old song "Where Could I Go But to the Lord." He asked Jim to consider joining them for this event.

When they gathered that day, there were twelve people present. After the song was finished, Bill suggested they just sing some old numbers around the piano before they all departed as they might never be together like this again. As they continued to sing, people were being blessed, and soon the tears began to flow. Then Larry Gatlin of the Gatlin Brothers shared that he had previously lost his voice, and he had to cancel all of his country dates. Hearing this, Vestal Goodman asked if Larry would mind them gathering around him for prayer. Larry accepted the offer, and as they began to pray, God's anointing spirit fell on everyone present. When they had finished praying, Larry, with tears running down his face, asked if he could sing, "I Bowed on My Knees and Cried Holy." When he was finished, they were all in tears. They had no intention of going there to make a video. Bill had filmed the event as he wanted to retain a memory for his personal enjoyment.

The next week after reviewing the recording, he called Jim Hill telling him the recording was out of sight. After some editing, the recording of this exciting gathering became the first of many Homecoming videos. In that first Homecoming video, we can capture a glimpse of what was felt that day, and Jim, never letting go of those words he heard that day while beneath the raging battlegrounds of Korea, has often reminded us, "I'd rather write a gospel song than to be president."

* * *

Ray McGinnis grew up in Columbus until 1975 when the family returned to his father's hometown of Portsmouth. Ray was exposed to gospel music at an early age as his father traveled full-time as an evangelist and songwriter. It wasn't an easy lifestyle. Ray recalls, "My dad always kidded and said it was chicken one week and feathers the next." That's the way they lived, never having anything left over, but God always took care of their needs. Ray's wife, Nancy (Bales) McGinnis, and her brother, Mark Bales, also came from an evangelistic background. Using an old Model A Ford, Nancy's grandparents would travel all over singing the gospel. They would line their seven children up like stair steps, and while grandpa, Pat Payne, would play the guitar, they would sing.

Traveling as the Singing Payne Family, they became very well known around the Portsmouth area and even in the Dayton area. Nancy's aunt, Marilyn (Payne) Bowling (Ida Payne's sister), grew up singing with the Payne family. She later married Chip Bowling and sang with the Southern-Aires.

The Bales Family started singing in 1959 and traveled full-time by faith as they worked their way through every state in the nation. Nancy traveled with her family from the time she was three years old until she was married at the age of eighteen. While growing up, the Bales family actually saw more of Ray's father than Ray did because they would often be working camp meetings and revivals together. Although Brother Bales still leads the song services at his home church and Ida, his wife, still plays the piano, their families have come off the road and are no longer an evangelistic team.

In 1978, feeling the Lord directing them to start a music ministry, Ray, Mark, and Nancy formed a new group known as the Good News Trio, most often simply referred to as "Good News." God has truly blessed their ministry, and they have sung almost every weekend since the group started.

Once they were traveling back from Flemingsburg, Kentucky, where they had sung at the high school with two or three other national groups including the Cathedrals. It was late, and they were on an old Kentucky road. All of a sudden, the back wheel slipped off the berm, and John was standing up fighting with the steering wheel. He wiped out a few road signs before ending up spinning and sliding down the road with the back wheels in one ditch and the front wheels in another. There were fifteen people on the bus, and everyone except the driver was falling down and bouncing around. There was screaming and yelling and, of course, plenty of prayer as the bus continued to slide. The old bus was scraping the road as it continued to slide, but it never turned over. Adding to the excitement, they soon realized they were headed straight for a big barn. Everyone was convinced they were going to hit that barn, and it was going to be very ugly. Just as they got to the barn, somehow God reached down and turned that bus. It came out of the ditch, headed down the road, and they never even stopped. No other cars came along during the slide, and praise God, not one person was injured.

Nancy has written close to 150 songs. She has probably twenty-five songs lying in a drawer that haven't even been sung. Hearing a tune in her head, Nancy creates the lyrics to a song. Then Mark, using the guitar, actually writes the music. The Hoppers recorded one of her songs called "I'm on the Rock" and it reached the top 20 of the *Singing News* chart in 1985. The Nelons recorded a song Nancy wrote called "Stepping in the Steps of Jesus." It was on their Grammy album entitled *Come Morning*. Rex Nelon was always a good friend and the family had a lot of respect for Rex. Referring to the passing of Rex Nelon, Ray said, "I think that we really lost a great ambassador for southern gospel music."

Joy (Bales) Jones, sister to Nancy and Mark Bales, began singing at age four. In 1996, she joined a group called New Journey as a featured vocalist. During the late 1990s, she performed on several Gaither Homecoming videos, and in 1999, she was voted favorite soprano by the Kentucky Gospel Music Association. In 2000, she started a solo ministry traveling with her two sons as the Jones Family.

In September 2003, the Good News Trio won the NQC Talent Search with the song "God's in Control," which earned them a spot on the Son Sound Music Group Platinum Label. "God's In Control" was written by Nancy right after the terrible 9/11 tragedy that took place in New York City in 2001. They have been privileged the last two years to sing with Jim Hill at their 50 Miles of Hero Celebration held in Portsmouth. Ray considers Jim a wonderful gentleman of gospel music.

The Good News Trio had been asked to sing at a fall fair in Lancaster. The fair board had brought in a small country church building where the groups were to sing. They parked the bus and walked into the little church building to find only two or three people had stopped by to listen, and the group finishing their portion of the program appeared to be somewhat defeated. To make things worse, they were required to use the fairground's sound system.

Having prayed on their way there that the Lord would help them to be a witness, they decided to give it their best. They got up to sing, and after a couple of songs, the Spirit filled that little place, and they began to notice that people were stopping outside, and pretty soon the little church was full. Before they stopped singing, a crowd of over two hundred people had formed outside the church. People were leaning in the windows, and some were raising their hands with tears streaming down their faces. Mark gave an altar call and people were crying out to the Lord just like the old revivals meetings of tw hundred years ago. They were only supposed to be singing for thirty minutes, and the next group, instead of being aggravated and upset, simply joined in and began praising the Lord. They had church that day!

Ray says, "I will never forget how the Lord takes a simple situation, and His Spirit can be felt even by people who normally wouldn't know what to call it. But they felt the Spirit of the Lord, and it just arrested them in their tracks."

Good News is unique in that they have retained the same group members for twenty-nine years. Mark is pastor of a church, and Ray runs a financial service office for MetLife. It has been challenging at times traveling almost every weekend in their motor home. Ray believes it is worth the effort, and he says, "It is a true blessing when you are up there and people seem encouraged, when you see the smiles on their faces or perhaps witness a sinner fall at an altar and give their heart to the Lord. They have had a rough day sometimes, and then they come and kind of forget about all of that and they hear you tell that God's in control."

One time during a service in which they were singing, an elderly gentleman near the back of the church jumped up to shout. The place was packed, but he jumped up and ran to the front of the church. Turning toward the center aisle, he continued to shout and headed for the back of the church. He had taken about three steps when he fell victim to a slippery back brace, and his pants dropped, exposing red-hearted boxers. Working to get his pants pulled up, he hurried to the back of the church where he remained huddled under the coatrack trying to regain his composure. The group lost it and broke out into laughter—it couldn't be helped. He was a wonderful gentleman, and this was certainly an embarrassing moment. Yet the Lord gets glory even in the strangest situations. When the group started laughing, those in the first four or five rows who didn't see what happened thought they were getting blessed. It soon became a chain reaction. The laughter turned into a time of spiritual blessing, and before it was all over, they had experienced a wonderful service.

Ray, as Sunday school teacher, often tells the youth in his class, "If you pull up to a red light, and you have gospel music playing in your car, and the person beside you can't tell what kind of music it is, you may need to ask the Lord, 'Am I doing the right thing?'"

* * *

Radiant Heart is a ladies trio from the Portsmouth area. The group began singing in 1995. Founding members include Lori (Crawford) Reed, a cousin to the late Keith Whitley, Kristina Napier-Locher, and former member Linda (Tingler) Reynolds who is the sister to Greg Tingler of the Gospel Harmony Boys. Other former members who have been a part of Radiant Heart include Kim (Patrick) Lutz, the daughter of Harold Patrick who was with the Golden Keys, and Ruth Marie Hymer who grew up singing with her family.

A family of ten children, they traveled the tristate area known as the Singing Harr Family from Bradford. The family started singing, in 1963 and several of the sisters continue singing today as the trio the Sisters of Light in Marion. Several of Ruth's uncles on her mother's side sang together as the Robert Family from Marion. They started traveling together in the 1970s and continued until sometime in the 1990s.

After singing at the Ohio State Fair, Radiant Heart exited the stage, and as the people were leaving, Lori and Linda found a copy of the *US Gospel News.* Casually flipping through the pages of the magazine, Linda discovered their song entitled "No Other Name" had made it to the top 100 chart, and she quickly showed it to Lori. They were in total shock and amazement and desired to share the exciting news, but to their disappointment, no one could be found.

Radiant Heart has been privileged to share the stage with some of the nation's finest artists including the Dove Brothers, the Hayes Family, John Darren Rowsey, and Jeff & Sheri Easter. A special combination of voices, this female trio produces some beautiful harmony. They have sung at Renfro Valley, the NQC Showcase, and they won first place at a Boyd County Fair competition in Kentucky. Radiant Heart never hesitates to give the Lord all praise and credit for the harmony and talent He has given them. Their main objective is to be used by Him and share their testimonies of how God brought them from the deep dark place of additions into his forgiving love and grace.

* * *

Marilyn (Payne) Bowling came from the Portsmouth area. Her parents sang together, and as Marilyn and the other children came along, they were all taught to sing. Marilyn started singing at age four. and later with the help of her sister Opal and her brother Jimmy, they formed the Payne Trio, singing together for about fifteen years. Her sister Ida's children later formed the group the Good News Trio. Her sister Mary's family formed the Slaughter Family Singers. Mary's daughter joined the group One Accord. Jimmy writes some good songs and now sings with his two sons in a group they call Third Generation.

In 1971, Marilyn married Chip Bowling. Chip's mother was from the Dayton area where she was part of the Singing Setter Sisters. Before getting married, Chip was in the air force for four years. He spent most of his tour in Germany where he put together a little sixties rock band called the Shy Five. After returning from his air force tour, he sang for a while with his siblings. He married Marilyn, and they sang as the Bowling Trio for four years with the help of his sister. Chip and Marilyn were then offered a position singing with the Voices Triumphant in Flatwoods, Kentucky, and they remained with them for two years.

In 1977, Chip and Marilyn started singing with the Southern-Aires. After about six years, they left the group and started singing as a duet. Later they teamed up with Richard Brown, prior member of the Crownsmen Quartet, to form the Representatives, which stayed together about two years. Then with the help of Dick Puckett, they created another group called Inheritance that lasted for another three years. Finally, they ended up back with the Southern-Aires where they remained until 2004.

From 2004 until the time of Chip's passing in 2005, they continued to sing as a duet. Marilyn now plays piano in her church and plans to develop a solo ministry. She has written over two hundred songs, and both the Mid-South Boys and the Singing Cookes have recorded some of her songs. Having written the song in only five minutes, she considers the song entitled "He Did It All for Me" to be her best effort. One evening, while they were singing this song, a man came into the church. After the service, the man told them he had planned to end his life, but after hearing the words to this song, his life was changed.

* * *

Greg Tingler was born on October 17, 1955, in Portsmouth. His mother, Evelyn Tingler, was a piano player. She played southern gospel music. She played at the Ryman Auditorium during a Wally Fowler All-Night Singing when she was only fourteen years old and received two standing ovations. She was a great pianist and played for a radio quartet called the Gospel Tones in Portsmouth. The group was together for twelve years. They did two programs a day and sang concerts in the evening. She played at 6:00 AM for the morning program and again at 4:00 PM for the evening program, and then they would leave the station to go sing in the evening, and then they would get her home so she could go to school the next day.

Greg's father, Clarence Tingler, met his future wife at a gospel event and was later instrumental in forming the Sunrise Quartet in Portsmouth. The group was together for about twenty years.

Greg started singing when he was about four years old. Growing up, they never had any other kind of music in the house except southern gospel music. His parents soon left the quartets, and they became revival singers working revivals all the time. At home, it was mom, dad, and his sister. They all had chores to do, but when they would finsh their chores his mom would go in and start playing the piano. That was the queue for everybody to hit the living room with their instruments. Evelyn had a little french poodle, and when she would start playing the piano, the poodle would jump up on her lap and wouldn't leave until the music was over. Even the dog got involved, and this was the only lifestyle Greg knew until he was thirteen and left the family to travel with the Payne Family. He never went to a prom or any of those things. First, his church didn't believe in dancing, and second, he was always on the road singing.

The next-door neighbor, Jim Hill, had written a song, and prior to sending it down to Ben Speer for publishing, he brought it over to Evelyn requesting she play it through. Sitting down at the piano that day, she played, for the very first time, the manuscript to that great song entitled "What a Day That Will Be."

At age fourteen, Greg helped put together a group called the Messengers. As there were so many groups with some form of *messenger* in their names, somebody came up with the name of the *Gospel Impressions*. Greg says, "At that time any kind of a different name just threw people. We were called everything from the 'Gospel Compressions' to the 'Gospel Depressions.'" They were a male quartet traveling as far as Memphis, Tennessee, and they remained together for two years.

Harold Patrick, piano player for the Gospel Harmony Boys, and the guy who introduced his mom to his dad came to see if Greg, age sixteen, would be interested in going with the Gospel Harmony Boys as a bass player. So at age sixteen, he started traveling with the Gospel Harmony Boys. After playing bass for five years, Harold had a heart problem, and the group ended up on the road one evening without a piano player. So Greg went over and started playing the piano. This turned into a four-year stint with Greg as the group's pianist. It is interesting that Greg ended up playing piano for this group because fifty-five years earlier, when his mother was playing for the Gospel Tones, Leonard Adams, the guy who along with Harold Lane originated the Gospel Harmony Boys, came to his mother telling her that if she was a man, she would be playing for the Gospel Harmony Boys.

One reason he got a good start with the Gospel Harmony Boys was they had already recorded a song he had written called "His Love was so Boundless to Me." The LeFevres heard the Gospel Harmony Boys sing the song and ended up recording it also. Rex Nelon later took it and put it on the charts. So he had his first chart song when he was only sixteen. It must have been exciting as a teenager to be receiving letters from the LeFevres and cashing those royalty checks.

A short time later, Greg got married and started having a family. In the early 1980s, he, along with Harold Patrick and Dean Hickman, who took Jim Hill's place with a group called the Golden Keys, started a group called the Sentries in Portsmouth and sang together for several years. It was during this time that Greg received his biggest claim to fame. He wrote the song called "He's Coming Back," which made it to number one as recorded by Jimmy Swaggart. Greg told his wife, "I feel like Moses looking over in the Promised Land, here we are at number one, and next month there is going to be nothing." Sure enough, the next month—nothing—it was all gone. But thanks to the amazing reach of Jimmy Swaggart's ministry, the song has actually been put out in over forty different countries.

Greg had become acquainted with Ivan Parker when he was with the Singing Americans. So during a Gold City concert, he was standing at their record table talking with him, and Greg told him they had beaten him out of a number one song. Ivan told him if it was any consolation, they had just recorded one of his songs entitled "Movin' Up." Growing up, Greg had to learn to read shaped notes (do, me, so, do), which inspired the song "Movin Up," an old convention-style song. Gold City later did another song written by Greg entitled "What a Glad Day."

Then the evening the Dove Awards were being shown on TV, Greg had taken his two little girls to see *Sesame Street*—live. On the way home, they stopped by his wife's family to pick something up. While there, her cousin came to the door and told them they needed to watch the Dove Awards at midnight as one of his songs was to be performed. The song was "What a Glad Day."

Not long after that, Gold City put out another one of his songs on their *Windows of Home* album called "Not Made with Hands."

The Hoppers did a song of his called "Love's Sweet Song," and every time they hired a new female singer, including Kim Hopper, they would record the song again. The Florida Boys have also done some of his material. Greg possesses a wealth of experience as a gospel artist, musician, and songwriter, yet he is quick to acknowledge that he is just a vessel being used by God to reach the World.

Greg sang for a while with a group in Renfro Valley called New Voice. The group was started by bass singer Tom Graham who was from Columbus. In fact, Tom is the guy that took J. D. Sumner's place with the Stamps Quartet when J. D. passed away. Tom kept calling Greg and wanting him to sing with him. Greg finally agreed, and they sang for about four years together until 1997 when an opportunity came open for him to return to the Gospel Harmony Boys. He came back as the lead singer, and in 2002 when financial difficulties made it advantageous for them to discontinue their ministry, they celebrated their fiftieth anniversary with a huge reunion concert to bid farewell to well over a thousand supporters who turned out for the event at the United Methodist Camp in Stoutsville on a beautiful Labor Day weekend. After a short break, the group reunited, and as of 2007, the group was still going strong.

Greg owned a music store for a while but sold it around 2007.

While in Portsmouth, we had a great view of the Ohio River. In Portsmouth, we also stop for lunch at Fazoli's Restaurant. Driving through town, my wife is confident that the Wal-Mart was not here during her last visit. Leaving Portsmouth, we travel east along the Ohio River Scenic Byway (U.S. 52) and passed through New

Boston. Taking a left on Ohio River Road, we arrive at Wheelersburg, home to the Pop's Drive-in Restaurant, a Scioto County icon for many years. Pop's is a drive-up restaurant where you park under the awning, and a waitress comes out so you can order from the painted-on menu on the exterior wall of the building. Inside, you could order any daily plate special you chose, and you were certain to run into someone you knew, always! Speaking of someone you know, have you ever heard of the True Gospel Sounds?

In 1975, Rick Schweinberg, Dan Ward and his wife Debbie, all of Wheelersburg, formed the True Gospel Sounds. Rick wrote the song "When the Lord Saved Me" as recorded by both the Hoppers and Triumphant. He also wrote "My Friend," recorded by the Dixie Melody Boys, and "The Man with the Whiskers" and "Be Sure Your Sins Will Find You Out," both recorded by the Jeff Treece Band. Rick was the southern gospel DJ and operations manager for both WPAY in Portsmouth and WXIC in Waverly.

In 1978, Teresa joined the group, and in 1980, she became Mrs. Rick Schweinsburg. That same year, the group took first place in the gospel music competition held at the Ohio State Fair. Dave Morrison started playing steel guitar, banjo, and lead guitar for the group and wrote the song "If It Hadn't Been," which was recorded by the Hoppers and Teddy Huffam and the Gems. He later wrote "It Took a Carpenter from Nazareth," which was recorded by the Primitives. Keyboard player Jerry Moore previously sang with the New Life Quartet in Minford. Jerry wrote the song "Too Much Thunder" that was recorded by the Dixie Melody Boys. He later sang with the Royalaires in Circleville.

When the True Gospel Sounds stopped singing in November 1998, Debbie and Danny Ward went on to sing with a group called Sincere in Huntington, West Virginia. In 2004, Rick and Teresa's son, Micah Schweinberg, became drummer for the Crabb Family and the Crabb Revival in 2007 all from Hendersonville, Tennessee. Rick now works for Daywind Records and New Day Distributing in Hendersonville, Tennessee.

* * *

The group By Grace started as a trio in 1998. In 2003, the name was changed to Day 3. Their mother, Lavonda Bailey, sang with the Gospel Tones in Portsmouth, and their sister Debbie Ward sang with the True Gospel Sounds in Wheelersburg.

Their nephew Bobby Wampler played drums for the group. He resembled Randy Owens of the group Alabama. While traveling in their first bus, a Silver Eagle, which they had purchased at an auction, Bobby would often stand at the front of the bus, and upon spotting him, people would follow them thinking they were the group Alabama.

Leaving Wheelersburg, we take SR-552 back to U.S. 52 where we continue east along the Ohio River, passing the Hanging Rock Recreational Area where you can get a great view of the Ohio River Valley. Continuing east along U.S. 52, we soon turn right on SR 93 to Ironton, recognized as Ohio's southernmost city and home to Bobby Bare and Rich Adkins.

Richard "Rich" Aaron Adkins was born in Ironton on July 31, 1972. When Rich was two years old, his parents relocated to Middletown. At a very young age, Rich's dad was diagnosed with terminal cancer and went on to be with the Lord at the age of thirty-two. His mother continued to raise her two little boys in a Christian home. Every church service you could find, these three were lifting up the name of Jesus in word and song. Rich has a special disease inherited from his father that resulted in the removal of his large intestine when he was just in sixth grade. Rich started singing in the children's choir, and as time passed, he became an intricate part of the praise and worship team with his brother Danny leading the way as the church pianist.

From 1988 to 1998, Rich sang with his family in a group called the Singing Lively Stones. They sang at school functions, local churches, nursing homes, and local radio stations. Rich was often asked to sing the national anthem at his high school basketball games. His senior year, he was voted Most Talented and was asked to write and perform a song for his graduating class. He celebrated the joy of performing at his graduation shortly after his return from New York City, where he and his high school choir performed at Carnegie Hall. After graduation, Rich worked as an activity assistant at a local nursing home. His job was to sing and entertain the residents, and he counts this as one of his most rewarding jobs.

When Rich was nineteen years old, he met his wife, Jody Ann Lipps, at a church fund-raiser. Four short years later, they married and started a life of their own. Rich has a special love for his wife and often tells people that God clipped the wings of heaven's most beautiful angel and sent her to complete his world.

Rich has always walked through every door that God has opened for his ministry without hesitation. Recently, Rich auditioned for the Dream Big talent show held in St. Mary's, at the St. Mary's Theatre & Grand Opera House. After twelve weeks of competition, Rich walked away with the grand prize, a *new car* and the opportunity to open for such country superstars as John Berry, Jimmy Fortune, and T. Graham Brown. Rich now lives in Carlisle, and in 2006, he competed in NQC Talent Contest winning a recording package with Son Sound. While at the NQC, the Sons Family introduced Rich to the legendary Eddie Crook. A few months later, Rich signed an exclusive recording contract as an artist and writer for the Eddie Crook Company. The Called Out Quartet recently released his song entitled "God Wrote My Name."

* * *

Gary Morgan was born on February 24, 1956. Growing up in Ironton, he worked as a newspaper delivery boy. One day while delivering the paper to a member of the New Life Quartet, the man asked him if he could sing. The next thing you know, he had started his music career singing for the New Life Quartet at age sixteen. He remained with the group fourteen years, and after leaving the group, he later sang with the Noblemen Quartet in North Carolina. Also with the Nobleman at that time was Avis Adkins who later formed the Dixie Melody Boys.

Gary later started singing with a group called the Journeymen from West Virginia. The group's bass singer was Aaron McCune, who started singing with them at age sixteen. Aaron then went on to sing with the Palmetto State Quartet and is presently singing with the Gold City Quartet. Gary remained with the Journeymen until 1998, when he formed the Gospel River Boys. Gary's son also sang with the Journeymen and now sings with the Gospel River Boys.

Songwriter John Darren Rowsey works closely with the Gospel River Boys providing top-quality songs. Over the past year, the group has been featured on such networks as Daystar Network Channel 61, Great American Country (GAC), as well as the Gospel Music Television Network. The desire of the group is to encourage Christians and win the lost for Christ. The Gospel River Boys became a full time ministry in 2002. Hearing this group, you will be exhilarated, ministered to, and entertained, an evening that will remain in your heart and mind for a long time to come.

Leaving Ironton, we follow the cobblestone roadway down along the Ohio River past the old train depot, and working our way back through town, we end up going the wrong way on a one-way street. The drivers are courteous of our ignorance, allowing us an opportunity to make a turn onto the right street. Back on track, we head north on SR-93, cross under SR-52, and stop at the historic site of the Old SR-75 tunnel. Shortly, we are back on the road and continued north, and after making several turns, we turn left onto SR-141. Passing through Hecla, a young man on an ATV pulls out on the highway and goes flying up the road. Traveling around forty miles per hour, we are unable to catch him. As we continue along SR-141 we enter into some back country farmland, and the terrain becomes very hilly. Winding back and forth across Symmes Creek, we pass through several small communities. Enjoying the scenery, we spot something unique, a huge rock with a large tree growing on the rock. Passing through several small towns, we continue to repeatedly cross Symmes Creek and each time the water gets closer to the road. A few miles further, we make a sharp turn to the right and quickly come to a stop as all that lies before us is water. It seems the Symmes Creek is in high-water stage, and as far as the eye can see, the road is under water. At this point, we have no choice but to turn around, and using our GPS, we wind our way back and forth from gravel road to gravel road, including one called Blessing Road, until we find a bridge high enough to cross Symmes Creek and make our way back to SR-141. My wife is relieved to once again be on paved roads. Shortly after we returned to SR-141 we arrive at Gallipolis, home to the male quartet called Forgiven 4.

George Dillion and his brother sang in a group called the Greasy Ridge Quartet from Lawrence County. They were offered a chance to go to Nashville, Tennessee, in the 1930s but turned it down because of family obligations. Later George formed a group called the Dillion Family, and his son Rich sang with the group throughout his childhood.

In 1987, Rich gave his heart to the Lord and started singing with a group called Exodus in Lecta. Exodus was a mixed quartet at first and eventually became an all-male quartet. Rich sang with them until 1994. In 1996, he started singing with a quartet called Released. The group purchased a bus from the Singing Echoes, and they had to completely remodel the interior because everything had been designed for short people, and Rich was a tall man.

Once they were scheduled to sing in Elkhart, Indiana. They had hired a truck driver to drive the bus for this trip. On the way home, Rich explained the gear-shift pattern and headed to his bunk to get some rest. Awakened by the sound of horns blowing, Rich rushed to the front of the bus. Somehow, the driver had accidentally shifted into reverse, and they were traveling backward on a four-lane highway (SR-32). Rich quickly took the driver's seat and managed to get things under control.

They signed a recording contract with Morning Star, and the group remained together until 1999 when Rich left to form a quartet called Forgiven 4. Rusty Ballinger was with Forgiven 4 four years until sometime in 2002 when the group disbanded, and he started singing with the Gospel Harmony Boys in West Virginia.

In 2003, Rich Dillion joined the JoyFM Trio. No longer a trio, they changed their name to the Glorybound Quartet. They continued with that name until August 2005 when they revived the name Forgiven 4. Leslie Lemley sings baritone for the group. He has been singing since he was a child traveling with his family. He sang with the Gospel Messengers for about fourteen years.

During a service at a small church in Prestonsburg, Kentucky, they were singing the song "Midnight Cry" to a standing-room-only crowd. All of a sudden, the Spirit started moving, and people were filling the altar. It was a wonderful experience. Then sometime in 2006, they were singing in Summerville, West Virginia, when five people got saved. Before the service was over, they had taken those five people down to Elk Creek were they were all baptized.

Before we leave Gallipolis, we turn left on Second Street (SR-7) and stop at the Shake Shoppe for a restroom break and a delicious milkshake. Back on the road, we make a few turns, and taking U.S. 35, we start traveling northwest. We make a quick stop at the first rest area—that milkshake didn't handle traveling too well. We reach SR-325, turn left, and head to Rio Grande, where we drive to the site where the Bob Evans Restaurant chain started from a single truck stop diner on the Bob Evans Farm in 1953. The restaurant chain started as a result of patrons continually telling Bob Evans his sausage was the best around. Many folks also considered the Concords the best gospel group around.

Doug Miller, a distant cousin to Dall Miller of the Southern-Aires, was born in Ironton on December 24, 1958. In the 1970s, he started singing with the Evangelistic Quartet in South Point, and in 1980, he decided to start his own quartet. Purchasing the name from Jim Black, he formed the Concords. The group traveled full-time, and one of the original members was Brad Dashiell who had previously traveled with the Mid-South Boys. Also with the group was Carrie Huckada who also had been with the Mid-South Boys and the Hinsons. Later, Doug purchased all rights to the group and moved the group to Ohio. In 1973, the group reformed and continued as a trio in Rio Grande with Doug, his wife, Patricia, and Butch Garey.

Butch attended church with his grandmother on a regular basis, and she had a huge influence on his life. He started playing the guitar at age fourteen and quickly joined with other players in his hometown. Influenced by such greats as Chet Adkins, Butch became an accomplished musician and plays several instruments. Butch Garey started singing in high school with a group called the Eternal Youth, traveling throughout the local states. Butch is also an active songwriter. His song "Straight for the Gate" was recorded by the Harmony Boys in Georgia and became a national single. Butch left the Concords to focus on local church ministry and spend more time with his family. Butch continues to write music, and for over twenty-five years now, Butch has been actively involved in forming praise and worship teams in local churches.

The Concords sang at NQC for seven years and were nominated as Ohio's goodwill ambassadors. During the mid-1980s the *Singing News* labeled the group as "The fastest growing gospel group in America." The Concord album entitled *More and More* was one of their more popular albums, and the single "You Did It All for Me," written by Butch's sister, Tina Bright, who also sang in the Eternal Youth, became a very popular and much requested song for radio airplay across the nation. Traveling full-time from Texas to the eastern states, they maintained a schedule of about two hundred bookings annually until the group retired in 1990. Today Doug and his wife live in Patriot and continue to sing with their daughters.

Leaving Rio Grande, we continue west along U.S. 35 and miss our exit. We turn around and exit right taking SR-327 north, passing a huge elk farm on the right. After passing through the town of Wellston, we pass a General Mills plant. Merging onto SR-93 we drive through Hamden, passing Roller Coaster Road. Sounds fun for a bus ride! Reaching McArthur, we view a really neat hotel and turn left onto U.S. 50. Then driving through a heavily wooded area, we end up on Goose Creek Road. Traveling along Goose Creek Road, we pass some beautiful waterfalls and some huge rock outcroppings on the way to South Bloomingville. While in South Bloomingville, we visited with some of the group members of Family Heritage.

Before 1990, the group Family Heritage sang together as the Davis Family. In 2005, they were awarded the New Horizon Award, and in 2006, they were awarded Band of the Year, both by the Ohio Christian Association.

Leaving the 2006 NQC, they were traveling along Interstate 64 on their way to Parkersburg, West Virginia, to sing for a Sunday morning service. It was very foggy, and they could hardly see. Suddenly, the bus, which was recently purchased, started smoking. Pulling off to the side of the road, they found a large hole in the exhaust pipe. Soon a car pulled over, and a man, who also traveled in a gospel group, offered some assistance. Working on the bus until 2:00 AM, they were able to temporarily fix the hole. They quickly headed down the road, and within five miles, the hole had blown open again. As no phone service was available, they sat on the bus along the side of the road and prayed for assistance. Finally, a local man came by and took them to a local park facility where they could freshen up and make contact with their families. Families later picked up several of the group members, leaving the bus and three members to solve the problem. At about 10:00 PM Sunday evening, the bus was fixed with help from a local garage. The bus arrived home safely around 2:00 AM Monday morning, and everyone was grateful for the protection God had provided.

They have performed at Ohio's famous Westfall Gospel Sing several times and have completed two Florida tours. They often sing at the Gospel Music Barn in eastern Tennessee. They have also sung several times at the Guernsey County Gospel Sing in Cambridge. They continue to travel, performing on the road almost every weekend, spreading the message of Jesus in song, and they are one of the few groups today that use all live instruments.

Leaving South Bloomingville, we take SR-664 traveling through Hocking Hills State Forest. Passing through the Old Man's Cave and Cedar Falls area, I was reminded of the time my wife and I were hiking along the Cedar Falls Trail with our son. Noticing my wife stepping over what appeared to be a big stick, I grabbed up our little boy as we watched the stick, a really big snake, cross the trail. Leaving the park area, we turn right onto SR-374 taking a scenic drive to SR-56 where we turn left and travel east to SR-93. Turning left onto SR-93, for the third time today, we make a quick drive north to Mount Pleasant. The Society of Friends, more commonly known as the Quakers, settled in eastern and southern Ohio and established Mount Pleasant. In 1817, Quaker Charles Osborn of Mount Pleasant published *The Philanthropist.* It was the first antislavery newspaper in the United States.

Sid Wheeler was born in Mount Pleasant. During high school, he sang with a group simply called the Quartet, and they took first place in the state competition. In 1983, he moved to West Virginia and started a solo ministry in southern gospel. Sid now travels throughout the eastern United States and is known as the soft-spoken man with the powerful voice.

Leaving Mount Pleasant, we turn around and head south on SR-93 to SR-56 where we turn left and travel east to New Plymouth where we merge onto SR-328. Working our way along the creek, we travel north to Union Furnace, passing some deer grazing in the field with the cattle.

Homer Alvan Rodeheaver was born in those beautiful Hocking Hills on October 4, 1880, on a small farm in Simcoe Hollow, a couple miles from Union Furnace. Homer grew up in Jellico, Tennessee, and to make money for the family used an old blind mule to haul lumber for the mill.

In 1896, he started college at Ohio Wesleyan and while at Ohio Wesleyan, having an ear for music, he learned to play a slide trombone he had purchased for only seven dollars. Leaving college in 1904, he toured with evangelist William E. Biederwolf. In 1909, Homer joined up with Billy Sunday leading the music and playing the very same trombone he played while at Ohio Wesleyan. During his stay with Billy Sunday's organization, he led millions in song. In 1911, as the need to provide songbooks for the crusades continued to grow, the Rodeheaver Publishing Company of Chicago was founded, and in a short while, he published his first work entitled *Somebody Cares.*

In the early 1900s, with the development of phonograph records, Homer produced some of the first gospel recordings and aired, over radio station WDKA, one of the first programs of gospel music ever heard. In 1918, he served five months in the Spanish-American War as a trombonist in France. After returning from the military, he rejoined the Billy Sunday organization but left in 1929 because of health problems. Rodeheaver made an appearance on the *Haven of Rest* radio program in 1934, and in 1935, he took part in a memorial service when Billy Sunday passed away of a heart attack.

At the passing of Virgil Oliver Stamps in 1940, Homer referred to that great bass voice with these words: "They will probably let all the rest of the bass singers in the heavenly choir take a vacation, at least for a little while, and just put Virgil O. Stamps in their place."

Because of the rapid growth of the publishing business, they later bought out two other companies, and the name was changed to Rodeheaver Hall-Mack Company. Rodeheaver founded the Rainbow Ranch for underprivileged boys located near Palatka, Florida. On December 18, 1955, at the age of seventy-five Homer Rodeheaver passed away, and in 1960, the Rodeheaver Hall-Mack Company was acquired by Word Music.

Leaving Union Furnace, we continue east on SR-328 to U.S. 33 where we turn left and travel north along U.S. 33 to U.S. 22. Turning left onto U.S. 22, we travel west for several miles until we reach the Ohio Christian University where they hold some great gospel concerts each year. Shortly after passing the university, we reach Circleville, a town laid out in a circular pattern by Daniel Dresbach and recognized as the largest producer of broomcorn in the United States. Benjamin Hanby, composer of "My Darling Nellie Gray" and "Up on the Housetops," grew up in this community. Boasting a water tower painted as the world's largest pumpkin, Circleville hosts the Pumpkin Show every October.

The Haddox twins were born in Circleville on October 10, 1945. They had several uncles that used to play violins, guitars, and other instruments. On Sunday afternoon, all the people would gather around the piano and play before taking their afternoon naps. Kermit left the church for a while, but he finally came back home. They attended a little church, and they would watch singing groups come in, and it just stirred something up within those two boys. The preacher would say, "Hey, you boys want to sing?"

He played the guitar, and the boys started humming and singing a little bit, and one thing led to another. Then in the late 1980s, the Homelighters were formed by Kermit Haddox and his twin brother, Kenny. They have never put a price on their ministry, always going by faith and accepting freewill offerings. Kermit says, "We are in the soul-saving business. If we are up on the platform and somebody comes to the altar, it doesn't bother us a bit, we just stop and go down and pray with them."

Once, the Homelighters were scheduled to sing at a place back in the hills of Ohio near New Haven. Arriving in their van, they noticed a couple of guys standing at the door holding shotguns. As the brothers started looking at each other, the men motioned for them to come on in. The church was a log cabin with a dirt floor. It had bus seats for pews. Kenny said, "Are we suppose to sing here?"

The man quickly responded, "Yeah, we got boards up here for your speakers." They only knew about four songs, but the people loved it, and they ended up singing those four songs over and over. After letting them take a short break, they had them sing them over again. After the service was over, Kermit asked why they had the shotguns. They told him that some people in the area didn't want church going on in that little hollar, and they were told if they had any singers or any preachers there tonight, that they were going to kill them. Kermit said, "What!"

They told him, "Don't worry, boys, we're going to guard you and take you right on out of here."

Well, it so happened that they kept their word as the group all survived, and that's the truth!

Before joining the Homelighters in 1994, Don Kontner sang with the Master's Men in Reynoldsburg for about five years. The Master's Men were a popular group and sang with a number of professionals. They disbanded for a while when the manager retired and moved to Tennessee. Their manager returned and has reorganized the group, but they just sing in their local church.

Leaving California in 2002, Dennis Reed moved to Ohio bringing with him thirty-five years of experience. He has performed in the Madrigals and several theatre musicals. He sang with the Jericho Quartet in Chino Hills, California, for two years and hosted a southern gospel music program on radio KPRO in Riverside, California. He currently plays in the Pumpkin Show band in Circleville. In 2002, they won an award from the governor at the Ohio State Fair—the Quartet of the Year.

Mark Wyman, one of the prior members, went on to sing with Teddy Huffam and the Gems. Bass singer Tim Lockbalm later went with the Southern Men in West Virginia. In 2005, both Gary Haynes and Rob Watson, who had previously sung with the Cornerstone Quartet, went on to sing with the Masters Four from Groveport.

They were scheduled to sing in the childhood church of Loretta Lynn in Kentucky, and their sixteen-year-old drummer was getting set up when the preacher came in, and taking one look at the drummer, he was going to have a heart attack, they thought. He said, "Oh, boy, I don't think that's going to work. This church will never hold still for those drums."

And Don told him, "Well, you have two options. He stays, or we go. Because we are not about to tell him he can't play gospel music when he could be playing rock-n-roll." Don suggested they go to the back of the church while they were setting up and pray about the matter before he made a decision.

They went back for a long season of prayer, and when they got up, he said, "I'm going to let him stay." The service started, and in the middle of the first song, the church congregation, approximately two hundred people, got up and started moving around. They were crying and hugging one another, and the Spirit was moving. The preacher came from the back of the church, grabbed Don by the neck and, almost pulling him off the podium, said, "Son, I want to thank you. I've been the preacher of this church for twenty-five years, and I have never seen anything like this in this church."

They picked up a 1965 Buffalo bus in Bakersfield, California, for $4,500. The Lord has always supplied their needs. They have sung in many churches, and they have sung in barns, tents, and even fields where they just took a tractor, went in, and mowed it all down. They sang in a barnyard where a guy had built a big stage for them. While singing, they happened to look down, and there were some old sows lying right there close to the stage just snorting away.

* * *

Jerry Metzler grew up right in Circleville. His father was a preacher, and the family moved to Jackson when he was in junior high school and stayed there for four years until they moved back to Circleville. When Jerry graduated, he left town and went to work for the Kroger Company as a meat cutter, and he would sing on the weekends.

Jerry Metzler and his wife started singing with another couple, and the Royalaires were formed in 1963 as a mixed quartet. Jerry's wife played the keyboard. After ten years singing as a quartet, the other couple had to move out of town, so they became a trio and have remained a trio ever since. They have had several different members in the group including Susan Peck, who now sings with Karen Peck and New River. She started singing with the group in 1987 and sang with them for three years. When Susan Peck was still with the group, they were vacationing on a cruise, and her sister Karen was singing with the Nelons on a cruise.

The Rhythm Masters had been doing the tour but were no longer available so Maurice Templeton asked Karen Peck if the Royalaires could do the chapel service one morning. After the group sang, they requested they come back and do the chapel again next year. In time, they were not only doing the chapel services but some of the evening concerts too. The group has now sung on over twenty-three cruises sponsored by Templeton Tours.

Mary Alice Brashear also sang in the group for five years. While performing with the Royalaires on a Singing at Sea cruise, Mary Alice Brasher met Tim Lovelace who was traveling with the Florida Boys. In 1995, after the development of a long friendship, Tim flew to Mary's hometown in Ohio where they had their first official date, and they were soon married. Today Mary and Tim travel as a team, and Tim has become one of the top humorists in the southern gospel realm.

The Royalaires had a nice Silver Eagle. Jerry rented a big barn, and some man from the Columbus Custom Coach came and customized all the interior of the bus. Jerry installed a new suspension system, a new engine, and an automatic transmission. It had a washer and dryer and even a shower. It was nice! In 1998, Jerry's wife was diagnosed with cancer, and in 2002, after singing by his side for forty years, she passed away. Jerry decided to sell the bus the year she died. He prayed for the Lord to send a buyer, and soon here came a buyer from Florida, and the bus was sold.

Tracey Leggett sang in the group for eight years. When Tracey left, she was replaced by a lady from Atlanta, Georgia, named Michelle Davis. Michelle sang with the LeFevres in Atlanta twenty years prior when she was only seventeen years old. She's been singing with the group for about three years. Tracey Liggett returned to the group and now flies from Spartanburg, South Carolina, almost every weekend to travel with the group.

Jerry has remarried and his present wife, Susan Metzler, is singing with the group. In 2007, the Royalaires sang at Ohio Christian University in a new auditorium along with Greater Vision, Crystal River, and Michael Combs before a crowd of two thousand people. The group continues to sing doing approximately two weekends a month, but they are cutting back as Jerry, at age seventy-six, says he is getting too old to keep going. No longer having a bus, they simply travel in a van and do a lot of dates in Florida during the winter time.

Jerry Moore sang with the Royalaires, and he wrote a song called "The Book, the Blood, the Blessed Hope." The Inspirations recorded the song, and the first three months they had it out, they sold ten thousand copies. It was piggybacked on another song that finally went to number one called "I'll Not Turn My Back on Him Now."

One weekend, they were down in South Carolina. It was Memorial Day weekend, and they were traveling home along IR-77. There was a mountain at Fancy Gap, Virginia, called Fancy Gap Mountain that was seven miles long with a 5 percent grade. Heading up the mountain, Jerry shifted the bus down into third gear and worked his way very slowly up the hill. When they got close to the top, he could hear banging and kicking at the rear of the bus. Pulling over to check things out, he found they had burned up the rear end. He hitched a ride and was taken to a little farmhouse somewhere in Virginia. He called everybody he could find in the book and finally got hold of a guy named David Smith. He came and picked him up and towed the bus into his shop. Jerry's wife worked for a guy in Circleville who had a private four-passenger plane so they got hold of him, and he flew down and picked up Jerry's wife and two other ladies that were in the group, leaving Jerry there. At first, he slept on the bus until they got ready to do the work. He then had to stay in a little motel for ten days that had a black-and-white TV, air conditioner in the window, and a telephone down at the office. He would walk about six miles each day up to the garage from that motel and check on how things were coming. And finally, his wife even wired him some money. Most people never realize what the groups go through from time to time as they travel down the road.

Returning Home

Leaving Circleville, we turn onto U.S. 23 and travel north along a scenic route to IR-270 where we enter IR-270 west taking it to IR-70. Entering IR-70 west, we head for home. Merging onto IR-75 north and taking the U.S. 40 exit to Vandalia, we end Tour No. 4.

HIGHER CALL

PFEIFERS

PFEIFERS

PFEIFERS

PFEIFERS

DIEHLS

Paul Minney

ATONEMENT

ATONEMENT

GOLDEN KEYS

Danny Gaither

Jim Hill

Jim Hill with STAMPS

Jim Hill with STAMPS

Jim Hill with STATESMEN

GOOD NEWS TRIO

RADIANT HEART

Marilyn Bowling with
SOUTHERN-AIRES

Greg Tingler with
GOSPEL HARMONY BOYS

TRUE GOSPEL SOUNDS

Rich Adkins

GOSPEL RIVER BOYS

FORGIVEN 4

FAMILY HERITAGE

HOMELIGHTERS

ROYALAIRES

ROYALAIRES

Tim & Mary Alice Lovelace

Chapter V

Mansfield Tour

In My Robe of White

I'll hear the trumpet sound; all the saints will be heaven bound
We will cross over Jordan wide; stop and view the other side
There I'll see those Holy Hills; and my mansion He has built
I'll be the first one in the line to see my name in the Book of Life

It's going to be a wonderful time; when I get to the other side
See my loved one's gone before; we'll be parting nevermore
We'll be walking on the streets of gold surrounded by riches untold
When I look upon His face; I'll be saved by His amazing grace

In my robe of white I will fly away
To that land so far, meet my Jesus there
It will be so grand when I get to that land
In my robe of white I will fly away

—Geniece Spencer Ingold
(Used with Permission)

Leaving Vandalia, we head east on national road (U.S. 40) crossing over Taylorsville Dam where the water is backed up behind the dam because of some recent storms. We continue east, and just before arriving in Springfield, we pass the beautiful Ohio Masonic Home that has the appearance of a castle. Continuing along National Road, we enter Springfield, where the first town jail was guarded by a black bear. Turning right on High Street, we drive past the Westcott House at 1340 East High Street, a sprawling two-story house that has all the features of Wright's prairie style and is the only Frank Lloyd Wright prairie-style house in the state of Ohio.

Marlene Burton sang with her sisters in a group called the Cooper Sisters. The Cooper Sisters sang on WIZE Radio for the *Negro Business Hour* program in Springfield. Around 1980, Marlene formed a family group called the Burton Family Singers. Marlene gave birth to fourteen children and adopted another, and she taught them all to sing. The Burton Family Singers have been honored to sing several times to teenage inmates at the Clark County Juvenile Detention Center. For years, they traveled the United States, including Alaska, even doing tours in Jamaica and the Cayman Islands. The family stopped singing as a group in 2004, but some of the children continue to sing.

* * *

The Heaven-Aires started singing in 1971 and even had a number one song on the charts for nine weeks. In 1990, after the tragic loss of their tenor singer to leukemia, they stopped singing. In March 2004, several former members of the Heaven-Aires reorganized as the group One Accord.

One Accord offers a variety of music that includes traditional and southern gospel. Debby Craig Seymour was born in Portsmouth yet has lived most of her life in Springfield. Following a long heritage of southern gospel, she dedicates her life to lifting up the Lord's name in song. Marsha Moats began her gospel singing career as a young lady. She has been an inspiration to others giving all the glory to the Lord. She took some time off for a while, but today she enjoys singing His praises after more than twenty years. Mike Stroup has a wonderful ear for music and works hard to make the various parts of the group come together. His talent on the piano speaks for itself!

* * *

At the age of eight, Vickie Lynn (Sibole) Gaines became the youngest member of the Dimples Quartet. At fifteen, she started traveling with the Maranatha Singers and experienced the thrill of performing at the *Grand Ole Opry*. She also sang in a trio with her sisters and later sang with her sister Rhonda in the Master Sounds. She now sings with her husband, Elden Gaines, in their duet Two for Calvary. Elden previously sang with the Joint Heirs Quartet in California and with the Master Sounds for a time.

Rhonda (Sibole) Moore started singing with her sisters in 1969, and they sang together until 1973, calling themselves the Faith Trio. Rhonda grew up in a poor environment, and often when they went out to sing, they wouldn't receive enough money to cover their expenses. Many times on the way home, they would repeatedly sing "We've Come This Far By Faith" because they were about to run out of gasoline.

In 1989, Rhonda started singing with her husband, Elzie Moore, and his brother who wrote several of their songs in a group called the Master Sounds. Marla Conrad later joined the group. She had previously sung with the Masters Quartet for sixteen years. After singing with the Master Sounds for two years, Marla left to start a solo ministry and has been singing solo for about six years. Since Marla left the group to go solo, the Master Sounds continue singing as a duet.

Marla has a nineteen-year-old daughter named Kiley who is blind with multiple handicaps. Marla finishes many of her programs with her daughter singing that great old song written by Jim Hill "What a Day That Will Be." Marla considers herself in full-time ministry and has traveled as far as Florida.

* * *

Blake "Squirrel" Powell was born in Springfield on September 7, 1986, and started singing with his mom as a ten-year-old. While Blake was still a young boy, his eighteen-year-old brother was crushed by machinery in an accident at the Honda plant. During this difficult time, Big John Bledsoe from Journeyman Quartet of Huntington, West Virginia, was a big source of support for Blake.

At age fourteen, Blake started singing with a group called New Creations from Cincinnati. When Blake turned sixteen, he started traveling full-time with the Journeyman. He sings tenor for the group and occasionally plays the piano. Sometimes they even let him drive their big 1993 Silver Eagle bus.

* * *

Janie Kenerly, Keith Echols, Michael Kenerly, and Leah Wilkerson started singing together in the mid-1980s after getting together for a special choir rehearsal where they were the only four people who showed. Since they had all four parts, they decided to learn a song and this began the Rescued Quartet. The primary focus of their ministry is working with inmates at the various prisons. The group sings mostly a cappella, and they enjoy asking the audience for special requests. As a result, they have had some unique experiences. Once, during a singing at the Civic Center in Cambridge, someone called out for the group to sing "The Old Rugged Cross." When they started singing, people began praising the Lord, and an old man came running down the aisle with both hands held high. He was truly receiving a blessing from the Lord. Another time, they were singing at a midsummer service when someone requested they sing "Silent Night" a cappella. The song was a blessing confirming that Christians can celebrate the birth of Christ any day of the year.

The gentleman who produced most of their work is Biney English, brother of Michael English. Janie says, "Biney would always introduce us as the black group who sings white." Rescued is pleased to have won a Top in Sound contest and another contest sponsored by WCVO radio.

Leaving Springfield, we continue east on U.S. 40 and pass through Harmony. We turn right onto IR-70 and travel east for several miles to IR-670 and, crossing the Olentangy River, exit onto U.S. 23. We turn onto Broad Street and enter Columbus, home of artist James T. Mason who designed a topiary recreation of George Seurat's 1887 masterpiece *A Sunday Afternoon on the Island of La Grande Jatte* at the Ohio State School for the Deaf and Dumb Park. The piece contains fifty-four human figures, eight boats, three dogs, and a monkey.

Chuck Larkin was born in Columbus on June 14, 1942. He grew up singing solos in his local church, and in 1962, he started the Challengers Quartet. In 1967, John Evans joined the group, and with the help of the Holy Spirit, he and Chuck built the group into a very powerful ministry to the youth of that time. They performed all across the country at college and high school assemblies. Many young people came to know the Lord through their ministry.

Another member of the group, Ed Crawford, joined to sing lead in 1973. He went on to sing with the Singing Americans and the legendary Kingsmen. He now heads up the Mystery Men Quartet.

Also a member of the group was Jeff Isaacs, formerly of the Imperials. Once while traveling through Missouri, the Challengers stopped for food and fuel. They finished and loaded the bus and were quickly off down the road. After traveling about halfway through Indiana, someone realized they had left Jeff Isaacs in Missouri.

The Challengers were privileged to share the stage with many quartets including the Statesmen, the Oak Ridge Boys, and J.D. Sumner and the Stamps. They also worked the fair circuit with the *Hee Haw* road show. The Challengers went full-time in 1972 under the ownership of Chuck and their bass singer, John Evans. That same year, Danny White joined the Challengers.

Danny was introduced to southern gospel music by his parents and started learning to play the piano in 1954 when he was seven years old. During high school, he was in three rock-and-roll bands playing at sock hops and band contests. They rehearsed in his garage until someone called the police because they were making too much noise.

Growing up in the 1950s and 1960s, he would be taken to gospel concerts by his folks to hear such greats as Hovie Lister and the Statesmen, the Blackwood Brothers, the Speer Family, the Blue Ridge Quartet with Elmo Fagg, the Oak Ridge Boys and the Imperials with Joe Moscheo at the piano. Danny loved southern gospel and was always impressed with the low sounds of the bass singers and the versatile piano styles. His four favorite bass singers were J. D. Sumner because of how low he could go, Noel Fox with the Oak Ridge Boys, Richard Sturban, and Armon Morales with his smooth harmony.

In the fall of 1968, he got a call from his first quartet. He met with the group at church for an audition. They were amazed at his style and welcomed him to the group. He traveled with this group in an old Cadillac limousine for two years, and Danny cut his first album with these guys, just four vocals and piano. Influenced by the rhythm of Hovie Lister, the simplicity of Ben Speer, and the diversity of Tommy Fairchild, Danny borrowed a little from each to create his own unique piano style.

He played his first concert in 1969 sharing the stage with the Happy Goodman Family at the Logan Memorial Field House in Logan, West Virginia, at the age of twenty-one. Holding down a factory job and playing southern gospel music every weekend, Danny was having a blast. It wasn't long before he was singing with the Challengers, and although he wasn't making much money, he had reached his goal of touring with a gospel group and traveling in a big bus.

Their first two years on the road, they sang on the main stage of the NQC in Nashville, Tennessee, and in 1973, they were nominated for the Horizon Award. Danny White wrote the song "Give Your Life to Jesus" as recorded by the Challengers. Danny had an uncontrollable high-pitched laugh, and one day while watching Laurel and Hardy in an Iowa restaurant, he started laughing, and before he quit, everyone else in the place was laughing.

Danny White later sang with the Capitol City Boys. His song entitled "The Rapture's Almost Here" was recorded by the Capital City Boys, and he remained with them a couple years. Danny went on to play keyboard for the Jordanaires and later broke away from the gospel circuit to work in country music with an artist named Don Frost, from Nashville, Tennessee. In March 1977, he was hired as a staff musician at the Wheeling Jamboree in Wheeling, West Virginia, and in March 1978, Danny went on the road with Faron Young and the Singing Deputies. He later went on the road with the Tiny Wellman Band from Columbus. When Tiny became a born-again Christian in the 1990s, they retired from doing the clubs and started doing festivals and fairs. Danny was with the Tiny Wellman Band about thirteen years.

Born with no fingers on his right hand, Danny had taken a lifetime to overcome this physical challenge. Danny was forced to battle severe anxiety and panic disorder all his life. It progressively got worse as the years went by to the point where he could not function at all. His fingers, arms, and legs were sometimes out of control, and his vision was blurred. He experienced loss of balance, disorientation, and his speech was restricted. Danny went through some tough times, but in October 2003, he returned to the altar and rededicated his life to Jesus Christ. In the words of Danny White, "I can never go back to what I was. I know I am saved, healed, and on my way to heaven. Old things are passed away and all things are new. Praise the name of Jesus forever!"

Danny remains busy working in the praise band at his church. He also has a small studio in his home.

The Challengers auditioned for the *Jimmy Dean Show* but never got on the show. The Challengers backed up various artists including Crystal Gayle and shared the stage with Bob Hope and the *Lawrence Welk Road Show*.

One evening, while driving home from a concert, they spotted a Pizza Hut. As it was still open, they pulled the bus into the parking lot, but before they could get off the bus, someone working in the restaurant turned off all the lights and closed the restaurant.

In 1975, they were traveling down the road when the front tire exploded, throwing their GMC 4101 bus into a truck. It was a serious accident, and a passenger on their bus, Bob Day, died in the accident.

Later that same year, Chuck Larkin left the group, and in 1978, he joined the Capitol City Boys. The Capitol City Boys changed their name to the Capitols in 1979. The Capitols went on to record some country hits and even had a short stint in a nightclub. When Chuck left the Capitols in 1986, he didn't sing for a few years until 1989 when he joined a group called HIS from Tampa, Florida. In 1991, he joined another group in Tampa called "Spiritual Harmony."

In 1995, he joined yet another group from Tampa, Florida called the Sunshine State Quartet, which is very active to this day. Jim Harville, the lead singer for the Sunshine State Quartet, has a wonderful testimony of the healing power of the Lord Jesus Christ. During a robbery, Jim was shot between the eyes at close range with a .38-caliber hollow-point bullet and is here today because of the power of prayer and healing.

After leaving the Challengers, Terry Kauffman joined a group in Branson, Missouri. Jack Krum went on to sing with the Revelators.

* * *

A group called the Gospel Clouds of Joy started back in the early 1950s. One of the members, Anthony Byrd, was born in Columbus. Anthony was a former member of the Gospel Recruiters and also sang at the professional level with the Gospel Interns. Anthony and his wife live in Jonesboro, Georgia, where he has been singing with his family since 1989 in a group called Peaceful Harmony.

Timothy Patterson was born in Warren. He plays a variety of instruments, his specialties being acoustic and steel guitars. He previously played for the Kansas City Melodyairs. He has been playing professionally for over forty years.

Jimmy McGee was born and raised in Columbus. His father, originally from a small area in Independence, Louisiana, passed on some of those country values and customs including the traditional red beans and rice and the fried fish in corn meal. Jimmy thanks his father for not sparing the rod and thanks his mother for not telling dad every time it was needed. His mother was very involved in church, and as a child, he went to church two times during the week and twice on Sunday. Church is where he developed his love for music. He sang and played drums in church and picked out a few songs on the piano. By age twelve, he had also started playing the guitar. Before graduating from high school, he had some great times playing for several local quartets such as the Mighty Sons of God, the Praising Sons, and of course, the Gospel Clouds of Joy.

* * *

James Edward "Eddie" Saunders was born in Covington, Kentucky, in 1909. He attended West Virginia State University and Wanzer Vocal School. In 1937, after touring the country with a gospel group called the Kings of Harmony, he moved to Columbus where he formed his own group called the Gospel Trumpets. In 1944, working with local radio station WTVN, he produced the programs *Helping Hand* and *Swanee Hour*. Saunders became Ohio's first African-American disc jockey and later joined WVKO, Columbus's first African-American station. He worked with WVKO until 1979. Saunders received recognition from the National Urban League and other organizations.

* * *

Born into a military family, Ron Lay, Jr. sang in several school choruses, but he wasn't exposed to southern gospel music until a visit to Tennessee with his parents in 1999. That same year, he moved to Columbus and became actively involved in his church, and as a result, the group Grace Harbor, a mixed trio, was formed in 2000. The group consisted of Ron Lay, Jr., his wife, Lori Lay, who sang with the Flower Family before getting married, and Randy Snodgrass.

Randy was raised in West Virginia and exposed to gospel music at an early age. His family would often gather around the piano after dinner and sing hymns. He started singing in church as a young child and at eight years old he was singing in his first group with his mother and his aunt. They called themselves the Praisers Trio. By the time he was twelve years old, Randy was playing piano for the CoPilots based in Charleston, West Virginia. He later sang with the Harvest Trio and the Gospeleers in West Virginia. He also sang with an Ohio-based group called Manna. Randy has written several songs and his song "Glory Is Waiting" was recorded by the Proclaimers Quartet from West Virginia.

In 2003, Grace Harbor was on their way to sing in West Virginia. They had stopped at a truck stop for lunch. While there, Ron had to get something out of their vehicle. In doing so, he temporarily placed the group's clothes bag on top of the vehicle. After eating lunch, they jumped into the vehicle and were off down the road. As they started down the freeway, they noticed something fly off the top of the vehicle, and soon there were clothes blowing all over the freeway. Realizing it was the group's clothes bag, they quickly got off at the next exit and headed back down the road. Arriving at the scene, they started running all over the road attempting to pick up what was left of their belongings. About that time, a law official pulled over and told them to move along before someone got hurt. Having no other clothes, they were forced to sing in the same clothes they were wearing. Needless to say, the group has often, in good humor of course, reminded Ron of his responsibility in this little mishap.

* * *

Founded by Arthur Dennis in the early 1950s, the Five Star Harmonizers represent a long history of gospel singing excellence and have persevered for over five decades. Steeped in gospel tradition, the group has blended a variety of musical influences to produce its own unique style and sound.

One of the first members, Bruce Fletcher, has been with the group for over fifty years. Bruce was born in Athens, Alabama on December 27, 1933, and grew up on a farm learning to pick cotton and plow with a mule. He remembers riding to church on an old farm wagon pulled by mules and hearing the sound of singing coming from the church far down the road as they approached.

The group traveled by car, often squeezing seven men into one car. Once while driving home from an event in Roanoke, Virginia, they were traveling through Charleston, West Virginia, when suddenly the driver lost control of the car. If they had not crashed into the bridge, they would have plunged into a deep portion of the river. When the rescue team arrived, the group members were all taken to the hospital for minor injuries, and because of his fear of needles, several of the other members had to hold Bruce down so the doctor at the hospital could give him a shot.

Various members, representing some of the nation's finest gospel music talent, have participated in the group over the years. Theodore Smith sang with the Mid-South Singers from Detroit, Michigan, and the Lyric Supremes in Columbus for thirty years. Sam Jamar sang for five years with the National Hummingbirds in Columbus. Frank Tate previously sang with the renowned CBS Trumpeteers, one of the early pioneers of gospel music. Bobby Garfield "Tree" Jackson previously played guitar for the Highway QCs. Both Theodore Good and Terry Ragland traveled with the Blind Boys of Alabama, and Terry also played bass for the Pilgrim Wonders. Mark Hairston also sang for the Pilgrim Wonders.

The group has shared the stage with several groups, including the Soul Stirrers, the Fantastic Violinaires, the Mighty Clouds of Joy, and the Swan Silvertones. Over the years, the group has made several recordings including the 1994 release of "He's Coming Back" on Columbus-based Valiant Records. The group has been blessed to receive numerous awards including Best Male Group of the Year and the 2006 Gospel Legend Award. Although the ebb and flow of life has required changes in personnel, the determined will of the group's only remaining original member, Bruce Fletcher, drives the group to reach for greater heights. In addition to their local concerts, they continue to sing at an annual event in Huntsville, Alabama with the Deep South Singers.

* * *

Willard Meadows was saved in the mid-1960s and has been singing gospel ever since. The Heavenbound Singers began in 1966 as a trio with Willard, his mother, Lena Neal, and his sister Doris Baer. They started out traveling in a 1954 Flex bus, which they used for many years. When his mother and sister decided they couldn't travel anymore, he formed a new trio with the help of some friends, and they traveled together under the same name until the end of 1972.

During her first marriage, Ruth lived in Cleveland and had two children. In November 1972, she married Willard, and in December of that same year, she, Willard, and their daughter, Tama reformed the Heavenbound Singers, and they have been traveling together since. Their daughter started playing piano at age five and began playing for the Heavenbound Singers at age eleven. She has played for the church choir and different events, but her main job is to play for the Heavenbound Singers.

At one time, they had several young boys playing instruments for the group, and back then, the group members would all dress alike. Ruth was the official keeper of the clothes. She saw that they were clean and on the bus ready to wear. Finally, the group decided they weren't going to dress alike anymore and would simply wear regular clothing. Then one day, they were traveling down the freeway to their next appointment, and one of the guitar players discovered a button had come off the white shirt he brought for that evening. He diligently tried to sew it back on while they traveled down the road. Unable to get the button to stay on, he became irritated and certain that their old matching clothes were hanging in the back of the bus, he threw the shirt out the window. Later when preparing for the concert, he went back to the closet, and the clothes were gone. When they decided they would no longer wear matching clothes, Ruth had removed them from the bus. The only thing he could find on the bus was a white blouse that belonged to Ruth. So that night, he had to play wearing her white blouse.

David Wycuff has been playing bass for the group for over thirty years. Occasionally, Dave sings with them allowing them to do some quartet arrangements. He is a very quiet person and had traveled with them many years before they were aware that he could sing. They did a television program for three years with a local pastor. They are also known for their love for revivals, singing many throughout the year. In fact, in 2006 they sang at eleven revivals. They traveled throughout the region singing in Indiana, Kentucky, West Virginia, and Ohio for many years, but now, they travel in a fifteen-passenger Ford van, and their travels are limited because of age as both Willard and Ruth are in their seventies.

When not singing, they enjoy listening to good gospel music, and sometimes, they attend the singings held at the Der Dutchman Restaurant in Plain City where they recently heard the Booth Brothers sing some great old songs like "Still Feeling Fine."

* * *

In 1997, a group called Notes, a dynamic men's trio, was formed ministering through a variety of music styles. Later that same year, they sent some envelope-sealed promotional information to a church belonging to Just Joy Enterprises, a company owned by Bob Black's wife Joyce. When the posters were returned to the group, they read, "GOSPEL SING: JUST JOY." Believing this was a special blessing from God, the group name was changed to Just Joy. This name depicts the personality of each member and emphasizes the group's desire to spread joy.

In 2000, one member resigned but was quickly replaced, and they continue to provide a unique blend of harmony as they sing those old hymns a cappella. They have sung at churches, camp meetings and fairs throughout Ohio and even did a tour in New York. They have performed on WTSF TV 61 in Ashland, Kentucky, and TV 39 in Marion.

* * *

Elliott McCoy was born on June 11, 1945, in the hills of Pike County, Kentucky. In connection with the famous Hatfield-McCoy Feud, his father was killed while working in a coal mine in Kentucky, and Elliott was raised by his grandparents. They were godly people, and Elliott thanks the Lord for the heritage they provided to him and his brother. Growing up, he always went to church. His Grandpa McCoy attended a Primitive Baptist Church. Their singing and their style of music was a little different, a quiet type of worship. His grandparents on his mother's side would go to church at the Pentecostal Church of God in Cleveland, Tennessee. Elliot's Grandma Roberts didn't want to sing anything that dragged, calling it "dead music," so it was a very interesting contrast.

All of Elliott's uncles were musicians and singers. Growing up on a farm where there is not much to do other than work, Elliott remembers that in the evenings, they would all gather on the front porch and sing. Many people talk about front porch fellowship, but in Elliott's case, that's the literal truth as that's what they did in Kentucky. He learned to sing and play instruments as his uncles could play any instrument with strings on it—guitar, mandolin, or banjo. He never honed his instrument skills as his real love was singing. Elliott's inspiration for singing came from his childhood in Kentucky. When he was fifteen, they moved to Ohio where the churches were a little different, but he soon was singing in his high school choir and glee club.

Like most teenagers, he began listening to rock-n-roll music and wanted to be a rock star. His idols were the Beatles and Elvis Presley. At age sixteen, he started singing rock-n-roll in bars and clubs and had to lie and get a forged ID to be able to enter the bars.

When he was eighteen, before becoming a Christian, he was playing at a bar in Michigan. They were replacing a band at a big club in Ann Arbor, and the band they replaced had a phenomenal eighteen-year-old lead singer.

Arriving early so they could see who they were replacing, Elliott met the lead singer, and he said, "That guy's going to go some place, you can just tell." The lead singer's name was Bob Seger, and he went on to be very famous in rock-n-roll.

In December 1963, Elliott married a young girl from Ohio and remained in the Columbus area most of his life. He was saved in 1967 and became heavily involved in church. He quit singing in the rock band, got a regular job, and was introduced to gospel music. Then a couple in the church invited him and his wife to go to a gospel event in Columbus at the Veteran's Memorial Auditorium. The concert featured the Statesmen Quartet, the Blackwood Brothers Quartet, the Speer Family, and a trio called the McDuff Brothers. One concert and he was hooked! He enjoyed all of the groups, but the McDuff Brothers captured his attention and remained one of his favorite groups in gospel music. Elliott says, "They sang with conviction and with anointing and you could tell they were the real deal."

Several of years later, he put together a trio in Columbus called the Timesmen. One of the members was Bill Pitts, a talented singer who went on to pastor a church in Lancaster. After singing with the group he was introduced to the Laymen Quartet, and in 1971, he joined the group.

The Laymen Quartet was formed in 1966 by George Curnutte and some other members attending the Whitehall Church of the Nazarene in Columbus. The group was named the Laymen Quartet as they were laymen for Christ. Their first transportation was a six-door 1960 Plymouth Airport limo that was later replaced with a 1948 Flex bus. George's wife, Dottie, made suits for the group as well as table banners for a number of the groups at the NQC. She often sewed on buttons for singers like Rusty Goodman and George Younce. One night, Jim Hamill and London Paris had spent the night at their house, and when Jim was backing out of the driveway, he ran into their garage door.

They sang at a number of Nazarene churches and worked with a Nashville promoter named Sonny Simmons. Sonny promoted large gospel events in Columbus and Akron, as well as Charleston, West Virginia, and Louisville, Kentucky. The Laymen Quartet would work the circuit with him. In those days, they were referred to as a semipro group because they still had full-time jobs to make a living. They were one of the first semipro groups to sing at the NQC. They also sang at the first Westfall Gospel Sing held at Westfall High School and sponsored by the Monroe Men's Club. As of 2008, the Annual Westfall Sing remains a very popular event. The Laymen were one of the first local groups to land a major recording contract with the QCA Recording Studio in Cincinnati. QCA was the first manufacturer to produce a full-color stock jacket for albums, and the Laymen did two projects with QCA that were released nationally.

In the 1970s, the Laymen Quartet was the host gospel group every night at the Country Music Cavalcade held at the Great Southern Hotel in Columbus, sharing the stage with such artists as Roy Clark and Estelle Parton. They had achieved some success, but it was difficult to work all week and try to sing on the weekends. They even did a two-week tour in Haiti. As they became more popular, they worked a full-time schedule singing on Friday, Saturday, and Sunday every week and working about fifty weeks a year.

Elliott was with them for about six years and retains some fond memories. When George Curnutte's daughter, Debbie (Curnutte) Chuvalas, was nine years old, George Younce took her up to the stage, and as she sat on his lap, he sang the laughing "Bumble Bee" song. In 1972, she quit school and moved to Memphis, Tennessee, to work with Brock Productions promoting Elvis Presley and setting up his concerts. This lasted about six months until her father called her home to sing with the group where she remained for three years until she was married.

The Laymen Quartet was on its way to Louisville, Kentucky, shortly after midnight when they stopped at a roadside rest to check the oil. You had to constantly check the oil on the bus back in those days. Elliott, who was driving, pulled over, and he and George Curnutte got off and headed to the rear of the bus to check the oil. George opened up the engine compartment, and Elliott was standing at the side talking with him. While talking, he noticed, from of the corner of his eye, somebody getting off the bus. Though he never actually looked at them, he was certain someone had gotten off the bus. When they finished the work, they got back on the bus, and George got behind the wheel, and they took off. Traveling down the road, they were sitting there talking, and everybody else was lying in the bunks asleep.

After about five minutes, Elliott suddenly remembered seeing someone getting off. He quickly told George, "*Hey*, I think I saw somebody get off the bus."

George said, "I didn't see anybody get off."

Elliott agreed to take a head count. They had a piano player named Maurice Frump who had played for several groups including the Crusaders. Thinking the person who got off the bus looked like Maurice, Elliott asked if Maurice was on the bus. Everybody said, "Yea, Maurice is back there sleeping."

He yelled back to Maurice but didn't get an answer, so he went to the back, and sure enough, Maurice was not on the bus. Getting off at the next exit, they turned around and headed back to the rest area. By the time they got back to him, about forty-five minutes had passed. There he sat, and man, he was mad. He was mad because he thought they had done it intentionally, and all weekend, he wouldn't even talk to the other group members. Finally, on the way home for the weekend, Elliott said, "Hey, buddy, I am sorry. We did not intentionally do that."

By this time, Maurice had calmed down and responded, "Well, I got to thinking about it, and yea, I believe you didn't."

While traveling with the Laymen, Elliott received a call from Ed O'Neal of the Dixie Melody Boys. Ed said, "Hey, I need a lead singer."

With excitement, Elliott replied, "Hey, man, I would be interested." Financially, the offer was only about one-fourth what he was currently making, so he had to turn him down.

The Laymen were singing in West Virginia at the big annual Mount Nebo sing. They had worked it five years in a row, and there were usually seventy to eighty groups there. Typically, the groups would show up, sign in, and sing one song and be done. Sometimes on Saturday night, they would let a group sing another song if the audience gave them a big ovation. The crowd loved them, and often, they would end up singing about half an hour, they wouldn't let them quit. There was another group from West Virginia called the Calvarymen which consisted of Squire Parsons, his brother Virgil, and two other men. The Laymen would start singing on Saturday night, and after about half an hour, as the crowd wouldn't let them quit, they would bring the Calvarymen onto the platform, and they we would sing together for another half hour.

In 1975, they were singing at Mount Nebo to a crowd of about forty thousand people. While singing, Elliott noticed a young lady taking pictures, and she just sort of stood out. Afterwards, he approached her inquiring as to why she was taking pictures. She indicated she was working with the *National Geographic Magazine*. She was a freelance writer, and she was doing a story on the state of West Virginia. He asked why she would come to a gospel sing, and she responded, "Well, because it was attracting so many people." That was pretty unique.

After they had finished singing their afternoon session, some guy came up to them and told them that if they would sing "The Glory Road," there was a guy in the crowd that would get saved. Explaining they were only allowed to sing one song, the man then asked the director who initially said, "No!" The director then asked, "Man, What's so important about that song?" When the man replied, "Somebody getting saved," the director said, "Okay, okay, one song."

Sure enough when they started singing the song, the man came running to the platform. When he knelt at the foot of the stage, the whole crowd erupted. The young photographer continued taking pictures, and in the June 1976 issue of the *National Geographic*, the article came out and the caption read "Joyful Noise Saves Sinners."

Once while the Laymen were on the road, Elliott had parked the bus in front of the church where they were to sing. While parking the bus, he noticed a big tree that had recently been pruned. It was full of little branches so you had to really look close to see the big branches. Their tenor singer, Russ Bailey had this phobia; they called it "adjusting the bus." Whenever they would park the bus to unload, he thought he had to move it as it just wasn't located quite right. So that day, Russ was adjusting the bus and pulled forward, hitting what appeared to be a little tree branch. Directly behind that little branch was a big branch, and before he could stop, it came crashing into the front of the bus—right through the window. He was going fast enough that it came into the bus lifting the bus off the ground. The windshield was shattered; it tore out the headliner—just a horrible thing. They shook it, trying everything, but could not get the bus off the tree. They had to call a wrecker to pull the bus off the tree.

Because of their ties to Sonny Simmons, the Laymen worked every major show from Louisville to Akron. They would do the Akron Rubber Bowl once a year. One night at the Akron Rubber Bowl, Sonny had brought in a number of groups, and there was a crowd of over eight thousand people. The event went late into the night, and being close to a lake, the fog soon started rolling in. By 12:30 AM, the singers couldn't even see the fans. The police came in about 1:00 AM and told them they had to turn it down because the neighbors were complaining.

The Laymen worked regularly with groups like the Oak Ridge Boys, the Rambos, and the Goodmans—some of the top groups in their day. One night, the Laymen had to follow the last two big groups on the program, the Oak Ridge Boys and the Downings. These two groups had presented an excellent performance, and to make things even worse, they came out together for the last five minutes, and doing a song together, they tore the place up. When the stage was clear, Sonny said, "All right, the Laymen Quartet."

Somewhat nervous, they were preparing to enter the stage when Dwayne Allen of the Oak Ridge Boys told them, "Hey, it doesn't make any difference. You got people here that would rather hear you than the Oak Ridge Boys."

With those words of encouragement, they stepped out on the stage. The crowd was still buzzing with excitement, but the quartet knew that when you walk out onstage after a group has just overly thrilled the crowd, you better go soft and easy. So they opened with an old song entitled "Nearer My God to Thee," singing it a cappella. The crowd quieted down to listen, and when they finished the song, they received a standing ovation.

Around 1977, although he continued to live in Columbus, Elliott put together a part-time group based in Cincinnati called the Premiers Quartet. That's when he first started singing with Carrol Rawlings. A guy named Carl sang bass. Russ Bailey, who had sung with Elliott in the Laymen Quartet, sang the tenor part. Elliott says, "This was one of the better groups I had sung with at that time. We had a real top-shelf, good, professional sound."

They were a very strong regional group and stayed together four years. When Carrol Rawlings left, they hired Bill Dykes, and when Russ Bailey left to sing with the Senators, they hired a tenor named Gary Throckmorton who had sung with several groups including the Southern-Aires.

Carol Rawlings had a number of contacts through his father that allowed them to work a number of interesting and rather large Baptist conventions. They worked several big evangelistic meetings with Rex Humbard, as well as some good work with Dr. Rawlings. About once a month, he would jump on the bus, and they would travel some place where they would sing before he preached. The Premiers performed at Kings Island during a special Christian day event. Jerry Falwell flew in, and both he and Rex Humbard spoke. They often sang at the big annual sing held at Akron Baptist Temple. In the 1970s, Baptist Temples were some of the biggest churches in the nation, and that was a good circuit if you could get your foot in the door. In all this, the Premiers performed for the Lord. They felt that was their ministry, and that's what they wanted to do.

Sometime later Carl, the bass singer, decided he was going to retire and didn't want to travel any longer. Elliott, Bill Dykes, and Gary Throckmorton tried to keep it together for a little while as a trio, but it never was the same, and around 1981 or 1982, the group folded. Elliott got out of gospel music and became heavily involved in his church and his work. He was in the car business at that time and was a general sales manager at Germaine Toyota in Columbus.

In 1988, he got together with Bill Dykes and Roy Tremble who had previously been with the Cathedral Quartet. They put together a group, and Bill had just moved to Columbus from Nashville where he had been singing with Larry Orrell in a group called Chariot. Since that group had folded, Bill suggested they call themselves Chariot, and that's what they did. This new group had a great sound because those two guys were phenomenal singers. Roy was with them less than a year when he got married, and he and his wife decided to go into their own ministry. He was replaced by Gary Throckmorton, but after about a year, Gary got another job offer and moved to Virginia. They replaced Gary with an old pro named Tank Tackett who had sung with several groups from Ohio including the original Weatherfords Quartet. He also sang with Jerry and the Singing Goffs in the 1970s. They kept it together for two more years until Tank moved to Nashville to sing with the Statesmen Quartet.

By 1993, Elliott's kids were no longer little, and he had some success in business so he started talking about relocating to Nashville, where he had always wanted to live. About that time, Tank called telling him that Jake Hess was going to be leaving the Statesmen, and he said, "Why don't you come and sing with us?" Elliott thought that would be a great opportunity, so he called several guys for advice. They told him the group wasn't going to last as Hovie Lister was having health problems. Despite the advice given, it sounded like a wonderful opportunity, so Elliot took the position, and they moved to Nashville.

At the end of their third road trip, they pulled up in front of Hovie's house, and he announced that he was folding the group. The remaining group members organized a group called Southern Tradition, but they only kept the group together about a year.

When the group disbanded, Elliott's sons were all grown and had left home, and the only one they had left at the house was their daughter. They wanted to find a good church with a good youth program, so they got plugged into Cornerstone Church in Nashville. At the time, the church was running about 350 people and had grown to over 6,000 members by 2008.

Elliott started singing in the choir and joined the praise team. Even though this was not his first love, he wanted to do something for God. Occasionally, they would need a quartet or a trio number for the service, so they would have him put together a quartet for the song. There was a man in the church named Mitch who had moved to Nashville from North Dakota just a few years before Elliott arrived. Mitch had never sung southern gospel. In fact, he was an old rock-n-roll singer that had gotten saved. One day, Mitch asked Elliott, "Hey, do you think you would like to put together a group?" Elliott indicated he had been thinking about putting together a group, so they agreed to work on it together. But they still needed a tenor.

Then on July 4, they were sitting in the choir when a young girl sang an incredible song called "Dear Captain." After church, Elliott asked the young girl who wrote the song. She said her mother and stepfather cowrote it with another man. The song was about praying for the president and was written 1999. In 1999, nobody wanted to pray for the president—they only wanted to talk about him. After sitting around a table talking about President Clinton, these three people went home, and one of them felt convicted and called back telling them that they should pray for the president, not talk about him. And out of that conversation developed the song called "Dear Captain"—the captain of the country, the president. They pitched that song to over two hundred artists, major artists, and they all said no, but it's all God's timing.

Getting permission to record the song, Elliott took it to a producer in Nashville requesting they produce a soundtrack. Changing the arrangement, Elliott told the producer he wanted a track that when it is heard, it will be an instant classic. When the tragic September 11 event hit he had the track about half finished. As Elliott sat in his home watching the planes crash into the building, Mitch called expressing his concern. While talking with Mitch, it was as if a light went off, and Elliott knew the song needed to be heard as people needed to be praying for the president. Calling the producer, he said, "I need this thing done as fast as you can get it."

Once they found someone to fill the tenor part, they wanted to ship the song to the radio and see if they would play it. The people didn't know who they were, and they didn't even have a name. They decided to get some pictures made of the group, so they contacted a photographer named Paul Ward. He does all the major groups in gospel music and does the *Singing News* cover. Paul asked, "What's the name of your group?" Liking the word *bridge*—they wanted to be a bridge to Christ and as there were three people in the group—the group Three Bridges was officially formed. They provided him a copy of the song, and the next day, Elliott got a call from a big attorney in Nashville wanting to talk to him about the song. Elliott went down and met with him and shared his desire to find a record label that might be interested. The next day, he received a call from Sunlight Records, which was, at the time, one of the biggest in southern gospel. They signed Three

Bridges, shipped the song out, and in the next six years, they had ten top 40s, six top 10s, and two number ones. It was unbelievable, and few people still know who they are. Some of the old-timers know who the Laymen Quartet is, but most people have never heard of Three Bridges.

George Curnutte Jr., prior member of the Laymen, often drives bus for Three Bridges. Singing frequently in the Columbus area, they recently sang in Logan at the Nazarene State Camp Meeting before a crowd of about three thousand people. Residing in Hendersonville, Tennessee, Elliott continues to travel and sing, maintaining a deep commitment to his family. After forty-four years of marriage, he and his school sweetheart, Terri, have six kids and twelve grandkids.

* * *

Providing the blended sounds of both three- and four-part harmony, New Jerusalem is a multitalented family and bluegrass gospel group from central Ohio. Although the family had been singing at their home church and small gatherings for some time prior, New Jerusalem actually started in 1997. Diana Boggs comes from a long line of musicians. Her grandparents sang together in a group called the Turbervilles, which remained together for a period of twnety-five years. The piano player for the Turbervilles went on to play piano for the Revelators, another group from Ohio. Diana's parents also had a group called the Sagar Family, and this group was together for twenty years. Both Diana and her husband were a part of this group. The Sagar Family group disbanded shortly after Diana's mother passed away.

New Jerusalem has received several awards for their instrument skills, and one year, they were acknowledged by the governor of Ohio as the "Horizon Group of the Year." They have made television appearances throughout the Midwest, and their music is played across America. They have performed at the Roy Acuff Theater and the Gibson Cafe both in Nashville, Tennessee.

When their daughter Calina Boggs was only fourteen years old, Randy Renigar commented, "She belts out a song like nobody's business . . . a young jewel, a real find, and has loads of talent." Calina was also one of the artists featured on the cover of *Power Source Magazine* as, "Artists to Watch for in 2007." Calina won the *ICM Talent Show* in Nashville and has been winning fiddle competitions since age seven. Her little sister Candy is also following the family heritage as an award-winning vocalist and a multitalented musician.

* * *

Charlie Hodge was born in Decatur, Alabama on December 14, 1934. At the age of twelve, he had his own radio show in Decatur, Alabama. He later graduated from the Stamps-Blackwood School of Music along with a fellow student named Bill Gaither. Around 1954, Charlie, Bill, Danny Gaither, and a friend of Charlie's formed a gospel quartet called the Pathfinders. They sang anywhere the door was opened, and in an effort to gain exposure for the group, they moved to Columbus. At this time, Danny left the group and returned to finish school.

The Pathfinders got a job doing a fifteen-minute radio show on Worthington radio station WRFD as sponsored by Pennington Bread. They were privileged to open for the Statesmen/Blackwood Brothers tour, and the Pathfinders soon produced their first record, an old 78 featuring the song "Suppertime" and that old spiritual "Rain, Rain, Rain."

Soon the group began to struggle, and after a concert at the county fairgrounds in Van Wert, they called it quits. Bill Gaither headed back to Indiana taking a job at Cox's, a local supermarket. Gaither enrolled at Taylor University, but retaining his love for gospel music, he would often listen to the Weatherfords on radio. Then one day, the Weatherfords stopped by, offering him an opportunity to go on the road, but his father said, "No!"

Sometime later, with the help of his sister, Mary Ann Gaither, Bill formed the Bill Gaither Trio. When Mary Ann left the newly developed group to get married, they were left short handed with a commitment to sing for a Sunday evening service at the Maiden Lane Church of God in Springfield. As the date rapidly approached, they were unable to find a replacement, and Gloria Gaither, Bill's new wife, reluctantly agreed to help. That evening in Springfield, calling themselves the Gaither Trio, they performed their first concert singing a Henry Slaughter song entitled "I Never Loved Him Better Than Today" and a Doris Akers song entitled "Sweet, Sweet Spirit." As Gloria began to share words from her heart, God's spirit filled the auditorium, and those present were truly blessed. After years of touring as the Gaither Trio, Bill created the Gaither Vocal Band. Now known to the world, Bill Gaither continues to actively preserve southern gospel music through the promotion of his Homecoming productions.

Charlie Hodge had a great love for gospel music. He sang with the Marksmen for a while, and by age twenty, he was singing lead for the Foggy

River Boys. As they traveled, he would take a Coke crate along to stand on as the rest of the guys towered over him.

On one appearance in Memphis, Tennessee, on an ABC Network show, Elvis Presley came backstage to meet the Foggy River Boys. Later while stationed at Fort Hood, Charlie and Elvis met again. Traveling together on the same military ship to Germany, a friendship began to develop, and when Elvis's mother, Gladys Presley, passed away, Charlie was there for Elvis, and a close relationship was established. Elvis and Charlie remained extremely close, and Charlie actually lived at Graceland for seventeen years. He was given small roles in a few of Elvis's movies, including *Clambake* (1967), *Speedway* (1968), and *Charro* (1969). Charlie faithfully traveled with Elvis, playing guitar and singing some backup, until that last concert held on June 26, 1977. Charlie passed away on March 3, 2006.

* * *

In 1997, a trio named Pure in Heart was formed. To gain exposure, they attended the NQC and handed out free cassettes of the group. Although they completed six recordings, their ministry was short-lived, and the group stopped singing in 2005.

* * *

The Revelators Quartet was organized in 1956 by Jack Krum and Lloyd Farley. The group started in West Virginia, and in 1961, they relocated to Columbus. They sing at revivals, churches, and even did several all-night singings. Their deep-south spirituals and hymns were done with a true sincerity and reverence to God.

* * *

After several years of solo ministry in Columbus where she was born, Katy Van Horn started singing soprano for the Nelons. She sang for two years with the Mike Speck Trio. In December 2003, Katy married Troy Peach, and they make their home in Hendersonville, Tennessee. While singing with the Nelons, Katy met J. P. Miller, who was working at the Southern Gospel Music Association in Pigeon Forge, Tennessee. J. P. teamed up with friend and mentor, Lou Wills Hildreth, a legend in gospel music, to host the weekly talk show on Gospel Music Television called *Inside Gospel.*

Katy and Troy became good friends with J. P. and his wife Tyanne when J. P. asked them to sing background vocals and Troy to produce his solo project. This friendship proved to be long lasting and brought them together into their current ministry of First Love. Reaching the lost for Christ through their music is one way to honor their First Love. Their purpose is to remind Christians that God's grace is sufficient. They also want to encourage the weary to return to their First Love.

* * *

Lanny Wolfe was born on February 2, 1942 in Columbus. His father, Pearl, was a railroad engineer. His mother, Precious, was the daughter of a Methodist preacher, and she sang and played the guitar in revival services all across the Midwest as a teenager. While growing up, Lanny, along with his mother and his two siblings, faithfully rode the city bus to church every week. At age nine, he began to take piano lessons, and two years later, when his teacher moved away, he started improvising and taught himself to play by ear. In 1963, he got married, graduated from OSU, and got a job teaching in the Columbus public school system for two years.

In 1970, while he was dean of the school of music at Gateway College in St. Louis, Missouri, he formed the Lanny Wolfe Trio. The trio traveled all over the United States singing in churches on weekends while Lanny taught at the Bible College and worked on a master's degree in music. Lanny has penned over seve hundred songs including "Greater Is He," "God's Wonderful People," "Surely the Presence of the Lord Is in This Place," and "More Than Wonderful." Lanny was voted SESAC's Gospel Composer of the Year for 1975 and 1976. His song "More Than Wonderful" won a Grammy Award for the duet performance of Sandi Patty and Larnelle Harris. The song was also voted Song of the Year in 1984 by the Gospel Music Association. It was the first time ever that a song from a musical had been chosen for such honor. In 1984, he was also honored as GMA's Gospel Songwriter of the Year.

In addition to his folio of songs written, Lanny has written fourteen musicals including the very popular *Noel, Jesus Is Born* arranged by Don Marsh.

* * *

Talk about walking side by side, the group Side by Side seems to have the plan. Brad Griffis and Gary Brown have been singing together since 1999. Prior to forming Side by Side, Brad sang with a group called Reverence in Hilliard. In the early 1980s, Brad was a third-generation singer with the Vogues, which was a chart-topping pop/easy listening vocal trio originally formed in the 1960s. Remember the song "Turn Around, Look at Me."

Following four years with the Vogues, Brad sang full-time with a chart-topping country band called Atlanta. Among other things, they performed on the *Merv Griffin Show*. Brad, an accomplished songwriter, has written over seventy-five Christian/southern gospel songs.

During high school, Gary Brown sang with the Followers in Columbus. In 1978, he started singing with the Lancers Quartet remaining with them for several years. He later joined the Hilliard group Reverence and remained with them until they disbanded in 2005.

In late 2006 Gary, really wanting to sing, posted a request at the online site (singingnews.com) for a chance to audition with other groups. There were many inquiries, but one really caught his eye. A fellow by the name of Dan Ramirez sent an e-mail making reference to a long-ago gospel music relationship on the east side of Columbus. Turns out that Danny and Gary had sung together off and on in the 1970s, but time and distance had caused them both to lose track of one another. As a result of that *Singing News* posting, their forgotten friendship was rekindled.

Prior to moving back to Columbus, Danny lived in Albany, Georgia, and sang with a well-known group called the Gracemen Quartet. God's hand was at work because Danny had also been corresponding with Bruce Landis who had previously sung with the Riegal Brothers in Dayton. Bruce was also part of a musical group called Deliverance while in high school.

Then one cold and blustery afternoon in December 2006, the potential members, who as of that time had not even been personally introduced, met at the Cracker Barrel Restaurant for lunch. They had a lively discussion about God's goodness and the excitement felt when singing quartet style. As a result of this meeting, they decided to form a new group, and as they walked out of the restaurant, Bruce suggested they try harmonizing. So standing on the sidewalk they sang "Amazing Grace" along with a few Christmas carols as curious restaurant patrons passed by on their way to lunch.

Several months later when the group needed someone to help with set up and run the sound system, Danny suggested they contact his friend Doug Taylor with whom he had previously sung. Doug had sung with the

Mastermen and Majestic River. Accepting the position, Doug, in addition to his other responsibilities, soon became the all-around go-to guy concerning all group issues.

Danny Ramirez left Side by Side in March 2008 to join a trio called Damascus Road. Fortunately, Doug Taylor stepped in as full-time baritone, and the group has not missed a beat.

What is so unique about this group is that they are all equal—no one owns Side by Side except the Lord. All the members have sung with other groups bringing a wealth of experience to what they believe is a refreshing and heartfelt new sound as they go forth proclaiming to a lost and broken world that there is hope and love to be found in Jesus and Him only.

Leaving Columbus, we drive through Upper Arlington. Then turning right onto Riverside Drive (U.S. 33), we travel north along the scenic Scioto River. Turning left onto SR-161 we drive west for a short distance where we take IR-270 north and shortly enter IR-71. Merging onto IR-71, we travel north to U.S. 36. Turning left onto U.S. 36, we travel north, passing through several small towns until we arrive in Mount Vernon, where Paul Lynde from television shows *Bewitched* and *Hollywood Squares* was born on June 13, 1926.

Helen VanScyocs was born in Newark on June 2, 1952. Her father, Bob Erwin, was raised in Vinton County and was tagged as "the meanest man in the county." In July 1986, she moved to Nashville to pursue her country music dream. She played for a local gospel group for about three months. It was a family group, a mixed female trio. She moved back to Ohio in 1987, and in 2000, she began singing with a ladies trio known as Heartsong.

In 1988 the VanScyocs started a family group with husband-and-wife teams Jim and Helen VanScyocs and brother Jeff VanScyocs and his wife, Cris. They were privileged to open for many professional groups, including the Cathedrals at a Labor Day singing event in 1988. In 1990, they sang on stage with Gerald Wolfe.

Once they were singing in a church, and they had set up behind the pulpit. As they stepped out on the platform, they raised their microphones and started singing. That was everyone except Jim—his microphone stand was stuck. He had no choice but to start singing down at a lower level, and I don't mean singing bass! One side of the church could see his dilemma and started laughing intently while the other side remained serious, totally unaware of the problem. Helen had to look the other direction to avoid laughing herself. This day is often referred to as the day Jim the Dwarf sang gospel music.

Another incident took place the day after Helen turned fifty-five. Someone complimented her on how her dress sparkled. Looking at the dress, she found she had put her dress on backward, and the sparkles were not in the front where they belonged. Oh, the joys of old age.

In 2003, at their fifteen-year anniversary concert, the VanScyocs sang with the Wilburns, and the Pfeifers were special guests at their sixteenth anniversary concert. Helen, on the encouragement of John Pfeifer, has written a book sharing her testimony, which has been an effective tool in their ministry.

After Jeff and his wife left the group, Jim and Helen continued as a duet until May 2007 when they joined the Singing Smiths. Jerry and Ruby Smith had been traveling as a duet for nineteen years. Jim and Helen traveled with the Singing Smiths until December 2007 when the Smiths decided to take a sabbatical from traveling to pursue a ministry with their family. Jim and Helen now continue their ministry as a duet, traveling and singing wherever God opens the door.

Leaving Mount Vernon, we turn left onto Sandusky Street (SR-13) stopping at McDonalds for a quick restroom break and an ice cream cone. Back on the road, we travel north passing through Bellville to IR-71 where we head north to SR-301. Taking 301 North, we travel a short distance to West Salem, home of the Pearly Gates, a family group consisting of six vocalists that started singing southern gospel in 1992.

About one year after the group started, Andrea Ball joined the group to play the keyboard. Shannon Shaw left the group to start a solo ministry and was replaced by Pearly Gates group member Stacy's oldest daughter, Jennifer. The group has experienced a number of personnel changes but continues to minister throughout the Ohio region. The Pearly Gates have appeared on television programs in both Lewisville and Wadesworth. In their spare time, the group members remain actively involved in their home churches.

The Pearly Gates were scheduled to sing in a parking lot at a street fair held in Perrysville. The group performing right before them was a rock group. When the rock group was finished, and they got up to sing there was only one person who remained in the parking lot to hear them sing. They didn't realize there was a raffle momentarily taking place, and as they began to sing, the crowd returned. Before it was over, a huge crowd had gathered to listen. When they had finished singing, the bass player for the rock group came up to tell them he enjoyed their message.

OHIO 5

Leaving West Salem, we head northeast on Buckeye Street (U.S. 42) to Salem Road where we turn right and cross over IR-71. After passing through the town of Burbank, at twenty-five miles per hour, we drive to Creston, where in 1881 William Stebbins agreed to help his neighbors and began lending some of his hard-earned savings to those whom he considered responsible men and women. Buying a safe and a desk, he moved into a small storefront in downtown Creston and founded the Stebbins National Bank. The bank has a unique history of robbery events. In 1928, the tellers were held up by two of the Wadsworth brothers. Then in 1954, two Rittman brothers took several thousand dollars from the bank at gunpoint. And finally, in 1971, a third pair of gun-toting men entered the bank and, within a matter of minutes, left the bank with money taken from the cash drawers. In 2004, the Stebbins legacy came to an end when Wayne Savings acquired the bank.

Also from Creston, the Copenhavers have a much shorter history than the bank, having formed as a trio in 2005. The group consists of two brothers, James Russell and Joshua David, along with their mother Karen. Karen grew up playing piano for the church where her father preached. Having played the piano for many groups over the years, Karen now gives piano and voice lessons in her spare time. Before helping form the trio, Jim sang with the Royalaires for about one year. Josh is an avid southern gospel history buff.

OHIO 6

Leaving Creston, we continue east driving up a long steep hill to Rittman, home of the Ohio Boxboard Company, the largest integrated carton factory in the world. Also with a long history in Rittman, the Regents Quartet started in 1968. Larry McElroy, one of the original members, previously sang with the Gospel Tones for five years. Later he put together a mixed trio called Ransomed. In 2003, he joined the group Higher Calling in Wooster. He remained with them until 2007. Jim McElroy, who was also a member of the Regents, had previously sung with the Vanguards. Harold Shock, known to many for his smooth baritone voice, previously helped to found the Lordsmen Quartet.

Leaving Rittman, we turn right on Sunset Drive and make a wrong turn. Back in Creston, we take SR-3 north and reach Medina where we pick up SR-57 and then quickly lose it. We then continue north on SR-42 and pass through Brunswick where we turn left on Center Road (SR-303). After making several turns, we manage to get back to SR-57 where we turn left and travel northeast to Grafton, where settlers migrating from the western part of Massachusetts lived in a log cabin on a hill overlooking Willow Park. Two large hotels were constructed near the railroad station, and many tales have been told through the years of outlaws having stayed in these hotels. He is no outlaw, but some of those terrific songs written by Mike Payne possess the power to shake the gates of hell.

Mike Payne started his singing career in 1972, creating gospel songs by changing the lyrics of country songs. With the help of his two brothers Mark and Keith, he soon formed his first group called the Mike Payne Trio. Several others joined the group including Mike's soon-to-be wife, Loreen Caudill. The group's name was changed to the Glorious Gospel Heirs in honor of their home church, the Glorious Church of God. Mike's songwriting ability began to get attention as other groups started recording such songs as "God Delivers Again" and "That Same Spirit."

In 1981, at the recommendation of group member Rudy Pierce, they changed the group name to simply the Paynes. Their signing with Windchime Records resulted in a succession of radio hits that touched many lives. Their first single "Ready or Not" debuted at number 20 on the chart and "Out of This World" held the position of number one for four months.

The Paynes introduced the first southern gospel concept video entitled *I'm a Jesus Fan*. Coauthored by Mike Payne and Ronnie Hinson and recorded on the *I'm a Jesus Fan* project, that classic song "When He Was on the Cross" was named Song of the Year in both 1985 and 1986.

In 1986, Mike Payne was named head of Eagle One Publishing in Cincinnati.

The Paynes continued to produce chart-making songs, recording a live album entitled *Fire on Stage* at Dayton's Memorial Hall. One of the songs sung that night "Angels Step Back" remained number one for five straight months.

The Paynes songs talk about things of the spirit and show the path to redemption. No concert was complete without first giving the listeners the opportunity to personally become acquainted with the King of Glory. In 1990, shortly after Mike was called to preach, the Paynes disbanded. The group temporarily reunited in 2000 for a special reunion concert. Mike and his wife, Loreen, along with their daughter continue to minister as a family.

Leaving Grafton, we turn right onto Main Street, and passing the Goose Crossing sign, we turn right onto SR-10 and head to IR-71. Traveling south on IR-71, we exit right onto Bagley Road and drive to the Comfort Inn where we spend the night. After checking in, we drive to a local Road House and enjoy a delicious dinner while a local snowstorm dumps about three inches of snow on the ground. Waking up the next morning, we find a total of eight inches of snow on the ground. After cleaning all the snow off the car, we leave the motel and head north on IR-71. God seems to have a sense of humor for as we head north on IR-71, the first exit we pass is called "Snow" Road. Passing Progressive Field, home of the Cleveland Browns, we enter Cleveland, home of the first Christmas tree in America. The evergreen tree was placed in the foyer of Zion Evangelical Lutheran Church on Christmas Eve 1851. Just like the many different decorations on the Christmas tree, the city of Cleveland holds claim to a variety of gospel artists.

Sherri Farmer was born in Louisville, Kentucky, and later moved to an area east of Cleveland. Heavily influenced by listening to the Gospel Singing Jubilee, and having accepted Christ as Savior at age eight, Sherri started singing gospel music at a young age. After relocating to Colorado for her husband's employment, Sherri sought to develop a strong solo ministry. She now travels nationally, and at every concert, Sherri seeks to remind Christians to whom we belong.

* * *

The Foggy River Boys were originally formed as the Marksmen Quartet in Dayton. The group consisted of Danny Koker (the group's manager), Jim Hamill, bass singer Don Taylor, and Earl Terry. In 1960, when Earl Terry left the group, David Young was hired to take his place.

Born Lester David Young on August 5, 1938 in Unaka, North Carolina, he began formal piano lessons at age eight. While still in high school David formed a quartet in Lenoir City called the Kingsmen. This group was a precursor to the famous Kingsmen Quartet based in Asheville, North Carolina.

They were quite active at churches, and they also appeared on Ted Mack's *Amateur Hour* television show.

David joined the Sons of Song in 1958, a new trio comprised of Don Butler, Don Robinson, and Calvin Newton. David stayed with the Sons of Song until 1959 when he was offered a job playing piano for gospel music legend Wally Fowler. He stayed with Fowler for two months, long enough to acquire the nickname Little David. Then David joined Bill Crowe in Winston-Salem to put together a brand new group called the Victors. David received another call from Don Butler that would once again change his plans. As a result of that call, David joined a new quartet in Atlanta called the Ambassadors. He remained with the Ambassadors until joining the Marksmen.

The Marksmen would occasionally back up Red Foley and were regulars on the Ozark Jubilee. The group was doing well, but it wasn't long until Don Taylor was drafted for military service. A short time later, Jim Hamill left the group to join the Blue Ridge Quartet. The Marksmen got David's old friend Bill Crowe to replace Hamill and moved to Cleveland to work with Dr. Cecil Simmons. Shortly after moving to Cleveland, the Marksmen became a full-time group and changed their name to the Foggy River Boys. They pioneered the first all-night sings in the Cleveland area. They also did several concerts in the Detroit area for Lloyd Orrell. Their arrangements featured dual piano accompaniment by David and Danny Koker, and they were quite inventive. Despite numerous personnel changes, including Ron Van Horn, Mack Evans, Charles Yates, and even Bob Thacker, they remained one of the top groups of the time.

In 1961, Danny Koker was hired by the Weatherford Quartet to work at the Cathedral of Tomorrow with Rex Humbard. David Young also left the Foggy River Boys in 1961 to join the Prophets Quartet in Knoxville, Tennessee, but was drafted to the army that same year. Returning from the military in 1963, David's dream job soon became reality. He joined the Couriers who had recently sung at Carnegie Hall. David loved the Couriers but he began to feel the need to settle down and raise a family. So in 1965, he told the Couriers that he would be resigning and would never travel full-time with another group. In 1980, for only a brief period of time, David started up a group called the Victors.

Today, David lives comfortably near Dahlonega, still singing occasionally with Colleen, his loving and devoted wife of forty-two years. Their four daughters sing together, calling themselves the Seasons. David was inducted into the Gospel Piano Roll of Honor in 2004 at the Grand Ole Gospel Reunion and in 2008 his son Mike Young continues the family heritage actively singing tenor with a popular group out of Nashville, Tennessee called Southern Sound.

* * *

Loren Harris was born on May 25, 1969, in Cleveland. His parents, Rev. Donnie and Sandra Harris, sang in regional groups throughout eastern Tennessee from their hometown of Unicoi, Tennessee. Loren started singing with his family at about age three and was led to the Lord in 1977 by his uncle Rev. Ed Davis. Loren remained with the family group for twenty-four years and then sang with the Miracles and Greater Heights. Loren met his wife, Cindy, at Wal-Mart while going through her checkout line. He soon fell hard for her, and the two were married in August 1995.

Loren studied music under Steve Hurst for three years before joining the Wilburns, filling the vacancy left by Tony Peace. After Loren had been with the Wilburns a few months, Jonathan Wilburn left to join Gold City and was replaced by a great young singer and songwriter by the name of Ricky Atkinson. Loren had been traveling with the Wilburns for four years, and although he loved the group, he was driving several hours each week just to meet with them. So when he heard the Perrys were seeking a lead singer, he gave them a call, and in May 2000, he started traveling with the Perrys.

While singing with the Perrys, the songs "I Rest My Case at the Cross" and "I Wish I Could Have Been There" became number one hits for Loren. Loren's family has always supported his career. His parents told him to chase his dreams and be the best he could be, and to keep God first. Leaving the Perrys to spend more time with his family, he now lives in Elizabethton, Tennessee, and is currently on staff at his home church, Valley Forge FWB Church, and doing some selected solo dates.

Having grown up listening to some of the greatest groups in southern gospel, Loren now collects old southern gospel albums and has a love and respect for the pioneers of gospel music. Two of his biggest influences are the late Jim Hamill and the late Rusty Goodman. Loren says he enjoys traveling and meeting people. Possessing an outgoing personality, he is a friend to all and doesn't have an enemy in the world. Loren is currently traveling on a limited basis in a group called Ricky Atkinson & Compassion. Loren is a talented singer and as Tracy Stuffle of the Perrys says, "That boy has an amplifier built into his voice box."

* * *

Growing up in Cleveland, John Nordquist started his piano career at age twelve when he accompanied the Spurr Trio. In 1958, he assisted during the Cleveland crusade. Winning a teen talent contest at the Youth For Christ convention held at Winona Lake, New York, he later became involved in extensive radio and television work. Later while attending Houghton College located in New York, he became a member of the Houghton College Trumpet Trio.

* * *

Sallie Martin was born in Pittfield, Georgia, on November 20, 1896, and in 1917, she moved to Cleveland. Some time in the 1920s, she relocated to Chicago, Illinois. In 1932, she joined a gospel chorus put together by Thomas Dorsey and Theodore Frye and later sang with Dorsey's University Gospel Singers. They were featured on the WLFL radio station singing many of Dorsey's compositions. When Mahalia Jackson became the featured soloist, Sallie focused on running the Dorsey House of Music until her departure in 1940. Teaming up with Kenneth Morris, they opened the Martin and Morris Music Company. In an effort to market their music, Sallie formed one of the first ladies' quartets known as the Sallie Martin Singers. They toured through both the United States and Europe until the group disbanded in 1975. In 1985, Sallie was honored as an "African American Living Legend" by the Los Angeles County Public Library. Sallie passed away on June 18, 1988 at the age of ninety-two.

* * *

Friendly Womack sang gospel with his brothers down in the coal-mining country of West Virginia calling themselves the Womack Brothers. Friendly promised the Lord that if He would give him five sons, he would see that they carried on the tradition and would sing for His glory. He moved to Cleveland and started working in the steel mill. Before long, God had answered his prayer, providing him five sons named Bobby, Cecil, Harris, Curtis and

Friendly Jr. After moving to Cleveland, Friendly started a new group called the Voices of Love. They would often practice at his house, and his boys would listen in. Sometimes, the boys would do imitations of the various members, creating joyful laughter throughout the house.

The middle son, Bobby Womack, would often sneak and play his father's guitar while he was at work. As he was left-handed he had to figure out his own method of playing with the strings upside down. By the early 1950s, Friendly was keeping his promise and had his boys singing gospel at churches around the area.

In 1953, he asked the Soul Stirrers if they would open for them at a program to be held at a local church. The Womack Brothers were a big hit, and Sam Cooke made sure the congregation provided some funding to the family for their expenses. The $73 collected seemed like a million dollars to nine-year-old Bobby. The Womack Brothers career took off, and they began traveling the gospel highway. They worked with such groups as the Staple Singers and the Five Blind Boys of Mississippi. The Blind Boys were impressed with young Bobby's guitar work and took him on the road with them.

Roscoe Robinson, born in 1928, became one of the most seasoned travelers on the Gospel Highway. Singing with a number of groups during the 1950s, he eventually was asked to join the Five Blind Boys of Mississippi, becoming successor to the legendary Archie Brownlee. Roscoe later sang with the Blind Boys of Ohio. Having listened to the Womack Brothers, Roscoe firmly believed in their potential and encouraged Sam Cooke to promote them. Sam Cooke was himself a gospel artist. He started singing with the Nobleairs when just a teen.

It wasn't long until Sam was encouraging the boys to cross over into secular music. At first, the boys were reluctant, but through the persistent coaxing of Sam Cooke, they finally agreed, and their name was changed to the Valentinos. Reworking the lyrics to a gospel song Bobby had written entitled "Couldn't Hear Nobody Pray," they came out with the song "Lookin' for a Love." It sold two million copies and remained on the charts about eight weeks during the summer of 1962. The crossover to secular music was unacceptable to their father, and even with their success, he suffered much anguish.

* * *

The Shields Brothers started singing together in 1928 and continued to minister for about seventy years singing both in churches and on the radio. After singing with the Jubilee Four in the 1940s, Claude Shields, Jr., son of Claude Shields, helped reorganize the Shields Brothers Quartet. Clifford Phelps, another member of the Jubilee Four, went on to sing with the Harmony Echoes.

* * *

The Friendly Brothers traveled the USA during the 1950s, singing songs written by Bill Spivery such as "Can't Thumb a Ride." In the 1960s and 1970s, Bill helped lead a group called the Sons of Truth. In 1977, he put together a female group called the Operators.

Remaining on the air for over forty years, Bill won an award for the most favorite gospel radio personality in 1993 and was later inducted into the Broadcasters Hall of Fame. Bill wrote "Operator, Get Me Jesus on the Line" and received national recognition for a song entitled "Mr. John," which was written in memory of President John F. Kennedy.

Note: For additional reading on the vast number of African-American gospel groups in the Cleveland area, I recommend the book entitled *Cleveland's Gospel Music*, written by Frederick Burton.

While in Cleveland, we pass by the Masonic Auditorium where some great gospel concerts have been held over the years. Then turning onto a side street, and after watching a car drive down the sidewalk, we cut through a church parking lot that is surrounded by a six-foot chain-link fence and are forced to turn around. Heading west along Superior Avenue, we continue through town, and crossing the Veteran's Memorial Bridge, we get our first view of the partially frozen Lake Erie. Leaving Cleveland, we cross the Rocky River and head west along the Lake Erie Coastal Trail Tour (SR-6). Passing through Sheffield, my wife is enthralled with a library that is located right on the shore of Lake Erie. Driving through Loraine, we pass over a drawbridge on the Black River. Continuing west, we reach Vermilion, named for the abundant red clay in the area used by the Indians. While in Vermilion, we stop for lunch at Big Ed's Main Street Soda Grill, a small place with a basic menu boasting fried bologna and a 1930s décor. After an enjoyable lunch, we are soon back on the road and continue traveling along Lake Erie. Shortly, we view in the distance those spectacular Cedar Point amusement rides and soon arrive at Sandusky, home of the Merry-Go-Round Museum, the only museum with a working merry-go-round. Similar to that Merry-go-round, people got on and off as the Freeman family changed group names and family members throughout the early years of their ministry after starting out as the Pathway Quartet.

Harrison Darrell Freeman was born in Amorst in 1957 but was raised in the Sandusky area. While Darrell was growing up, his family attended the Tiffin Avenue Church of God where most of the people, including his parents, were from the south, and their services were filled with singing and music. While Darrell was still a young child, his parents, Wilma and Ralph Freeman, with the help of another couple named Diane and Mack Allen, formed a quartet in Sandusky called the Pathway Quartet. At first, their music was provided by Mack playing the acoustic guitar. In 1967, Ralph Eddie Freeman, Jr., Darrell's older brother, joined the group. And by 1969, his middle brother, David Freeman, was playing bass.

In 1970, the Pathway Quartet was in a bad automobile accident in Toledo. While traveling in their van, they were hit by a drunk driver, throwing Dave out the widow of the van and onto the road. The van then crashed through some trees, breaking the windshield, and they actually had to crawl out through the broken windshield to get out of the van. As they slowly approached Dave lying on the road, they were certain he was dead. His head was severely banged up, but he was okay.

Darrell was playing the snare drum for the group at the time, but he had stayed home to watch his younger sister.

After the accident, Dave no longer desired to travel with the group as he had come too near death. When Dave left, the group decided Darrell would have to play the bass, and although he had never played, he agreed to try. Mom and dad had already recorded several albums, so sitting there in his living room at 324 East Washington Street and listening to their albums, young Darrell learned how to play the bass guitar. Within two weeks, he was on the road playing bass, and he traveled with them until they disbanded.

Later, Mack and Diane left to start a group with their son Terry and their daughter Carolyn called the Allen Family. They only sang together for about three or four years.

Darrell's father changed the name of group, and they simply called themselves the Pathways. Then in 1980, Darrell married a talented young singer named Chris Hawkins who was living in Kentucky and traveling with the Hinsons.

Chris (Hawkins) Freeman was born and raised in Bakersville, California, and started singing when she was just a little girl. She traveled singing with her mom and dad until she was a teenager. In 1974, as a seventeen-year-old, she was hired to sing with the Hinsons. She performed with the Hinsons for seven years, and in both 1976 and 1977, she was voted the youngest Queen of Gospel Music ever. In November 2006, as a past member of the Hinsons, she became one of the newest members of the Gospel Music Association Hall of Fame. She remains one of gospel music's greatest singers and is still going strong.

Chris became a valuable part of the Pathways, and they continued traveling as a family until Darrell's father decided to come off the road. After dad left the group, Darrell and his brother decided to change the name of the group to the Freemans. Their dad really didn't like the idea, but they did it anyway. They traveled together another year or two until Darrell's brother decided he had rolled a lot of miles and was tired of traveling.

On February 6, 1982, Chris gave birth to a precious little girl they named Misty. Born in Florida, mom and dad were a little worried those first few weeks after her arrival. Then before Chris and Misty were able to travel, dad had to return to Ohio to make some emergency home repairs. On his way back to Ohio, Darrell experienced an interesting flight, being almost frightened to death by a bursting balloon and then being interrogated by security upon arrival at the Cleveland airport. It was probably those jeans and the little backpack he was carrying.

With Darrell's brother no longer in the group, Chris and Darrell had some decisions to make, and as it was sometimes difficult to travel out of Sandusky because of the winter weather conditions, he and Chris decided to pack their bags and head to Nashville, Tennessee. Chris's sister, Diane Hawkins had come out from California and was presently living with them. She had been very helpful to Chris and had become a terrific babysitter. So in 1984, when they made their move to Nashville, Diane agreed to come along.

They were making plans to move to Nashville, but they had no band and only one car. They loaded all the equipment, and everything they owned onto an old bus that dad agreed they could use until they found some money to pay for it. When everyone was ready, they were off to a little town called Greenbrier, Tennessee. They left in February, and of course, it was very cold. Yet they were encouraged, knowing they were headed to a warmer climate where the weather was going to be much nicer. The next day after they arrived at their new home, Tennessee had the biggest snowstorm they'd had in ten years, and they were unable to move their furniture from the bus to the house for a couple of days.

Greenbrier was a very small town, and when Darrell walked in the hardware store looking for a snow shovel, the man said, "A snow shovel—what's that?" They told him it would melt in a day or so, and there was no use in fooling with it. Nonetheless, he worked hard shoveling the snow all the way to the house, and just as they had told him, a day and a half later, it was gone.

Darrell, Chris, and Diane now made up the Freemans, and hiring a piano player from Logan, West Virginia, Ronnie Sego—Naomi Sego's son—to play the drums, they were once again on the road. Later when the piano player decided to move back home, they called a cousin, Joe Freeman, from Kansas, who was only seventeen years old. He actually played drums and a little bit of keyboard, and when they asked if he was ready to come down and play, he thought he would be playing the drums. When Darrell told him that he would be playing the piano, he said he wasn't very good, but Darrell simply said, "You'll get there." Soon he was on his way to Tennessee and has been with them ever since. In 1994, two years after marrying Joe Freeman, Diane came off the road to have their first child. At this time, Joe became the third voice for the group.

Darrell and Chris's daughter, Misty Freeman, started with them when she was fourteen years old—playing acoustic guitar—and she now has her own albums and is writing many songs. She has cowritten their new single called "I Need a Drink." Misty married Bryce Callaway on May 13, 2006.

Then their son, Kaylan Freeman, who was born in Madison, Tennessee, became their drummer on stage, and he's been playing now for five years.

They were traveling one afternoon, and Darrell was up in the front of the bus all alone. Everybody else, of course, was back in the lounge relaxing. As they approached Atlanta, Georgia, Darrell heard something in the engine and became concerned that there was a problem. He got off at the next exit and pulled off the road behind a Burger King restaurant. Putting on the parking break, he got off the bus to check the engine. Opening the engine door, he listened for the noise he thought he had heard. After a few minutes, unable to detect anything wrong, he closed the engine door and got back on the bus. Turning back onto the freeway, he continued traveling, and when he was about forty miles down the road out of Atlanta, he started hollering out names, "Chris!" No response. "Joe!" No response. "Misty!" No response. "Hey, is anybody back there?"

After he traveled another ten miles down the road, he began looking around and was wondering if the rapture had come, and he had been left behind. At the next rest area, he pulled the bus off the road, and walking to the back of the bus, he found no one. Darrell turned the bus around and traveled almost fifty miles back to the exit where he had stopped at the Burger King. Exiting the freeway, he pulled into Burger King, and behold, there they were.

Excitedly entering the bus, they began to explain that they thought he had pulled off the road to get something eat. They were all in the restaurant when he pulled away. Chris was crying a little bit and shared with him that two nights before she had seen where a husband went crazy and walked away leaving his whole family.

In 2007, the Freemans were presented with the *Singing News* New Style Award as a result of their number one song, written by Rick Hendricks and Angie Hoskins, entitled "He Chose Me." Taking only eleven weeks to reach the top, it was one of the fastest climbing hit songs in southern gospel music in the past thirty-five years.

* * *

The group One Less Stone was started in 1985 as a trio, and in 2005, they became a male quartet. Singing part-time they have traveled the tristates appearing on several television programs, and in 2005, they won first place at the NQC Talent Contest.

Once, on their way back from making a recording, the group stopped to sing at a church in Rand, Washington. After the service, the pastor was expressing to the group how disappointed one of the elderly members was because they were unable to attend the service. They asked the pastor, and he told them she only lived a couple blocks from the church. They agreed to go sing for the woman and began walking to her house. Arriving at the house, they sang several a cappella numbers including that great old song "Haven of Rest." The woman was overwhelmed with joy, and the Spirit seemed to hover over their little group as they ministered to her. They left that day not certain who received the greater blessing, the little ole lady or the group. A short time later, the pastor contacted the group informing them that the woman had passed on. That was probably her last gospel concert here on earth, but the sounds she's hearing now are heavenly.

Once while Eric was driving his private van to Chattanooga, Tennessee, for a singing engagement, the transmission went out and had to be replaced. Two weeks later, while using one of the other group member's trucks, the transmission went out, and they had to drive all the way home in second gear. Then just a short time later, while using the group's custom van, they were on their way home from a singing appointment, and the transmission went out. Three strikes and you're out!

OHIO 10

Leaving Sandusky, we take SR-2 East, and crossing Old Woman Creek, we turn right on Baumhart Road. Heading south on Baumhart Road, we drive under the Ohio Turnpike to Garfield Road and into Oberlin, where temperance advocates formed the Ohio Anti-Saloon League in 1893, believing that American society was in moral decline and that people were violating God's desires by consuming alcohol.

The Fisk Jubilee Singers, the first group to perform spirituals throughout the world, left the campus of Fisk University of Nashville, Tennessee in 1871. Their first concert, consisting mostly of classical music, was held in Cincinnati. At that time still an unknown group, their turnout was low, and things did not go well. One Cincinnati newspaper labeled them "a band of Negro minstrels who call themselves Colored Christian Singers."

Later in Oberlin, while on the same tour, they were asked to sing at a Congregational Church ministers' convention. Enchanting the audience with a new song entitled "Steal Away to Jesus," they began to establish a name for themselves. By the time they reached Brooklyn, New York, a concert had been arranged, and after the concert, they became the toast of the town. Before ending their first singing tour, they sang for President Ulysses S. Grant at the White House.

OHIO 11

Leaving Oberlin, we drive through Oberlin College and continue south on SR-58 passing through several small towns. As we reach Sullivan, it seems the snow is disappearing. Passing through Ashland, we pick up U.S. 42 and soon pass the First Baptist Church where we once heard the Gospel Harmony Boys in concert, and they thanked my wife for her encouragement as she was smiling throughout the concert. Continuing south we arrive in Mansfield, home of the Living Bible Museum where more than 175 figures are on display representing forty-one different scenes from the Bible. Mansfield is also known as the "Carousel Capital of Ohio."

The Lordsmen later became the Colonial City. The Colonial City Quartet started singing around 1985 and was based in Mount Vernon. They took their name from a sign that said, "Mount Vernon is the Colonial City." Two of the members, Asbury Adkins and Ralph Linkous, previously sang with the Lordsmen a quartet started by Harold Shock in the 1960s also from Mount Vernon. Asbury Adkins was born on October 20, 1929 in Wayne, West Virginia. His mother was from the Toney family, and she is a cousin to the original Toney Brothers.

Mike Deane had previously sung with the Liberty Quartet and the Harmonaires of Bellville. Tim Campbell sang with his family before joining the group and his son David Campbell put together a group in Mansfield called Heaven's Harmony.

Colonial City was doing an engagement at a church service in the Columbus area. Tim Campbell had been dieting, and while the group was up singing, Tim's suit pants started sliding down his silky dress-shirt. As there was no place to slip away and resolve this matter, Tim was forced to explain the problem to the congregation. The rest of the group gathered around him, creating a temporary wall, so he could fix the problem. Needless to say, the next song was a little difficult to sing. The next time the group was preparing to leave for a singing, Tim entered the bus to find there were about eight pairs of suspenders hanging from the ceiling of their big MCI bus.

Wynn Baker later left the group to start a solo ministry, and Kim Brown and Steve Feazel were both part of a short-term group in Lexington called the 2nd Chance Quartet.

Asbury, a distant cousin of Harold Lane, later moved to Huntington, West Virginia, where he sang with the Gospel Harmony Boys. From there, he moved to Wichita Falls, Texas, to take a position with the original Dixie Melody Boys, and after a short term in the military, he spent some time singing with the Swanee River Boys. In 1957, choosing to remain home with his family, Asbury turned down a contract to sing with the Statesmen Quartet when they were looking for Cat Freeman's replacement. Rosie Rozell got the job and the rest is history.

Asbury later helped form the Adkins Brothers in Columbus. The Adkins Brothers ministered throughout the Midwest, and after traveling for ten years, the group disbanded, and Asbury joined Colonial City. He sang with

Colonial City for another ten years until he left to reorganize the Adkins Brothers Quartet with his sons.

Colonial City was in a studio recording their *Stand Firm* project when they received news of the tragic 9/11 event in NYC, and in 2005, Colonial City held a reunion singing at the Renaissance Theatre to a crowd of over a thousand people.

* * *

JB Spencer was born in Millstone, Kentucky, on September 7, 1935. JB was the tenth of twelve children, and sometimes, he tells people that his parents had so many kids they ran out of names and started using initials.

When he was a young boy, his older sisters taught him a few chords on the guitar, but he never really played much until after he was a teenager and had moved to Winchester, Ohio. When he was sixteen, he came to Shelby and got a job at Ohio Seamless Tube Company the next day. After working there for thirty-one years, he retired in 1984.

In 1954, the company went on strike, so he decided to visit his parents for a few days. While visiting home, his sisters introduced him to a girl named Barbara. She had sung in church since she was five and learned to play the guitar when she was eleven. So how did she win JB's heart? She would play and sing to him almost every time they were together. On a bright sunny day, September 30, 1955, JB and Barbara were married in Winchester, and they have remained in the Mansfield area ever since.

Barbara was born in Waynesville on December 5, 1939, and was the eighth of fourteen children. Her parents, Cledus and Gracie Lamb, were both born and raised in the Berea/Corbin area of Kentucky. They sang in church often, and they both played the accordion. Barbara was saved at the age of six and grew up in a church that had a lot of music and singing. She and her sister Ruby sang specials together on a regular basis. At age eleven, Barb began begging her dad to buy her a guitar. Finally one day, he brought one home that he had picked up at the Goodwill. Barbara says, "That was the happiest day of my life even though it was one of those old guitars with a square neck."

In 1958, JB went to the altar and got saved, and that's when they started singing in their home church. When they started singing, JB didn't know how to sing harmony, so Barbara had to teach him. She also helped him improve his guitar playing. Until 1972, they sang mostly in their local area. On October

26, 1956, their first child, Geniece, was born. Wade was born on February 25, 1958, and Kevin was born on March 30, 1961. Wade started singing at age three, and before he started school, he, Geniece, and Kevin were singing three-part harmony. When Geniece was eleven, she took piano lessons but played mostly by ear. In those days, JB worked second shift, and evening after evening, Barbara, not realizing she was preparing them for their lifelong ambition, would work with the children teaching them how to sing. When Wade was eleven, he became interested in playing the mandolin, and Barbara taught him the only three chords she knew and gave him her mandolin. He is self-taught and is quite well known for his mandolin playing.

In 1972, a man named Les Morgan who attended the same church as the Spencers came to them and told them they should make an album. He told them he would cover half the cost, but they weren't very interested in the idea. He talked with them again, offering to pay the entire cost. After thinking about it for a while, they decided to check out a studio in Barb's hometown where her cousin was the engineer. They set a date, and their first recording entitled "The Unseen Hand" was soon completed. They had five hundred albums produced, and JD told Barbara, "These five hundred albums will sit in our closet from now on."

How wrong he was! Once the news was out, people began buying them, not only for themselves but also for their family members, sometimes buying ten to fifteen albums at a time. Within two weeks, the group had to reorder. Needless to say, they paid back the money to Les Morgan that he had spent on the album. Les remained a big fan of the Spencers, and each time they made a project, he always received a free album. When making their first recording, they played their own music except for the bass guitar. They hired a studio musician to play bass and liked it so well they told Kevin, who was only eleven at the time, that if he could learn to play the bass guitar, they would buy him one. He was confident he could, and in two weeks, he was playing in church. He hit some sour notes for a while, but it wasn't long before he was a very smooth bass player, and he played on their very next album.

After their first album, the Spencers' singing engagements began to escalate. They developed a mailing list and sent newsletters to over thirty-five thousand families on a regular basis. They also promoted their songs on the radio by sending out 45s and CDs to hundreds of radio stations. The Spencers have recorded close to sixty albums. For many years, the family has owned their own publishing company entitled Peaceful Stream Music. While all five of the Spencers write songs, they are very aware that it is a God-given talent.

Around 1982, they started traveling full-time as a result of their song entitled "In My Robe of White," written by Geniece. The Spencers first recorded it on their *When I Crossed That River* album. Shortly after the song was recorded, they sang with Gold City in Pennsylvania, and upon hearing the song, Gold City requested permission to record the song on their next album entitled *Live in Atlanta*. They took the song to number one, making "In My Robe of White" their first big hit. Having it on the charts at the same time, the song went to number 19 for the Spencers. Their version of the song became popular everywhere, even in some foreign countries including behind the iron curtain. This was a stepping stone, a real milestone for the Spencers, opening up a lot of doors. Geniece wrote many other Spencer songs, including "Hallelujah Morning" recorded by the Bishops. Wade's song "When I Cross That River," the title song of the album, went to number 20 on the charts, and it was recorded by the Singing Cookes. On that same album was a song entitled "It's so Peaceful" that Barb wrote, and the Cathedrals recorded it on one of their live albums.

One night, most of the family was asleep, and Barbara's brother Orville was driving the bus. JB was sitting up front talking with him. Hearing a noise, he began to smell smoke, and suddenly, there was screaming from one end of the bus to the other. Orville pulled the bus off the road, and they determined that a belt had burned, causing the smoke and the smell. The Lord had watched over them, but they still needed some time to allow everyone to calm down. Sitting there on the bus, they began to share story after story about what they thought was happening. Suddenly, Wade looked down and said, "Well, I'm sitting here in my underwear!" He then made a beeline to the back to get dressed. They all had a big laugh and never have let Wade live that one down.

In 1976, Geniece married Ernie Ingold, and in 1987, she left the group to raise her family. Ernie had sung in church with his sister Barb Ingold before getting married. When Holli, their oldest child, was thirteen, they sat down at the piano to see if they could get a trio going. They were surprised at how well their daughter could sing. So in 1991, Geniece returned to the road with her husband, and they are known as the Ingolds. The other two children, Heather and Jared, joined them, and sometimes the three children would sing trio. For years, when the kids were growing up, they traveled and sang, mostly in the neighboring states. They also sang in Alabama and Florida. Having been married thirty-two years, the Ingolds live in rural Shelby. By the way, have you ever heard of the Shelby bicycle? You guessed it! That's where they were made. The Ingold children are all married now. Holli sometimes sings at her church while Heather, and her husband, Merle Wentz, are now part of the Ingold group. Geniece says, "I'm so thankful for the life we've had because it showed our children how to have a heart for ministry, and they are all three serving God and married three wonderful Christians. I would like to think we have affected people in a positive way by sharing the Gospel."

In 1989, the Spencer's song "Coming Soon" (written by Gene and Val Johnson) went to number one for three months in America and for eight months in the Virgin Islands. Besides singing in the islands, they have sung from Maine to California and in Canada and Jamaica. In 1990, they filmed a sixty-minute live concert on the British Virgin Island of Tortola. This project took months of preparation along with the help of a large recording crew from Nashville, Tennessee. The Spencers returned several times over the next few years, singing on different islands. They would get up at daylight, and traveling by boat, they would work their way to a different island each day. Their song "Let's Meet by the River," written by Kevin and Barbara, not only went number one but also became Song of the Year for the *Singing News* in 1990. It was also 1990's most played gospel song in the United States. JB believes this is the biggest honor they ever received. Their third number one song was "It'll Be Worth it after All," written by Barb's cousin, Denver Lamb. Besides the three number one songs, God blessed them with many top 20 and top 40 hits over the years.

For many years, the Spencers were part of the Greenland Park Sing held annually in the mountains of Kingsport, Tennessee. Hosted by James Lane, there would be thousands of people in attendance as well as several well-known singing groups. They experienced some wonderful services there as the Lord would often come down and bless, and people were getting saved. Their greatest memory was once while singing the song "Coming Soon." People were shouting and having a wonderful time in the Lord. There were people coming up around the stage to pray, and people were even kneeling to pray out in the crowd and under the trees. That was in 1989, and people still talk about that service today.

While traveling in Kentucky in their second bus, a 4905, the engine blew. After having somebody pick them up and take them to their appointment, JB called a company in Columbus and talked to a salesman about a new MCI bus. JB told him he would take it, and the man said, "I'll have it ready for you tomorrow." So that night after the concert, borrowing a car from a cousin, JB and Wade left Kentucky, and driving through the night, they arrived home at seven the next morning. Taking a short nap and a shower, they then headed to Shelby to get a loan for the bus. After getting the loan, they drove to Columbus and picked up the bus. The Spencers were singing in Ironton at Calvin Evans's annual camp meeting that night, so Barb's cousin brought her and the equipment to the venue. By the time JB and Wade arrived, it was getting dark and was almost time for the service. When the service was over, having made no arrangements for the night, they simply put some foam mattresses on the floor of the bus, and that's where they slept. The bus had no furniture or partitions, so they hung up sheets to create temporary rooms. Good thing it was a family group!

A short while later, a company in Georgia did a beautiful job customizing the interior of the bus.

From Kentucky, they traveled to North Carolina to do a service with a famous radio preacher, Maize Jackson. After the service, they started their long journey home, but before they even got out of the parking lot, they knew something was wrong with the bus. The fuel had gelled and was bogging down the engine. They called a man to come and fix the problem, and after working on the bus all night, he still couldn't get the engine to prime. As a last resort, he finally ran a hose from the gas tank, which is in the front, to the engine at the rear of the bus with a hose hanging along the outside of the bus from one end to the other. God knows how to keep us humble. When they got back to Columbus, they drained all the fuel out and finally got the engine primed and running properly (without the hose).

In 1992, Kevin left to form his own group. His group has been traveling full-time since 1993 touring across America as well as several foreign countries. For years, he hosted the Winter Fest in the Renaissance Theater in Mansfield, bringing in many major groups. Kevin has written several popular songs including the one he cowrote with his mom "Let's Meet by the River." Kevin Spencer and Friends just released a brand new CD project entitled *Remembering Rusty* with that song, plus a collection of Rusty Goodman classics like "Who Am I?", "I Wouldn't Take Nothing for My Journey Now," and "Leaving on my Mind." He also owns a music publishing company known as "Some Dawning Music, BMI." Kevin has appeared on different Gaither videos, and those of you familiar with those videos might remember Kevin singing "I Heard About a Stone." Living in Ashland with his family, Kevin continues an active ministry.

One night as they were driving through Alabama on I-65, Kevin woke up around 2:30 AM and had no idea where they were. He had been sleeping for a while, but something told him to get up. Working his way to the front of the bus in the dark, he very softly spoke to the driver, Ken Hilty, so he wouldn't frighten him out of the seat. A few seconds later, Kevin yelled, "Ken, watch out! There is a semi in the road blocking both lanes." Ken quickly hit the brakes, slowing the vehicle down, and using the median, they safely drove around the semi. Kevin firmly believes it was our Lord that woke him up.

After Kevin's departure from the Spencers, JB, Barbara, and Wade stayed together until 1998 when JB and Barbara decided they needed to slow down. Instead of doing 180 dates a year, they are now doing an average of 50, and from time to time, they do family reunions.

After his parents retired, Wade continued on with the Amish Country Jubilee for a few years. Wade has written a few songs including one he cowrote with his sister Geniece called "Joseph's Story." Wade and his family live in Perrysville, and he currently sings about 160 dates as a soloist. His wife, Theresa, now travels with him as he tours across America and the Bahamas. He also takes mission trips to Uganda and Kenya, Africa, and to the Ukraine where he sings in prisons, schools, and orphanages. He has reached many people for Christ and has a real heart for the less fortunate. Speaking of traveling, Wade says, "I still have a lot of the old friends I enjoy singing for and staying with while on the road."

Since JB and Barbara retired, they now lead a much more relaxed life singing from time to time and spending more time in their home church. Barbara enjoys homemaking and loves cooking for company and is an avid reader. JB is a news hound, and he loves hunting, especially turkey hunting, and he even went hog hunting once while down in Alabama. He tells people he has insomnia and that he sleeps all right at night and in the mornings but is restless in the afternoons! This couple is to be commended for their fifty-two years of marriage. They have ten grandchildren and three great-grandchildren. If you were to talk with the Spencers today, they would be quick to tell you the Lord has blessed them far beyond their expectations and are very thankful for all the years they have spent singing the Gospel and that nothing is more satisfying than to sing under God's anointing and knowing you have helped others through your song or testimony.

Leaving Mansfield, we take U.S. 30 west for about nine miles looking for the Lincoln Highway. Unable to find the Lincoln Highway, we exit right onto SR-61 and take it to Crestline, the hub of Ohio. Early settlers in the village incorrectly believed that the town was the watershed of the state, where streams to the north emptied into Lake Erie and those to the south emptied into the Ohio River, thus the name Crestline. Just as the streams flow in different directions, so it was with the life of Tony Hall, founder of the gospel group known as the Hall Family.

The Lord spoke to Tony Hall one evening during a rock concert. From that time forward, his life was changed, and in 1989, the Hall Family started singing as a trio. Tony's wife, Beverly, possesses a strong Christian heritage, and their two daughters Laynia and Lyndsey are both talented singers and aspiring musicians. Some time later, Rick Romans and his family also joined the group. Rick was drafted by the Kansas City Royals and pitched for three years. In addition to his singing ministry, he is currently a scout for the Atlanta Braves.

Returning Home

Leaving Crestline, we take U.S. 30 east to SR-314 where we head south back to U.S. 42. Reaching U.S. 42, we continue south, passing through a number of small towns, until we reach Plain City. At Plain City, we stop for an enjoyable dinner at Der Dutchman Restaurant. Having eaten more then we should have, we get back on the road, and following U.S. 42 south, we soon reach IR-70 and travel west in the dark for about fifty miles to IR-75. Taking IR-75 north to Vandalia, we end Tour 5.

BURTON SINGERS

MASTER SOUNDS

Blake Powell with JOURNEYMEN

CHALLENGERS

GRACE HARBOR

FIVE STAR HARMONIZERS

Elliott McCoy with PREMIERS

Elliott McCoy with
THREE BRIDGES

* Bill Gaither & Ben Speer

* Bill Gaither with
GAITHER VOCAL BAND

Charlie Hodge

Charlie Hodge with
FOGGY RIVER BOYS

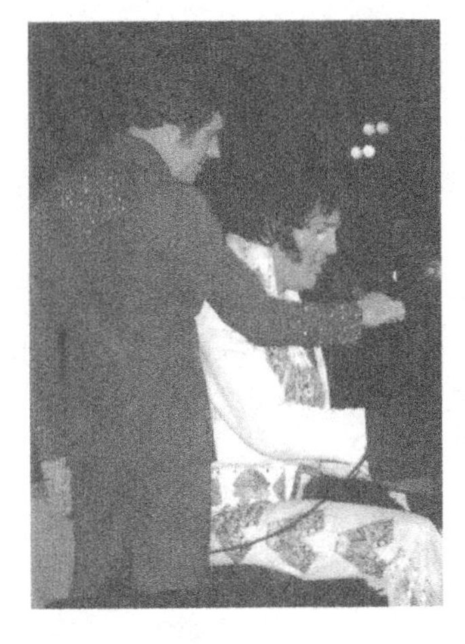

Charlie Hodge with Elvis Pressley   Lanny Wolfe & Sandi Patty

SIDE BY SIDE

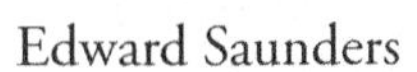

Edward Saunders

COPENHAVERS

PAYNES

PAYNES

Sherri Farmer

FOGGY RIVER BOYS

FOGGY RIVER BOYS & Dr. Cecil Simmons

David Young

David Young with the Couriers

Loren Harris

* Loren Harris with PERRYS

WOMACK BROTHERS

FRIENDLY BROTHERS

Bill Spivery

SHIELDS BROTHERS

PATHWAYS

* FREEMANS

FREEMANS

* Daryl Freeman

Chris Freeman with HINSONS

* Misty Freeman

ONE LESS STONE

FISK JUBILEE SINGERS

COLONIAL CITY

SPENCERS

JD & Barbara Spencer

Wade & Theresa Spencer
at 2002 NQC

KEVIN SPENCER & FRIENDS

HALL FAMILY

Chapter VI

Cincinnati Tour

He Loves Me

Why did He go to Calvary
Why was His life's blood shed for me
Why did He suffer as no man has ever done
There's just one reason, I am the one

When I'm sad, He loves me
Even when I'm bad, He loves me
When it seems no one cares for me
I talk to Jesus, He loves me

He loves me, He loves me
Jesus loves me
He loves me, He loves me
Jesus loves me

—George Amon Webster
(Used with Permission)

Leaving Vandalia on a cold cloudy morning, we take Dixie Drive north to National Road (U.S. 40) where we turn right. Then after making a quick stop at the post office and the BP to fill the gas tank, we continue east to IR-75 where we travel south driving through the famous "Malfunction Junction." As the traffic slows down we catch a view of the beautiful Art Institute off to the right where several groups have taken photos for album covers. Continuing south, we merge onto U.S. 35 eastbound, passing Cornerstone Baptist Church where many groups performed in the past. It is also the current the home church of the New Life Trio. Reaching Xenia, we take the U.S. 35 bypass headed to U.S. 68. As we travel through Xenia, we are reminded of the tragic tornados that had passed through this area. There were many losses, and Bob Walls who was with the Golden Tones lost his wife during one of these tornados. During one of the tornados, my wife witnessed a station wagon driving down the road with part of a tree sticking out of the window. While talking about the tornados, we drove past the U.S. 68 exit, forcing us to travel on to IR-71 taking it south through flat farmland back to U.S. 68. After a quick stop at McDonalds, we head south on U.S. 68, and soon driving past the site of the old ice cream shop, we arrive in Wilmington, where folks at Hazard's Drug Store created the first banana split in 1907. If we planned better, we might be pulling in during their annual festival celebrating the famous dessert. No banana splits for us. We'll stop instead at the local Perkins restaurant, a favorite of the group Eastern Sky.

Eastern Sky formed within the group's home church when group member Darren moved back to Ohio in 1995. They performed on Dayton's Access Television, and twice they won third place at the Smithville Tennessee Fiddlers Jamboree. When Eastern Sky sings, we see Howard Kelly, who has been playing for forty-five years and had previously played with the Blue Ridge Mountain Boys. Harlon White, who traveled and sang together with Francis Parker, is also there. Harlon was once asked to sing with Ricky Skaggs before Ricky became famous. Eastern Sky frequently stops at the Perkins restaurant in Xenia when traveling through the area. If we plan it right, we may even get there one of the times they set up their instruments outside in the parking lot and perform for the public after having a bite to eat at Perkins.

Leaving Wilmington, we turn left onto U.S. 22, and passing Wilmington College, we continue east to Sabina, known as the Eden of Ohio. Sabina is also the home of Eugene. On June 6, 1929, residents of Sabina discovered the body of a fifty-plus-year-old African American man. Officials believed that the man died of natural causes and named him Eugene after a person who lived nearest to a Cincinnati address found in the dead man's pocket. The Littleton Funeral Home embalmed the body and placed him in an outbuilding, where people could view the body, hoping someone would reveal the man's true identity. Between 1929 and 1963, more than 1.3 million people viewed the body. In 1963, the funeral home finally decided to bury Eugene in the Sabina Cemetery. When a person gets saved, sometimes—like Eugene—the world is unable to recognize them, in this case because they have become a new creation. Sharing this message with the communities throughout Ohio is a bluegrass group from Sabina called New Creations. The group was formed around 1995 with the original group members all coming out of the same church. They continue to maintain an active church and prison ministry often singing at the London Correctional Institute. New Creations also sings in some nursing homes and was privileged to sing for the 2000 Ohio Chautauqua on the campus of Wilmington College.

Leaving Sabina, we pass a unique little diner called Kim's Classic Diner, and we also pass the road we were supposed to turn on. Turning around, we travel back to SR-729 where turning left we head south and continue through flat farmland that brings back memories of living in Kansas. Shortly after turning left onto SR-72, a helicopter goes flying by so low that we can read the writing on its side. Reaching the town of Leesburg, we turn right onto SR-62 where we drive through the town of Samantha, passing a car delivering the daily mail and crossing Clear Creek we enter Hillsboro, home of the Dalton Gang.

Born in southern Ohio, Tom Dalton grew up in Lebanon and moved to Hillsboro with his family when he was sixteen years old. He grew up in the church, and his mother had purchased an album of the Looper Trio. She played that album over and over as Tom was growing up. One evening while Tom was attending church, Joe and Lily Isaacs came in and sat down on the back pew. Joe had married Lily and brought her back from New York City. Tom remembers, "Lily had something over her head, and then some time during the service, Lily knelt down on that back pew and gave her heart to the Lord." Soon they started attending Tom's home church.

Cheryl (Looper) Dalton is a native of middle Tennessee. Growing up in Tennessee, her family has always been in gospel music. Her father, Coleman Looper, was part of a group that was very popular in the 1960s and early 1970s called the Looper Trio. In fact, RCA tried to sign them, but her grandmother didn't want them to go to Nashville.

When Cheryl was fifteen, she started singing with her father in their family group, Coleman Looper and the Way Travelers. They were in full-time ministry travelling throughout the local states and were involved in a number of large concert events. They frequently worked with the Pathways of Sandusky, who later become known as the Freemans. They also played with the Singing Cookes and their very good personal friends the Isaacs.

One time, Coleman Looper was hosting an annual event on a Fourth of July weekend in Tennessee at the Overton County Fairgrounds. Joe and Lily Isaacs and the Sacred Bluegrass, as they were called at the time, came down for the event. They brought Tom Dalton with them and introduced him to Cheryl. Tom and Cheryl started dating, and in May 1980, they were married in Crossville, Tennessee. Denver Lamb was the best man, and Lily Isaacs sang in the wedding. Denver is Tom's first cousin, and the one who wrote that great song "It'll Be Worth It After All," which became a number one hit song for the Spencers.

Cheryl's brother who was singing baritone had gotten married and left the group. So after marrying Cheryl, Tom took her brother's part in the group, and they traveled as Coleman Looper and the Way Travelers for one year. Feeling the need to be a "normal" family, they came off the road and settled down in Tennessee. After only one year, they were going crazy, and it only took some singing in the living room, during a visit from Cheryl's brother Justin, to convince them they needed to be back on the road. Before long, they were being invited to sing in other churches, and soon became known as the Dalton Gang.

They remained in Tennessee for another year and then moved to Winchester, and around the same time, they made their live album at the McKamey's Homecoming. They lived in Winchester for four years. During this time, they went out to California and played on TBN with LaVerne Tripp, Rusty Goodman, and Walt Mills and had a wonderful time. While in California, they sang at Dr. Stewart McBernie's church that seats ten thousand people. They returned from California to discover their answering machine had taken so many calls it had broken. They were able to play the messages back, but that was the end of that answering machine. Even a machine can only take so much.

Once they received a call from the chamber of commerce in Meade, Kansas. Meade was the town where the notorious Dalton Gang, the real bad guys, had their hideout. The town holds a big event each year and typically brings in several big country artists, but they had been contacted by many of the local churches requesting the Dalton Gang partake in the event. Their portion of the event was held in a football stadium, and it was absolutely full. It was a wonderful trip, and many of the local churches supported the event.

They continued as the Dalton Gang until Tom developed some health issues, causing them to come off the road in 1988. He was then offered a job in Nashville, Tennessee, running a gospel publication on Music Row for the parent company Multimedia. They had a magazine called *Music City News*, which took care of the country music world and had started a southern gospel music magazine called the *Gospel Voice*. They asked Tom to come down and run this new magazine for them. Believing the Lord was in this change, they quickly moved to Nashville, and Tom took the job. In 1991, he started a business called Brentwood Talent and Marketing, working with the Crabb Family, the Melody Boys, and others. He also worked in promotions for Farrell Records when they switched over to southern gospel.

In 2001, Tom came home and said, "Cheryl, we are going to have to start traveling again. The Lord is really dealing with my heart, and we've got to do our music ministry again."

His health was pretty much in check at that point, so the Dalton Gang went back on the road again full-time. The gang is now a trio comprised of Tom, Cheryl, and their daughter, Troye, who was born in Nashville, Tennessee. She says, "Home to me is the bus. It seems I've spent most of my life on the road."

During their ministry, they have sung at Dollywood, Renfro Valley, Kentucky Apple Festival, and on December 23, 2005, they sang at the White House in Washington DC during the Pageant of Peace.

Because Tom's father has passed away and his mother is in her eighties, they now split their residence between Nashville and Ohio. They are based in Ohio during the summer months and travel south for the winter months. During the 2007 NQC, they did the Round Table with Solid Gospel on Friday, and then they did a showcase on Saturday morning.

"God has entrusted us with the awesome task of telling people of His saving grace, and we want to do our best," Tom says.

Leaving Hillsboro, we follow U.S. 62 through town, passing the historic Belle Opera House. Heading south, we travel through some hill country and pass through New Market. Arriving at Fincastle, we watch as a farmer works to resolve the mess created by the dumping of a hay wagon carrying rolls of hay. Continuing along U.S. 62, we pass through Macon and Ash Ridge where you can buy a bale of hay for six dollars. After passing through Russellville and Red Oak, we come to U.S. 68 where we turn left and travel south to Ripley. Turning right, we cross Red Oak Creek and drive through the business district passing the old Hotel Bodmer. One of the more interesting sides to the history of gospel music lyrics is its double meaning. The African Americans often used song lyrics as a source of secret communication among the slaves to pass on messages regarding their plans to escape by such means as the Underground Railroad. For example, the song "Swing Low Sweet Chariot" refers to the town of Ripley, located at the top of a hill adjacent to the Ohio River. It was one of the stations along the Underground Railroad that welcomed runaway slaves and provided assistance on their journey to freedom.

Leaving Ripley, we take a scenic drive along Front Street located on the Ohio River where we had a delicious lunch at Coheart's Riverhouse founded in 1987. I had their famous zip burger with sweet potato fries and my wife had a catfish sandwich and corn nuggets. After lunch, we head back north on U.S. 68 (Simon Kenton Memorial Highway), and just north of Ripley, we pass the historic Red Oak Presbyterian Church, another station on the Underground Railroad. The church cemetery is the burial site of a more recent personality, Rosa Washington Riles, known for her portrayal as "Aunt Jemima" of Aunt Jemima Pancake Mix fame. We continue north about twenty-five miles, passing through Wahsburg and crossing Straight Creek to Mount Orab, an area that has yielded countless specimens of trilobites (fossils) as seen in museums around the world. In addition to countless fossils, Mount Orab was also home to the Big Gospel Singing Round-Up held each summer at the Brown County Fairgrounds back in the 1970s. The area has also produced several families who sang gospel music.

Ralph Green began singing as a youngster with a family group called the Green Brothers and Linda. When the family group was no longer together, Ralph continued to use his abilities for the Lord playing for the Segos, Smitty Gatlin, Bob Wills and the Inspirationals, and the Men of Music.

* * *

The North Family, consisting of three sisters (Karen, Sharon and Judy) and one brother (Winford), started singing in 1966 traveling throughout the United States and Canada.

The late 1970s brought big things for the group. In 1976, they were featured as special guest on one of Kash Amburgey's Holy Land tours. In 1979, they were nominated for a Dove Award; they won a singing contest in Goldsboro, North Carolina; they signed a contract with QCA Recording; they performed on the *Archie Campbell Show*; and they began a tour with the Dixie Melody Boys that continued into the next year.

Winford wrote the song "Peace of Mind" that was later recorded by the Perrys reaching number 28 on the *Singing News* chart. After the group had stopped singing in 1981, Winford sang with the Crownsmen for five years. In 1995 Karen, Sharon, and Judy came back together for a three year reunion stint. This was the beginning of a singing career for Ashley Foster, Karen's daughter.

Of special memory to Karen was the time they sang in a Catholic church in Quebec, Canada. Karen has been traveling solo since 1997. In 2001, she won the Ohio Gospel Music Association Female Vocalist of the Year at the Ohio State Fair. Sharon has also continued as a solo artist, and Winford currently sings with his wife and daughter. At times Sharon, Judy, and Elizabeth, Winford's daughter, sing together as the North Star Ministries.

Leaving Mount Orab, we head south, taking U.S. 68 to SR-125 where we turn right into Georgetown, the boyhood home of Ulysses S. Grant until 1839 when he entered West Point. The brick home, built by his father in 1824 still stands along with the school he attended. Gospel concerts have been held at the Gaslight Theatre. This town is also home of some dedicated young men—members of the group Soul'd Out.

Matt Rankin was saved when he was sixteen years old, and shortly after becoming a Christian, his youth director gave him Gold City's CD *Standing in the Gap*. Matt quickly fell in love with southern gospel music, particularly quartets, and it became his dream to sing in a quartet.

In June 2001, Matt tried out for the lead position with the Kingsmen Quartet from North Carolina. He traveled with them for one weekend, doing the lead part on some of the songs but didn't get the job. Matt turned this disappointment into an opportunity in July 2001 when he played a major roll in forming Soul'd Out.

One Sunday night, they were singing at a Nazarene church in Bethel. At the time, they were still singing trio, and it was the tenor's first weekend with the group. They had not yet fine-tuned their sound, but their hearts were in the right place, and they wanted to have a positive impact on the people. They saw real confirmation of their efforts as the Lord blessed the service and thirteen teenagers answered the altar call, giving their hearts to Jesus.

In May 2004, the group went on the road full-time as an all-male quartet with Matt Rankin singing a strong lead part and Matt Fouch, from Indiana, singing the bass. And if there weren't already enough Matts, Matt Clark, originally from California, now lives in Jamestown, Tennessee, and plays the piano for the group. A young man from Bethel named Brent Hopper provides the tenor part, and Joel Trimble covers the baritone, lending a smooth blend of harmony. Joel used to play the piano for a group called Young Harmony from Chattanooga, Tennessee.

The group has been nominated twice for Horizon Group of the Year. Matt Rankin has written several songs, and the Kingsmen have recorded a couple of his songs including "Jesus Knows My Name."

The Soul'd Out Quartet was in an accident on Wednesday, February 7, 2007. The group was headed home after singing at Bill Bailey's Winter Convention in Palmetto, Florida. They were only a few miles from Cincinnati when they lost control of their vehicle and ran into the concrete median on Interstate 75. The quartet praised the Lord that no members had to be hospitalized and that there weren't any other vehicles involved in the accident. As the group's van was totaled, it was necessary to look for a new one; but they were soon able to acquire a recreational vehicle.

They had another travel incident in July 2007 while driving through Arkansas. Matt Rankin was asleep in the back, and they stopped at a Wal-Mart. He woke up questioning why they had stopped, and the guys hollered back telling him, "We're going in to get food and some supplies."

After they had left the RV, Matt decided to go ahead and get dressed and also went in to get some food and look around. Matt was in the store for quite a while, and when he came out, the RV was gone. They had left without him because they thought he was still in the back sleeping. To make matters worse, he had left his cell phone on the RV. The group had been gone for twenty minutes before Matt was finally able to borrow someone's cell phone. Calling Brent's cell phone he said, "Hi, this is Matt."

"Matt who?" the tenor responded.

Losing his patience he said, "Matt, your road manager. You left me at Wal-Mart."

As soon as they realized Matt was not with them, the group turned around and went back to Wal-Mart.

Normally, two Wal-Mart visits in one day would be a shopper's dream. While in the store, Matt had bought ice cream bars, and it was 110 degrees that day. So he stood outside in that blazing heat watching his ice cream bars melt away. For Matt, it was a chilling experience to say the least.

Witnessing nearly four hundred decisions for Christ within the short-term of their ministry, the group's focus is clear. Concerning the future Matt says, "We are just going to keep doing what we are doing. I would love to write a number one song but, if that doesn't happen, God has allowed us to make a living ministering and fulfilling the call that He has place on our lives. And I am just excited doing what I love to do." I'm certain from the response of the crowd while this group performed on main stage at the 2008 NQC, we will be hearing more from this group.

Leaving Georgetown, we travel northwest along SR-125, passing through Yankeetown and Bethel where we stop for fuel across the road from an old 5-10 Ben Franklin Store. Continuing west, we pass through Bantam and arrive at Amelia, named in the 1830s for the wife of the toll-booth keeper. The town became famous for its abundance of gladiolas and was one of the world's largest suppliers of goldfish. In addition to the fish and flowers, Amelia has also provided a couple of fine "Jims" to southern gospel music.

For many years and in several capacities, Jim Boggs has blessed countless numbers of people from coast to coast, whether singing an old hymn or a new release. In 1962, Jim started a duet ministry with his wife. Before singing with his wife, Jim had the opportunity to play the upright bass for the Happy Goodmans. Since the passing of his wife, Jim has continued the ministry as a soloist. Based on a recommendation by another group during a radio interview, he is known today as "God's Southern Gentleman."

* * *

Jimmy Dooley began singing in his grandfather's church at age five. At age fourteen, Jimmy accepted the call to preach. Just three years later, he felt the call to go into a special music ministry. Just seventeen and ready to start his music career, Jimmy fell seriously ill. He was hospitalized as his condition continued to worsen until doctors gave him just months to live. Refusing to give up hope, and through many prayers from God's saints, Jimmy was healed and has been sharing his testimony ever since.

Jimmy later formed a southern gospel trio, but after only a few years, he left the group to develop a solo ministry. In 2002, Jimmy married his longtime fiancée, April, who has been a tremendous asset to his ministry. He also opened a recording studio called the "Cross Connection Studio." Jimmy has written a number of songs that have been recorded by such artists as the Gallaways, Palmetto State Quartet, the Beene Family and Ivan Parker. Since starting his music career, making a difference has been the focal point of his ministry. But first and foremost, his goal is to see the lost accept Jesus Christ as their personal Savior.

Leaving Amelia, we turn right onto Church Street to Chapel Road. As there is no road sign, we pass Chapel and have to turn around. Turning left onto Chapel Road, we take it to SR-132. Turning left onto SR-132, we travel north along a winding road to Batavia. In 2000, Mohamed Atta purchased flight deck videos for Boeing 747-200 and Boeing 757-200 models from Sporty's Pilot Shop—forever linking Batavia to the terrorist attacks of September 11, 2001.

In 1991 something much better took place in Batavia when the group Trinity started as a duet, and in 1997, they became a trio. Prior to joining Trinity, Todd sang with the Pfiefers of Washington Court House for almost four years.

Leaving Batavia, we continue north on SR-132 to SR-32 west where we turn left on Old SR-74 and drive through Mount Carmel, home of the Woodruff Family. Barry Woodruff and his brother Steve grew up singing as part of the Woodruff Family. Barry was so young when he started singing that for him to be seen they had to put him on a chair. In 1981, they organized the Sonmen trio, and six months later, they grew to a quartet when bass singer Gordon Steger joined. Prior to joining the group, Gordon was popular among barbershop quartet enthusiasts.

In 1985, the Sonmen won the NQC talent contest, and though the group signed a long-term recording agreement with Bill Dykes and Eagle One Records, they committed to remain local. Jeff Perkins, the group's piano player and baritone, later became director of Advertising and Promotions for Eagle One. The group disbanded around 1987, and Barry, Steve, and Gordon formed a group called Sonsation for a two-year stint.

Continuing west along SR 32, we pass through Newton turning right onto Round Bottom Road. We then turn left onto Valley Avenue, right onto Church Street and left onto Wooster Pike where we pass through the Swiss-modeled village of Mariemont. From Mariemont, we travel west to IR-71 where we turn south. We exit onto SR-562 and drive to Norwood, nicknamed Little Kentucky because of the large number of Kentuckians who migrated to the city in the middle of the twentieth century. In 1938, Cal Lindner and his son opened the first United Dairy Farmers store, in Norwood. Their chocolate ice cream was voted the best in the area in 2005 by the *Cincinnati Enquirer*. Migrating north, those Kentuckians had to cross a huge bridge to reach Ohio, so it seems rather fitting that the group who hails from Norwood would be called the Bridges.

The Bridges formed in 1960, initially as a trio, and later became a quartet. Before becoming a quartet, the trio won first place at the Southwest Indiana Singing Convention. The group traveled throughout eleven states doing a large number of concerts in Georgia. They sang at the Williamsburg Courthouse Square in Kentucky and also had regular radio broadcast performances from Middletown.

While traveling to Virginia to sing at a local church, they discovered a hole in the bus radiator. The assistant pastor of the church agreed to work on the bus while they sang, and during the service, his daughter gave her heart to the Lord. The group felt sorry that he was unable to be present for this special occasion.

Once while they were singing at the Armory in Barbourville, Kentucky, for a crowd of about a thousand people, a woman in a wheelchair came forward and got saved. This was a true blessing for the group.

The original trio remained together throughout the thirty-one years spanned by their ministry. They all continue to minister in their home churches.

Leaving Norwood, we travel south along U.S. 22 passing a unique castlelike building occupied by WCPO, Channel 9 TV. As we enter Cincinnati, we are welcomed by the beautiful ringing of the church bells. Traveling through this busy town, we view many tall buildings and historic sites including the home of the famous Cincinnati Reds baseball team, the first professional baseball team and one of the original eight members of the National League. Cincinnati was nicknamed Porkopolis around 1835 when it was the country's chief hog-packing center and herds of pigs traveled the streets. Since then, the city has been known by more dignified names including the Queen City and the City of Seven Hills.

Perhaps it was the scenery inspiring this last nickname that also inspired Thomas Dorsey. While traveling by train from Indiana on his way to Cincinnati, and seeing the peacefulness of the countryside, Thomas wrote the words to the beautiful song "Peace In The Valley."

* * *

The Brown's Ferry Four formed at AM radio station 700 WLW in Cincinnati in June 1943 when a group called the Drifting Pioneers left the station. Alton Delmore recruited his brother Rabon, Grandpa Jones, and Merle Travis to form this quartet. While shopping for black gospel records at a record store in Cincinnati, they met Syd Nathan, one of the most important contacts in their history. Over the following three years, Brown's Ferry Four became one of the top country gospel groups in the nation.

Within six months of their first performance, three of the four members departed for military service. Travis joined the marines, Alton Delmore went into the navy, and Jones joined the army. The radio station owned the name and kept the Brown's Ferry Four alive by recruiting other members throughout the duration of the war. After the war, Syd Nathan, who had founded King Records in 1943, orchestrated the reunion of the original members of the Brown's Ferry Four. In 1946, Nathan produced a number of recordings by the Brown's Ferry Four including several classic numbers such as "Everybody Will Be Happy (Over There)" and several originals by Alton Delmore. These recordings soon became some of the most heartwarming gospel music ever recorded.

The group continued on the air for years singing many songs written by Albert E. Brumley. The group's repertoire consisted almost exclusively of gospel music. They learned the basics of shaped-note singing, but in order to add some range and diversity to their programs, they added black gospel numbers (known at the time as Negro spirituals). A broadcast version of the Brown's Ferry Four continued to appear regularly on WLW, but their next recording session didn't take place until 1951.

The Delmore brothers, Jones, and Red Turner assembled for the group's final recording session in August 1952. The Brown's Ferry Four disbanded following the death of Rabon Delmore in late 1952. Although the group made very few personal appearances, they managed to become one of the most beloved country gospel groups through their radio broadcasts and the promotional work of King Records.

Grandpa Jones, remembering the Brown's Ferry Four's style, helped form the Hee Haw Gospel Quartet, an offshoot of the television show *Hee Haw*.

* * *

Keith Waggoner was born and raised in Indiana. He moved to Cincinnati in 1995 to attend God's Bible College. During his time there, he traveled with a college quartet named Assurance. Keith remained in Cincinnati after he graduated, serving as minister of music for the Immanuel Church of the Nazarene in Highland Heights, Kentucky, just across the Ohio River. He also sang part-time with Allegiance, a Cincinnati area trio. Keith left Cincinnati in 2004 when he answered a call to serve at Grace Baptist Church in Nampa, Idaho.

In 2006, Liberty Quartet offered Keith a position singing tenor. Realizing God was giving him the desire of his heart, he accepted the position and now travels full-time with Liberty. They travel over fifty thousand miles annually ministering from churches to prisons as the Lord directs. They also sing in several large conventions including the Great Western Quartet Convention and the Gospel Music Fan Festival in Canada.

* * *

Charles Fold was born in Atlanta, Georgia, on June 4, 1942. His family moved to Cincinnati when he was four, and in just a few years, Charles began playing piano in his local church. A classmate of the Isley Brothers, young Fold was influenced by their musical abilities. While attending college in Detroit, he met the gospel legend James Cleveland and began playing piano for the Meditation Singers. After returning to Cincinnati, he formed a group called the Messengers, and they became quite popular in local churches. In 1970, Fold left the group, desiring to return to the music of his home church. When several other members decided to leave, Fold's plans were changed, and the Charles Fold Singers were created in 1971.

Acclaimed as one of Cincinnati's finest voices, the group was invited to sing backup for James Cleveland. They continued to work closely with James Cleveland, making several recordings. The group recorded the song "Never Will I Turn Back," one of its greatest hits, for Savoy Records. The Charles Fold Singers have received four Grammy nominations and have performed with the Cincinnati Symphony Orchestra.

Charles Fold became music director at the Lincoln Heights Missionary Baptist Church in Cincinnati and later became board member of the Gospel Music Workshop of America. Fold once told the *Cincinnati Enquirer*, "Music can make you cry. It can make you laugh."

* * *

Alan Wayne Godsey was born in Cincinnati on July 8, 1952. He starting singing with the Upchurch Family at age four and remained with them until he was sixteen. Moving to Fort Wayne, Indiana, he started singing and playing bass with the Singing Jubilees at age 19. On December 18, 1971 he married a young girl from Marion, Indiana named Cathy Wallace who also started singing and playing with the Singing Jubilees. At age 36 Alan left the Singing Jubilees and started singing tenor for the Northmen, a quartet from Fort Wayne, Indiana. He continued to sing tenor until his son Scott joined the group. At which time he started singing the lead part.

Alan has hosted the Northern Gospel Singing Convention for ten years and also hosts the Northernfest. Maintaining a close relationship with Buddy Liles, the Northmen have often opened for the Florida Boys. Alan was healed of cancer in 1996 and in 2007 he received the Eddie Crook Leadership award for his outstanding leadership ability and his promotional achievements. Having performed in over thirty states and four foreign countries, the Northmen are still going strong in 2008.

* * *

Glen Steely was born on June 18, 1944 in Williamsburg, Kentucky. He sang in choirs in high school and college. Glen and his family would often attend the Mull Singing Convention held at the Civic Auditorium in Knoxville, Tennessee, and sometimes at the Bill Meier Baseball Stadium. He also listened to the Blackwood Brothers and the Statesmen on the radio and really enjoyed the sound of that male harmony. Glen was a teacher for thirty-one years in the West Clermont school system beginning in 1964 with his first fifth grade classroom. Despite this incredible teaching career, Glen managed to find a little time to sing.

His first group was a mixed group called the Gospel Four from the hills of Kentucky. Glen attended an old-time singing school at a church where he learned to read shaped notes and sang a couple of times on a radio station with some of the people from the school. When the station invited the group from the school, they were a trio in need of a bass, so Glen was invited to join them for that appearance.

Steely traveled with a group called the Kentucky Wonders of Williamsburg, Kentucky, for several weekends while their regular bass was unable to perform with the group. He also started singing with the Nationals Quartet, a little group that was trying to get off the ground in Cincinnati. The group was unable to make it and soon disbanded.

He sang with a group called the Vibrants for about one year. In April 1968, the Crownsmen Quartet was organized with Emmitt Spears singing tenor, Art Sears singing lead, Doug Sharp signing baritone, and Glen Steely singing bass. Playing piano for the group was Bill Hettinger. When the group started, they had to borrow money to purchase their first suits and to get a sound system.

The first weekend the Crownsmen was on the road, they were forced to deal with some real difficulties. They needed several cars to haul all of the equipment, and while on their way back to the Cincinnati area, Emmitt Spears's brand-new Buick LeSabre overheated. To get the car home, they had to make numerous stops along the way, and the frequent overheats resulted in a cracked engine block. During one of those stops, Art's car also overheated. While Doug was attempting to loosen the radiator cap on Art's car, the hot fluid came gushing out, hitting him in the face and requiring medical attention. Needless to say, better travel arrangements had become a necessity.

In December 1968, they purchased their first bus, a 1948 Flexible four-cylinder diesel. They remodeled the interior and used that bus for four years until they bought a 1948 GM 3751 Silverside bus from Spartanburg, South Carolina's, Blue Ridge Quartet.

The Crownsmen traveled throughout the Midwest states singing with some of the nation's finest groups. Taking an annual vacation to Florida together, the group would sing at churches along the way and various places in Florida.

One year, they were singing on a Dayton area program that featured Rusty Goodman. Rusty had just begun his solo career at that time. Charlie Feltner was singing lead for the group, and Charlie and Rusty were friends. While doing a sound check, Rusty was backstage and heard them sing. He invited them to his van where Rusty asked them to back him up on one of his songs. They agreed, and after two or three solos, Rusty called them out. They performed the song, and the crowd responded so well that Rusty asked them to stay. For the next twenty minutes, he sang old Goodman songs with the Crownsmen as backup. Recalling the performance, Glen said, "That was kind of a neat experience."

Charles Feltner was with the group for two and a half years until heart problems forced him to leave.

Jamie Ragle sang tenor with the Crownsmen for a while. He went on to sing with the Dixie Melody Boys. Today, Jamie is a full-time evangelist. Ken Ankney also sang tenor for a brief period. Ken sang with several more groups and is presently singing with his son Bradley in a group called the SonShip Quartet. Bill Dykes sang with the Crownsmen a short time. Bill sang with several other groups including the Rhythm Masters, the Cathedrals, and Jerry and the Singing Goffs.

Gary Throckmorton sang first tenor for a while. Gary wrote a song called "Let Your Fingers do the Walking through the White Pages" that got some chart play but never made it into the top 50. One Saturday night, they were preparing to sing on WAKW, a Christian radio station in Cincinnati. They were using the station's microphones, which were downstairs in an auditorium. Dr. Sam Deets, program host, was upstairs in the control room. Cutting to a commercial, he called down on the microphone and said, "Okay, guys, get a song ready. We'll be going to prayer time pretty soon. But after this promo, we will go straight into your song."

They had determined to sing Gary's song "Let Your Fingers do the Walking."

Making final preparations, with microphones in hand, they patiently await the signal. Suddenly, Dr. Deets called back and said, "Fellas, a man just called in requesting prayer as he was injured today in an industrial accident. So let's send this next song out for him."

Then he said, "He almost had three fingers severed in this accident."

It was probably not the best time for "Let Your Fingers do the Walking." They avoided an awkward moment with some quick thinking as they picked a different song to perform on that radio show.

Ronnie Jones played steel and lead guitar for the group until leaving them to join the LeFevres. Through the years, the group had a number of piano players. Bill Neal who had played piano for several groups was with the group a short time. Then while still in high school, Debbie McQueen played piano for the group. She later played for the Weatherfords, and now she and her husband travel full-time as Forgiven.

When Jason Webb was at the music conservatory in Cincinnati, he spent his free weekends traveling with the Crownsmen and playing the piano. And when he wasn't there, Scott Kelly would play.

Gary Bailey worked at Artist Recording when he was traveling with the group. A young man who was going to go into full-time ministry asked Gary to play piano for him, and soon Gary left his job, and they went to Florida to hold a revival. Arriving the day before the revival, they were on their way to where they would be staying. As it was not far, they decided to spend some time at the beach. While crossing the road, Gary was hit by a drunk driver and killed instantly. His parents were contacted to inform them of what had happened. Within thirty minutes of hearing this news, Gary's mother died of a heart attack. A double funeral was held where fellow Crownsmen, Doug Sharp and Glen Steely served as pallbearers.

Deciding they wanted to get their itinerary out to different areas, they started writing a little paper. It had their upcoming performances on the back and usually some recipes inside. Glen started providing information about where they had been over the last several dates, and the paper was named *Glen's Gleanings*.

For twenty years, they sang during the Easter service at a Nazarene church in Richmond, Indiana. One Sunday, they had left Richmond and where traveling through Liberty, Indiana, on their way home. Glen was driving the bus and talking, reminiscing with Doug Sharp. All of a sudden, Scott Rawlings, grandson of Dr. John Rawlings, who was singing lead for the group at the time, started laughing. Glen questioned, "Scott, what's so funny?"

"Do you realize that you and Doug have been talking ever since we left the parking lot of that church back there, and neither one of you have finished a sentence yet?"

By 1995, things were slowing down, and Doug was already singing with a group called Forgiven on Sundays when the Crownsmen were not singing. So in 1995, after doing a weekend performance in St. Louis, Missouri, the Crownsmen came to an end. As Glen and Doug owned the group, they simply divided everything, releasing the other group members to go their separate ways. Glen did not sing in another group until 2001 because of problems with blood clotting in his legs.

Then in 2001, receiving a call from the Ball Family, he told them he couldn't travel as he had to keep his leg elevated to reduce the swelling caused by blood clots. Nelson Ball told him he could prop his leg up on the bus so he agreed to give it a try. Traveling with the Ball Family, Glen has traveled as far as a little town called "Nashville" on the edge of Texarkana, Arkansas.

About performing Glen said, "When singing, you have to take ownership of a song. You are not singing it because somebody else sang it, you are singing it because you want to get the message across, and so you have to take that song as yours. Vestal Goodman—never heard her sing a song that you didn't feel like it was her song. She just took it over and from then on, it was a Vestal song. And so I think that's the way it should be with any singer. If they are delivering the song, then they have to get into it and it has to be them, it has to be real. Otherwise they are just singing the song." While addressing the National Singers Association (NSA) Glen stated, "There is no purpose in gospel music without Jesus Christ."

* * *

Early in his gospel music career, Herbert Ball sang with the Cumberland River Boys of West Virginia. He filled in for the Swanee River Boys several times. In 1949, he put together the Dixieland Quartet based in Cincinnati singing with Charles Ball, James Shell, and Charles Thacker, all from Ohio. Charles taught for the Vaughn School of Music for a number of years.

The group had a program on WCPO and WKRC. The also sang on *The Bob Braun Show*, with Bob Braun, filling in for group members from time to time. After singing at Cadle Tabernacle with the Dixieland Quartet, they offered Herbert Ball an opportunity to go on the road singing as sponsor for the R. J. Reynolds Tobacco Company. This would have included an opportunity to sing on the *Arthur Godfrey Show*. They declined the offer stating that they didn't smoke and would not work for a company that promoted the use of tobacco. The group once sang at Renfro Valley, and the owner of Renfro Valley offered Herbert a full-time position with the Renfro Valley 76 Quartet, but he declined this offer also. Herbert passed away in 1981.

Herbert's son Nelson Ball was born in 1937, and in the late 1950s, following in his father's footsteps, he started the Good News Quartet. Two of the members, Phil Meabon and Ron Gunter were from Ohio. The group stayed together for about ten years.

Around 1965, Nelson joined the Portals Quartet from Cincinnati, and in 1968, he formed the Ball Family. The Ball Family has sung with many national groups on the Sonny Simmons program. They were in concert with Bill Gaither when he was still traveling part-time. They were privileged to perform in Branson, Missouri, on the Barbara Fairchild program. Their piano player, Carol Hill, taught at the Stamps-Blackwood School of Music for many years. The group continues today as a family group made up of Peggy (Ball) Arnold, Nelson Ball and his wife, Sarina Ball. Replacing Herbert on the bass part is the well-known singer Glen Steely, previously of the Crownsmen Quartet.

* * *

In 1939, at the age of twenty, Ernest Jennings "Ernie" Ford studied voice at the Cincinnati Conservatory of Music. In 1956, among his many accomplishments, he recorded an album entitled *Hymns* that remained on the weekly *Billboard Magazine Album Charts* for over five years. It became the first record of Christian songs to achieve "gold record" status. Ford was inducted into the Gospel Music Hall of Fame in 1994.

* * *

In 1961, Jesse Willingham organized the Golden Aires, one of Cincinnati's oldest gospel groups. The group started out with King Records and, in 1970, signed a national recording contract. Continuing to grow, the group had several hits during the 1980s, including "Peace in the Valley." Then in the 1990s, Charles O. Collier became the new manager for the group, and with his talent and songwriting experience, the group has continued to reach new heights.

* * *

Cloid Baker was born in 1947 in Huntington, Indiana. His parents were typical farmers of that time. He started singing with his folks when he was almost four years old doing revival meetings the like. At age fifteen, he began singing with a group of full-time evangelists from his home church, traveling with them during the summer when not in school. After high school, Cloid traveled with a group from Vincennes, Indiana, called the Masters Quartet. He later sang with Randall Clay in a Dayton group called the Camp Meeting Singers.

During his youth, he had developed a friendship with a group from Alexandria, Indiana, called the Bill Gaither Trio. In 1969, while Cloid was with the Camp Meeting Singers, they performed a concert in Muncie, Indiana, with the Bill Gaither Trio. Cloid was talking with Danny Gaither, telling him that the Camp Meeting Singers were losing their piano player because Ralph Seibel had just taken a job with the Klaudt Indian Family. During this conversation, Danny told Cloid that they had just purchased their first bus and were looking for someone to play bass and help Danny drive the bus. Danny asked if he had any interest in the position. Cloid was interviewed by Bill and hired to be bass player for the Gaither Trio. He traveled with them until 1975.

Cloid was with the Gaithers when they were writing some of their most beloved songs like "Because He Lives." He remembers being thrilled at the crowd's spontaneous reaction as Danny would sing "Something about That Name," and when they would do "The King Is Coming," people just stood to their feet before the song was even over.

While living at home, he also became friends with a gospel group—one of his dad's favorites—called the Weatherford Quartet. Sometime in the early 1970s, while doing a Gaither/Weatherford concert in Wilmington, Delaware, he met a young girl named Debbie who was singing with Earl and Lily Weatherford.

"That's where she fell madly in love with me—that's my story, and I'm sticking to it," Cloid says.

It's not certain who fell first, but it wasn't long before a wedding was held at the home of Bill and Gloria Gaither in their beautiful flower garden to unite this love-struck couple.

Prior to playing for the Weatherfords, Debbie accepted her first musical position playing for Doug Sharp and the Crownsmen Quartet. While playing for the Crownsmen, they appeared in a concert with the Weatherfords. As a result, Earl offered her the job, and wanting to travel-full time, she started traveling with them. In 1972, after getting married, Debbie left the Weatherfords and moved to her new husband's hometown in Fairmount, Indiana. When the Gaithers stopped doing Sunday dates, Cloid and his new wife Debbie, and Cloid's father, Ray, would go out singing as the Baker Trio, which was a forerunner of the group Forgiven.

In 1976, while vacationing at Disney World in Orlando, Florida, they learned the Weatherfords were in need of some help. At that time, Cloid's mother had become quite ill, and it was no longer possible for Cloid's father to continue traveling. So they were hired to sing with the Weatherfords—Debbie for the second time and Cloid for the first.

When Cloid and Debbie were traveling with the Weatherfords, Earl and Lily lived out in the middle of Oklahoma. In those days, especially out west, there weren't as many sanitary regulations as there are today. On the way home from one road trip, they took their hometown exit and stopped along the ramp, as was customary, to dump the waste tank from the bus toilet. It was late at night, so Cloid checked the mirrors to make certain no other vehicles had pulled in behind them. Then Earl called up and asked, "Is it okay, Clodhopper?" (He always called him "Clodhopper.")

Checking in the mirrors again, Cloid said, "Let her go, Earl."

Then moving along at a slow pace, they began to dump their waste. About the same time Earl had pulled the plug, Cloid spotted headlights behind the bus. The car was pulling off to the side and had turned on its windshield wipers. It wasn't far down the road to Earl's driveway, and when they turned the corner, the car followed them. Cloid began to panic thinking, *This guy is really mad.* The car continued to follow them, and when they pulled into Earl's driveway, the car pulled into the neighbor's driveway and stopped. Then recognizing the car, they breathed a sigh of relief. That is until reality set in, and they realized that the car they had just covered with waste belonged to their neighbor. The neighbor was very understanding and handled this matter nicely. But you can probably guess who washed the car.

While traveling with the Weatherfords, the Bakers had only one child, a daughter who was three years old. When Debbie became pregnant with their second child, they realized it would be difficult traveling full-time on a bus with two young children and made the decision to stop touring. Earl and Lily were very understanding. So having the house in Fairmount, the Bakers went home, but they were not sure what they were going to do to make ends meet.

Arriving home they pulled in the driveway and walked into the house, and the phone rang. It was Danny Gaither, and he began to share that he had made the decision to leave the Gaither Trio and start his own ministry. He wanted to know if they were interested in singing with him on the weekends. As it was just going to be weekends they accepted the offer, but of course, they were soon traveling full time again. They continued with Danny for a number of years until their daughter was old enough to start school. Believing they should not try to raise the kids on the road, they once again pulled out of touring and started working in the church. During their work at the church, they always maintained some type of group that would occasionally go out and sing when their schedule would allow.

In 1985, they moved from Fairmount, Indiana, down to the Cincinnati area. They actually live in Bright, Indiana, which is just across the state line from the Cincinnati area. Cloid says, "I have always liked this area, it's kind of different from where I grew up in the flat farm land, we actually live in the little foot hills at the edge of Indiana, and it's quite nice, a beautiful place to live."

Shortly after moving to Bright, Indiana, Cloid was working at Friendship Baptist Church in Cincinnati, Doug Sharp started coming over to Friendship when he was not singing with the Crownsmen, and they would sing together, rekindling a friendship of nearly twenty years ago. Soon they started picking up dates, and people were requesting them to sing for various church functions. When after twenty-eight years, the Crownsmen finally stopped singing, Doug continued singing with the Bakers. That was how the Cincinnati group Forgiven was started with Doug Sharp singing baritone, Cloid singing lead, and Debbie singing the alto part. They were soon keeping a busy schedule, and as Doug was older than the rest of the group, he finally decided to retire. Cloid and Debbie decided that the timing was right for Forgiven to be a full-time ministry, so Cloid left his position at the church, and they began accepting dates all over the country, year round.

They had picked up a young man named Brian Worley who lived in Kentucky, but because of family obligations, he only remained with them for one year. Brian now sings with a group called the Worley Brothers, and the two groups maintain a close friendship.

Once, while Forgiven was singing at a country church in Alabama, someone requested Brian sing "Oh What a Savior." He had never sung the song with Forgiven but was willing to try. Not knowing in what key they should sing the song, they left that matter to the church pianist. That was a mistake. Realizing the song was pitched three or four steps too high, Cloid jumped in at the high part singing the lead part an octave lower. Before singing the second verse, they requested the pianist to lower the key, thinking he would know how much to lower the song. They were wrong! It was still a couple keys too high, and Brian almost passed out, his face turning very red, before they finished the song. The crowd was gracious providing a standing ovation and an invitation to return.

When Brian left the group, they hired a talented singer named Tank Tackett. Tank was singing with the Weatherfords when Cloid and Debbie first met. After Tank joined Forgiven, they maintained a heavy schedule, spending a lot of time traveling back and forth to Florida. Tank had diabetes, and after traveling with them for a little over a year, his condition worsened. The doctor finally told him his health condition was getting far too serious, and it was going to kill him if he didn't stop the rigid tour schedule. It was hard for Tank to part with the group, but he knew it was necessary so he left the group. Tank later went on to sing with Jerry Goff and the Singing Goffs, and even later in his career, he sang tenor with Hovie Lister and the Statesmen.

Tank was replaced by a young man named Jes Adam. As churches began moving to contemporary music, Forgiven made a decision that they would always sing a few old hymns during their programs. Not shy about his feelings toward this movement, Cloid says, "Some people may think it doesn't matter, but I think we are foolish as a church body, and I'm talking now of the whole body of Christ, not just one church, to discard those inspired treasures written by some of the greatest songwriters of the past."

* * *

Willie Crawford was born on August 13, 1930 in Columbia, South Carolina. In 1958, Willie started singing with the Gospel Giants, remaining with them for several years. Then in 1961, at the home of Rev. John Mackey, Willie helped form the Mighty Echoes of Glory.

The 1960s was filled with racial unrest and was a difficult time for a group of African American singers to get their start. While traveling through the southern states, the Echoes experienced some difficult times and had to be careful where they traveled. The group demonstrated "mighty echoes of perseverance" as they continued to minister in the face of these difficulties, traveling from Chicago to New York and going as far south as Mississippi.

Rev. Willie Crawford sings lead for the group and plays the guitar. For seven years, Willie hosted a local telecast called the *Gospel Praise Hour* featuring a variety of gospel artists.

Once while the group was traveling through Indiana, they stopped at a small-town restaurant to get a bit to eat. They were seated, and soon the waitress was preparing to take their orders. One of the women in the group, coming from a fast-food oriented metropolis area, simply ordered a hamburger. The waitress asked her, "How do you want it?"

She seemed confused and simply replied, "I want it cooked!"

The group now uses many live instruments, and Willie's wife Nancy Crawford plays the guitar and does some singing in the background. They have sung with such groups as the Blind Boys of Mississippi and have been performing annually at the Blues and Gospel Festival held in Cincinnati since the early 2000s. Although they had to slow down because of some health problems, the power this group continues to put forth can best be expressed by the title of one of their latest recordings simply called "Jump."

* * *

Julie Greatorex was born on December 18, 1987, in Cincinnati, Ohio and has been singing southern gospel music her entire life. Before Julie came along, her mother Patricia Gunter sang with her sister Doris and Sheryll Harris in a Cincinnati trio called the Haloettes. Once at the NQC, Mosie Lister played the piano for them.

When Julie was a young child, the family traveled as a group called Legacy. They continued traveling until Julie was twelve years old. In 2001, the family came back on the road under the name Haven. After Julie graduated from high school, the group started traveling more. Even though they later took some time off, they continued to sing for the NQC.

Once when the family was singing as Haven, they entered the Swannee River Jubilee talent contest held in, Live Oak, Florida, and hosted by the Dixie Echoes. Julie was having one of those days, feeling miserable and believing nothing was going right. Not wanting to sing, she managed to pull herself together and give her best effort. Much to Julie's surprise, Haven took first place! With their first professional talent contest win, they were awarded some recording time at a studio owned by Randy Shelnut. From that connection, the family developed a close relationship with the Dixie Echoes.

In 2004, the family came off the road again, and in 2006 when Julie graduated from high school, she took a position with a group called "Griffith & Company," originally called the "Griffith Family," from Sylacauga, Alabama. She has been singing with them for almost two years. As a result of singing with her family, she has become acquainted with many of the nation's top gospel artist. She says, "One of my closest friends, Steve Weatherford, has known me since I was a little girl and has given me some pointers on the ups and downs of the southern gospel industry."

One of her older brothers, Joey Greatorex has driven the bus for Hissong and Squire Parsons.

* * *

Raised in Cincinnati, the first generation of Isley Brothers were encouraged to begin a singing career by their parents. Their father was a professional vocalist, and their mother was the church pianist. The original group consisting of Ronald, Rudolph, O'Kelly, and Vernon Isley started out as a quartet with their mother playing piano for the group. Vernon was killed in a 1955 bicycle accident.

In 1957, leaving their Christian heritage, the brothers moved to NYC, seeking recognition as a doo-wop group. Their popularity continued to grow, taking them as far as England. In 1986, O'Kelly died of a heart attack, and in the 1980s when Rudolph retired from music to become a minister, it appeared the Isley Brothers were finished. However, through the efforts of Ronald, a remnant of the group continues to sing though they never returned to their gospel roots.

* * *

The Mason brothers were all born in Kentucky and later moved to Ohio. At one point, all of the brothers worked for the Sterns & Foster Mattress Company. Before forming their own group, two of the brothers sang with the Knisley Quartet. In the 1930s, they put together a group called the Mason Brothers Quartet. The group included all of the brothers, with the sisters helping out at times. They traveled mostly throughout south central Kentucky using their own vehicles and singing for revivals and special services. They never accepted any money for their ministry. All expenses were paid by the group members. After almost fifty years of ministry, the group came to a close in the 1980s. Some of the brothers continue with solo careers. At age ninety-four Lowell, the only living Mason brother, lives with his wife in a Florida nursing home.

* * *

Don Harper played bass guitar with the Mansion City group in Cincinnati. He later played steel guitar with Dwayne Lee & Eternity for about two years.

Later, while playing piano for the River City Quartet, he began working with Steve Wilson. A few years later, Don and Steve left the group and formed the Ohio Valley Boys. After about four years, Don left the Ohio Valley Boys and formed the Harpers. Steve Wilson continued with the Ohio Valley Boys.

The Harpers was comprised of Don Harper, his wife, and two daughters. Their daughter Britni Harper has been singing since she was big enough to hold a microphone and is an outstanding soprano singer. One evening after singing on stage with the Dixie Melody Boys, Ed O'Neal approached Don Harper, giving his daughter a great compliment by telling Don that if Rex Nelon were still living, he would probably want to take Britni on the road. Derrick Loudermilk now sings in place of the Harpers' oldest daughter. The Harpers have sung at the SGM Fanfare in Chattanooga, Tennessee, and they sing on the NQC Regional Artist Showcase every year.

Steve Wilson sings in the Ohio Valley Boys with Gary Crawley. Gary has an impressive heritage in gospel music. His father, Jim Crawley, sang with several groups and was privileged to sing with Buddy Liles. Gary began his career with the Gloryland Quartet from Lebanon but only sang with them for about six months. He then sang with the Gospel Mariners in Dayton for eight years. While with the Mariners they were regulars on the *Good Ship Zion*, a weekly television program. He later sang with the Compassion Quartet out of Georgetown, Kentucky, for seven years. He then filled in with the Journeymen Quartet of Mason for another two years. Leaving the Ohio Valley Boys, Gary now sings with the Victors Quartet from Middletown.

After changing several group members, including the addition of a young female singer named Scarlett Monday, the name was changed to the Ohio Valley Quartet to accommodate the mixed-group status. The group has sung with such groups as the Dixie Melody Boys and Kevin Spencer & Friends. In addition to all this, Steve also pastors a local Baptist church. The group recently teamed up with the Harpers and several other groups in the area, and with the help of Homer's Restaurant in Evendale, they formed the Greater Cincinnati Southern Gospel Music Association designed to promote and preserve southern gospel music in the Greater Cincinnati area.

* * *

Harold Reed was born in Cincinnati on February 28, 1971. He accepted Christ as personal Savior as a teenager in his pastor's home. Harold was exposed to southern gospel music at an early age. He saw the Kingsmen Quartet in concert when he was young and, from that moment, knew southern gospel music was his calling. As soon as Harold graduated high school in 1989, he traveled with Squire Parsons for one year. Squire was very helpful to his future providing advice and vocal tips.

After traveling with Squire, Harold joined the Melodyaires and spent three years with this South Carolina-based group. While he was singing with the Melodyaires, they booked the Dixie Melody Boys to sing at their Homecoming in South Carolina. During the event, Eric Ollis questioned Harold as to whether he had an interest in singing full-time. Harold was interested, and two weeks later, McCrae Dove called to verify his interest in the job. At the time, Rodney Griffin was singing baritone for the Dixie Melody Boys, and he put together some songs for Harold to learn.

A week later, Ed O'Neal called and officially offered the position to Harold. His first date with the Dixie Melody Boys was on December 30, 1993. On the road, in addition to singing, Harold was responsible to set up and run the sound equipment. He also sat up on nighttime bus drives to help keep driver Eric awake. Harold loved traveling with the Dixie Melody Boys and was thrilled to work for Ed O'Neal.

Harold was married on July 2, 2002, and in 2004, Harold left the Dixie Melody Boys to start singing with the Florida Boys. In 2007, possibly because of the upcoming retirement plans of the Florida Boys, Harold joined the Kingsmen Quartet fulfilling his childhood dream. Harold has become one of the favorite tenor singers in southern gospel music and has one of the highest and most recognizable tenor voices on the road today.

* * *

Charles Novell was born in southwest Virginia on August 31, 1942, and grew up listening to southern gospel quartet music. A quartet from Wilmington, North Carolina, came to sing for his church, and young Charles was enthralled with their sound. When Charles was eight, Doyle Blackwood visited his church to sing and left a lasting impression on this young man. Through Charles's teen years, the family would travel to Winston Salem, North Carolina, about four times a year to attend a gospel event at the R. J. Reynolds Auditorium promoted by C. R. McClain. The first concert he attended was a "shuttle" concert held in Mount Airy, North Carolina. A "shuttle" concert is where three local gospel concerts are held at the same time at three different locations. Held at the National Guard Armories, the groups would switch stages, traveling from one concert hall to the other, singing at all locations before the evening was over.

In 1961, Charles moved to Cincinnati to attend the famous Cincinnati Conservatory of Music. He formed a quartet in his church, but it soon disbanded. He later formed a trio along with Jerry Daniel and Ron Medley. They began calling themselves the Galileans. Upon learning that another group in the area already was using this name, they went looking for another name. While listening to the radio one day, Charles heard someone make reference to a regent. They said a regent was someone who served in the absence of the ruler. Believing this was exactly what they were doing, Charles shared his thoughts with the other two members and in 1967, the group became the Regents.

The trio traveled the Midwest states managing 100-150 bookings annually. They sang for many camp meetings including the annual Church of God General Assembly, which was held at many locations throughout the United States. Jerry left the group in 1970 to go into the ministry and was replaced by Charles's wife, Barbara Novell. She remained active with the group and continues singing today with Charles and Rod Medley.

In 1971, the group purchased a 4104 bus from well-known gospel singer Sammy Hall. The first weekend they owned the bus, they were so excited to ride it that they drove to their appointment somewhere in Indiana without any license plates on it. In 1973, the group was involved in a bus wreck along SR-747. A truck ran a red light and hit the bus in the front door. The bus was a total loss. The other group members were only treated for minor injuries, but Charles sustained facial injuries that required surgery. The group traveled by car, pulling a trailer, for the remainder of their ministry.

Some time in the mid-1970s, Ron left the group to go into an evangelistic ministry and was replaced by Stan Bowling. Stan was only with the group for a year and was replaced by Rod Solomon who had previously sung with the Rhythm Masters Quartet. The Regents stopped traveling around 1976. After disbanding the group, Charles took a position as music minister at his church.

In 1976 J. D. Sumner requested that Charles take over the Stamps School of Music. The school's name has been changed, but Charles continues as administrator of the Christian Music Conference School of Gospel Music held annually in Murray Kentucky. The conference carries on the tradition that started in 1924 with gospel music legend V. O. Stamps. It was originally known as the Stamps School of Music.

In 1988, holding a doctorate of music degree, Charles started teaching private piano and vocal lessons. He has been the vocal coach and teacher for the Blackwood Brothers, Kenny Bishop, Ivan Parker, Charlotte Ritchie, and many others. He had been involved in gospel music as a songwriter, arranger, recording producer, and performer for over thirty-five years. He has performed on TBN and CBN television networks and for major concerts throughout the United States and the world. Charles developed a Christian recording studio called Counterpoint and has produced almost one thousand seven hundred projects. Some of the artists he has worked with in the studio are Perfect Heart, the Blackwood Brothers, J. D. Sumner and the Stamps, the Kingsmen, the Hoppers, and Bobby Clark.

Charles' son Rob Novell traveled with the original Perfect Heart from 1991 to 1995 as their bass guitarist. He is also involved in studio work at Counterpoint and has been private instructor for Adam Borden of Gold City, Jason Selph of the Carolina Boys, and Jason Clark of the Nelons. Rob recently moved to Georgia where he plans to continue his studio work.

* * *

A native of Danville, Virginia, Kay Francis Barksdale once traveled the nightclub circuit singing rhythm and blues. Moving to Cincinnati in the early 1950s, she continued her nightclub circuit. In 1961, she was named Miss Cincinnati and became the first African American to hold the title. In May 1977, she was at the Beverly Hills Supper Club in Northern Kentucky along with three thousand other people when around 9:00 PM, dense smoke was discovered in the Zebra Room. The fire department rushed to the club, but the fire spread rapidly, and the large crowd was unable to find the exits quickly. Over 160 people lost their lives in that fire, and another 200 were injured.

Surviving the fire, Kay told investigators that a chef led her to a room where she was safe from harm. According to investigators, there was no chef to match her description, and the room she identified could not be found. Was it an angel? The facts may never be known, but it seems clear that God had a purpose for rescuing Kay from that terrible event.

Kay had suffered vocal damage in the fire and was unable to speak or sing for about two months. During this time, Kay prayed to God, promising Him that if he would restore her voice, she would never again sing the world's music. Known today as Cincinnati's Gospel Jewel, she has kept her promise telling her story and singing for the Lord in many local churches, the Lebanon Correctional Prison, and on center stage in Cincinnati's Music Hall. Singing all over the United States and Canada, she has appeared on national television and in the movie *Say Amen Somebody* with Tommy Dorsey. Kay has the presence to enter a room full of strangers and leave with everyone her friend. Her ministry continued to grow through the 1990s. She has traveled across the country, won numerous awards, and made appearances at the request of powerful and important people. Kay has known fame, but when asked who she is, she will most likely reply, "I am a child of God."

* * *

Milton "Ace" Harry Richman was born in Cincinnati on August 14, 1916. Feeding on the influence of pop music, he started making music with the banjo, saxophone, and bass fiddle. Ace organized his own ten-piece orchestra called the Sophisticates of Rhythm. After learning to sing shaped-notes, he formed a group called the Red River Rangers singing a combination of country and gospel.

The Smith brothers, John "Tennessee" Smith (tenor), and his brother A. L. "Smitty" Smith, formed their first string band while they were still children. In 1938, they crossed paths with Ace Richman while working at a radio station in Cincinnati. Teaming up, they moved to Columbus where they worked with Hank Newman and the Georgia Crackers. The trio was joined by Pat Patterson and formed the Sunshine Boys, historically known as one of the most versatile quartets in gospel music.

Their first home was Macon, Georgia, where they performed on radio station WMAZ. They moved to Atlanta, Georgia, and performed regularly on radio stations WAGA and WSB. In 1942, Pat Patterson left the group to join the military. He was replaced by Eddie Wallace, a talented pianist with a great gospel musical pedigree. The addition of Eddie motivated the group to include gospel music in their repertoire. They demonstrated their versatility on radio station WAGA by performing as two different groups. They would perform a fifteen-minute radio program as the Light Crust Dough Boys, a western swing band with full instrument accompaniment. During a thirty-second commercial break, Eddie Wallace would move to the piano, swing the microphones around, and the Sunshine Boys would sing a fifteen-minute gospel program. This setup lasted for several years and was so effective that it fooled most listeners into thinking they were two different groups.

In 1945, the Sunshine Boys traveled to California where they appeared in a series of Western films. These films also featured stars such as Eddie Dean, Lash Larue, Smiley Burnette, Charles Starrett. The Sunshine Boys would be inserted into the film singing Western songs and spirituals where appropriate.

The Smith brothers, more interested in pursuing country and western music, left the Sunshine Boys in 1949 and, remaining in the Atlanta area, performed country music as the Smith Brothers. Ace Richman and Eddie Wallace continued in gospel music, performing for a short time as the Travelers Quartet. Later, hiring a bass singer from Florida named J. D. Sumner and a tenor from Covington, Georgia, named Fred Daniels, the Sunshine Boys were back on the road.

In 1951 the Sunshine Boys starred in the famous western movie *Prairie Roundup* where Ace and J. D. Sumner can be seen wearing cowboy hats and sitting around the campfire singing a song while they rest from a long day on the roundup.

In addition to their varied music, stage, and screen appearances, the Sunshine Boys were recruited to help sell a number of products in major brands over their careers. Their advertisements helped make some of those products into household names.

On June 30, 1954, an airplane tragedy shocked the world of gospel music, as Bill Liles and R. W. Blackwood of the Blackwood Brothers were killed in the crash. The event initiated a round-table of bass swaps. First, the Blackwood Brothers hired J. D. Sumner to sing bass. In turn, Johnny Atkinson was asked to sing bass with the Sunshine Boys. Burl Strevel left the Blue Ridge Quartet and joined the Sunshine Boys in 1956, replacing Atkinson. In 1964, Strevel returned to the Blue Ridge Quartet and replaced George Younce.

While the NQC was still being held in Memphis, Ace took the Sunshine boys down to sing. At that time, the Sunshine Boys were still a part-time group, so J. D. Sumner informed the group he couldn't put them on the stage that year. The evening was going well when around 10:00 PM, the lights in the auditorium suddenly went out, creating total darkness. The lights were only out for a few minutes, and when they were turned on again, Ace Richman stood center stage. He immediately greeted the audience, "Good evening, ladies and gentlemen. We are the Sunshine Boys, and we're here to entertain you."

The Sunshine Boys continue to perform annually at the Grand Ole Gospel Reunion. In honor of longtime group member Fred Daniels who passed away in November of 2007, please remember the next time you cook a pot of Minute Rice or make a purchase from General Foods, the gospel quartet that helped to make them famous in the 1950s was the Sunshine Boys!

* * *

Leonard Franklin Slye was born in Cincinnati on November 5, 1911. His first home was a tenement on Second Street in the same location where Riverfront Stadium was later constructed. The Slye family moved to Portsmouth in 1912. They navigated the Ohio River on a houseboat they build from salvaged lumber. Leonard's parents purchased land with plans to build a home, but that proved unnecessary. The Flood of 1913 floated the houseboat onto their property, and they continued living in the houseboat on dry land. In 1919, Leonard's family moved to Duck Run where he learned much of his musical ability including his famous yodeling. The family moved back to Cincinnati when Leonard was seventeen and his father took a job at a shoe factory. Before his movie career, Leonard drove a farm truck, was an active cowhand, and worked in the same shoe factory as his father.

Moving to California in 1930, this young man connected with some other musically talented people forming a western trio, which eventually became known as the Sons of the Pioneers. In 1937, finding an opening with Republic Pictures, Leonard played several singing cowboy roles as Dick Weston before taking on his famous pseudonym Roy Rogers in 1938. In 1941, he was reunited with his old friends the Sons of The Pioneers, and after making eighty-nine western movies, he became known as the king of the cowboys.

On December 31, 1947, Frances Octavia Smith, a Texas girl better known to the world as Dale Evans, was married to Roy Rogers and became an active part of his acting career and ministry. Dale wrote a popular gospel song entitled "The Bible Tells Me So."

Following wonderful careers using their acting and musical abilities, both Roy and Dale continued their ministry recording inspirational albums. They established the Happy Trail Children's Foundation and, in 1965, opened the Roy Rogers-Dale Evans Museum in Victorville, California. Roy became an honorary member of the Country Music Hall of Fame in 1988 and, in 1991, participated in the recording of an album entitled *Tribute*—a musical salute to his career. In downtown Portsmouth, you can find the Roy Rogers Esplanade with a concrete slab that contains Rogers' handprints and footprints.

* * *

Reverend "Chief" Bruce Thum, a Cherokee Indian combining his talents with Charles Verness launched their first revival crusade in Springfield. The crusade was a success, and thus, the Sunshine Evangelistic Party was created. In 1950, Bruce met a young lady of German decent, Ruth Sess, from Cincinnati who won his heart, and they were soon married. With the addition of her voice to the Sunshine Party, they were soon in demand in some of the nation's largest churches. Charles younger sister, Violita, soon joined the group. She had a well-trained voice and played several instruments. They were soon traveling the world carrying the good news of the Gospel. The Cathedral of Tomorrow in Akron, one of the nation's most modern churches, hosted one particularly successful crusade. They also appeared on both the *Art Linkletter Show* and the *Bob Crosby Show*.

* * *

Jim Brady was born May 19, 1970, in Clare, Michigan. His father was a traveling evangelist, so he grew up on the road. His father has been in evangelism for forty-six years, and as of 2008, he is seventy and still preaching! Ever since he was old enough to talk, Jim loved to sing. Along with seven brothers and sisters and his mom and dad, they traveled as the Brady Family Gospel Team based in Houston, Texas. Many people simply referred to them as "God's Brady Bunch." Using RVs, buses, and motor homes, they traveled across the country holding revivals and crusades. Jim says, "There was a bunch of us, but we had a great time just singing and ministering, you know, in evangelism. What a great heritage it has been. It has kind of developed and shaped who I am and prepared me for what I am doing now. It has been a joy, an awesome thing!"

When Jim was sixteen, he started writing songs. He met a girl from Cincinnati named Melissa Shuler, a native of Dayton, at a gospel concert in Atlanta, Georgia. They fell in love, and were married on March 6, 1993. Melissa grew up around southern gospel music and even sang as a fill-in with the Martins and Lordsong (on the Mark Lowry tour) until a position could be filled. She continues to do solo work and teaches at the Steve Hurst School of Music in Nashville, Tennessee.

Melissa's father, Jack Shuler, previously started his musical ministry with a group called the Songmasters in Miland, Tennessee. The Songmasters featured singers such as Dale Shipley, who went on to sing with Perfect Heart, and Debra Spraggs who went on to sing with the Hoppers and then the Talleys (as Debra Talley). Jack Shuler played the steel guitar for the Songmasters and occasionally sang.

After Jim married Melissa, he moved to Morrow, and for the next ten years, they spent most of their time traveling and singing all across the country with the family group called the Shulers. The group consisted of Jim, his wife, Melissa, and her father Jack Shuler, evangelist and musician. The Schulers were best known for their family harmony and original songs written by Jim and Melissa. In 1997, the Shulers were nominated in the *Singing News* fan awards as Horizon Group of the Year and by SGMA as New Artist of the Year. It was during his time with the Schulers that Jim received an invitation to sing with the Booth Brothers.

Contacting him on a Monday or a Tuesday, they shared that they had heard him sing and were requesting he fill in until they could fill the position. Jim agreed, and when he questioned as to when he would be needed, they responded, "This coming Friday." He told them to overnight him their current music, and he met them on Friday in Nashville, Tennessee, at the Gaylord Arena for a Gaither Homecoming concert. What a daunting challenge to have your first appearance with a new group come at a Gaither Homecoming. Jim said, "Everybody on the Gaither tour was so encouraging, and they embraced me and treated me like family, and encouraged me, and it was a wonderful night."

He sang with them that entire weekend and then a few more weekends. Jim soon realized that not only were they like minded in music, but they also shared the same ideas about ministry. When the Booth Brothers finally asked if he would stay and be part of the group, he was confident God was the one orchestrating the situation. When he joined the group, one of their first nights out, the great songwriter, Mosie Lister told Jim, "You know, you could be a real brother because you sound like one."

Jim often tells people, "Michael and Ronnie are blood brothers, and I am a brother in the Lord."

While the group was traveling on the Gaither tour, Jake Hess told Jim, "Man, you fit this group."

Later Ben Speer, another great hero and a great legend in gospel music told Jim, "Man, you have really added something, you know, your own spark to the group."

After joining the Booth Brothers full-time, Jim and Melissa moved to Florida for a short time. More recently, they moved back to Nashville,

Tennessee, the music hub for gospel music. Traveling every weekend from Nashville is much easier than Ohio or Florida, allowing Jim to fulfill all of the recording, booking, writing, and publishing requirements for the group. Living in Nashville also allows the group members to be home with their families providing them real quality time. The group's hectic travel schedule, 150 dates a year, combined with their needed studio time, would have kept them from home much more if they lived somewhere else.

"So we are blessed," Jim says, "to do what we do and it is just very rewarding. I mean the sacrifices are being away from our family, but the rewards are just wonderful. The people have been so kind to us, and to see lives changed and see the songs we sing reach the heart—you can't beat it, we are loving it."

In the early spring of 2007, they had sung in Kalispell, Montana, and were headed east through Wyoming. While traveling along the interstate, the weather began to deteriorate. As they approached Sheridan, Wyoming, there was an accident that shut down the interstate. The highway patrol directed everyone onto a small mountain road that was to detour them through Sheridan and back to the interstate.

After about an hour of traveling along that small road, with the weather continuing to worsen, the traffic came to a stop. Some trucks had jackknifed in the poor conditions, and traffic was once again at a standstill. They were unable to turn back, and they couldn't go forward. It appeared they would be stranded on that little back road somewhere near Sheridan, Wyoming, for quite some time.

There they sat, on that big bus with very little to do. They had no cell phone service and no internet, but the Lord provided. When the highway patrol arrived by helicopter, they were able to get messages to their families to let them know they were okay. They had some snack food on the bus, so although it wasn't steak, they wouldn't starve, at least for a while, and they had a generator on the bus to provide heat so they could stay warm.

Some of the people of the community started showing up on snowmobiles bringing sandwiches, snacks, and water along with other necessities, and the guys were very thankful. Realizing that it had taken a lot of fuel to climb up the mountain, they began to worry that they might run out of fuel. By the third day stranded, they were indeed running out of fuel. As the Lord would have it, there were some people in a truck behind them who had just filled two reserve tanks on their truck with three hundred gallons of fuel. Little did they know when they were filling those tanks that they were getting fuel for the Booth Brothers. The generous people in that truck allowed them to come down and siphon as much fuel as they needed to keep their bus running. The Brothers paid for the fuel and, thanking them, told them if they got cold on their truck to come over and get on the bus. At one point, there were several people on the bus just warming up.

As time went on, the close confines of the bus began to wear on the men. The snow drifts were amazing; some were as high as the bus. The snow was blowing sideways—it was a blizzard. Everyone was anxious to get home, but they managed to get along. They would sit up in the front of the bus for a while telling stories, laughing, and having fun. They would probably admit they became a little slap happy as the time went on, but they were having a good time. Jim says, "It seemed like something from an old movie, it got funny because we couldn't believe this was really happening."

They continued to siphon diesel out of the neighboring truck until the fourth day when they were able to start moving again. They were soon following behind a snowplow as it plowed a path along the road ahead of them. When they finally left the mountain, they were amazed to discover they had more fuel than when they headed up on the mountain! The Lord provides.

Their families were obviously worried, and the promoters had to call and cancel appointments. In all, they canceled four concerts, but through the whole experience, God was watching over them. He provided for them and saw that they had everything they needed.

Jim has won several awards and written numerous songs. His most popular song "Truth Is Marching On" has been recorded by Legacy Five, Gold City, and the Talleys. Jim says, "The awards and things that come are really neat, and they are appreciated, but it's not the reason we sing. I just hope that we sing something or say something that will help people. These songs actually become part of these people's lives. And if we can help them and give them strength, hope, and encouragement to keep the faith and to walk with God, then I feel like we have accomplished something."

On the Booth Brothers award-winning CD *The Blind Man Saw It All* is a song called "The Eyes of Heaven" that Jim had a part in writing. The song was written for people whose work for the kingdom receives little or no recognition—teachers and small-church pastors and evangelists, like Jim's father. You may not know their names, and they are not on TV and they don't sign autographs, but they are faithful to their calling. Jim says, "That's why I wrote that song, to encourage those people."

* * *

Standing six feet tall, Aycel Soward had a bass voice that seemed to go down endlessly. Aycel studied voice at the Cincinnati Conservatory of Music and worked hard to produce the best sound possible. Although he had trouble with maintaining rhythm, his voice was one of the great basses of his day. Aycel sang with a number of groups before passing away on April 1, 1956 at age forty-two.

* * *

From the collaboration of Steve and Diana Folenius and Joseph Netto, Stedfast was established as a trio in 1994. Steve previously worked with the Southern-Aires in Dayton. His wife, Diana, has performed for Kentucky Governors, has taken first place in several talent contests, and was honored to present a special rendition of "The Star-Spangled Banner" during the nationally televised Operation Desert Storm rally. Joseph Netto has been singing since he was a young boy. His light humor provides comic relief for the group as they seek to provide a dynamic ministry.

* * *

Buford Abner was born on November 10, 1917, in Wedowee, Alabama. He began singing with his brother Merle in 1935, and in 1937, they formed the Vaughan Four. In 1939, they took a suggestion from Archie Campbell and formed another group called the Swanee River Boys, in memory of Stephen Foster's song "Way down upon the Swanee River." The group had a unique style with smooth harmony very similar to an old-time African American group. During World War II, Buford and Merle were called to military service in the Pacific. Lee Roy Abernathy and Bill Liles temporarily replaced them. After returning from the war, Buford and Merle sang on the legendary WSB Barn Dance in Atlanta. In 1948, the Swanee River Boys were hired by Cincinnati radio station WLW to replace the Mills Brothers. They performed two to three shows daily on air.

In 1955, the group moved to Indianapolis where they sang for twelve years without a personnel change. They were privileged to work with Bing Crosby, Bob Hope, Dean Martin and Jerry Lewis. In the 1960s, the group traveled with the USO performing for the U.S. troops overseas. The group continued to perform into the early 1970s.

In 1970, after performing for thirty years and writing over one hundred songs, Buford Abner left the group. Buford was eighty-five years old when he sang at the Grand Ole Gospel Reunion in Greenville, North Carolina.

* * *

Daniel Brink Towner was born on March 5, 1850. He began his musical development at an early age and attended the Cincinnati Conservatory of Music as a part-time student. While at the conservatory he accepted an invitation from Dwight Moody to join his association of evangelists and musicians. In 1893, when Moody moved to Chicago, Daniel became the head of the music department. While in this position, he developed a music curriculum for preparing gospel musicians and authored a number of textbooks. Towner became a prolific hymn writer. Two of his best known hymns are "Trust and Obey" and "At Calvary."

Leaving Cincinnati, we take IR-75 north traveling along in bumper-to-bumper traffic for about eight miles to SR-126 (Ronald Reagan Highway). We travel west for about five miles to SR-127. Turning right onto SR-127 we drive north to Mount Healthy. Some say the town of Mount Pleasant became known as Mount Healthy as a result of the community's effort to avoid the cholera epidemics of nearby Cincinnati. While this may be a rumor, the town was in fact officially renamed Mount Healthy in 1893.

One current resident of Mount Healthy, Bill Phelps, has not always been in the best of health.

Born on October 31, 1938, in Elmwood, Bill was raised in a very musically oriented family. Bill began playing "Jesus Loves Me" on an old upright piano at age three. Bill's father was a business associate of George Carrier who sang with the Swanee River Boys. When George would stop by for a visit, Bill would plead with him to teach him some new chords on the guitar. He started learning music in school but was later dismissed from the school band for repeatedly adding notes to their arrangements.

In 1966, while riding motorcycles with some friends, Bill made a sharp turn. One of his tires was low, causing the motorcycle to fishtail. Bill was thrown across a patch of grass and sent sliding down a blacktop road. He was taken to the hospital with severe injuries to his wrist. The doctors expressed a belief that the injuries would prevent him from playing the piano ever again. Bill asked the Lord to help him recover, promising he would only play for Him in return. Both ends of this bargain held up as Bill regained the ability to play and later turned down a secular music job in Las Vegas.

That was not the end of Bill's health valley. Cancer was found in his right thumb that, if not for a skilled Indiana doctor, would have required the removal of his thumb. Demonstrating his resolve, Bill fashioned a homemade aluminum splint on his thumb and wrapped it with electrical tape in order to play the piano that very weekend. He even performed a piano solo that evening, playing "When They Ring Those Golden Bells" to a standing ovation.

Bill has played for numerous groups in his career. The first was the Fellowship Christian-Aires Quartet in Cincinnati. He was with that group when they did the Country Jamboree Show on WKRC TV. He sang with the Crawley Brothers out of Cincinnati and even did a short stint with the Pine Ridge Boys. In 1966, he completed a tour through Montreal, Canada, with Jerry and the Singing Goffs. He played once for the Florida Boys while Darrell Stewart was in the hospital. He also played several times for the Crownsmen in Cincinnati and was with Coy Cook and the Senators for a short while.

Bill went on a two-week tour with the Hemphills that included one particularly memorable moment. They were singing on the *Grand Ole Opry* show at the Ryman Auditorium in Nashville, Tennessee. Grant Turner was the emcee for the program. During one of their songs, Bill was sliding the piano stool back and forth on the floor as he played. Suddenly one of the legs fell off the stool, but Bill managed to keep on playing until the song was finished. At the end of the song, he stood up with a flourish, sending the stool flying across the stage.

He was later with the Premiers for one year and did a short tour with the Prophets at the end of their career. His longest stint was with the Rhythm Masters from Lockland, and one of the last groups he played for was the Keynotes in Cincinnati.

After taking a few wrong turns, we travel back to SR-126 and leave Mount Healthy. We take SR-126 east five miles to IR-75 where we turn north and travel the short distance north to Lockland. The community was plotted in 1828 as a direct result of being located along the Miami & Erie Canal. This portion of the canal has since been replaced by IR-75. Also located in Lockland is the Lockland Baptist Church where Dr. John Rawlings was pastor.

In the mid-1960s, the Landmark Quartet was formed as a radio ministry of the Landmark Baptist Temple in Cincinnati. They quickly established the quartet as a major group and were signed to a recording contract with Heartwarming Records in Nashville, Tennessee. In just a short period, they found themselves on a western tour with two of the nation's top groups, the Stamps and the Imperials. The original group consisted of Mack Evans, Carrol Rawlings, Don Norman and Carl Noe with Jack Clark at the keyboard. Jack started out with the Homeland Harmony Quartet and both Don Norman and Jack Clark were previously with the Harvesters Quartet from North Carolina. Don Norman later when on to take a position as soloist for the Jerry Falwell Ministries. Mack Evans had sung with the Goss Brothers, the Rangers, and the Klaudt Indian Family. In 1966, their bass singer, Carl Noe, was replaced by Buddy Liles.

Born in Newport, Kentucky, Buddy had previously sung with the Notemen Quartet in Dayton, and in 1963, he took his first full-time position singing with the Orrell Quartet out of Detroit, Michigan. Their pianist was Lorne Matthews, who had previously played for the McDuff Brothers and went on to play for the Cathedrals. The Orrell Quartet traveled full-time singing throughout the USA and Canada, and appeared in over a hundred radio broadcasts. The group disbanded in 1969.

The Rhythm Masters Quartet was formed in Birmingham, Alabama some time in the 1950s. Then in 1967, when Dan Hubbard relocated to Ohio, they connected with Homer Milan and formed the "new" Rhythm Masters. This group consisted of the two original Rhythm Masters, Homer and Dan, Grady Nix joined as tenor, Clyde Burns as baritone, and Bill Phelps on piano. Buddy Liles joined in 1969 after the death of Homer Milan, and later, Carrol Rawlings came on as baritone.

Once during a concert at a Nazarene church in Trenton, they were singing their most-requested song, "I'll Have a New Life," and suddenly without any prodding, people started coming to the altar, and soon the altar was full and many gave their hearts to Jesus.

Grady later left the group to join the Prophets Quartet and became known as "Chico." He stayed with the Prophets Quartet until he retired from full-time ministry. Carrol Rawlings, and his wife, Linda, continued the Rhythm Masters until the name was retired in the early 1990s.

Carrol Rawlings was born in Cave City, Arkansas, in September 1939. His grandfather Henry Mobley taught singing lessons at the Stamps-Baxter Singing School. His uncle Clark Mobley, was a songwriter for the Stamps-

Baxter Company, and a piano teacher to, among others, the now-famous Roger Bennett. Carrol's father, John Rawlings, was instrumental in the promotion of gospel music in Texas and in Ohio. In the 1950s, most of the major groups were guests at the Lockland Baptist Church where Dr. John Rawlings pastored. Carrol wrote the song "One of These Days," recorded by the Cathedrals.

In 1972, Buddy left the Rhythm Masters to join the Florida Boys where he remained for a number of years. Buddy now travels as a solo ministry, and in 1995, Buddy was awarded the Marvin Norcross Award. He was later inducted into the Gospel Music Hall of Fame and has appeared on many of the Bill Gaither Homecoming Videos. The late Jake Hess said of Buddy Liles, "I have known him to be a man of character and integrity, a man who loves his family and whose life is devoted to the Lord."

Another member of the group, Bob Cameron, was born in Swiss, West Virginia, and lived a portion of his childhood in Ohio. At the age of six, with the help of his father, he began singing. Bob's career included a stint with Bob Wills and the Inspirationals of Fort Worth, Texas. He presently lives in Shreveport, Louisiana, and sings bass for the group One Accord based in Many, Louisiana.

Dennis Whitaker played bass and filled in as tenor for the Rhythm Masters for seven years. He also did some studio work with LaVerne Tripp. He also played with several Ohio-based groups including the Gospel Journeymen, the Miami Valley Boys, and the Proffits. He filled in with the Lindamen in Cincinnati for a while and did a short tour playing for Teddy Huffam and the Gems when they were in Brooklyn, New York.

The Rhythm Masters have several fond memories from the road. Once while at an outdoor event in Meridian, Mississippi, they were on stage with the Thrasher Brothers when they experienced an electrical grounding problem requiring everyone to quickly exit the stage. In all the hustle, the Thrasher Brothers hurriedly removed their equipment from the stage, loaded their bus, and drove down the road. They stopped for fuel and began straightening up the bus. That was when they realized they had taken Dennis Whitaker's bass guitar on their bus. Oops.

Another time, they were traveling in an old GMC 4104 bus, previously owned by Rex Humbard, when the engine blew. They managed to get home and worked twenty-four hours nonstop to put another engine in the bus before their next trip to Maryland. Covered with grease, they fired up the engine to take the bus for a test drive. They put the bus in first gear to pull forward so

Dan could remove the blocks. Suddenly, the bus was going backward. Dan began to yell. Stopping the bus, they determined all the gears were operating in reverse. They had put the engine in backward! They got the engine switched around, but on a subsequent trip to Indiana, the replacement engine blew a rod. Oops and oops again!

On one road trip, the Landmark Quartet was staying on one of the higher floors of a hotel. Outside the window of their room, a couple members noticed some pigeons sitting on a ledge. Having nothing to do to keep them out of trouble, they caught a couple of the birds and took them to the elevator. Opening the elevator door, they pushed the button for the first floor and quickly tossed the birds into the elevator. They ran down the stairway and sat quietly in the lobby to watch as the elevator door opened. When the doors opened, there was an explosion of feathers as the birds made their escape into the lobby. Remaining calm, they returned to their room and burst into laughter. No oops about that one.

Carrol Rawlings's wife, Linda, became the Rhythm Masters pianist shortly after she married Carrol. Linda became the church pianist at her home church at age nine and is considered by many to be one of the finest gospel pianists around. From 1970 to 1985, the Rawlings owned the Artist Recording Studio in Lockland. The development of recording tapes forced the studio to close its doors. A later version of the Rhythm Masters consisted of the trio of Carrol Rawlings, his wife, Linda, and Bill Dykes who had previously sung with the Cathedrals and Jerry and the Singing Goffs.

In 2003, with the help of their daughter, Lindsey, and three talented young men from Kentucky, Carrol and Linda formed a new quartet called the Harvesters based in Florence, Kentucky. Carrol believes, "God has helped us assemble a group of young men who not only meet the necessary musical standards, but also the spiritual standards, to make a cohesive, talented gospel quartet that has a message to bring to a lost and dying world."

In 2008 Jack Clark continues to teach music theory and piano at the Ben Speer's Stamps-Baxter School of Music.

Leaving Lockland, we take Forrer Avenue north to Shepherd Road where we turn right and cross over IR-75 to Smalley Road. Turning left onto Smalley Road, we continue to Reading where we turn left onto SR-42 and travel about four miles to Sharonville, originally named "Sharon" in 1788 after a small town in Pennsylvania. Sharon became a stopover for stagecoaches traveling from Cincinnati. Just as those stagecoaches were on a journey, the Gospel Journeymen were on a mission for God.

Darwyn "Tookie" Wilson was born in Nancy, Kentucky, on June 16, 1935. In 1971, he formed a group called the Gospel Journeymen and with some other members of his church. The group started as a trio but became a quartet within their first year. They traveled in a fifteen-passenger van for a while and later purchased a nice Scenic Cruiser bus. They continued to sing until the early 1990s.

One evening while traveling on U.S. 65, the freeze plug blew out of the engine block, causing all of the oil to drain out of the engine. This called for some quick ingenuity, so using a toothpaste cap, some duct tape, and a couple metal clamps, they fixed the leak and were back on the road again. TV personality McGyver would have been proud of them. The patch job allowed them to get home, but when it came time to properly fix the problem they, had a difficult time removing that toothpaste cap.

Phil Morris sang tenor for the Gospel Journeymen and later joined the Dayton Ambassadors. After leaving the Dayton Ambassadors, with the help of his son James Morris, he formed a group based in Batavia called the Parables.

JB King, Francis Chamberlain and Wendall Davis, all members of the Dayton Ambassadors, played for the Gospel Journeymen while the Dayton Ambassadors were temporarily off the road. In 1994, the Journeymen held a reunion concert, and at the end of the program, they gave away all of their old recordings to those who attended the performance. Other members of the Journeymen include Stan Poe, who later formed his own trio in Milford, and Jim Bradley, who went on to sing with the Masters Quartet.

Returning Home

Leaving Sharonville, because of road construction, we are directed by a traffic officer to travel the wrong direction on a one-way road (Main Street) all the way through the downtown section. Finally, through the detour we turn left onto Lebanon Road (SR 42) and continued north to IR-275. Turning west onto IR-275, we travel a short distance to IR-75. Turning north onto IR-75, we traveled fifty-five miles to U.S. 40 where we exit to Vandalia, ending Tour 6.

DALTON GANG

NORTH FAMILY

NORTH FAMILY

SOUL'D OUT

Jim Boggs

BRIDGES

FORGIVEN

Tank Tackett, Don Baldwin &
Cloid Baker

Keith Waggoner with LIBERTY

Alan Godsey with the NORTHMEN

CROWNSMEN

CROWNSMEN

CROWNSMEN

HARPERS

Harold Reed

Harold Reed with
DIXIE MELODY BOYS (2003)

* Harold Reed with FLORIDA BOYS

Charles Novell

REGENTS

Kay Francis Barksdale

Ace Richman with SUNSHINE BOYS

Roy Rogers & Jim Hill

Ruth Sess with SUNSHINE PARTY

* Jim Brady

BRADY FAMILY (Jim's first album, age 3)

Melissa (Shuler) Brady

Jack Shuler & Jim Brady

Jim Brady with BOOTH BROTHERS

Aycel Soward

LANDMARK QUARTET

Buddy Liles

Buddy Liles with REBELS

Buddy Liles with FLORIDA BOYS

Jack Clark

Jack Clark with Homeland Harmony

Jack Clark and Don Norman
with Harvesters

RHYTHM MASTERS

RHYTHM MASTERS

Carroll Rawlings with HARVESTERS

GOSPEL JOURNEYMEN

Chapter VII

Cambridge Tour

I Just Want to Thank You Lord

I just want to thank You Lord for every time you heard me pray
Just want to thank You Lord for always being there
When I was so down and out,
You came along and made me want to shout
I just want to thank You Lord, thank You Lord

If I had a thousand lives to live I'd give them all to my Lord
He's been so good to me that is the least I could afford
He's made the Good times out number the bad,
been the best friend I've ever had
I just want to thank You Lord, thank You Lord

I just want to thank You Lord for every time you heard me pray
Just want to thank You Lord for always being there
When I was so down and out,
You came along and made me want to shout
I just want to thank You Lord, thank You Lord

—Judy Marshall
(Used with permission)

Leaving Vandalia on a cold winter morning, we take Dixie Drive south to Benchwood Drive where we turn left and head to IR-75. Turning left we enter IR-75 and travel north a short distance to IR-70. As we prepare to turn onto IR-70 east, the car in front of us hits a patch of ice and starts spinning in circles. Once they recover we enter IR-70 where we are immediately surrounded by those beautiful orange construction barrels. We travel about sixty miles in mild traffic to Columbus. Passing by Columbus we spot a huge antenna that looks like a giant tuning fork. We merge onto U.S. 33, pass a huge USA flag blowing in the wind, and travel about ten miles to Gender Road. We exit to the right and enter Canal Winchester, home of the Barber Museum that traces the profession's contributions to both hair and health care as many barbers were also surgeons. The red-and-white barber pole symbolizes the days when barbers would hang their bloody surgical rags out to dry. No doubt Glenn Marshall was very familiar with the barber pole.

Glenn "Chester" Marshall was born on March 20, 1926, during the Depression when times were hard. No matter how rough things were Chester always had a sense of humor and developed the gift of singing at an early age. Having no television, the family would gather around the old stove to sing or listen to the *Grand Ole Opry* on the radio. It was their way of relaxing. As a result, Chester and his brother Mennis were soon playing and singing for local revivals. The duet became a trio when Chester married Angeline, and it wasn't long until the singing group called the Marshall Family was created.

Just simple country folk living near Canal Winchester, the Marshall family were quite well known for their harmony. The Marshall kids were raised in church often attending two or three times a week. During revivals, they went every night and still had to get up for school. Although Chester wasn't there at times, he was always supportive of his wife, making certain the children were in church. When they were still quite young and singing in church, the family began to work on their harmony often singing a cappella at home to practice. Judy gives their dad a lot of credit for their harmony because he had such a sharp ear for it. He was persistent, and if anyone got a slight bit off key, he would stop everyone and find the culprit. Judy says, "You had to be right on pitch, or he would stop everybody and say, 'Now, let's get it right, we've got to get this right.'"

They continued to sing at their little home church in Obetz, and soon they were branching out to other churches all over the state of Ohio and then the surrounding states. Their ministry was growing rapidly even though they were still very young and attending school. As their popularity increased they were invited to sing on a television program on Channel 8 in Charleston, West Virginia. This was an exciting opportunity for the group and opened many doors for them.

Dave Marshall was a big fan of Ralph Stanley and was responsible for the group's appearance at a big traditional bluegrass music festival with Ralph Stanley in May 1974. Later that year, they signed on with Rebel Records, one of the largest bluegrass labels at that time. That first festival in 1974 with Ralph Stanley certainly opened a different door for the Marshall Family. They were soon receiving many requests to sing as they started traveling throughout the United States. They started out traveling in just a van. Later they had a station wagon and finally a motor home.

Singing in large secular environments such as fairs and festivals the crowd would often be hoopin' and hollerin', having a good time when it was time for the Marshall Family to sing. Stepping out on the stage, they often witnessed the Lord's calming spirit moving through the crowd, and by the time they would get to the second or third song, much of the crowd was often sitting down and listening.

Once they were traveling in their van headed to Nashville to appear for their first time on the Bill Monroe's Bluegrass Program for the *Grand Ole Opry*. Dad was driving, and their brother Danny was sitting in the passenger seat. They had just passed Cincinnati when the carburetor started making a sputtering noise. As the engine could be accessed from inside, they removed the engine cover, and soon Danny had figured out a way to keep the engine running. Every time the engine started sputtering, he would raise the engine cover and peck on the carburetor with a wrench. Danny was good at keeping time with his music, and he soon figured out the timing on that engine, so he knew just when to hit the carburetor before it would start sputtering. Danny continued his motor musical all the way from Cincinnati to Nashville. Thanks to their brother Danny they arrived at the *Opry* as scheduled, and although somewhat nervous, they had a wonderful evening sharing the stage with such artists as Bill Monroe and Ricky Skaggs. Things went well that evening, and they continued to appear on the *Grand Ole Opry* at other times throughout their ministry.

Between 1974 and 1981, they were very busy and traveled many miles doing most of the major bluegrass festivals. Judy became manager for the group, and she worked hard trying to arrange their appointments, so they weren't headed to Texas one day and returning to New York the next. The Marshall Family reached out to a lot of people, and although they never actually traveled overseas, they received letters from people living in England, Japan, and other countries who enjoyed listening to their music.

They had started making plans for an overseas tour with some other gospel bands, but before the tour was finalized, the family group disbanded. A factor that strongly influenced the discontinuance of the family group was the passing of their mother due to cancer in 1983. Mom was the rock of the Marshall Family, a very godly woman, who continually provided encouragement to the family members. Although she never sang, while traveling all those years to further the Gospel, they had a precious little mother at home praying and fasting for her family. Truly mom was the inspiration that guided the Marshall Family to their full potential.

Their mother wrote a little song entitled "I like Walking in the Spirit." Judy and her mother used to sing this song in church together. Mom would start singing the first verse, but then she would get happy and just start shouting, leaving Judy standing up there all alone. Judy would have to quickly move to the microphone to finish the song. Having fond memories of this little song, it became part of Judy's first solo project completed in 1985. When hearing the song, sometime later, Alison Krauss expressed a desire to start singing the song.

After the group disbanded, the family members went their separate ways. By 1985, Judy was living in Florida and began to feel the Lord tugging at her heart. Her mom was gone, and though they couldn't bring her back, she knew mom would want the family to continue singing. She contacted her brothers, agreeing to move back to Ohio if they would go back on the road. To her disappointment, they expressed no interest in putting the group back together. Still feeling a strong desire to minister and acknowledging that the Lord had given her many more songs to sing, she stepped out in faith and produced a solo project entitled *Judy Marshall, Country Gospel.* The project was first released in 1989 on Turquoise Records.

God continues to open doors, and in March 2006, Judy went on the road full-time. Judy currently lives north of Nashville, in Gallatin, Tennessee and her little saying is, "I want to do what I can while I can." Judy has written many songs, but probably the most popular by far would be a song she wrote when just a teenager after a miraculous healing from the Lord entitled "I Just Want to Thank You, Lord." The Bishops recorded her song "Waiting for the Master to Come." Some of the churches Judy frequently visits have created drama teams as a reaction to Judy's song entitled "Soldier" where Judy wears a dressy army outfit during her performance with the drama team wearing army camouflage outfits.

Judy's sister Donna and her two daughters Angie and Crystal have formed a new group called Mere Image. Crystal writes much of the group's material, and one of her songs was recorded by Young Harmony. Mere Image has appeared on Gospel Music Television (GMT) and has shared the stage with several of the nation's top groups. They also were privileged to perform on the *Christian Country Music Awards Show* held at the famous Ryman Auditorium in Nashville, Tennessee.

At the young age of five, Donna was experimenting with the effects of sound. Their dad worked midnight shift, and one morning, standing outside his bedroom door, she plugged her ears and screamed as loud as she could, believing no one could hear her because she couldn't hear herself. Suddenly, dad opened the door, and he was not too happy. But he soon realized she was just exercising her vocal chords, which paid off in the years to come. Donna has one of the most beautiful tenor voices in gospel music today. Her voice blends beautifully with those of her daughters. Their harmony is superb!

OHIO 2

Leaving Canal Winchester, we continue on Gender Road to Lithopolis-Winchester Road where we turn left and travel south through some rolling hills for about three miles to Lithopolis, birthplace of Adam Willis Wagnalls. Born in 1943, Adam attended Wittenberg College in Springfield with Isaac Kauffman Funk. He later became the cofounder of the Funk & Wagnalls Company in 1877 and a Tudor-Gothic-style Wagnalls Memorial was later built on Columbus Street using native stone from a local quarry. With and abundance of natural stone in the area, it was only natural the local gospel group call themselves the Cornerstone Quartet.

In 1996, Mel MeLoy put together a mixed group called the Cornerstone Quartet. All members of the group graduated from Bloom-Carroll High School. They have completed several recordings and recently signed with Eddie Crook. In 1997, they sponsored the first annual Memorial Day Gospel Sing, a benefit event in Lithopolis and, as of 2007, the group has raised $75,000.

Leaving Lithopolis, we continue south along Lithopolis Road passing through the small town of Greencastle. Near Patten Lane, we spot a beautiful little gorge nestled in the trees. Reaching Lancaster, we realize we missed our turn, and after a few more turns we reach Memorial Drive where we turn left and travel through historic downtown Lancaster, passing by a unique red brick McDonalds Restaurant. Lancaster is the hometown of Civil War general William Tecumseh Sherman and the present home of Robin Douglas Kirk who was born in Columbus on December 7, 1961.

Moving to Ohio from Eastern Kentucky, Robby's parents were raised Primitive Baptist in the Old Regular Baptist Church where no one played music. At age eleven, Robby played with some bluegrass guys, and they gave him a guitar. By age thirteen, he was playing that guitar pretty well and was traveling on the road playing bluegrass gospel music with a group called the Edenaires. While playing for the Edenaires, Richard King requested he travel with the King Family. He traveled with them playing the flattop guitar for about two years. At age sixteeen, he moved on to another group called the Liberty Gospel Singers based in Columbus who had been singing for nearly forty years. Today they are called the Heartfelt Singers. At age eighteen, Robby left the group and was soon married to a young lady named Karen. While off the road, he worked as a youth evangelist at his home church.

In 1983, feeling a calling to go back on the road, he started a family group called Generation of Faith Southern Gospel Singers with the help of his wife, Karen, and his sister Linda. Robby says, "They've wore out several conversion vans and two greyhounds just having a ball serving Jesus and winning souls." The group makes its home at the Hilock Fellowship Baptist Church in Columbus. Robby plays several stringed instruments including a little steel guitar. They traveled with a five-piece band for a number of years, but now, they use performance tracks that display their song writing abilities.

The group has shared the platform with many of the nation's top groups. For over thirty years, Robby has maintained a close personal friendship with the Singing Cookes. He enjoys time spent with the Cooke boys and Darrel Freeman when they are in the same area. He also talks with his close friend Daniel Maharrey from Alabama, about three times weekly. Robby feels God has taken a little bit of talent and blessed it, allowing him to meet some of the most fantastic people in southern gospel music.

Another member of the group, Robby's son Jeremy Kirk, has written many original songs. Several times during his young ministry, desiring to remain with the family, Jeremy has turned down numerous offers to play piano for well-known artists. Robby acknowledges the style of worship is changing, and the next generation of gospel artists is following close behind. He considers this a simple passing of the torch, claiming that's just how God works. As this new generation steps in place, they will be called the "new" Generation of Faith.

In 2005, the group was awarded Ohio's Gospel Group of the Year by the Ohio Christian Music Association (OCMA), but Robby reminds us, "You can be the greatest guitar player in the world, but if you are playing for the wrong reason and souls are not the main priority, you're just an entertainer."

* * *

The King Family is a trio consisting of Sue King and her two children Sarah and Jonathan. In 1996, after singing in their home church for many years, they stepped into full-time ministry. They first started singing in nursing homes and now travel across the nation. Sue has written a large number of the songs as recorded by the group. The group specializes in diversity, performing everything from inspirational violin duets to the twin fiddling of bluegrass style. In 2001, the King Family was honored by OGMA as Gospel Instrumentalist of the Year. Both Sarah and Jonathan have received numerous awards and trophies for their classical violin and fiddle playing. The group has performed at many fairs throughout Ohio and at the Renfro Valley Entertainment Center in Kentucky. Sue says, "Our desire is to sing and to play music unto the Lord in order to reach the lost, to encourage those who have already accepted Christ and to inspire young people to get active in church work."

* * *

Originating in the late 1960s as a male quartet, the Songsmen traveled extensively throughout Ohio and the surrounding states presenting the gospel of Jesus Christ in testimony and song. Their music ranged from southern gospel favorites to easy listening contemporary Christian music. They later became a mixed quartet and eventually a trio.

Ministering at festivals, fairs, and many church services for an assortment of denominations, they always use live accompaniment consisting of a keyboard, drums, and a guitar. They were featured on both the radio and television before coming off the road in 2004.

Having managed the group for over twenty-five years, Bud and Debbie Bibler continue to promote gospel music by organizing and hosting several gospel music events each year.

Leaving Lancaster, we continue east along U.S. 22 for about fifteen miles. Soon realizing we had missed SR-664, we traveled back along SR-22 for about five miles to SR-664. Back on track, we soon enter the town of Rushville, the birthplace of Benjamin Hanby who wrote the famous Christmas song "Up on the Housetop."

Reminding some people of the North Pole, it gets pretty cold in South Dakota where Rhonda Lee was born. Her parents later moved to Ohio where her sister Debra Lee was born. The Lee Sisters started singing as a duet in 1990s.

In 1999, with the addition of Carolyn Saddler, they formed a trio known as Lee & Saddler. Before joining the group, Carolyn sang with Dolly Parton's aunt, Dorothy Jo Owens, in a gospel group called the Mountain Melody Singers, which also included Dolly Parton's sister, Willadeene. Lee & Saddler hosted a benefit in Zanesville where Stella Parton appeared as a guest singer for the group. Lee & Saddler remain involved in revivals and have retained a personal relationship with the Parton family in Pigeon Forge, Tennessee. They have traveled and sung throughout the USA appearing on numerous TV programs in Ohio, North Carolina, and the *Don Frost* TV Show in Nashville, Tennessee.

Rhonda became an ordained minister in the 1970s. As a result of her battles with polio, Rhonda was forced to leave her full-time employment. Using her struggles to the glory of God, she enjoys using humor in her messages and, at times, becomes a character called "Miss Priscilla," a God fearing, bible-toting lady who states that regardless of one's appearance, God looks on the heart.

In addition to handling all computer issues for the group, Debra is secretary for the Lancaster Methodist Campground. Lee & Saddler have written many songs which inspired them to form the Lee & Sadler Publishing Company.

Leaving Rushville, we follow SR-664, now a very winding two-lane road, passing through the village of Bremen. We enter Hocking County, and the road continues to curve back and forth as we are awestruck by the beautiful ice hanging from the rocks. Somewhere along the way, we have to stop at an intersection that has blinking stop signs. Finally we arrive at Logan, home to the Columbus Washboard Company, the last washboard manufacturer in the country. Most of their current sales are to the Amish.

Although she probably never used a washboard, Sharon Hardman was raised on a farm in the beautiful Hocking hills region of Southeast Ohio and grew up with plenty of exposure to southern gospel music. Her father sang with the Crawford Brothers Quartet. Sharon sang with her siblings as the Revelations for fourteen years. She started her solo ministry in 1999. Sharon has shared the stage with many of the nation's top groups.

* * *

In 1998, Andy Good joined his father in an a cappella group called the Harmony Four and sang with them for three years. Andy later sang with the Gracemen Quartet in West Virginia for one year. His father filled in with the Gracemen Quartet from time to time. Shannon Troyer, who also sang with them, is now singing with a group from Plain City. In 2002, Andy sang with the Circleville Bible College Quartet for one year. The piano player for the group was C. J. Davis of Family Heritage.

Leaving Logan, we turn left onto U.S. 33 and travel south through a beautiful valley following the Hocking River to Nelsonville where we stop for delicious lunch at the Coffee Cup Restaurant established in 1971. Passing the Hocking Hills Train Station, we continue along SR-33 through the Wayne National Forest until we reach SR-682 where we turn right and head to The Plains, home of Mike Douglas who has been singing gospel music for about thirty-two years.

Mike became interested in gospel music when he first heard the Oak Ridge Boys, and their energetic style of presenting the gospel had a great influence in his life. Deciding to use his talent for the Lord, Mike later formed a trio with the help of his brother John and their sister.

In 1970, after experiencing a few changes in personnel, they changed their name to the Harvest Trio. In 1983, they recorded with the Eddie Crook Company in Nashville, Tennessee, on the Regency record label. Mike cowrote a song with the piano player Randall B. Snodgrass, which did very well across America. In 1987 and 1988, the Harvest Trio sang at the NQC in Nashville,

Tennessee. After a couple more changes in personnel and making a brief effort to go full-time, John and his wife Sue were called into a full-time preaching ministry. Mike sang solo for a while and did some evangelistic speaking at some of the local area churches. Mike later sang lead with the Proclaimers Quartet based in Parkersburg, West Virginia, for six years.

After much prayer and searching, Mike connected with two young men, Jimmy Howson and Justin McBride, and formed the group DaySpring based in Athens. Jimmy Howson had been involved in gospel music since he was nine years old. He was a member of a group at his home church called the Ambassadors for Christ. Later in his career, he joined a mixed gospel quartet called Headed Home. After singing with them about one year, he and his long time friend, Justin left the group forming a duet. Justin also sang with the Ambassadors for Christ about eight years prior to singing with Headed Home. Jimmy and Justin have since left DaySpring, but with the help of his wife and his brother John and his wife Sue, Mike continues to sing while he seeks new personnel.

OHIO 7

Leaving The Plains, we continue south along SR-682 for about five miles to where we cross the Hocking River and drive through Athens where a barn built in 1914 was once a part of a dairy farm at the Athens Lunatic Asylum and milking cows was part of the patients' therapy. Driving on cobblestone roads, we pass through the campus of Ohio University, and finding U.S. 50, we turn east and travel about four miles to Guysville where we exit onto SR-329 and continue to Stewart where we pick up SR-144. Turning right, we follow the Hocking River through some hill country as we travel along SR-144 to Hockingsport where we turn right onto SR-124. We continue on SR-124 for about five miles to Reedsville, located along the Ohio River and home to Shelburne Films, an independent film and video production company, specializing in educational, news, and documentary titles since 1972. Their recent production *Opening the Door West* is a two-hour television documentary about the first legal pioneer settlers of the Old Northwest Territory and the story of life on the Ohio frontier in 1787.

Also from Reedsville is a family trio called Delivered, who started singing in 1995. All self-taught musicians they write all their own music. They were named as the Upcoming Group of the Year in 2001 at the Ohio State Fair by the OCMA.

One evening the group was traveling home on their bus, and having a bad day, they were somewhat beaten down. All of a sudden, someone started singing, and soon they all began to join in. Before long, God's Spirit had filled the bus, and pulling over to the side of the road, their spirits were lifted as they enjoyed a little worship service of their own. In 2002, they sang at a fair in Parkersburg, West Virginia, and because of bad weather conditions, only one person showed up. Nevertheless, they put on a complete program. Sometime later while they were traveling, they ran into this person again, and she shared how God had really touched her at that previous concert.

Before leaving Reedsville, we drive by and take a look at the Belleville Lock & Dam. We then turn right onto SR-144 and travel along the Ohio River to Coolville where we turn right onto SR-7 and continue northeast about thirteen miles. Passing Ohio's smallest church, we arrive in Belpre, home of the Lee Middleton Original Doll Factory specializing in porcelain and vinyl collector's dolls.

Pat Topolsky, a native of Belpre, started a gospel group while in school. After college, possessing a strong desire to provide quality sound equipment, he was soon providing advice to gospel groups regarding their sound equipment. One of his first business calls came from Danny Gaither wanting to purchase equipment for the Bill Gaither Trio, and things moved forward from there. He has been featured in the *Singing News Magazine*, and he has also been awarded numerous RIAA Awards for his work with gospel music videos. Later forming Top In Sound, Inc. he has installed over two thousand church sound systems. Over the years, many top-name gospel groups have trusted Top In Sound to keep them sounding great.

After a quick restroom break at McDonalds, we leave Belpre traveling west along SR-618, also the SR-50 Business Loop. We turn right onto SR-339 and travel about four miles north, passing through the village of Corner and Veto, to Sweetapple Road where we turn left and drive into Vincent, home of Carolyn (Richards) Butcher who started singing country music at the weekend jams her parents would hold in their home.

Developing a close relationship with Christ later in life, Carolyn began to seek a career singing gospel music. Since that time she has been nominated for several awards including New Female Artist of the Year by the Eastern USA Country Gospel Music Association. Her husband Dave Butcher attended church as a child but as a teen drifted far down the road to destruction. He became a cheat, liar, and even a thief. After a spiritual experience at age twenty-five, his life was turned around. In 2005, he was elected International Reciter of the Year at the CGMA International Convention held in Branson, Missouri, and from 2005 to 2007, he was voted Reciter of the Year by the Country Gospel Music Association. Dave and Carolyn continue traveling today under the name of Spiritual Road using their talents for God.

OHIO 10

Leaving Vincent, we continue north along SR-339 for about four miles to SR-550 where we turn right, passing the Lighthouse Baptist Church in Barlow where the Gospel River Boys will be singing Sunday morning. We continue along SR-550 passing through a tunnel and the village of Pinehurst to SR-7. Turning left, we travel about two miles to Marietta, where on Friday, April 13, 1973, an All-Gospel Homecoming Concert was held. This event was promoted by Sonny Simmons, who was born in Akron and was one of Nashville's dynamic promoters. Singing for the event was international recording artist Connie Smith, who was born in Marrietta, along with one of America's number one quartets the Oak Ridge Boys.

OHIO 11

Leaving Marrietta, we turn left onto SR-60, and winding through the Scioto River valley, we drive by Marietta Bible College, passing through Devola, Lowell and Coal Run on our way to Beverly. While in Beverly, we stop for gas and visit Lock No. 4. Beverly has three remaining locks from the Muskingum lock system, which is the only hand-operated lock system in continuous use from the 1800s. In March 1907, much of Beverly experienced a devastating flood. Coming from this quint little setting is the Clark Family.

Marvin and Deana Clark have been singing gospel music since 1990. Marvin comes from a strong musical background, and Deana grew up playing piano in her home church. They started out as a trio with the help of a family member, and as their four daughters learned to sing and play instruments, they became a part of the group. The Clark Family travels as a country-gospel-bluegrass group singing at fairs, festivals, and churches across the country. The Clarks founded and managed the Ohio Valley Opry, a traditional music show, held monthly in McConnellsville at the historic McConnellsville Opera

House. Their ministry is a testimony of faith as their three oldest daughters were all diagnosed with a genetic lung disease called cystic fibrosis at a very early age, but all are doing wonderfully well.

Leaving the lock, we turn right onto SR-60 and then turn left onto SR-530 where we wind up a very steep hill and enjoy a beautiful view of the countryside. Arriving at Warren, we turn right onto SR-821 and drive to Lower Salem. Driving through Lower Salem, we turn left onto SR-145 passing a church that could only be entered by crossing a little bridge that looks like a drawbridge. We continue along SR-145 winding northeast to Harriettsville, home of the Chapel-Aires.

Jim Blair remembers as he was growing up, the neighbors would gather around in the evenings and sing. Jim started singing country music in 1959, and then in 1976, he and his wife started a group called the Chapel-Aires. They started out as a duet and, in 1984, became a trio when Paula Preston joined the group. Paula previously sang with her family and is a very versatile singer. The Chapel-Aires travel throughout the Midwest states and often sing at the Guernsey Gospel Sing.

The Chapel-Aires were singing at a church one evening, and near the end of the service, in preparation for the altar call, Jim planned to have the congregation stand to their feet, bow their heads, and close their eyes. But stepping to the microphone, this is what he said, "Please stand on your hands, bow your eyes, and close your head." The congregation understandably lost it, and for some unexplainable reason, the group has never been invited back to that church.

Leaving Harriettsville, we take SR-145, passing through Stafford to Carlisle where we turn left onto SR-724. In the warm light of a beautiful sunset, we then turn right onto SR-260, and continuing to spot deer along the way, we turn left onto SR-78. After passing through Caldwell, we turn right onto SR 821. We continue along SR-821, and after passing under IR-77, we spot a huge sign on the right that says, "Jesus Loves You." We travel about four miles, passing through Coal Ridge, to Ava where in September, 1925, the *Shenandoah Dirigible* was ordered to conduct an ill-advised publicity tour of Midwestern state fairs. Less than twenty-four hours into its flight, the world's strongest airship, the *Shenandoah Dirigible*, was caught in a thunderstorm at Ava, torn to pieces, and scattered across the rolling hills of Noble County in Southeastern Ohio.

Commander Zachary Landsdowne of Greenville was killed, but amazingly, twenty-nine of the forty-three crew members survived.

Also from Ava, Darla Wheeler, now the mother of two adult children, started singing when just a child. Making her first recording in 2001, she has now completed three projects. She plays piano in her home church while maintaining an extensive nursing home ministry, and she remains actively involved in the Guernsey Gospel Jubilee Association. She has been privileged to share the stage with such groups as the Toney Brothers, Brian Free & Assurance, and Naomi and the Sego Brothers.

Leaving Ava, we continue north along SR-821 to SR-313 where we turn right and drive to IR-77. As the sun is setting behind us, an owl sweeps down across the road right in front of our car. We take IR-77 north to IR-70 where we turn west and travel a short distance to the Cambridge exit. Spending the night at the Comfort Inn, we enjoy a nice dinner at the American Restaurant, one of those all-you-can-eat places. The next morning as we leave the motel, we take SR-209 north into Cambridge stopping at a vintage McDonalds along the way to view the 1950s décor that includes a 1956 Chevy. Reaching downtown Cambridge, we turn right onto U.S. 22 and drive east through the hilly section of town where, in 1806, a group of early settlers from the Isle of Guernsey in the English Channel of England pitched camp because the women in the party refused to move on. Another woman, Denise Edwards Brown, refusing to change her beliefs, continues to take her stand for Jesus

Denise was born on January 16, 1973, in Cambridge. Denise started her musical career at the age of five when she sang in the Zanesville Junior Choir. At the age of nine, she had her first TV appearance when she sang on the Channel 2 Cambridge Praise Gathering. With this exposure, it wasn't long until she was receiving multiple requests to sing, and she was soon on the road. Her father, Quincy Edwards, would drive Denise to all of her singing appointments.

Through her ministry, she later met Marlin Brown, the man who would become her future husband. Before getting married, Marlin was with New Generation from Batesville, Indiana, and New Covenant in Charleston, West Virginia. He then traveled full-time with Homeward Bound in Illinois and the Ron Blackwood Singers of Branson, Missouri. He was singing with the Manships in Paoli, Indiana, when he married Denise.

After they were wed, Marlin went full time with the Wilburns in Carthage, Tennessee. In 1994, Marlin and Denise formed a trio called Majority based in Franklin, Indiana. The group was together for about 10 years. Since that time Denise and Marlin have continued their ministry as a duet. For twenty years, her father Quincy Edwards, founder of the Guernsey Gospel Jubilee Association, has been holding outdoor gospel sings at Spring Valley Campground on Dozer Road in Cambridge.

Leaving Cambridge, we continue east on U.S. 22 where we soon drive over a portion of Salt Fork Lake, and passing through Winterset, we come to Antrim where we turn right onto SR-513. Driving along SR-513 we spot some deer and pass a house where some clothes are hanging on the line, and they were probably frozen stiff. We travel along SR-513 for about six miles to where we merge onto IR-70 east and travel about twenty-one miles to U.S. 40. Along the interstate, the ice-covered trees are glistening in the morning sunlight. Reaching U.S. 40, we exit IR-70, winding down the hill on a horseshoe-bend curve to U.S. 40 where we turn right and continue east, winding back and forth under and over IR-70. We drive through Lloydsville, passing a big Friends Church on the right, and cross over IR-70 and enter Saint Clairsville, home of the Clarendon Hotel built in 1890, one of the oldest continuously operating hotels on National Road (U.S. 40).

The Coleman Family is a family band from Saint Clairsville who enjoys entertaining with bluegrass, old time and gospel music. Starting in 1995 they have performed at a number of fairs and opera houses. They have sung in many churches throughout Ohio and West Virginia also performing on Jamboree USA. In 2008 their ministry was going strong.

Leaving Saint Clairsville, we head back through town to SR-9. After turning the wrong way on SR-9, we turn around and travel south for about five miles to SR-149 where we turn left. Unable to find Okay Road, we drive back to County Road 56, and turning left, we cross a very small one-lane bridge. Shortly after crossing the bridge, we spot some longhorn steer grazing in a field along the left side of the road. We continue along the county road taking a right onto County Road 5 and a left onto OR&W Station Street and a right onto Ramsey Ridge to Jacobsburg home of the Believers.

Jack Palmer started out singing solo around 1982. His wife, Anna, joined him to form a duet, and when their granddaughter joined up with them, they became the Believers. They have sung on the radio and have done several television programs. Their ministry focused on nursing homes, revival meetings, outdoor concerts, and churches. They were also involved in the Feed the Children campaign by Mountain Vision. For fourteen years, they sponsored a local weekend called the Singing Gospel Jubilee, and Quincy Edwards ran sound for the event. While working as trash collector, Anna's husband later lost part of his thumb but still manages to play the guitar. He is also full-time minister at Hillcrest Bible Church in Belmont. As a result of medical problems, Anna has lost sight in one eye, but she also continues to sing for the Lord.

Leaving Jacobsburg, we turn left onto County Road 56 and drive about one mile to Mills Hill Road where we turn left, cross the creek, and travel to Pipe Creek Road. Turning right onto Pipe Creek Road we follow the creek about five miles to SR-7. The icicles along the stream are dazzling in the sunlight. Turning left, we travel another twenty-three miles north along the west bank of the Ohio River, watching the large barges pass by. Passing through Martins Ferry, we watch the smoke rise from the Cardinal Nuclear Plant. Exiting right onto SR-151, we pass through New Alexandria. Realizing that our wonderful GPS has messed up, we follow SR-151 back to SR-7 passing through Mingo Junction, a local ironworks community. Back on SR-7, we continue north to Steubenville. Exiting on Dean Martin Boulevard, we drive to the site of Fort Steuben, built in 1787. A town full of churches, Steubenville is called the City of Murals because over twenty-five murals can be found in the downtown area.

David Wayne Mathes was born in Steubenville on April 23, 1933. He attended high school in Fairborn and graduated from the University of Tennessee in 1966. David started singing with Jake Hess and the Imperials in 1966, remaining with them for one year. From there, he went on to sing with the Frost Brothers Quartet. "On the Jericho Road" was one of his most popular recordings.

Leaving Steubenville, we drive along West Market Street watching people walk up the road with Bibles in their hands. After turning right onto SR-43, the road merges with U.S. 22, and suddenly, we're lost. Pulling into a service station for fuel, we talk with a lady getting gas, and she provides some direction. Back on the road, we soon find U.S. 22 near the Lover's Lane exit. We merge onto U.S. 22 and travel about sixteen miles to U.S. 250. Reaching U.S. 250 we take a side tour through the town of Cadiz to visit the birthplace of actor Clark Gable. Back on U.S. 250, we travel along the northern edge of Tappan Lake, where we watch the geese walking on the ice-covered lake. Reaching the dam, we make a loop across the dam and continue toward SR-800. Reaching the town of Dennison, we turn the wrong way and have to turn around. Soon back on track, we continue north on SR-800 one mile to Uhrichsville, the previous home of William Ely, born in Harrison County on August 25, 1825. William's father, a native of Ohio and a blacksmith by trade, was instantly killed in 1883 by the bursting of an emery wheel while at work. William followed his heritage of blacksmithing for thirty-three years, working fourteen years at his trade in Uhrichville. He started a dairy in 1882, supplying the local communities with milk.

In 1994, Jose Pena helped form the Gospel H.I.M.S. Quartet based in Uhrichville, Ohio. The word *H.I.M.S.* is an acronym for "He Is My Savior." Sheila Carl of Tusacarwas, the group's pianist, was choir director for twenty years and has played piano for several churches. Randy Meece of New Philadelphia had previously sung with the Victory Quartet in New Philadelphia. Another one of the original members, from Port Washington, is Jeff McDonald. The group is always encouraged when someone finds salvation as a result of their ministry. One Sunday morning while singing in Middleborne, West Virginia, a sixty-eight-year-old woman gave her heart to the Lord.

Once, on the way to sing in Pleasant Point, West Virginia, they noticed the steering on the bus seemed a little abnormal. At a rest area they checked the bus and determined the front tire was separating. They called AAA, and someone showed up about two and a half hours later. The repairman they sent had just lost his wife to cancer and his house to a fire. The group counted it a blessing that they were able to witness to this man and provide some comfort as a result of their little inconvenience. They made it to Peasant Point for their appointment, and they stopped at Wal-Mart on the way home to have the new tire mounted. Wal-Mart wouldn't mount the tire, and they had to take it to a local garage called Possums Garage. The man who mounted their tire was the janitor. He and his family were cleaning the garage for business Monday morning.

Randy and Sheila have left the group being replaced by Doug Seevers, one of the original members and Jose's brother-in-law, and Brett Jackson from Dennison, Ohio.

Before leaving Uhrichsville, we stop at KFC across the street from Jerry's Restaurant for lunch. After eating, we take Water Street to U.S. 36 where we travel west for thirty-three miles to SR-541. We turn left onto SR-541 and drive to Coshocton home of Edgar J. "Texas" McNabb, a famous right-handed pitcher for the Baltimore Orioles in 1893. Out of twenty-one games, he pitched twelve complete games. The next season, he was released and signed with a minor league. Shortly thereafter, in the winter of 1894, he died a tragic death.

Speaking of tragic deaths, Jonathan White's parents were killed in an accident caused by a drunk driver in 1992. After the tragedy, Jonathan and his wife took on the role of parenting his younger siblings. Jonathan grew up singing with his family as they traveled throughout the country doing revivals. About one year after the accident, Jonathan started a solo ministry. He also started singing with the Brotherhood Quartet in Barberton. He remained with the quartet for two years.

One of the unique things about the Brotherhood Quartet was that they traveled to many of the concerts wearing leather jackets and riding on Gold Wing motorcycles while the bus followed behind. Once they were in South Dakota driving through the Needles. While they were stopped at one of the sites, they started singing and were passing out free recordings of the group. A man came up to them and wanted to know if he could have a different recording as he already had the one they were passing out. He said he had gotten it when they were singing in a restaurant somewhere in Colorado the previous year.

While traveling, they would often sing in the restaurants where they ate along the way. Shortly after the group was formed, they were traveling through Pennsylvania. They stopped at a little roadside restaurant, and while eating, they noticed a big husky guy working his way to the juke box. They started singing a song. When they were finished, he walked up to their table, and without even a smile, slapped a dollar bill down on their table and said, "I get four for a dollar, so you've got three more songs to go."

In 2000, Jonathan White joined up with Sheldon Mencer and Steven Cheney to form the trio Mencer, White & Cheney. Sheldon wrote a number of songs including, "Lead Me to the Rock," recorded by Janet Pascal, and

"Only God Knows," recorded by Gold City. Sheldon and Steven wrote the song "Sweet Peace," which was recorded by the Kingsmen. Coming off the road around 2005, the group still does a few appointments, and Jonathan White continues his solo ministry. Jonathan's daughter was born with Down's syndrome, and God has opened the door for Jonathan to minister in many hospitals across the country.

Leaving Coshocton, we take a quick drive through historic Old Town to SR-83 where we turn left and travel to Tsego where we wind up out of the valley, passing a small herd of deer. Following along a windy ridge road, we pass through Bloomfield to New Concord. Turning right onto U.S. 40 we travel a short distance to the old S Bridge. Built in 1830 and located along U.S. 40, the bridge was constructed in an *S* shape as it was easier and cheaper to build a stone arch at a right angle to the stream and bend the road at the approaches. Claiming New Concord as home is a group called Friendship Four.

Singing throughout Ohio and West Virginia, Tim Thomas, founder of the Friendship Four, is a third-generation gospel singer. His grandfather attended the Vaughn School of Music and later provided shaped-note training. Tim's father, Boyd Thomas, formed the Thomas Family Quartet in West Virginia and provided a radio program entitled the *Thomas Family Hour.*

Having strayed from God during his youth, Tim attributes his gospel music heritage as the avenue that reminded him he was lost and that God still loved him. Tim sang with the Thomas Family Quartet in Parkersburg, West Virginia, for five years. Then in 2000, after singing solo for three years, he formed the Friendship Four, a mixed quartet. The group considered it an honor when they were afforded the opportunity to open for the nationally known gospel group Brian Free and Assurance.

A desire to serve the cause of Christ in the mission field has taken the Friendship Four to the small country of Belize in Central America where the group formed a bond with the people living in the village of San Narciso, Belize. Partnering with Shalom Baptist Church of Byesville, the group continues its mission outreach by assisting with the educational costs of several youth of the village as well as working toward completion of a hurricane proof home for a family in the village.

The quartet has appeared at such places as *The Living Word Outdoor Drama*, Franklin County and Muskingum County Fairs, the Noble County

Correctional Facility, the state hospital at Cambridge, and the David Ring Crusade at Secrest Auditorium in Zanesville. The group continues today as a trio, singing predominately southern gospel music.

Leaving New Concord, we head west on U.S. 40 about five miles to Zane Grey Road where we cross over IR-70 and bear to the left at the Pine Lake Road split to avoid a steep hill at the intersection. We continue to Green Valley Road where we turn right and continue to SR-313. Turning right, we take SR-313 for a short distance to SR-146 where we turn left to Chandlersville, a village named for John Chandler, a local grist mill owner. Chandlersville is also home to the Singing Grannys, two sisters who started out singing with their father, and two other sisters in a group called the Heartmans out of Philo.

Forming their own group in 1997, the Singing Grannys continued to sing primarily in nursing homes and fairs and still take a few bookings today. One of the sisters, Wava Shuster has also done some singing with her husband.

Leaving Chandlersville, we take SR-146 to Zanesville where we merge onto IR-70 west and travel twenty-five miles to SR-79. We turn right onto SR-79 to Hebron where completion of the National Trail (Now U.S. 40) ushered in an era in which stagecoaches and riders on horseback were coming through Hebron on a regular basis, sometimes spending a night at the inn. At the turn of the century, a disastrous fire destroyed most of the business district, bankrupting many villagers.

Sometimes God calls time-out. In 1957, believing they could no longer continue a full-time singing ministry, the Rambos moved to the little town of Hebron. Buck took a job managing a local grocery store and Dottie worked in a plastic factory. During their short stay at Hebron, Buck worked hard and long to keep the store from going under. In the process, he became a close mentor to a struggling employee who was walking the path of destruction. One Sunday morning, after they had been ministering to the congregation, this young man and his wife found their way to the altar accepting Christ and surrendering their lives to Him.

Shortly thereafter, their mission finished, the Rambos left Ohio moving to Kentucky where they regained their full-time ministry status. The young couple, believing God had sent them to Hebron to rescue their lives, followed them to Nashville where they retained a close friendship.

One evening, years later, while driving from her motel to a tent revival being held somewhere in Ohio, Dottie Rambo became captivated by a cloud formation that inspired the writing of the song "We Shall Behold Him."

Shortly after 2:00 AM on Sunday, May 11, 2008 Dottie Rambo (born Joyce Reba Lutrell on March 2, 1934) was involved in an accident while traveling through Missouri in a 1997 Provost bus. She was on her way to a concert in Texas. Several others were injured, and Dottie, at the age of seventy-four, was pronounced dead at the scene. Dottie will be missed, but writing over two thousand five hundred songs, her legacy will carry on.

Leaving Hebron, we head back to U.S. 40 where we continue west, passing the National Trail Raceway and continue to SR-310. We turn right onto SR-310 and travel about three miles to Pataskala. In 1805, Richard Conine and his wife, Sarah, visited the area, liked what they saw, and went back home to New Jersey to arrange the purchase of 2,000 acres of land. Returning in 1821, Richard plotted a village which he called Conine. In 1851, the village received its first Post Office and controversy grew over the village name of Conine until finally the town was renamed Pataskala, which is an Indian word meaning "Licking." Within this growing community we find a group known as the Trio of His Love, a unique gospel group of three sisters who started in their teens and have been singing together for around twenty-five years.

Leaving Pataskala, we continue west along SR-310 to SR-16 where we turn left and continue about three miles to U.S. 40. Turning right onto U.S. 40, we drive into Reynoldsburg, a fairly large town, and the birthplace of the tomato. The Tomato Festival is celebrated each September in honor of Alexander Livingston who developed the Paragon tomato billed as the first ever tomato bred for commercial use.

Although not her birthplace, Pamela Kay attended a boarding school in Ohio at age fourteen and has lived in Ohio ever since. An on-stage singer since age four, she is also a trained pianist with a special ear for music. Prior to starting her solo debut, Pamela sang lead for a group called Unity. Since 1993, she has embarked on a solo career and has been recognized by the mayor of Columbus and the Ohio House of Representatives for her work in the field of gospel music, receiving awards for her musical contributions.

In addition to her concert work, she has made many personal appearances throughout the eastern United States, including the Ohio State Fair and numerous camp meetings and revivals. Pamela records monthly for the *Country Gospel Time* on Ohio TV-39. She has also had the opportunity to sing twice on a cruise ship and has sung with Hosanna Integrity's Choir. Pamela worked with Scott Fowler and Roger Bennett in the production of her second group project entitled *My Song in the Night*. Pamela Kay has had many songs on the southern gospel chart and was named Female Vocalist of the Year by the Tennessee Country Music Association in 2002. She is a singer with a style of her own—an inspirational style with a touch of southern gospel otherwise known as Christian country. But with her rich vocals and strong emotional lyrics, you will always hear God's promises.

Leaving Reynoldsburg, we continue west along U.S. 40 to IR-270 where we turn left and travel west along IR-270 to SR-62. Exiting onto SR-62 we travel south just a short distance to Grove City, home of the Gantz Farmhouse. Adam Gantz built this house in 1832 as part of a hundred-acre farm. It was donated to Grove City in 1973. There are ten unique herb gardens on the farm. Grove City is also the home of Bill Dykes, who was born in Cincinnati at General Hospital on December 10, 1946. His father was a preacher, so he was raised in the church and started directing music when he was twelve years old. Bill says, "I didn't know what I was doing, but I got up there and waived my arms." His father ministered all over the country and Bill went to school while his father was pastor at Georgetown Baptist Church located about sixty miles outside of Cincinnati.

His music teacher in school was Ms. Louise Krum who had sang at the Metropolitan Opera. She was well trained and was also teaching at the Cincinnati Conservatory of Music. She was a very large lady, had a heart of gold, and for some reason, developed a liking for Bill and took him under her wing. He started in her music class, later sang in the choir and had the lead part for three years in school productions. Sometimes she would even sneak him into class down at the Conservatory of Music while she was teaching. Bill remembers, "It was just awesome for me because I was a kid in high school, and I was just in awe of her past, she was incredible, not only as a vocalist, but a teacher. She became my first mentor."

While growing up he listened repeatedly to a little 45 he had in his room of the Blackwood Brothers. He loved gospel music and felt this was what God wanted him to do. When Bill was nineteen he saw an advertisement in the paper for a gospel singer. He answered the ad, and it was Floyd Arthur with the Chancellor Quartet from Hamilton. Just a kid, he was going to school at night and working at a finance company, and now singing with the Chancellor Quartet on the weekends.

They were all Nazarene boys so they sang mostly in Nazarene churches. They traveled in an old Silverside bus with the four-speed on the column. Big Dave Stewart was a collector of old cars and had five old Hudsons that were in absolute pristine condition, and that's the way he kept their bus. Floyd Arthur was a building superintendent and the leader of the group. He had converted his garage into a recording studio, and that's where they rehearsed every week.

One night in 1968 the Chancellor Quartet was doing a session at Artist Recording Studio when Carrol Rawlings and Dan Hubbard approached Bill informing him that Carrol would be taking over the studio at Artist Recording and was leaving the Rhythm Masters. They asked if he would be willing to audition for the job. Bill was in awe, and after hearing his audition, that day in the studio, they offered him the job. Leaving the Chancellors, he joined the Rhythm Masters, who at that time consisted of Chico (Grady Nix), Dan Hubbard, who was running WHAK, a radio station in Cincinnati, Buddy Liles singing bass, and Bill Phelps playing the piano.

Bill Phelps, their piano player, was a very jumpy person. If you even acted like you were going to touch his leg, he would jump or hit whatever was in front of him. Once they were at Taft Auditorium and while the Stamps Quartet was up singing Buddy Liles came up to Bill Phelps and simply bumped his leg. Instantly, Bill responded jumping right out on stage where the Stamps were performing. He was so embarrassed.

The Rhythm Masters would often sing for the chapel services at Liberty University and Bill helped Don Norman and Jerry Falwell at the For Love conferences. Bill says Jerry Falwell was a really great man, and Dr. John Rawlings of Landmark Baptist Temple was Jerry's mentor. While Jerry was in Cincinnati to preach the funeral for Dr. Rawlings's wife, he and Dr. Rawlings were talking and poking fun at Jerry, he said, "You know, Jerry, you need to lose some weight. You are ballooning up there."

Jerry replied, "Yea, Doc, you will probably be preaching my funeral." In 2007, when Jerry Falwell passed away, that's exactly what happened. Dr. Rawlings preached his funeral.

After traveling together for a while, the Rhythm Masters had a meeting at the Sharon Road Holiday Inn in Cincinnati to discuss their future. It was called a "Come to Jesus Meeting." Feeling like they had gone as far as they could go as a regional group, they were going to break out and try to make it at the full-time level. They were all young, had a lot of energy, and replacing their old 4103 Bus with the Cathedrals old 4104 Flex Bus, they were set to go. They had worked a lot with a promoter named Sonny Simmons gaining a lot of regional recognition while cohosting many of his programs at Taft Auditorium. As such, Sonny was on board with their plan to make the full-time move.

After much discussion that evening at the Holiday Inn, Dan, who had a full-time job as an engineer and a part time career with a local radio station, decided he could not go. Based on this, they decided to look for individual career opportunities.

Later that year, Buddy and Bill drove to Nashville to the NQC, and while there, Buddy accepted an offer from the Florida Boys, and Bill accepted a position with Coy Cook and the Senators. As both groups were based in Pensacola, Florida, Buddy and Bill were able to remain neighbors. Bill Phelps went on to be with the Hemphills.

Bill only remained with Coy Cook and the Senators about a year and a half. But it was a great tour as J. G. Whitfield, the promoter who owned the Gospel Singing News, owned the group giving them immediate exposure. The group members would often work at the newspaper and they became his front group as they promoted the newspaper. Calvin Runyon, who also sang with the Kingsmen, was singing bass, Bill was singing baritone, and Coy Cook was singing tenor as they traveled in a 4104 bus they had bought from the Downings. Mack Evans was singing lead and a short time later he became part of the *All Time Gospel Hour* at Thomas Road Baptist Church home of Pastor Jerry Falwell.

J. G. Whitfield later sold the group to a man in Mobile, Alabama. This was upsetting to the group members, especially Coy because he had previously sung with and was dear friends with J. G. The new owner wanted to sing baritone, so Bill agreed to step down from the position and resigned from the group. After being sold, the group only lasted for a short period of time.

Just prior to Bill leaving the Senators, Mack Taunton and George Amon had left the Cathedrals. Returning to their hometown of Flint, Michigan, they started a group called the Mack Taunton Team. After George Amon left, they hired a kid from Illinois named Jim Garston to play the piano.

Bill's family was in Cincinnati, so he would soon be heading back to Ohio. Before leaving Pensacola, Florida, Bill became aware of these changes, and having done a number of shows with the Cathedrals, he called Glen Payne and said, "Glen, word has it you need a baritone singer."

And he said, "No, I need a tenor singer, Roy Tremble is singing baritone."

Convinced they needed a baritone, Bill told Glen he would be in Cincinnati when they were doing their concert at Fairfield Junior High School in Fairfield. He agreed to meet with them asking Glen to just give him five minutes to audition. He told Glen they could put Roy on tenor because he had known him since 1961 when he was singing tenor with a small group called the Lancers in Kansas. Bill said Roy could sing high in the clouds. He said they had the Lancers in every year for the youth camp held in Cincinnati, and the kids loved them. Finally Glen agreed. The Cathedrals, not well-known, had just left the Cathedral of Tomorrow and were trying to make their mark. Bill believed it was only a matter of time, and they were going to become popular and he wanted to be part of their ministry.

Bill headed from Florida to Fairfield nonstop so he could sell his plan to the Cathedral Quartet. It was a long trip, and arriving home, he had not slept for two days. His voice was hoarse from talking on the phone, but he felt compelled to give it a shot. He was exhausted and didn't look very good either, but he arrived before the concert and jumped onto their bus. Without wasting, any time Glen said, "All right, let's go into the school, find us a room with a piano and let's see what it sounds like." Bill had already talked with Roy to get him motivated about the change.

Entering the room, the piano player started playing and soon they were singing that great song "What a Day That Will Be." Bill says, "We just kicked it up and started singing, it was like magic. You should have seen Glen and George looking back and forth at each other. They didn't even know Roy could sing tenor." Turned out Roy was not only a tenor singer but also a good one! All of a sudden, Glen asked Bill if he had brought anything to wear for tonight. It just so happened he had every piece of clothing he owned in the car as he had just driven from Pensacola. So he told Bill to go shave and put something on.

That evening after the program started, they brought him out on stage and, after singing several songs with them, he sang "The Lighthouse" and received a standing ovation. When the concert was over, and after confirming that Roy was agreeable to singing tenor, they told Bill the baritone position was his. They then told him this was their first stop of a two week tour and they were leaving immediately. They requested he load his clothes on the bus and inquired as to whether someone could come by and pick up his car.

When everything was taken care of, he loaded the bus and was off down the road singing with the Cathedrals.

They made a sizeable mark in the business at that point in time, recording their first record at Cleveland Sound, and their breakout song was "The Last Sunday" with Canaan Records.

Jim Garston was a tremendous classically trained pianist, but he wasn't with them very long. He left to travel with a country artist, and George Amon Webster came back to play piano. George Amon did a great job playing the keyboard and also wrote that great song "He Loves Me," which was a monster hit for the Cathedrals.

Bill says, "Glen and George are the classiest guys in the world. They were a great bunch of guys to be around and, of course, George is absolutely, completely out of his mind. Just funny—he's always on, you know, unless he wants to be alone in his quiet time. I learned more probably from George Younce than any teacher I ever had. He would school me on placement, he would school me on breathing, and he would school me on so many things as we were riding down the road."

In the early stages, they actually were better known in Canada because of the TV shows. They would go up to Canada and would sell out of stuff the first two nights they were there. Their wild popularity was partly because Rex Humbard's Cathedral of Tomorrow ministry was so huge up in Canada. They tried to play every date available while in Canada.

The Cathedrals were in Canada performing with the Singing Goffs and the Gospelaires. Sometime during the evening Jerry Goff cornered Bill, presenting some pretty challenging questions like: How would he like to make some real money? How would he like to work out of Nashville, Music City, USA? How would he like to have some hit records? He then indicated he would soon be losing his baritone singer, and he would sure like for Bill to come to Nashville. Bill, still somewhat young and trying to work his way through school, postgraduate work, was hesitant to give him an answer. Jerry Goff was persistent, wouldn't let this matter rest, and finally made him a financial offer he couldn't resist.

Bill accepted the offer and told Glen and George he was leaving. As George Amon Webster was a great baritone, this would work well for them also as they could melt the group down to just four. It was a difficult decision, but he never regretted making the move as Jerry Goff was very good to him, and they had some major hit records and gospel music awards.

Based in Nashville, Goff was not only a promoter but also an evangelist. Sometimes the Singing Goffs would go into a church and do a three-day crusade. That was enjoyable to Bill because he got to do the praise and worship and lead the music. The group would sing, and Jerry would preach. Keeping a busy schedule, they spent much time eating at restaurants and staying in hotels.

Things really started booming around 1975 when they came out with that great song "I'll See You in the Rapture." They were the ones to take it to number one on the charts. It was an absolutely unbelievable experience because not only did their visibility become incredible but their bookings increased as well. Don Littleton, their booking agent, doubled their fees so they all got a raise, which was kind of nice, and they were selling twice as many records as they had been selling.

Shortly after coming out with "I'll See You in the Rapture," they were singing in Pennsylvania at the Rodeo Arena for the Courier's Annual Homecoming. It was a big event, and there were a number of groups present including the Kingsmen, who at the time were doing some incredible programs absolutely wearing out an audience. But when the Goffs started singing the "Rapture," they literally would not let them off stage. Back then, they ordered their records in twenty-five-count boxes as that's how they were shipped. It was Bill's job to make sure that the bus was stocked. Before they left town, he would have to go down to the local bus station and pick up the shipment loading the bays with these twenty-five-count records.

By the end of the night in Pennsylvania, because of "Rapture," they had sold out of records. Back then, the way the groups would get at each other was by stacking boxes. They called it "stacking empty boxes." If you were stacking boxes, it meant you were selling lots of records. Well, that night they stacked boxes to the ceiling in the outer area of that Rodeo Arena. They sold out! Jerry Goff got on the bus and commented that in all his years with the Thrasher Brothers and all his years with the Goffs, he had never experienced a night like they had that evening. The audience was incredible, and the singing was great.

Once while doing a three-week tour the Goffs stopped in San Antonio, Texas. It was a Tuesday evening, but the church was huge, seating around three thousand people, and the promoter had told them it was going to be an incredible service. They unloaded their equipment and set up the records as usual. Then while getting dressed, Tom looked out the window expressing concern that there were no cars in the parking lot. Prior to the service as people began to enter the sanctuary, Wally was running the organ, Barry was playing bass, Jerry was blowing that trumpet, and Bill was playing the drums. Soon it was seven-thirty, time for service to start, and only five people had showed up—only five people.

As the service started Bill says, "I will never forget this as long as he lives. Goff will typically sing and minister even if there is only one person in the house. It is no big deal to him." But that evening, Jerry stepped up to the microphone, and after telling the church how much he appreciated the five people that showed, he told them that tonight the group was going to take the evening off. He then requested each one of them to stop by the record table and pick up a set of records at no cost, so they could enjoy the group's singing in the comfort of their home.

Jerry Goff had just bought a beautiful new Silver Eagle bus and had the body shipped over from Belgium. He then had Celebrity Coach in Nashville customize the inside to unbelievable specifications. Back in the 1970s, the crowds were incredible, and it made all the difference in the world when you had a hit record. People wanted to hear it over and over again, and Jerry Goff could wear a crowd out. He could wear the guys on stage out, too. Bill wrote a song that was recorded by about fifteen different groups. It is called "This is Love," and it became a gold record while Bill was with the Goffs. With all of this attention, they had to be really, really careful to make sure that their motives and intentions were properly focused.

The Goffs were doing a tent crusade up in Des Moines, Iowa. They had finished singing, and Dr. Goff, such a powerful orator, was preaching a message called "The Cross," a most powerful message on the reason for the cross. The huge tent was packed, and the power of the Holy Spirit was soon filling that big tent. He hadn't even finished his message when people started coming forward. Sounds like the moving of the Holy Spirit was really incredible that evening!

In 1975, they toured all summer with Colonel James Erwin, an *Apollo 15* astronaut, and the Goffs opened for the 1976 World Olympics in Montreal, Canada. They were also doing *God and Country* shows at fairs all over the country and did a three-week tour with the Oakridge Boys out on the West Coast.

Sometime later at the NQC, Bill was approached by QCA Records in Cincinnati, and in addition to traveling the country with the Singing Goffs, he was soon producing albums for QCA. They would sing Thursday, Friday, and Saturday night then twice or three times on Sunday, and when they weren't too far away, he would try to fit in the production of a recording on Monday, Tuesday, and Wednesday at QCA Records or Artist Recording. Bill loved producing, and Charles Novell would often help him by playing keyboard. He produced over two hundred records providing some extra income along the way to keep the family going.

Around 1977, a representative from QCA approached Bill asking him to become director of A&R Marketing, signing gospel groups and producing records. They made him an incredible offer agreeing to provide a good salary, a car to drive, and an expense account. At this time, the Singing Goffs were busier than ever. During the previous year, they had done three hundred dates and traveled a hundredsixty thousand miles. It doesn't matter how nice the bus, that's a lot of traveling. So still in his twentiess, Bill came to Jerry and told him he was taking the position with QCA Records. Bill told him it was his hometown; he could finally be with his family; he could get involved in a local church and could still occasionally sing on weekends if he wanted. Jerry respected that and was very, very gracious.

Bill later put together a group called the Premiers. He also went back and sang for about three years as part of the second-generation Rhythm Masters. They had a great hit entitled "God Rides on Wings of Love" that went national. After that he put together a group called the Chariots.

Bill's wife held a birthday celebration in Mason for his fortieth year in gospel music, and people came from all over the country. Jeff Perkins, who had a couple of groups from Cincinnati, was there. A number of people called in during the evening including Jerry Goff from Florida. They had a wonderful time. His wife found all thirty-six albums that Bill had recorded. This was a real surprise because he couldn't find the one he did for Canaan Records with the Cathedrals entitled "The Last Sunday." The album contained a great story song and George did a story song probably better than anybody.

Then one day out of the clear blue sky, they received in the mail, an absolutely perfect, in the wrap, copy of the *Last Sunday* album. Their good friends Cloid and Debbie Baker of the group called Forgiven, knowing they were looking for this record, had found a copy of the album. His wife was ecstatic, needless to say. There was also a pristine *It's About Time* album from his second tour of duty with the Rhythm Masters. She had them displayed, and his daughter had put together a photo display for the event.

During the celebration, his daughter got up and shared what it was like having a father singing gospel music on the road full-time. She said, "The thing that I remember most about when we lived in Nashville, I would wait on Sunday nights for the phone to ring. Sometimes it would be two o'clock in the morning, sometimes it would be four o'clock in the morning, sometimes it would be six o'clock in the morning, but I always knew mom was going to come and get me out of bed, we were going to go up to the Waffle House because that is where the bus dropped dad off every time he came in from a tour, and we would have waffles together."

They had a great time! There were three different groups there that sang and a lot of people spoke. Bill says, "It was a very humbling experience, to be honest with you. And it was a real blessing."

At age sixty, Bill is still employed and does some singing on the side with a new group that includes Chuck Sullivan when he is not involved in his own ministry, Larry Orrell when not traveling the world, and Terry Blackwood when he is not traveling or singing with the Classic Imperials. They hope to have Big John Hall join them soon. Big John was previously with the Stamps and the Blackwood Brothers and the original Friends Four.

* * *

Ron McNeal was born in Jackson County on January 18, 1939. Growing up, Ron lived in a little place called Kitchen, which is outside of Oak Hill. Ron says, "Kitchen was one of them 'poke and plum' towns where by the time you get your head poked out the window, you are plum through it." The family grew up singing in church, and Ron was only three the first time he sang a duet with his mom. He stood up on the altar rail with mom right beside the altar. He held onto her shoulder in order to be as tall as she was. He sang tenor to the song "I Won't Have to Cross Jordan Alone."

All through childhood, different churches within the local area would have special services, and as the family didn't have a phone, someone from the churches would come over ahead of time and ask if they could come on a certain Sunday to sing. The church would come and pick them up and after the service the church would fix their dinner and bring them back home. This activity continued until all children were married and left home.

Ron remembers listening to the Chuck Wagon Gang. He always enjoyed watching the Gospel Singing Jubilee when they had groups like the Blue Ridge Quartet, the Prophets, and the Johnson Sisters. His favorite quartet through all the years they sang was the Cathedrals. In addition to their terrific sound, he liked them because they always stuck with good old traditional southern gospel music. Ron never had a television until he was married in 1959. Up to that point, it was radio only and if they couldn't hear it on the radio, they just didn't hear it because they lived way out in the country and didn't have a car. They couldn't travel to the concerts when people would come around in different areas. But if there was southern gospel on the radio, they would be listening.

In the mid 1950s, he had the opportunity to attend some of the concerts held at the Memorial Auditorium in Columbus. Being overwhelmed with the rhythm of the music and the sound of that four-part harmony, he would come home from the concerts dreaming about starting a quartet. Ron says, "Even as a young person not yet saved, southern gospel music spoke to me, it made you take notice, you know, of what they were actually singing. And I always felt like it was just preaching with a tune to it." At age fifteen, he got saved, and then on July 17, 1959 he got married.

The McNeal Family started as a family group in their church in 1961. About 1963, their sister got married and left for college. They were pastors of several churches in the area. It was at that time that they changed their name from the McNeal Family to the Crusaders.

They began their travels doing a lot of revivals. The first year on the road, Ron had an old 1959 Mercury. It was a big old long car, one that looked like a boat on wheels. They rebuilt the engine and the transmission and had a trunk big enough to fit their equipment. Then they would all pile into the car—the four singers, the piano player, and sometimes even Ron's wife. They put a hundred and fifty thousand miles on that car in a period of eighteen months. They would leave one revival on a Sunday and start another on Tuesday. They would have Monday off, but in the course of a year, they wouldn't even have two weeks in all the single days through that year when they weren't singing in a revival someplace. In this manner, they became acquainted with a number of major evangelists. It didn't matter what denomination—if they got a call, they went. They never sang for money even though it cost a lot of money to do what they were doing. If the church gave them an offering, that was fine. If they didn't, the group never said anything about it.

Sometime in 1968, a man knocked on Ron's door one evening and said, "Come out here." They went out, and in the yard, there sat a big Flex Coach bus. It had the big air scoop on top at the rear of the bus. This was when they first started putting the engines in the back, and it was so easy for the engine to get hot. You had to constantly watch the water and the temperature. Then the man said, "This is yours."

The Crusaders had held an outdoor concert in the streets of Darbyville, a little town where they lived and went to church at the time. In fact, it was the church where he met his wife. There was a local man whom the people considered the town drunk, an individual steeped in sin. He had one boy that was about eight years old. The boy really liked the Crusaders because they had drums and guitars. One evening, the boy talked his daddy into bringing him to a concert, and because of the message in the songs, his dad accepted Christ as his Savior. As a result, his life was drastically changed, completely turned around from the life he once lived. The people were astonished at the change in a man's life as it was so visible.

This was the guy that knocked on Ron's door and said, "This is yours." He had bought the bus and was giving it to them. He had a heart attack while driving a tractor and died a few years later, and Praise God, he died a Christian. That was the first coach they had. Since that time, they have had five or six different buses. Their last bus was a 1973 Silver Eagle that they got in Anderson, Indiana. It had been used to haul company employees to Chicago for daily visits to the dog tracks.

In 1972, the first year Larry Riley was with the quartet, they had a piano player named Maurice Frump who kept track of all the people that came to the altar. During that year, there were 1,576 people who came to the altar. People would get up at any time during the service and come to the altar, and the group would always stop and have prayer with them. Sometimes, the altar would be lined three times within any given Sunday concert. They always gave people time to give their testimony.

Leaving the Crusaders, Larry Riley went to the Challengers. They went into full-time and then switched over from singing gospel to country. Larry later struck up his own country band traveling coast to coast for a long while until his health started failing him, and he had to come back home. He later got back into southern gospel.

Around 1977, the Crusaders sang in a little church down on the other side of Athens. As the church wasn't big enough to provide sufficient salary to support a preacher and his family, the preacher also worked as a game warden.

After singing at the church that afternoon, Ron came home feeling completely discouraged. His wife asked what was wrong. Ron told her he just felt like they beat their heads against the wall and didn't get anything accomplished.

Then in 2003, they were down in Logan at the Central Ohio Church of the Nazarene Campgrounds, and this older gentleman came up to Ron and asked if he had time to sit down and talk. They sat down and the man said, "Now, you're probably not going to remember me." He said, "You won't remember the church you came to when we heard you sing."

Suddenly, Ron stopped him and said, "That was the church just south of Athens. The pastor was a game warden."

And he said, "You do remember." After Ron shared how he felt that day the man continued. He and his wife, age sixty-three, had never been in church in their life. Leaving the service that day, they could not get over what they heard and what their Spirit sensed during the service. Going home that evening, his wife fixed dinner, and they filled up their plates but just pushed it back as neither one could eat. So they got ready and went to bed, and they couldn't sleep. Together they got out of bed, knelt down on their knees in front of their living room couch, and accepted the Lord into their life. With tears running down his face he said, "My wife has already gone on to be with the Lord, but I am going to catch up with her one day soon." What an inspiration! This is a reminder that if we just do our part and take our hands off and leave it up to Him, He will accomplish what we can't even think of doing.

Another member, Rick Allred was a tall, heavy-set fellow who lived in Fulton. He sang tenor with the group until he was taken from the group by a car wreck. Bob Michaels played the bass guitar and was also with the Mariners for a while. Francis Chamberlain played steel guitar for a number of years until leaving to play for the Dayton Ambassadors. He now plays for a group called Happy Hearts in southern Kentucky.

In 1972, the Crusaders went to Nashville and made a recording at the Skylight Recording Company with Joel Gentry. The title was *Going Up*. The youngest son of Francis Chamberlain actually got saved listening to that album. There were several songs that he really liked, and he got saved while playing those songs.

One afternoon while they were singing in Springfield, at a concert promoted by Kenny Shiveley, a man came in the service walking on crutches. They were singing, and people were continually lining the altar. About the third time they started to gather around the altar, the gentleman on the crutches was sitting in the back of the sanctuary. Suddenly he got up, and leaping frantically on those crutches, he came running toward the altar losing the crutches about eight feet before getting to the altar. He plunged toward the altar, hitting his chest on the altar. He hadn't prayed very long before he came up shouting, and around the church he went. He was truly filled with the Spirit, and all you could hear him say was, "I've got it, I've got it, I've got it!" Soon realizing his crutches were still lying on the floor and that he was running around the church, he acknowledged that something truly special had happened.

Jim Chapman, from the Springfield area, sang bass for several years. Prior to joining the Crusaders, he sang with the Gospel Rainbows in Springfield. He's now in Nashville doing back up music and studio work for people like Loretta Lynn. He teaches in a school as an art teacher. When the Greater Dayton Gospel Music Association held their big event at the Montgomery County Fairgrounds, Jim painted little pictures on the kid's faces. When the Crusaders would sing, where they had tables set up with white table cloths, Jim would pick three or four people out of the crowd and do a pencil drawing of those people. Of course, those people would always cut out the pictures. He has quite a talent. Jim Chapman cowrote a song with his brother-in-law Steven Curtis Chapman that went to number one. The Cathedrals recorded it, and "I Can Feel the Touch" was the name of the song. On a side note, Steven Curtis Chapman married Jim Chapman's sister who didn't have to change her name when she was married.

Another bass singer, Dale Murphy, was with them about ten years. Dale later sang with several groups including the Apostles with Ken Ankney. One weekend, when Tom Lawson was unable to sing, Dale sang bass for the Dayton Ambassadors. During a recent concert, in Christiansburg, Dale got up and sang a couple songs with the Crusaders. He is not presently with any group.

At one point in their ministry, the generator on the bus needed repair, and the voltage regulator needed to be replaced. To fix or replace these items was going to cost $6,000, and they didn't have the money. To get by, they had a battery charger hooked up to the battery, and using a small portable generator to run the battery charger, they were able to continually charge the battery. They traveled this way for a while.

After one event in Maryland, they were coming back through Pennsylvania headed up Snow Shoe Mountain along U.S. 80 when the engine stopped running. They had the bus towed to a local garage where they determined the engine was locked. The mechanic told them they could leave the bus and pick it up the next week. The next week, they took a bus mechanic who had previously done some work on their bus. After arriving, he looked over the engine and determined a sleeve had cracked when the engine overheated and then one of the rings on the piston caught in the crack, and that's what locked the engine. He removed the damaged piston from the engine, leaving only seven cylinders instead of eight, but this would get the bus home.

They got the bus ready, and when they attempted to start it, the battery was dead. They went back and looked and someone had stolen their portable generator and the battery charger. They had a trucking company charge the battery, and the mechanic told them they could only drive about two hours until the battery would be dead, and then the engine would just stop. So they figured that they would drive about two hours, charge the battery, and drive two more hours repeating this cycle until they reach home that was about seven hundred miles away. They started out on the road, and the engine soon got hot because of fuel mixing with the oil. Pulling off the road, Ron caught a ride with a semi driver to the next truck stop where he purchased some oil and a pan to drain the engine. Ron managed to get a ride back with another semi driver. In the meantime, their mechanic had whittled out a little piece off a bush and drove the peg into that fuel injector so fuel wouldn't squirt in the oil.

They changed the oil and were ready to start again, but before getting back on the road, Ron suggested they have a little prayer meeting. Getting down on their knees, Ron told the Lord he felt like they were doing exactly what He wanted them to be doing—they were a long way from home and really needed some help to get the bus home. Back in the driver's seat, they started up the bus and headed down the road. Before long, it started to rain and becoming foggy and dark, they had to turn on the headlights. The mechanic said, "That's going to cut our driving time down, so we will have to charge the battery more often." But that's not what happened, for as they reached Youngstown, which was almost five hours of driving, the headlights were still as bright as could be on that bus.

They continued on to Cambridge where they turned onto IR-70 and traveled west. Then about four-thirty in the morning, they decided to pull off at a truck stop near Buckeye Lake and get something to eat and have the battery checked. After checking the battery, the mechanic at the garage told them, "I don't know what you've got in the battery, but that thing almost burned up my tester when I hooked it up, I've never seen a battery so hot in my life."

Their mechanic shook his head and said, "Ron, that's impossible, we've driven over six hours, and they told us two hours was the max we could drive without a generator." Ron said, "Well, we have a generator. We just can't see it, that's all." They brought the bus home and ended up driving it for two more years without having to do anything to the battery. Isn't God great?

Gene McCorkle was on the television station for a long while, and everybody simply called him Gene Mac. He sang and played with the group for a long time. When he was in the war, he got an infection requiring the removal of his leg. Sometimes he would get blessed setting at the drums and would get up, grab his crutches and shout around on the stage and then back to the drums he would go.

In 1977 and 1978, the group toured in Hawaii. There was a man that worked at a radio station who had played piano for the Imperials in the states. He contacted them and set up five concerts. They would go for a week at a time, and he would set up five concerts some place on the islands. One day, a school furnished a school bus to take everybody around. They went to a little Baptist church that seated about 170 people. When the service started, they were standing around the walls, people outside the windows ten and twelve deep that couldn't get into the church. It was a service saturated with the presence of the Lord. The pastor of that church wrote Ron a letter six weeks later and said they had taken in nineteen new families into the membership after that service was over. He said it really made a difference for them. They just like that southern gospel!

Born in Springfield, Debbie Domer started singing in 1978 with the Crusaders. After three years, the group disbanded, causing Debbie to move into a solo ministry. In 1997, Debbie formed her own recording company called "Wayhome Records."

* * *

After moving to Grove City in 2003, having over twenty years of experience in gospel music, Garry Jones formed his own group called Mercy's Mark. Then in 2005, the *Singing News Fan Awards* named them the Horizon Group of the Year.

Garry Jones was born in Fort Walton Beach, Florida, on September 16, 1962. At age three, Garry was involved in a life-threatening accident that resulted in his parents becoming Christians and changing the course of his life. Garry started playing piano at the age of seven and began playing professionally at age seventeen. Garry traveled with Gold City for almost fourteen years before touring with Grammy Award—winning Ricky Skaggs.

He was cofounder, producer, and developer of Signature Sound Quartet. Garry was also honored to be featured pianist for the Old Friends Quartet with those two legendary artists Jake Hess and George Younce. Garry was the original producer and arranger for many songs including such greats as "If God Be For Us," "For God So Loved," "There Rose a Lamb" and "Midnight Cry." He has received numerous awards and was inducted into the Alabama Hall of Fame. He has appeared on several television programs including the 700 Club, John Hagee Ministries and has appeared on the Grand Ole Opry.

Another member, Christian Davis, with his smooth bass voice, started singing when he was three years old. His mother was a DJ for a local gospel station, so he was exposed to southern gospel at an early age. He started singing full-time with the Sounds of Liberty, a recruiting group from Liberty University in Liberty, Virginia, in 1998. Later that year, he joined the Old Time Gospel Hour Quartet. When they decided to cut back on their singing schedule, he formed the Christian Brothers Quartet, remaining with them until leaving to sing with Mercy's Mark.

Brent Mitchell came from a long history of gospel music with his parents forming a family group called the Singing Ambassadors of Macon, Georgia.

* * *

Judy initially started singing in 1964 with a ladies trio called the Joy Belles. They sang for the original "Teens for Christ" convention back in the 1960s. Judy got married in 1966, and when one of the girls had to withdraw from the group, she was replaced by Judy's husband, Don Clapsaddle. The group then became known as the Sounds of Joy. The group disbanded in 1987 after the passing of Judy's mother and pianist, Wanda Castle. In 1994, the remaining members felt the call to return to their singing ministry. They made a fresh start under the name Soul Purpose believing "Your soul is their purpose."

Soul Purpose was singing at a church in Greentown, Indiana, one evening when the church lost all electricity. It was ninety-five degrees, and talk about hot! Off came the shoes, off came the jackets, and out came the candles, but the service went on as planned. It was truly a night to remember.

Using various combinations of music from solo work to four-part harmony, they have performed at churches and state conventions throughout the eastern USA, sharing programs with some of the nation's finest talent. They sing five years straight for the Arts in the Alley, an event held in Grove

City. Kevin Williams, with Bill Gaither's Homecoming Concerts, produces their recordings in Nashville, Tennessee. Their recordings have been played on radio stations throughout the east coast from New York to North Carolina.

At one of the churches where the group was singing, there was a little girl, around four years old, who had been born with something wrong with her legs, and she was unable to walk. She had surgery, but the doctors didn't know for sure whether it would help her. Well, that day, she was so proud because her legs were beginning to work, and she slowly worked her way to the group and shared that God had fixed her legs, and she could walk again. The simple faith of a little child, what a blessing!

Returning Home

Before leaving Grove City, we stop at Tee Jayes Country Place Restaurant for a nice evening meal. Then traveling in the darkness, as the sun has now set, we follow SR-62 north to IR-270 taking IR-270 north to IR-70. Taking IR-70 west ramp, we travel about seventy-six miles to IR-75. Taking IR-75 north, we continue about two miles to U.S. 40 where we take the Vandalia exit, ending Tour 7.

MARSHALL FAMILY

Judy Marshall

MERE IMAGE

CORNERSTONE

GENERATION OF FAITH

KING FAMILY

Sharon Hardman

DAYSPRING

Darla Wheeler

COLEMAN FAMILY

GOSPEL H.I.M.S.

Jonathan White

RAMBOS

Dottie Rambo

Dottie Rambo & BOOTH BROTHERS

Pamela Kay

Bill Dykes

Bill Dykes with CATHEDRALS

Bill Dykes with SINGING GOFFS

CRUSADERS

CRUSADERS

CRUSADERS

MERCY'S MARK

MERCY'S MARK at 2006 NQC

SOUL PURPOSE with
Vestal Goodman

Chapter VIII

Dayton Tour

I'll See You In The Rapture

If we never meet again on this earth my precious friend
If to God you have been true and you've lived above all sin
Then for us they'll be a meeting, a hallelujah greeting
I'll see you in the rapture some sweet day

To my loved ones let me say, there'll surely come a day
When the Lord shall come and take His bride away
So get ready now to meet him, with a hallelujah greet Him
I'll see you in the rapture some sweet day

I'll see you in the rapture; I'll see you in the rapture
I'll see you at that meeting in the air
There with our Blessed Redeemer, we'll live and reign forever
I'll see you in the rapture soon glad day

—Charles Feltner
(Used with permission)

Leaving Vandalia, we turn left onto Dixie Drive and travel south to Little York Road. Turning right on Little York Road, we head east down the hill and crossing the Great Miami River we turn right onto Rip Rap Road and enter Huber Heights, where through the dedication of a young man named LD King, the Kings Journeymen, a bluegrass group, was formed in 1977 and continued to minister to churches in the region until 1994. They performed at the Greene County Fair for several years on stage with the Southern-Aires. The Byrd brothers, Randy and Jeff left the group to start a bluegrass group called Higher Ground, which remained together about one year.

* * *

The Singing Northernaires, a mixed quartet, started in 1978 and continued to sing until 1990. Jeff Delorme changed positions with Tim McIntosh, bass player for the Blessings Unlimited, so Jeff could travel with his future bride, Michele Arthur, who at the time was playing piano for the Blessings Unlimited. Jeff later played a long-term stint with the Dayton Ambassadors.

* * *

In the mid-1940s, while attending Pilgrim Holiness College in Frankfort, Indiana, Agnes Mae Hower, known to all as "Sparkie," along with two other young girls formed a trio. They named the trio the Buckeye Trio as they were all from Ohio. They traveled extensively across eastern USA from 1945 through 1947, typically ministering at revivals, campmeetings, and other special services. A versatile trio, they played a variety of instruments including the guitar, accordion, piano, and bass.

In 1947, Agnes married Edmund "Doc" Wells, and he soon became a member of the group. At which time they changed their name to the Buckeye Gospel Quartet. Ed had formerly sung with the Echoes From Calvary Quartet also from Pilgrim Holiness College. A prolific songwriter, his first composition, "Three Square Meals," was published in a Pilgrim Holiness Church songbook in 1945.

In 1950, Ed entered the pastoral ministry. At which time, he and Sparkie continued their music ministry under the name Wells of Salvation. Then in

1956, he compiled and published many of his songs in a songbook entitled *Wells of Salvation Songs*.

In the mid-1970s, Ed hosted a successful radio ministry while pastoring a United Methodist church in Helena. They continued singing until 1982. As mom and dad stepped down, their two children Mickey Wells and Melody (Wells) Morris stepped up to the plate to carry on the family tradition as the Wells of Salvation Gospel Band.

In 2000, the group's satire number on church dinners "Until We Eat Again" won a national songwriting competition sponsored by Embassy Music in Nashville, Tennessee and was later recorded by Aaron Wilburn.

Although Edmond Wells passed away in 2005 and was followed soon thereafter by his wife, Agnes, the Wells of Salvation Gospel Band remained active in 2008 primarily in prison ministry.

Taking Rip Rap Road south, we turn left onto Chambersburg Road. Then turning left on SR-202, we drive a short distance to our home church where we partake in Sunday school and morning worship. Back on Chambersburg Road, we turn left and continue east enjoying the scenery as the bright sunlight glistens over the golden cornstalks. Crossing the Mad River, we pass Wright-Patterson Air force Base (WPAFB) where we get a close-up view of those big B-52 bombers. Soon we turn right onto SR-444 and arrive in Fairborn. As a result of the 1913 Flood two villages, Fairfield and Osborn, were combined to form a new city called Fairborn.

Another combination, Charles Thomas and his wife Julia, started singing together as a duet shortly after they were married. A few years later, in 1963, they formed the Faithful Four Quartet based in Fairborn. Over the years, the group struggled with numerous personnel changes, bouncing back and forth from a quartet to a trio. In 1970, they officially became the Faithful Three Trio.

During one memorable service, while singing in Peoria, Illinois, they witnessed over thirty people give their hearts to the Lord. Probably one of the highlights for the group was when they performed to a crowd of over seventeen thousand people at a big singing held at Mount Nebo, West Virginia.

The group traveled throughout a seven-state area singing almost every weekend, and after singing together for over forty years, the group officially stopped singing.

Leaving Fairborn, we continue along SR-444 to Kauffman Road where we turn left and take a side tour to the top of Wright Brothers Hill where we view a beautiful monument commemorating the work of the famous Wright Brothers, Orville and Wilbur, who started experimenting in the late 1800s with a machine that would fly like a bird under its own power. Their original hangar site is located on Wright-Patterson AFB and is maintained by the United States Air Force. From the hill, we also have a great view of Huffman Dam, one of the five flood control dams constructed as a result of the Great Flood of 1913. Leaving the park, we view a man preparing to mount his horse and ride down the trail, enjoying the long-awaited sunshine. Turning right onto Kauffman Road, we continue to National Road where we make a right turn and continue to Colonel Glen Road. Turning left onto Colonel Glen Road, we pass Wright State University. Turning right onto Fairfield Road we enter Beavercreek where we stop at LaRosa's Pizzeria for one of their delicious pizzas.

Beavercreek is home to the Stillwaters, a mixed quartet that was formed in 1969 to provide music for two small churches in western Ohio. Also from the Beavercreek area is the Carl Shiveley Family.

Carl Shiveley was born back in a hollow on February 27, 1935, in Rome, which is down along the Ohio River. He always liked music, and he remembers they had a radio, one of those with three big dry cell batteries. They would listen to three music programs, one from Chicago (*Suppertime Frolic*), one from Wheeling, West Virginia, and the *Grand Ole Opry*. The family left the area when Carl was six years old and moved to the Portsmouth area where he grew up. His dad, Bill Shiveley, only knowing three chords would play the guitar and his mother, Katie Shiveley, would sing.

Carl and his brother Gene Shiveley started singing when they were seven or eight years old. They would play the guitar and the mandolin, and with Carl singing lead and his brother singing tenor, they produced some pretty good harmony. They use to walk up to WPAY radio station every Saturday morning carrying their instruments and would sing on the kids program.

Every night of the week, they would go to church somewhere. One time at a church dinner on Rosemont Road in Portsmouth, when Carl was between twelve and fourteen years old, he and his brother sang with their mom and dad. Then a guy got up and said he wanted to take up an offering for the boys. Taking up an offering, they received $5.34. Later, Carl got an acoustical guitar, and he made a Hawaiian type (steel) guitar out of it. Then during a revival at the Township Hall, he played his homemade Hawaiian guitar. After he was finished, they collected an offering to buy him an electric steel guitar. They raised almost enough money to buy one.

The brothers continued to sing together. They sang at an amateur show in high school one year and won first place. Boy, did they think that was something! They got their picture in the paper and everything.

After graduating, Carl was working at the lumber company in Portsmouth. Prior to getting married, Carl had a little group from the church that occasionally sang around the area. While in Portsmouth, he started dating a girl he had went to school with named Billie Mangus. They attended the same church, and once in a while, Billie and one of her friends would sing. She didn't sing with Carl until after they were married.

After his sister moved to Dayton, she told him he could get a good job there. So he moved to Dayton in September 1953 and started work. On April 24, 1954, Carl and Billie were married. After moving to Dayton, Carl started singing with a group formed by Forest Pelfrey called the Pelfrey Quartet, a bluegrass group from Fairborn

After singing with the Pelfrey Quartet, Carl, Billie and their daughter Kim all sang with Kenny Shiveley and the Cadets for about four years. Kim started singing when she was about five years old, and she was always singing in the car. She started playing the auto harp a little bit, and then she learned to play the mandolin. When she was learning to play the mandolin, Carl was playing the organ at the church, and she would sit behind him and watch his feet as he did the foot petals, and she would know what chords to play on the mandolin. Then when they started singing with Kenny, she played the electric bass and sang with the group.

Zeke Hoskins had a bluegrass group called Zeke Hoskins and the Country Gospelaires. His son played banjo for the group, and he broke his arm, so Zeke asked Carl if he would play with them that weekend. They traveled to a church down in Kentucky. When they arrived, they were not aware that it was a snake-handling church. Zeke and Richard were up singing, Carl was playing the banjo, and Zeke's other boy was standing behind Carl playing one of those "dog house" basses. While they were singing, a man came through a door on the right side of the church, and he had some kind of box in his hand. Carl wasn't paying any attention as he walked up on the platform behind them. They finished the song, and Zeke's boy leaned up to him and said, "Did you see what that guy's got? He's got a snake!"

After that song, they did about one more song and sat down. When they were done, Carl put his banjo in the case, picked it up, and walked out the door. Carl was sitting on the bus, but he noticed a crowd on the outside of the church, so he walked over to the window. They had taken the snake out and had started handling it. Shortly, someone came out and said, "They want you guys to sing again." Carl told them he wasn't going back inside, and that was final.

After playing with Kenny Shiveley, Carl went to Mexico for a while, and after playing the banjo on a John Burke recording, Carl started playing with John's group John Burke and the Layman Trio. Carl remained with them almost two years. Larry Polley was playing the mandolin with the group, and they were riding somewhere one weekend when he told Carl he was thinking about quitting the group. He then told Carl if they ever started singing as a family, he would like to play the mandolin with them. Soon they were traveling with John on the weekends and singing on the side as a family group.

In August 1974, about six months after Carl left John Burke's group, they started taking appointments and traveling more as a family. Larry began traveling with them, and picking up a couple of other guys, they really had two groups in one, and that's what they called it—Two Groups in One. They did a recording putting the Shiveley Family on one side and the other group, called the Faithful Travelers, on the other side.

Larry, good friend to Talmadge Clark, fondly remembers Talmadge buying a new banjo. He bought one of those RB800 gold-plated jobs. It was quite expensive, and he didn't want his wife to know, so he hid it in the barn, and it was a long time before she ever found out. Larry Polley is a barber, and Carl Shiveley still goes to his shop for a haircut.

The Shiveley Family started out using a motorhome but Rosco Gray, who sang bass with John Burke kept telling him they needed to get a bus. He told them about one sitting by Harshman Road that was for sale and said he knew the people who owned it. Carl told him he wouldn't know how to work on it, but Rosco insisted they were easier to maintain than a gasoline engine. So Carl went to the library, checked out a book on diesel engines, and determined it should be simple. They bought the bus, and it didn't even have an engine. It was a 1948 model, and after putting an engine in the bus, they used it for eight or nine years. They then purchased one of the Southern-Aires old buses, a 4104. It had a serious breakdown, and Carl grew tired of working on it, so he gave it away. A man and his son-in-law worked on it for a couple of weekends and took it to Kentucky.

Ray Elam, one of the members of the Faithful Travelers, was one of Lynn's friends. They had gone to church together for a long time and played some music together, and Lynn really liked bluegrass music. Then the Shiveley Family was singing in a church down in Springboro where Lynn Blankenship attended church. After church, he came up to Carl and said, "I really like your daughter's singing." He wanted to come up to the house some night when they were practicing. Carl told him that would be fine, and he started coming to the house to hear them practice. Kim ran away and hid the first few times he come to the house. A relationship began to develop, and on July 3, 1976, about the time Larry quit the group, Kim married Lynn Blankenship.

Lynn had asked Carl to teach him to play the mandolin, but since Lynn was already playing the guitar, Carl suggested he just play lead guitar. He started playing lead guitar with the group, and then he started on the mandolin and fiddle.

Over the years, they've had different members of the family in the group. When Carl "Junior" Shiveley was eight or ten years old, he started playing the bass with them. He played several instruments for the group. Carl's oldest daughter, Beverly, played bass for a while and did some singing. Carl's grandchildren were with the group at one time as well. Tara Blankenship played the bass for a while, and one evening when her brother, Jeremy Blankenship, was around nine years old, they were at a singing, and someone asked them to play the instrumental "Wonderful Words of Life." Lynn was working that evening, but they agreed to play the request, explaining it wouldn't sound the same without Lynn. Jeremy spoke up and said, "Well, I can play it."

They didn't even know he could play, so Carl questioned him, "You can play it like your dad?"

And he said, "Yeah."

Without any further discussion, Carl started playing the song just like he always did, and Jeremy came in on Lynn's part and played like a pro. It just happened that the next week, Carl came home from work, and there was a letter lying on his desk from his son Junior indicating he was leaving the group. So Jeremy stepped in that next week and started playing. Lynn also plays for a local group called Firm Foundation where he gets to play a little more fiddle.

Some time in 1990, they were driving the 1948 model bus on a narrow, winding backroad between Vanceburg and Grayson, Kentucky, and the road was wet. They came around a curve meeting a woman head-on. When she saw the bus come around that curve, she slammed on the brakes and came sliding sideways, with a drop off right down into the creek bed on the right and a high cliff on the left. She continued sideways until the nose of her car smashed into the cliff and the back end of the car hit the corner of the bus, demolishing her car. They just barely kept the bus from going over that bank.

They were coming back from Tennessee one time and threw a rod. The rod went through both sides of the engine. When they tore down the engine, they found the rod had broken off right next to the piston, and it was still on the crank and was just whipping back and forth. It was a Detroit 671, which is a straight block, and the thing whipped back and forth, breaking both sides out of the block before the rod broke off. All that was left was the stub on the crank and the stub on the piston, and both sides were gone out of the motor. The bus sat down in Tennessee for a while. Carl told the guy that came to tow it in to put it somewhere where it could be stored until it could be sold as they were not going to fool with it anymore. They went down the next week to get their stuff out of the bus. As the man was taking them to the bus, they started talking about fixing buses, and he mentioned what it would probably cost to have the bus towed back to Dayton. Carl decided if they could get it towed back for a reasonable cost, he would get it fixed. So having it towed back home, he got another block and built another engine.

They are presently singing using one microphone as that seems to be working best for their harmony. Having completed over thirteen recordings, they continue to travel, mostly back and forth between Tennessee and Ohio. They've also been to North Carolina and Michigan. They sang with the Primitives and the Bishops a couple times, and they sang with the Isaacs before they hit the big time. They always enjoy singing with the Dayton Ambassadors, and Carl says, "I remember the Dayton Ambassadors were singing over at Enterprise Baptist on Stewart Street in Fairborn, and they sang the song 'He Wrote My Name,' and the tenor singer back then was Dale Hartley, a big guy who really put himself into the song. After hearing the way he sang the song, we learned the song and still sing the song often."

After a great lunch, we continue along Fairfield Road, passing one of the famous giant Beaver Statues, which are located throughout the city. Reaching U.S. 35, we turn right and travel west for two miles where we loop onto IR-675 and travel south to Indian

Ripple Road. Turning right onto Indian Ripple Road, we turn right and travel through a congested shopping area to Far Hills Avenue. Turning right onto Far Hills, we enter the city of Oakwood and realize we should have continued west to Patterson Road. In an effort to correct our mistake, we turn left onto Oakwood Avenue. Passing some beautiful historic homes, we travel down a cobblestone lane to Thornhill Road where we turn right. We then turn left onto Rummymede Lane, crossing over Houck Creek, and turn right onto Springs Drive. This is a dead-end road so it's back to Rummymede Road where we turn right and drive through a beautiful park area where many people are out for a Sunday afternoon walk. Turning right onto Oak Knoll Drive, we finally turn right onto Patterson Road where we pass an old lookout tower that looks like a castle and a huge monument honoring John H. Patterson. From Patterson Road, we make a quick left onto Schantz Avenue, and then turn right onto South Dixie Drive. Traveling north, we pass the spectacular Carrillon Bells. Entering Dayton, we gaze across the Great Miami River where we see the University of Dayton Stadium where Bill Gaither has held a number of Homecomings. Continuing north, we turn right onto Stewart Street. Then we turn right onto Brown Street (Erma Bombeck Way) and continue to Wyoming Avenue. Turning right onto Wyoming, we pass Woodland Cemetery the burial site of many well-known people: Orville and Wilbur Wright who gave the world the wings to fly shortly after the turn of the century; L. M. Berry, founder of the *Yellow Pages* phone book; Erma Bombeck, well-known humorist; Paul Lawrence Dunbar, African American poet; James Ritty who made the first mechanical cash register. Continuing along Wyoming Avenue, we turn left onto Wayne Avenue and drive into Downtown Dayton.

The electric refrigerator was created in Dayton and became a household word, rapidly replacing the ice box. The worst flood in Dayton history took place during March 1913. Several days of heavy rain produced a raging torrent claiming over three hundred lives, and causing one hundred million dollars in damages.

Turing left onto Fourth Street, we travel west to Jefferson Street where we turn right and travel north to First Street. Turning right onto First Street we pass Historic Memorial Hall where many gospel concerts have been held over the years.

One day, the Blackwood Brothers Quartet was traveling down the road, and while sitting on the bus, J. D. Sumner jotted down the words to a simple little song. That night they were singing at Memorial Hall in Dayton, and

James Blackwood, on the spur of the moment, suggested they sing the song J. D. had just written. So reading the words off a piece of paper, they sung their new song entitled "The Old Country Church" for the very first time. The song produced six encores and soon became one of the Blackwood Brothers most requested songs. J. D. Sumner is in the *Guinness Book of World Records* for having sung the lowest bass note in history.

* * *

Durand Brown sang with his family before putting together the Believers Trio, which included his son Mark along with another gentleman named Mike Pierce. The group started in 1973, and they were together for ten years. Durand was also music director for the Dayton Baptist Temple. The church had a television program entitled *An Old Fashioned Meeting*, and the trio often sang on the program.

* * *

Paul Russell Lewis, known to most people as Jerry Coulter, was born in Nashville, Tennessee on September 9, 1946. Shortly after birth, he was adopted and taken to Dayton where he grew up singing in the choir. He also sang barbershop with the Daytona Chorale. Jerry and his family routinely attended the gospel sings held at Memorial Hall in Dayton, and often, his mom would have some of the groups over to the house after the concert. Jerry became a fan of the Blackwood Brothers and was fascinated by the fabulous bass singing of J. D. Sumner. Jerry was married in 1970.

In 1971, having a strong desire to sing and possessing a very low range voice, Jerry started a mixed vocal group called the Chords of Faith. In 1973, he, along with some friends at the Prescott United Brethren in Christ Church, formed a group called the Blessings Unlimited, and within two years, the group became a male quartet.

In 1976, Jerry was privileged to sing on a program with his favorite group, the Blackwood Brothers. Sometime later, while Jerry was eating at a Frisch's Restaurant in Tipp City, his favorite bass singer, J. D. Sumner, stopped in on his way home after buying a Cadillac in Detroit, Michigan. Sharing this time with J. D. was the highlight of Jerry's day.

Because of his newly developing relationship with Michele Arthur, piano player for the Blessings Unlimited, Jeff Delorme, who was playing bass guitar for the Northernaires, became a member of the group by switching groups with Tim McIntosh to be with his newfound love.

After their tenor singer Ken Ankney left the group, they continued to sing as a trio.

On Sunday, June 12, 1983, the group was traveling north on Interstate 75 returning home from a Homecoming celebration in Mount Healthy. It was a beautiful warm summer day, and several of the windows on the old school bus had been opened to provide some fresh air. Jerry Coulter was driving, and the rest of the group had settled back for the long ride home.

Suddenly, flames engulfed the front of the bus, and responding quickly, Jerry managed to steer the bus into the median strip and bring the bus to a stop. As their equipment was stored in the back, they were forced to exit the bus at the front, requiring each member to pass through the fire. As flames began to fill the bus, Jerry hurried everyone along, refusing to exit until everyone was off the bus. Michele was hesitant to run through the flames, so Jerry, a big man, quickly grabbed Michele by the arms and tossed her off the bus.

Michele says, "We were talking and laughing as always, and I was looking out the window at some of the old Voice of America radio towers. The next thing I remember, I was on my feet feeling squished together at the front of the bus and seeing bright orange flames. I felt very calm and remember thinking I'm going to die. The next thing I remember is being at the side of the Road standing face to face with Perry Groves."

After exiting the bus, Danny Williams quickly dropped to the ground and began rolling around to extinguish the flames that were covering his body. While rolling on the ground, he became disoriented, accidentally rolling toward the burning bus, and soon the flames were covering his entire body. People were pulling off the road to help, and one man, spotting Danny on the ground, hurriedly took off his jacket and started putting out the flames that had overtaken Danny's body.

Debbie Barnhart and Jerry Coulter suffered severe burns. Exiting the bus, Jerry's shirt was in flames. Using an ice cooler belonging to someone who had stopped to help, Jerry continued to coat his burns by soaking his T-shirt in the ice water.

Because of the heavy traffic on Interstate 75, it took medical teams almost an hour to arrive on the scene. Upon arrival, they initiated treatment, and all group members were taken to a local hospital for treatment. The group received over a hundred visitors, forcing the hospital to limit the amount of visitors.

Everyone experienced burns to some degree, requiring extensive treatment over the next several months. Although Rod Barnhart and Jeff Delorme experienced only minor injuries, the emotional pain of this experience was overwhelming to each member and their families. Devastated by the trauma of this tragedy, the group immediately disbanded, and it would be quite some time before some of the members would be able to continue their individual ministries.

Danny never recovered from the multiple injuries suffered during the fire and passed away about a week later. That witty, kind-hearted, chubby, twenty-six-year old husband and father of an infant daughter had the voice of an angel. The baritone part was something Danny discovered and sang with such expertise and conviction. His love for the Lord was evident in his daily walk, and Danny continues to live in the hearts of all those who were privileged to know him.

Rod and Debbie had been married less than six months at the time of the accident. Debbie spent nearly three months in the hospital, and a high calorie diet was required to aid in her healing. Debbie gave birth to their first child the following April.

The group later took part in a special singing held at Stebbins High School in Dayton. During the evening, Jack Barrett sang the tenor part. Jack later sang with Kenny Shiveley and the Zionaires. As time passed, Jerry attempted to regroup with Ken Ankney, Mike Ankney, and Rick Bryant, but this only lasted for a brief term. Several years later, Jerry, with the help of past member Perry Groves, temporarily reformed the group, calling it simply the Blessings. Singing in this group was Dewey Armstrong and Richard Matthew Doran, son of Rick Doran who sings with the Dayton Ambassadors. During one of the Dayton Ambassador Anniversary sings, Rick Doran received a special blessing when his son Richard Matthew, singing with the Blessings, sang "The Shepherd," a song written by Rick Doran. Jerry later sang bass in another group with Ken Ankney called Touch of Grace. Because of health issues, Jerry no longer travels but continues to take part in musical activities from time to time at his home church.

* * *

David Oney was born on January 22, 1947, in Wayland, Kentucky. He came from a large family with a Christian background. All of his brothers were somewhat musically inclined, and they all played guitars and banjos, and just about any instrument. They often sat around at home picking and singing their way along.

In high school, David met a young girl named Beulah LeMaster. She lived in Sayersville, Kentucky, and he lived in Prestonsburg, about twenty-two miles away. He worked at Sayersville delivering stuff to her school. When he would come in dressed in his Prestonsburg ball jacket and his little flattop all the girls wanted to help him bring in the groceries. Beulah thought, *What's the big deal?*

She would often see him as she rode home with one of the teachers, and when they stopped at the store where he worked, he would come out and put the groceries in the back. He would have to lift up her seat as they didn't have four doors. They later became more closely acquainted on a blind date.

After getting married in 1965, they moved to Dayton and have lived there ever since. They lived in a small house in North Dayton. David's dad was a minister, so being raised in a Christian home, they would sing some gospel songs. The family would get together each week to eat together and play country music in the garage. They sounded pretty good, and soon people started to invite them out.

Then while playing for a picnic at Wright State University, things got a little out of hand. They weren't even saved at the time, but Beulah realized they shouldn't be doing this type of event. She didn't want her children in that environment—it just didn't feel right. So she went and got their truck, pulled up beside the group, and said, "We're loading up, we're going home, as this is not for us." Their brother Herbert Oney was a minister and was always trying to get them into church requesting they use their talents for God. He never gave up, and soon one by one, the family members were getting saved, and it wasn't long until they were singing gospel music. Thus in 1977, the Oney Family was formed, holding their first gospel concert in Dayton at the Byesville Boulevard Church of God where they sang only five songs. That evening, the Singing Jubilees of West Carrollton also sang.

After getting into gospel music, they started receiving a few bookings here and there, and things continued to grow. The group started out all brothers and sisters. Beulah took care of bookings, took care of babies, and helped get the bus ready. They enjoyed what they were doing and traveled by bus. Their first bus was a small city transit bus that was originally used to take people to the airport. They fixed it up and traveled all over the place with that vehicle. They later purchased a 1948, Model 4104 Greyhound Bus.

One time, they were traveling from Richmond, Kentucky, on their way to a pig roast in Elizabethtown, Kentucky. It was late in the night, and David told his brother Danny, "Let's go up by Lexington, and we'll stop off and get a sandwich and then drive on to Elizabethtown." Then David went back to take a nap. As he lay there, he heard a bad roaring sound. It sounded like the bus was getting ready to fall apart. He got up and walked up to Danny only to hear a truck driver on the CB telling Danny that their bus was about to stop, and he would send somebody back to help them. He then passed them as if they were sitting still. Danny said, "Everything is bogging down, and I can't get any speed." David thought that maybe the fuel filter or something was stopped up. He then looked down and realized Danny still had the bus in low gear. Once they shifted it out of low gear, it started picking up speed, and they were soon moving down the road. It was a while before he lived that one down!

After several of the members left the group, it just wasn't the same any more, so around 2000, they changed the name of the group from the Oney Family to the David Oney Family. At one time, they traveled with a full band, but the present group consists of two brothers and their wives. Their son went on to sing with the Brewer Family, but that group later split up when some of the members got married.

The David Oney Family primarily travels in a five-state area. They have done several showcases at the NQC and sang on a few cruises traveling as far as Cozumel, Mexico. Danny has to travel out of town frequently, and they often have to go without him. Sometimes they don't take the bus—they just pull a trailer. They were down around the Cumberland Gap traveling in their suburban and had just filled the fuel tank, which holds about forty-four gallons of fuel. They were headed to their next booking when suddenly the fuel pump went out. Their next booking was in Tennessee about seventy miles away. After making several phone calls, some people came out to help them, and they didn't miss the booking. They made it back home on only three hours sleep.

They often played at a little pizza house, and one night David thought, *What am I doing here? I'm tired, I hurried home from work to get here, and these people are not listening to me at all.*

All of a sudden, a little waitress came over and got down on her knees beside their table and said, "Can I talk to you for a few minutes? I don't normally listen to gospel music. I work here because I need the job. I bought one of your CDs because I heard a song I liked, and it changed my life."

That uplifted him, and she reminded him of the purpose. Then they were back down to sing some time later, and the mother of the little waitress came up to them and said, "You don't know what it means to me to have a daughter come and ask me to go to church."

Beulah said, "I was listening to Art Linkletter, and he's in his nineties and still going strong. He said he's not giving up. God has given him the strength, and he'll go on until he dies. That's how I see the David Oney Family. We do not believe it's time to give up."

David says, "We know that His coming is drawing near, and we must stay busy furthering the kingdom of God."

* * *

Wilse "Hick" Lawson was born in Barbourville, Kentucky, on December 17, 1913. As a young man, he studied music and sang in a quartet with his grandfather Lewis Lawson. Hick was a coalminer, and when the mines in southeastern Kentucky began to shut down, he moved his family to Ohio. He sang with his wife and directed music within his home church. Hick taught several singing schools in local churches in Ohio, and after teaching several men at his home church to read music, he suggested they form a quartet. As a result, in April 1967, with the help of his son Wade Lawson, the Dayton Ambassadors Quartet was formed. When the group started, they only used two microphones, and most of their songs were sung a cappella.

Their first appointment was at Friendship Baptist Church in Miamisburg. They'd only worked out four songs, and during the congregational singing, the church sang every song they were planning to sing. About a year after starting the quartet, Hick's youngest son, Tom Lawson, returned home from a two-year tour in the army, and Hick retired his position as bass singer to his son Tom and went fishing. He often came out to hear the boys, but in March 1973, Wilse was called home.

In 1975, the group sang for the Ohio State Fair, and later that same year original member, Fred Terrell, as a result of throat problems said good-bye to the group. It wasn't long after returning home from the military that Tom became a police officer for the Dayton Police Department. Shortly afterward, his brother Wade also became a police officer, and as other police officers began to join the group, they were soon nicknamed The Singing Policemen. Some time later, Dale Hartley, another police officer, started singing with the Dayton Ambassadors.

Born on October 20, 1924, Lewis "Dale" Hartley worked for the Dayton Police Department, and although he did a lot of barbershop singing, Dale lived most of his life without Christ. Then one day, Dale agreed to come out to hear the Dayton Ambassadors sing. God used Dale's love for music as a tool to reach his heart, and it wasn't long before Dale had accepted Christ, and through the vibrant witness of Dale Hartley, over thirty members of his family accepted Christ as Lord and Savior.

After the group appeared on the *Cas Walker Show* in Knoxville, Tennessee, an article appeared in the *Country Music Corner* written by Martha Ashcraft that said, "The Dayton Ambassadors appeared on the show and were just sensational."

Once a patient at Kettering Medical Center, who was suffering from leukemia, asked the group to come to the hospital and sing for her. When the group showed up at the hospital, they sang for over an hour. It was truly a wonderful experience, and Tom says, "That's what gospel music is all about!"

Growing up next door to the Lawson family, Rick Doran would have never imagined that someday he would be traveling with the Dayton Ambassadors, but in 1977, that's exactly what happened. While Rick was just a young boy, Big John Hall, one of the Blackwood Brothers' dynamic bass singers, shared some encouraging words with Rick preparing him for the future. After high school, he joined the air force, and while living in Wichita, Kansas, God placed a calling on his life.

After returning to Ohio, having a great love for gospel music, he often attended those local gospel concerts promoted by Lloyd Orrell, and he remembers the all-night singings held in Indianapolis, Indiana, where Jim Hamill of the Kingsmen could often be seen walking around with a towel over his shoulder and a bucket of Colonel Sanders Fried Chicken in his arms.

Attending the Stamps-Blackwood School of Gospel Music in 1976, Rick, with the help of his wife, Rita, and her father, Harold Kouns, who later drove the bus for the Dayton Ambassadors, formed a trio called the Gospel Harmonaires. Shortly after the group started singing, Rick received a call from Wade Lawson, and although singing harmony was a struggle for Rick, the group agreed to take him on, and soon he was traveling with the Dayton Ambassadors.

The group sang several times on a local TV show called, the *Sammy Steven's Gospel Hour*. They later did a program at the Lebanon Correctional Institute with Athletes in Action, and saw about twenty prisoners accept Christ as their savior.

Once after singing at a church in Middlesboro, Kentucky, they were attempting to turn the bus around along a country road and got stuck in someone's front yard. After a call for help, the police soon arrived, and while they were awaiting the tow truck, the police officer shared with them that yard where they were presently stuck belonged to a convicted criminal who was waiting to be taken to prison. Sounds rather fitting for this group, wouldn't you agree?

In 1978, when Doc Partin stepped down, the group picked up a young piano player named Clint Smith who had previously played for the Marlow Brothers in Dayton. At the same time, Wendall Davis joined the group to play bass. He was also a former member of the Marlow Brothers. He later did a short stint with the Gospel Journeymen. He also played for the Southern-Aires and the Allen Law Singers.

When Dale Hartley passed away, he was replaced by Terry Elliott who later moved to Tennessee. Herb Marlow, another member of the Marlow Brothers, became tenor for the group when Terry moved away. The Marlow Brothers were together for about twelve years and broke up when their brother, Gary Marlow, lost his life in a construction accident. Harold Marlow continues to assist Kenny Shiveley with the weekly events held at the Coming Together Center in Dayton.

In 1979, the group was proclaimed as Ohio's Goodwill Ambassadors of Gospel Music by the governor of Ohio. The group often sang in the Cleveland area working for a number of years with George Hux of C&H Gospel Music Promotions and later with good friend Chris Morley who used to drive bus for the Happy Goodmans and promoted several gospel concerts in Cleveland. It was during their many trips to Cleveland, that their young piano player, Clint, met a young girl named Lois.

On October 5, 1979, Rick Doran promoted his first gospel concert. It was an evening of gospel music held in downtown Dayton at the Victory Theatre featuring a number of the area's local groups including the Dayton Ambassadors, the Blessings Unlimited, and the Southern-Aires.

In 1980, Francis Chamberlain started playing steel guitar for the group. Francis had previously played for the Parks Family in Franklin and had played for the Crusaders in Columbus for five years when he left to join the Dayton Ambassadors. About the same time, JB King became the group's new rhythm guitar player. JB previously played with a local group from his church called the Joint-Aires of Grace for twelve years.

The Dayton Ambassadors have been privileged to perform on stage with some of the nation's finest groups such as Bob Wills and the Inspirationals, the Happy Goodmans, the Kingsmen, the Dixie Echoes, and Gold City.

In 1982, after graduating from high school, Clint Smith moved to Texas. While living in Texas, Clint married that young girl from Cleveland. After Clint left the group continued singing for a while with Bobby Gibson filling in at the piano but soon decided it was time to take a break and came off the road except for a few special concerts.

Then in 1987, shortly after Clint moved back to Ohio, the group started singing again with Phillip Morris filling the tenor part. Sometime later when Wendall Davis left the group, Phil's wife, Sandy Morris, started playing bass guitar for the group. As Phil lived over an hour from the rest of the group, the continual commuting combined with his difficult work schedule soon took its toll, and Phil was forced to resign. At this time, the tenor position was filled by Mike Ankney, brother to Ken Ankney who had filled in for the group several times.

The group has maintained a tight bond through the years, and whether it was Dale Hartley faithfully bringing along those bags of donuts, Clint Smith standing barefooted in his pajamas on the sidewalk of New York City gazing up at the World Trade Center, Wade Lawson at practice trying to keep everyone on their part, Rick Doran trying to sing that great old song "The Lighthouse" without crying, Mike Ankney mimicking Elvis Presley to an attentive crowd at McDonalds on a Sunday morning, or Tom Lawson repeatedly saying, "If you don't know this Jesus we have been singing about, you are living far below the dignity God intended for you;" the memories will be cherished forever.

When Rick Shoemaker, pastor of New Carlisle Baptist Church, asked the question, "How can you be a cop and be a Christian?"

Tom and Wade Lawson responded, "We couldn't be cops without Christ. He is what keeps us going." The Lawson brothers served with the Dayton Police Department, Homicide Division, as detectives for many years. After retiring from the police department, both men assumed investigative roles with the Montgomery County Coroner's Office.

Continuing the group's legacy, Tony Rankin who presently plays steel guitar for the group was chief deputy sheriff of Montgomery County for several years, and Brian Dershem, who plays the bass guitar, is a captain with the Montgomery County Sheriff's Department. Rick Doran works as a therapist at the Montgomery County Juvenile Detention Center. Clint Smith performed autopsies for the Montgomery County Coroner's Office for a number of years, and Tony's wife, Denise Rankin, who travels with the group handling the product table and operating the sound system, also works for the Montgomery County Coroner's Office as a forensic scientist.

In 2007, the quartet had just finished a Saturday evening appointment in Nashville, Tennessee. Everyone was on the bus, and they were headed to Huntsville, Alabama, to sing in a Sunday morning worship service. Several of the wives had come along on this particular trip, and they had prepared some special treats to eat along the way. It had been a long evening, and some of the group members were eager to have something to eat and then relax as they made their way toward the hotel in Alabama.

Denise and Tony Rankin had decided to change out of their church clothes into something a little more comfortable. They were in the rear bedroom of the bus and were in the process of changing when they heard the siren of an emergency vehicle. Suddenly without warning, Tom, who was driving the bus, locked the brakes. The force of the sudden stop propelled Denise into Tony sending them both into the bedroom wall of the bus, and hitting the wall, they heard something crack. They also could hear a tremendous commotion coming from the front of the bus.

They quickly finished changing clothes and went forward to learn what had happened. As they entered the front of the bus, there was a mixture of laughter and confusion. Tom was explaining that an emergency vehicle had entered the bus's path from a side street, leaving him no choice but to brake hard in order to avoid a collision. Others were still wiping themselves off. It seems that Lois, Clint's wife, had been taking some food out of the refrigerator in preparation for their evening snack. When Tom hit the brakes, Lois, holding a large plate of deviled eggs in her hands, went down landing on top of Brian Dershem, who was also at the counter preparing a sandwich. A portion of the deviled eggs now covered both Lois and Brian. The remainder of the deviled eggs had sailed through the air landing on several of the other group members. Thankfully, no one was hurt. They just had a damaged wall, and those deviled eggs were a total loss!

In 2008, after forty-one years, the group continues singing at local churches and special events. On several occasions, Aaron Morgan, the pastor at the church where Tom and Wade attend, has sung with the group doing a special or filling in for Wade when he was unable to sing. Aaron previously sang full-time with the Joint-Aires in Jacksonville, Florida, for three years.

In February 2008, the Dayton Ambassadors were privileged to sing in a historic church located on Kercher Street in Miamisburg. This was the church where the mother of the famous McGuire Sisters was pastor.

One Saturday morning in March 2008, the group boarded their 1968 Model 4703 Buffalo bus and headed south on a much anticipated early spring trip. After a hard winter, they were eager to experience the hint of warmer weather that the Nashville, Tennessee, and Huntsville, Alabama, trip promised. Stopping at the home of Francis (former steel guitar player) and Reba Chamberlain in Franklin, Kentucky, they enjoyed a great lunch including a piece of Reba's delicious coconut cream pie.

Traveling to a tabernacle northwest of Nashville, they enjoyed a great service and met some wonderful people. After the service, they loaded the bus and headed to Alabama. Tom was driving and along the way, he remarked that he did not remember the hills south of Nashville being so steep as the bus was negotiating the inclines a little slower than normal. Nevertheless, they arrived in Huntsville about midnight.

The next morning, they were delighted to visit with longtime friends, Pastor Ralph and Elizabeth Brown. After a heartwarming service, they enjoyed a delicious Southern-style meal in the fellowship hall, and then around 2:30 PM, they boarded the bus for home.

It was a beautiful day. Tom was driving, and the first part of the trip was uneventful. A couple hours into the trip, they began to realize something was terribly wrong. The bus just did not seem to have any power when climbing a hill. By the time they reached Nashville, the bus was really running slow. Tom decided to pull off the road and check things out. Nothing appeared out of the ordinary, so they decided to limp on home. Wade was now driving, and they did great as long as they were headed downhill! At the slightest incline, the bus slowed terribly, and on the bigger hills, Wade had to pull off to the side where the bus crawled along the shoulder of the highway. Time seemed to slow down on the bus as 10:00 PM, then midnight, then 1:00 AM passed by, and they were still a long distance from home.

Creeping up hill after hill, the bus traveled closer to home each time. Several truckers blew their horn as they passed by. Some of the members tried to sleep, but vibration from the rumble strips along the side of the road was making sleep a challenge. Everyone was getting tired, especially the driver, but they were having an enjoyable time, and humorous comments about getting up the next hill were flowing freely. They finally reached IR-75 around 2:30 AM, and somewhere near Florence, Kentucky, they were pulled over by a Florence police officer and a Boone County deputy sheriff. Inviting the officers on board, they explained the problem. The officers, believing it unsafe for them to continue, provided them a police escort to the next available exit. Tom's son Gary drove all the way from Miamisburg to pick them up in his twelve-passenger van. When Gary arrived, they quickly loaded a few essential items, and packing thirteen people into the van, they headed toward home. Arriving back at the church at four-thirty Monday morning, everyone hurried to their vehicles and headed home. When apologizing to Mike Ankney's mother, who had to be at work at 7:30 AM, she replied, "I wouldn't have missed it."

The next day, Tom and his cousin drove back to Kentucky, and after determining the problem, they put a new fuel filter on the bus and drove home without having any problems. Tom has always been comfortable working on those old buses. In fact, his first memory of Ben Speer was at Memorial Hall in Dayton when Ben, dressed in a pair of coveralls, was under their bus working on something.

* * *

Born in Dayton on February 8, 1953, Peggy Salyer attended Greenon High School. Her father, Ben Salyer, sang in churches throughout Ohio and then in eastern Kentucky. He led the singing in several churches, and there were always people over at the house singing and practicing.

When Peggy was playing for Gar and Gwen Stambaugh, she was still in school, and they would often sing all weekend. One weekend, they had driven all night long and were headed to Paintsville, Kentucky, to sing. Many of the churches down there would have an altar of prayer at the beginning of the service. They arrived at the church, and before the service, a number of people had gone up for prayer. Peggy also went up to pray and fell asleep at the altar. Everybody had returned to their seats, and there she was on the altar all alone and sound asleep.

Peggy later played the piano for the Homegate Quartet, and one evening, they were traveling, and it was raining hard. Suddenly, they hit an oil spot or something in the road, and the vehicle began to spin. The vehicle never left the road, and after spinning several times, it just stopped in the middle of the road. Peggy says, "I just know the Lord was with us, protecting us."

The Dayton Galileans were formed in 1963 and traveled throughout Kentucky, Indiana, and Tennessee. All of the members of the original group attended the Fairborn Freewill Baptist Church. In September 1965, Peggy Salyer started playing piano for the group.

Peggy's children, Tim O'Bryant and his sister, Tiffanie, have been singing since they were kids. They have sung in church together since they were little. Tim's favorite singer was Glen Payne. Tim says, "He is really special. He truly knew what he was singing about and was very genuine."

The family started promoting concerts and bringing other groups into town. One time when they had brought a group in, the crowd wasn't what they wanted it to be. After the concert, a teenager came up to Tim and told him he had gotten saved, and that made it all worthwhile. Soon folks who knew them were asking, "Why aren't you singing at your own concerts?" The family talked about it for a few years, and finally, Tim's wife, Rita, was a big encouragement in helping them make the final decision. The O'Bryant Family—Peggy, Tim, and Tiffanie—first started singing at other churches in 2001.

On a Saturday afternoon, they drove over to Indiana, and when they arrived at the church, they pulled in the parking lot. Checking the doors, they were all locked, so they sat there for a long time waiting, but no one showed. Finally giving up, they pulled around the other side of the church to exit, and as they were leaving the parking lot, they could see the other side of the church sign. It said "The O'Bryant Family—Friday Night—7 o'clock." Upon arriving home, Tim called the church and apologized. The church later had them back, and they showed up on the right evening. Not to make excuses for them, but this happened about the time they found out that Tim's wife, Rita, was expecting, so things were a little out of kilter, but it wasn't little Alison's fault.

Peggy says, "Singing and serving the Lord with my children, God could not give me anything in the world more than that. It is beyond any treasure, any gift, possibly the greatest blessing that God could ever give."

Another time, they were invited to sing at a church with the Anchormen. When they showed up, nobody was there. They were unable to get a hold of anybody by phone, but finally, they were able to get in the church. It was about thirty minutes before the service was supposed to start, so they quickly set everything up and changed clothes. It was about five minutes after seven o'clock when the pastor finally arrived. Jason Funderburg of the Anchormen and Tim approached the pastor, and Jason told the pastor that he and Tim had talked, and they had agreed the O'Bryant Family would go on first, and then the Anchormen will come up and sing. Suddenly, the pastor said, "Hold on here." Then looking right at Tim, he said, "I've never heard of the O'Bryant Family, and as far as I am concerned, they aren't singing tonight."

Tim very politely responded, "That's fine, we don't have to sing."

Jason quickly spoke up and said, "If the O'Bryant Family is not singing, neither are the Anchormen."

The pastor apologized, stating that the folks who set up the singing had failed to inform him as to who was singing, and he thought that the O'Bryant Family was just trying to edge their way onto the program. Everything worked out fine, both groups sang, and they all had a wonderful time.

* * *

Rusty Ballinger was born in Dayton on June 27, 1962. His father was in the air force and was stationed at Wright-Patterson AFB. When he was two years old, the family moved to Berea, Kentucky. Rusty grew up in Berea and was later in the army from 1980 to 1986. He did basic training at Fort Dix, New Jersey, and then went to Fort Knox, Kentucky, and was out the whole time teaching basic training.

Prior to joining the military, Rusty was involved in rock music and sang in his first bar when he was only sixteen years old. When he first started out, it was more like the top 40 disco because that was popular at the time, but it got harder as the years went on. They wrote their own music and the heavy sound was always there. He later played in some small bands at the NCO Club. He stopped singing rock in 1996, believing he just didn't want to sing anymore. Rusty said, "Everybody claims you are a juke box, you know, the smoky bars. I would sing and sing and sing, like thirty or forty songs a night. And I always tell everybody I could sing until I tasted blood in my throat. And now I sing for the blood."

In 1998, finding his way back to the Lord, he met a great bunch of guys from Gallipolis. They were putting a group together called Forgiven 4, and Rusty tried out. He was singing tenor when he first started, but they couldn't find a baritone singer, so he agreed to take the baritone part as they could find other tenor singers. He remained with them until 2002 when their bass singer had a heart attack, and they come off the road. He then joined the Gospel Harmony Boys in West Virginia, and in 2007, he was still singing with the Gospel Harmony Boys.

Rusty's father was killed in an automobile accident in 2006. Rusty is glad that his father was able to see him change his life around before he passed away. His dad was a preacher for about thirty-two years, and Rusty is certain he was an embarrassment for many, many years singing rock music while his dad was in the pulpit. Greg Tingler of the Gospel Harmony Boys says, "Rusty is a good man. He is a joy traveling with. That's for sure."

* * *

Pearl (Brady) Ford grew up in Tennessee and has been singing all her life. When she was growing up, her uncles taught her music. They would teach her the notes first and then sing the words. She struggled at first as she had to work often, so the learning came slowly. She moved to Ohio in 1943.

The Dayton Harvesters started at the house of Maggie and Verlon Lewis sometime in 1956. After church one day, they went out to their house for dinner on the ground. After eating dinner, they started singing, and liking what they heard, the group was formed. Hershel Creech was the group's leader, and he played the guitar. That was all the music they had at first. Their first appointment was at the First Church of God in Moraine City.

When they started, Maggie sang the tenor part, and she would have really bad seizures at times. She never had one while they were singing but once she had one while they were on the road. Using a van, they traveled all over the Ohio Valley and the neighboring states. Eventually, Maggie had to drop out because of health problems.

They were scheduled to sing at a Church of Christ in Christian Union Church in Weston, and when they arrived, there was a big church bell with a rope hanging down by the door of the church. Someone told them that when the pastor gets happy during the service, he runs back and rings the church bell. That evening while they were singing, a ninety-three-year-old lady got saved, and about that time, she saw the pastor start running for the bell. Without any forethought, Pearl ran to the front door and helped the pastor rang the church bell. After ringing the bell, she returned to the platform and continued singing. After the service was over, the group was invited to spend the night at the house of the ninety-three-year-old woman. Pearl says, "It was truly an experience, probably the best service we ever had."

At one time, Charles Feltner lived down the street from Pearl, and she would walk to his house to purchase concert tickets. Denver Lamb was at Pearl's house one day as he was somewhat dating one of her supervisors from the GM truck plant. They had all gone out to dinner, and when they came back to the house, Denver had written a new song entitled "Rescue Me." So sitting on the floor, he played and sang the song.

One time they were traveling and Pearl kept telling the boys, "We are going to run out of gas."

They would say, "Oh, we'll stop at the next station."

And so, Phil Hardin said, "Well, if we run out of gas, I will just have to walk and go get it." Sure enough, they ran out of gas, and he had to walk and go get some.

Once they were traveling through Chillicothe and stopped at a Bob Evans Restaurant. Entering the restaurant someone noticed the Happy Goodmans sitting in the restaurant. George and Phyllis walked up to say hello, and they invited the group to sit with them for breakfast. Pearl sat next to Vestal, and they had a very good time together. Then sometime later, while they were stopping for breakfast at the same Bob Evans where they met the Goodmans, Pearl had a light stroke. She became numb on one side of her face. Arriving at the church, they anointed her and prayed for her, and she could sing. But when she got done and sat down, she could hardly open her mouth. When she arrived home the next day, she went to the doctor and was admitted to the hospital for thirteen days while they ran tests.

Talmadge Clark sang bass with the Dayton Harvesters. Talmadge had traveled with several groups and was a good banjo picker, but Hershel's wife, not liking the sound of the banjo, wouldn't let him play that banjo. As it turns out, her son now plays the banjo.

They completed over eleven recordings, but after several of the group members passed away, they were forced to disband the group. Pearl's son Danny started out singing when he was four years old, and Pearl played the guitar. He later sang with the Camp Meeting Singers.

After not singing for about ten years, in the early 1990s, Pearl started singing with a local group called New Jerusalem with Kenneth and Jean Sloan, who had previously sung with the Dayton Harvesters and Tim Parker. Their first practice was on a Tuesday evening, and Pearl had forgotten some of the important elements of practice as she left her car running the whole time they were inside practicing.

* * *

Born in Harlan, Kentucky, Rod Burton had his first taste of gospel music at age five while singing on a local radio program, and from then on, southern gospel music was in his blood. He found salvation at age eleven and, soon after, moved to the Dayton area. When Rod was a teenager, he traveled with the Charles Feltner Singers, singing and playing bass from 1978 through 1983.

He enjoyed a brief time with a group called His Witnesses before moving on in 1984 to form his Christian rock band called T.A.S.K, which was together for three years. In 1993, he found his place once again with a southern gospel group called Destined.

A transfer to the Chicago area in 1997 ended his tour with Destined. Rod spent the next few years singing lead with another trio called Through His Blood. Then Rod spent some time singing as part of a worship team. In 2006, Rod once again found his way back to southern gospel music signing with Eddie Crook Recording Company in early 2007. Rod continues to travel as a soloist and says, "It's my desire to share with everyone that we're all just sinners, saved by His grace."

* * *

The Gospel Crusaders were organized in 1958. They traveled many miles on weekends doing concerts, revivals, and church services. J. D. Gentry, known for his warm and ready humor, sang bass and managed the group. He had previously sung with several groups before joining the Gospel Crusaders. Singing baritone was Charles "Chuck" Berry, a native from Springfield, who had been singing since his early teens. The spokesman for the group was Hugh Grimsley, a big and jovial tenor, who put all of his 240 pounds into his singing.

* * *

George Walker was born in Olive Hill, Kentucky, on April 14, 1929. His mother passed away when she was twenty-nine years old and left three boys to be raised by their grandparents. After their dad got out of the army in 1944, they left Olive Hill and moved to Columbus where they attended school for a while. When they left Columbus, they came back to Olive Hill, and from there, they moved to Baltimore, Maryland.

When they were in Baltimore, their dad had to go into the hospital with sickness. Times were hard, and George had two brothers who looked to him as their dad although he was only six years older. The three boys stayed in a room by themselves, and George provided the income, working at a laundry for $20 a week. His brother later shared that there were times that he was so hungry he would pass the local fruit stand and was tempted to take an apple, but he always remembered the words of their grandmother, "No matter how hard up you get, don't never steal." He said that was what kept him from taking an apple. In 1946, after their dad got out of the hospital, George joined the navy, and his two brothers went on to school and were in Baltimore for eight or nine years.

While in the navy, George traveled the world. After two years, he got out of the service and moved to Dayton and got a job at General Motors. He finally convinced his two brothers and his dad to come to Dayton, and he got them a job at General Motors. Up the street from where George lived, there were two older people, and they kept inviting him to church. He would say, "Well, one day I will." Then one Easter Sunday in 1949, he started going to church, and liking what he heard, he continued going back week after week. One Wednesday night, George accepted the Lord Jesus Christ as his Savior.

He liked gospel music, so it wasn't long until he was singing in his home church and soon singing in other churches also. Then he got together with two ladies in the church, and they sang together for about a year as a trio. From there, he joined another group and sang with them for a while. Then George, a guy named Perry Kuntz, and a guy that played the steel guitar, Henry Banner, put together a male trio named the Gospel Travelers, and they sang together for about two years.

Finally in 1962, with the help of Imogene "Jean" Chambers and Ann Chapman, they formed the Gospel Melotones. Jean had previously sung with the Sunset Quartet. The Gospel Melotones traveled a seven- or eight-state area and saw many souls saved. They had several radio programs. They sang at colleges and sang at a Catholic college up in Indiana with Smitty Gatlin, father of the Gatlin Brothers. They traveled together around twenty-eight years or maybe a little longer.

They were in Gary, Indiana, and George was driving a Fleetwood Cadillac at that time. It was around 1972, and the temperature that day was eighteen below zero, with a wind chill of forty below. They were going to Danville, Illinois. The car broke down, and no doubt they would have frozen to death if somebody had not stopped. George got out on the road and stopped a truck, a Canadian driver, who took him up the road about five miles where he stopped and asked some guy if he could come down and pull them in. He said, "No, I can't do it. I've got to get home. I've been working for twenty-four hours and there's no way I can come back and pull you in." George continued to plead with him and was able to talk him into coming back and getting the car and pulling them in. The contact points had frozen on the engine, and that's the reason it wouldn't run.

They finally made it to Danville, Illinois, and entering the church, you could see your breath inside the building. He talked with the minister asking if they should just cancel the service. He said, "No, I have had it advertised on the radio and paper, and I think we should go ahead and do the singing." So George agreed to sing, and when they got up to sing, it was so cold that the piano player had gloves on, and they all had their coats on. After singing about three songs to a crowd of about ten people, George told the preacher, "That's it." They tore their equipment down and left.

Sometime in the 1980s, they sang with the Happy Goodmans in the Chrysler Auditorium in New Castle, Indiana, to a crowd of about nine thousand people. They also sang with the Segos, the Inspirations, and the Rambos. They sang on stage with the Cathedrals in Toledo during the first concert they had with George Younce.

For about five years, they would take tours singing throughout Georgia and Florida. They traveled all over Michigan, Indiana, Ohio, Kentucky, and Illinois. They never had a bus—they always used a car or a van. They stayed in motels or at people's homes along the way. They recorded around sixty-five different albums.

They were singing at a little Methodist church down in Carlisle, Kentucky called Rousch Hill Methodist Church. The pastor told him to go ahead and give the altar service when they get through. So they went ahead and sang that morning for about an hour, and when he gave the altar service, there were two people that came to the altar. They kept singing, and before they were finished, about fifteen people had come to the altar and gave their life to God.

George's most requested song is "Zion's Hill," which George always sings a cappella. George lost his voice for about four months in 2003. He went to a specialist, and all he could do was whisper. They had nine appointments, so they decided to play their soundtrack and simply pantomime. The first place they went was in Jackson in southern Ohio. That night, they sang for about an hour and half. They did about thirty songs, and George couldn't understand why the people couldn't tell he wasn't really singing. He said, "I guess you all know that I'm pantomiming," but they didn't understand.

The next day, continuing to pantomime, they sang in a great big church, and after they sang, one lady said, "George, that's the best I ever heard you sing." Nobody said a word, and although he felt a little guilty about what he was doing, they had a good service. They then went to Marion, to a church that seats seven hundred. They got up, and right before the service, the pastor said, "You're a little hoarse, aren't you?" After they had sang for the whole service, the pastor said, "Sing my song, George, you know, 'Zion's Hill.'" George told him his voice was a little bit rusty, and he didn't think he could do that song. The pastor agreed to let them do it the next time. They ended up doing the pantomime routine for nine different churches.

When his wife passed in the late 1990s, George took a break from singing. Later on, he met Rowena, and when they were married, they started singing together. They have been singing about nine years as George and Rowena Walker. In 2007, George turned seventy-eight and doesn't go as he used to, only averaging a couple appointments a month. He plans to keep singing as long as he is able.

* * *

Bob Washington started the Gospelaires, a male quartet, in the early 1940s. Bob also sang with the Gospel Caravan Quartet. The Gospelaires were based in Dayton and started singing in local churches. Their ministry broadened to where they were traveling throughout the world and singing with such greats as Clara Ward.

One of the group's most memorable performances was in the mid-1960s when they appeared on the *TV Gospel Time* program. Perhaps you remember the sounds of the Gospelaires back in the 1960s when Bob Washington was slicing his hand through the air as the entire group jumped to the beat of that old classic "Somebody Touched Me," and those sky-high backgrounds of praise by Paul Arnold would often move the listener to gasps of disbelief.

Charles McLean, known worldwide as one of the greatest falsetto singers started singing with the Gospelaires at age seventeen. He later went on to great fame singing with the Keynotes. In 1984, Charles left the Keynotes but continued doing solo work for a while. He now pastors a church in LaGrange, Georgia, and continues his solo ministry.

Some time later, Bob Washington moved to NYC taking the group with him. All of the original members have since passed on, but the group name continues under the direction of Bill Allen working from Florida. Bill has been with the group thirty-three years.

* * *

After living in Southern Ohio for a few years, the Millers moved back to North Carolina before their son Dallas was born. Then on February 2, 1929, Dallas "Dall" Miller was born and grew up in the mountains of Glendale Springs, North Carolina. When he was thirteen years old, they had one radio station in Winston Salem, North Carolina, that would play gospel music around noon every day. Dall heard groups like the Golden Gate Quartet, the Rangers, and some of the older quartets. He would be working out in the field but made it a habit to get in before the show came on, and that's when he got hooked on gospel music. Some time in the late 1940s, Dall sang with Earl and Mary Hazelbaker.

There were only two factories in the area where Dall grew up—one was a cheese factory, and the other one was a chair factory. He had a cousin who lived in Clarksville and worked at National Cash Register (NCR). Coming down for a visit, he told Dall if he would come to Dayton, he would help get him on at NCR. The only work he had was some timber cutting and working with the corn, so at age seventeen, he headed to Ohio, and two days after his eighteenth birthday, he started working at NCR.

After moving to Dayton, like many of his peers, Dall was called for military duty in Korea, and when his squad leader was rotated back to the States, they picked Dall to be the squad leader. It was a machine gun squad, and he was in charge of eight men. He was fortunate in that all the time he was over the squad he never had one guy get killed. Some time later, the platoon sergeant rotated from the first platoon, so needless to say, they picked Dall as the new platoon sergeant, and he was now in charge of forty men. In October 1951, they were getting ready for a big offensive. The Chinese and North Koreans had dug in along the mountains. Some of them had tunneled down about three stories in the hills. Using a battalion of men and bombing the area two or three times, they tried to take a hill they called Old Baldy. Unable to take the hill, they decided by October 3 that they would push off with a whole core, which is about three divisions. This sounded really rough, but Dall had just been saved before coming to Korea and had promised the Lord, over there in those hills, that if He would get him out of that place and bring him back home, he would commit his life to Him.

One day, there were some heavy weapons coming, and for some reason that only the Lord knows, Dall felt like going back up to his bunker. Walking through the trench, he went into the bunker, and as soon as he sat down on the edge of the trench, he heard a mortar round coming in—you could hear them whistling. He quickly rolled off into the trench, and when he got up and looked around, one of the sergeants and the lieutenant had been blown to pieces—they didn't even know what hit them.

They probably lost more men in those three days than America lost over in Iraq in four years. Except for a couple little scratches and a bullet through the back that only missed his spine by less than an inch, Dall returned home safely. Not to be forgotten, over thirty-six thousand men were killed in Korea during a three-year period.

After returning from the military, he continued to work at NCR until the big layoff when he got a job at WPAFB in the model-making department.

In the early 1950s, Dall sang with his cousin and his brother. Dall would play the mandolin, and they traveled around doing a little bluegrass. They attended the Mia Avenue Pentecostal Church on West Third Street in Dayton, and the church often had gospel singings. They brought in groups like the Pathfinders and the Ken Apple Trio. Dall later sang in a trio with a couple of other people in church, but they only sang for a short time and didn't have a name. Dall also played the standup bass at Mia Avenue. Charlie Bowman also attended Mia Avenue and was in charge of the Morning Light Quartet. Charles headed the Montgomery County Singing Convention for years and was instrumental in helping the Southern-Aires get started.

Charles Feltner also attended the church, and in 1955, Dall got together with Charles Feltner, Charles's brother Lee Feltner, and Bob Michaels, forming the Southern-Aires Quartet. They sang that way, with Lee playing lead guitar for three or four months until Naomi, Dall's future wife, started playing the piano.

Naomi was born on September 13, 1933, and her father was a pastor. Moving from Washington Court House, he took a church on Wyoming Street in Dayton. Sometimes they would visit other churches, and they attended many of the Sunday afternoon sings. Then one day, Dall saw Naomi at one of those "afternoon" sings. One of the guys he sang with had met her earlier, and when he saw Dall talking to her, he told him she had a boyfriend. His friend was upset because she had refused to go out with him. After showing up at the sings for a couple months, someone asked Naomi and her father to sing. She borrowed a guitar only to find out later that it was Dall's guitar. They sang the song "I'm a Millionaire," and she often tells people Dall took the song literally. Later that night, he talked with her and found out that she knew Bob Michaels. Bob drove one of those electric trucks through the buildings at NCR. Dall asked if he could come over the next day at lunchtime, and when he came over, he asked her out. They started dating in May 1955.

And since they were only using guitars and a mandolin, she soon started playing piano for the group.

The Southern-Aires started out using a 1947 Cadillac Limousine. Sanford Wood was singing tenor at the time, and being in construction, he got the idea of building a trailer. He built it like a box, and it had only one little wheel on the back. On one trip near Charleston, West Virginia, the wheel broke off.

Dall and Naomi were married on November 1, 1956. During their honeymoon, they went to a Wally Fowler all-night gospel sing, and they heard the Statesmen, the Blackwood Brothers, the Speer Family, and the Johnson Sisters. At one point during the evening, they received a special treat as J. D. Sumner brought Elvis Presley out on stage. Later when they returned to the motel, Dall turned on the TV and Marty Robbins was singing "I Never Felt More Like Singing the Blues." When sharing the story, Naomi jokingly tells people, "I've been singing the blues ever since."

Charles Bowman Feltner was born on February 20, 1929 in Hazard, Kentucky with one leg longer than the other. He was the second oldest of twelve boys and had four sisters. Later in life, he started wearing special shoes so people wouldn't notice that his one leg was shorter. His mother's family was all musicians. They would come to the house, and sitting out on the front porch, they would sing while playing banjos, mandolins, and stuff like that. That's where Charles got his ability to play the guitar and sing.

Growing up in Kentucky, the Feltner brothers had an interesting childhood. The Feltner family came over on a ship from Austria in 1731. They had to leave because the Catholic Church was going to kill everybody that didn't join at that time, so they ended up in Hazard, Kentucky.

Their dad was a big man, and you could mention the name Sherman Feltner to anyone in Hazard, and they knew him. He worked in the coal mine and sold moonshine, keeping the whiskey hidden in the garden in a fifty-pound lard can. He was a pretty rough guy and would shoot you for bothering the family or just on principle. Once the family had to move to Ohio because their dad had shot a man, and they stayed out of Kentucky for seven years.

Once, he and the boys were up on a hillside doing something, and the boys heard a big noise. Looking back, they realized their dad had disappeared. The hillside had collapsed and buried their dad. When help arrived, they just started moving earth until they found him, and when they pulled him out, he had two broken ribs and a broken ankle. He died from old age and a worn-out body, but he accepted God before he died.

Betty was attending a local Church of God, and the first time she saw Charles, he was really bashful. When the preacher asked if he would come up and sing, Charles agreed, but while the preacher was doing something, Charles hurriedly snuck out the back door. Then the next time Betty went to church and he was there, the preacher, going to the back door so he couldn't get out, again asked Charles to sing. He went up and played a guitar and sang the song "How about Your Heart." After he got through singing, the preacher put his arm around him and said, "And how about your heart, Charlie?" Charles just grinned, went back, and sat down.

After completing high school, Charles left home and went to a business college in Louisville, Kentucky. He was the only one in the family to get a college education. Working in the cafeteria, he attended college about two years until he was drafted and sent to Korea. When he got there, the first sergeant asked what was wrong with his leg. When Charles told him that he had one leg longer than the other, they determined he couldn't go out on the battlefield, so the first sergeant told him he would have to be a cook. He wasn't on the field, but he was close enough that when the big bombs would hit. It would shake the mess hall where he was cooking. Perhaps this was God's way of preserving him.

His mother bought Charles a Gibson guitar for $14 while he was in the service and kept it for him in Hazard, Kentucky. Charles didn't follow in his father's footsteps, and he later became the instrument God used to bring his father to the Lord. When he came home from Korea, he walked up the hill to the house, and he had his uniform on, not his jacket, but everything else, and he was soaking wet. His brother Sherman hollered at mom and said, "Mom, you better come and look at Charles, he's wet." As he reached the house, mom asked him what in the world happened. He said, "I just got baptized."

He went to Korea before he and Betty were dating, but she wrote to him all the time he was gone. When he arrived home, he drove fourteen miles to see her at the drugstore where she worked. He said he came to get a newspaper, but she knew he really came to see her. They started dating soon after that.

Charles loved his music, and he used to bring his uncle, Warren Shepherd, and his brother along when he was dating Betty. Betty felt she was also dating his brother and his uncle. They would come up to the house with their instruments, and they would sing and play for her mom. Uncle Shepherd was an unbelievable singer and guitar player, but he was a rare bird. About a week and a half before he died, they went to visit with him in Michigan. They were sitting there, and he said, "Hey, let me tell you, we went over to the place where you buy your tombstone, and we talked to this guy, and as he started into his sales pitch, I said, 'Hold on just a minute, I've got a question for you.' The guy stopped, and I said, 'Do you have a layaway plan?'"

Charles and Betty dated for five or six months, fell deeply in love, and then were married on August 26, 1953. He soon went to Dayton, got a job, and rented an apartment. He then came back to Kentucky for her, and with the help of her brother, they moved to Dayton. In Ohio, he started working as a scheduler at Standard Register where he retired after forty years.

Charles first took Betty to a Jesus Only Church, and that wasn't her belief, but that's what he believed, and that's where he occasionally attended church and probably where he was baptized. Betty told him she didn't want to go to the Jesus Only Church, so they started going to Mia Avenue Pentecostal Church of God. They attended there for years until the church moved west of Dayton, and that was a little far for them to travel, so they found a church in Centerville.

Betty sang one time with Charles at the Mia Avenue Church. One day, they talked Betty into singing, and they sang "I'm Using My Bible for a Roadmap." This was her first and last time singing, and she said, "My legs played Yankee Doodle Dandy while I sang." When they got acquainted with Brother Prosser, they started going to the Fourth Street Church of God in Dayton.

Charles went to the Holy Land thirteen times, traveling with Kash Amburgey eleven of those times. He would take his little singing machine and sing on the trips. His Bible knowledge was excellent, and if you asked him anything about the Bible, he could give you an answer immediately. He was very good on Bible history, one of the reasons why he enjoyed going over to the Holy Land.

He started writing songs before he started singing with the Southern-Aires and wrote over three hundred songs. "I'll See You in the Rapture" is probably his most popular song. It is sung all over the world. Charles heard it overseas, and some of his royalties are from Switzerland and all over. Although Charles is no longer with us, his music continues on, and in 2007, the famous Booth Brothers came out with their version of that great song "I'll See You in the Rapture."

Another popular song was "I'll Never be the Same Anymore," recorded by the Happy Goodmans. Rusty Goodman told Charles, "That's my style, Charlie." They went down to where the Goodmans lived and spent a weekend with them, and Charles was on their TV show. The Singing Americans recorded Charles' song "The Bridegroom Cometh." Once, the Eddie Crook Company offered to buy all of his music for $1,000.

Charles sang with the Southern-Aires for twenty-one years and later sang with the Crownsmen in Cincinnati.

Charles, all the Feltner boys, and their sister Ann, would sing every year at their family reunion. That was always a big thing, and it was held at the big Feltner 4H Park in London, Kentucky. A member of the Feltner family worked in Washington DC, and he had the park built. Charles told his son Kim if he would sing with him that he would buy him a minibike. So Kim agreed to sing. Kim, Vanessa, and Charles sang a little bit down at church, but when Kim got his minibike, he wouldn't sing any more. Vanessa started singing with a little group at a church in Centerville. She later sang with both the Southern-Aires and her father. She is currently touring Asia as an entertainer, playing and singing in hotels.

Charles formed his own group for a while called the Charles Feltner Singers. A lady named Charlotte sang with the Charles Feltner Singers, and once, she got excited and knocked all the flowers over while they were singing the song "Song of a Soul Set Free." Another time, she started shouting and knocked a little crippled man out of his seat. She quickly picked him up and setting him back on the chair continued shouting. She was a wild one, but she could sing a song.

On her deathbed, Charlotte started hearing a tune in her head, so she crawled out of the bed, got a pen and a piece of paper, and wrote down the words she was hearing. Sherman eventually sang the song several times. When she was a part of the group, everybody was thrilled to hear them sing. She enhanced the group tremendously.

The Charles Feltner Singers were on their way to Manchester, Kentucky, to sing at a county fair. During the trip, Charles became very sick to the point that they thought he might have to be taken to the hospital. Darrell Webb says, "Upon reaching the fairgrounds Charles, refusing to cancel their engagement, stepped out onto the platform and sang his heart out, never making the crowd aware of his sickness."

Charles passed away on September 2, 2005, at Miami Valley Hospital in Dayton. Jim Hill spoke of Charles at the Coming Together Center (CTC) in Dayton. He said, "There's nobody like Charles Feltner. I loved that guy. His physical handicaps didn't bother him at all. He would come out on that stage with that smile and that coolness he possessed, just a great man."

Lee Feltner played the guitar and also sang with the Southern-Aires when they first started singing. When Lee was a young boy, he and one of his brothers were traveling in a truck with their dad somewhere near Indian Head, and a man was hitchhiking. They stopped to pick the guy up, and as he climbed up into the truck, he had a .45 pistol in his hand. Their dad grabbed the pistol and, pulling him into the truck, took it out of his hand. Then beating him half to death, he threw him out and left him in the middle of the road. When he reached the first little store, he told them they better call the sheriff and have someone go pick up the guy. He told them what happened and nobody ever came to the house. That's just the way it was back then in Hazard, Kentucky.

After singing with the Southern-Aires, Lee disappeared for twenty years until one day, with the help of a sister-in-law, they found him living in Las Vegas, and he was in poor health. So they went out and picked Lee up and brought him back to Ohio. He was in bad shape, had lost his self-respect, and fluently used foul language as a result of playing in bars so many years. So their brother James, who was a minister, and his wife, Cheryl, started working with him. After a while, they got him to where he would go to church, and his health restored to where he could play the guitar again. Not long after that, he became a Christian and worked in the church until he died. He had diabetes, requiring removal of one leg. After removal of Lee's second leg, Sherman walked into the hospital and said, "Now what are you up to today, buddy?"

He said, "About thirty-six inches," and while still laughing he said, "I won't need these legs in heaven." People just loved him to death. Sherman says, "I'm just glad that we had that sister-in-law that was smarter than all of us, that found out where he was so we could get him back and get him back on his feet. That way he ended up going to heaven instead of hell."

Soon Lloyd Orrell was asking the Southern-Aires to work with him and help out with promotions for his concerts at Memorial Hall in Dayton and in Bainbridge. The group shared the stage at the NQC with such groups as the Statesmen, the Blackwoods, and the Kingsmen.

They never had too much trouble out on the road with their buses, but one time, they were traveling home in their second bus, an old 1947 Silverside, and somewhere around Chillicothe, the fuel filter clogged up. They had been stranded along the side of the road for about an hour and a half when some guy came along to help them. He took them to a nearby parts store, but of course, it was closed. Returning to the bus, the man took a roll of toilet paper and told them he was going to put it in their filter. He told them it should last until their got home. It worked fine, and they made it home without any problem.

In 1970, as part of a Kash Amburgey tour, the Southern-Aires sang in Israel with Zeke Hoskins and the Gospelaires and the Lamb Family. The Lamb Family sang for several years in the Dayton area and a few other places. They later moved to Florida and didn't sing much after they went down there. While on tour, they sang in Jerusalem, McGinnis Hall, and they were told this was the first gospel concert ever held there. They also sang at the Shepherd's Cave, which was the one up on the hill known as Mount Olive.

In 1978, Chip and Marilyn Bowling started singing with the Southern-Aires. Chip and Marilyn lived with Dall and Naomi for about six or seven months while their boys were still living at home. After about six years, they left the group and started singing as a duet. They later ended up back with the Southern-Aires where they remained until 2004.

They were going down to the Carolinas, and the Gibson brothers were filling in for Chip and Marilyn Bowling because Chip had heart surgery. Those boys took enough food on the bus to last a week. It was probably around midnight, and they were driving through West Virginia. One of them was standing in the middle of the bus eating something when Dall took a hard turn around a curve, sending him into the wall. He knocked the window open, and his arm went out the window.

Another time, Charles Feltner was driving, and it started raining. Dall told Charlie he needed to be careful as the road was getting slick. Charlie said, "I'll handle it." Then as they approached the traffic light, it started changing. Suddenly, Charlie locked up the brakes, and the bus started fishtailing as it slid into the intersection. They ended up in the oncoming lane before the bus stopped, but the Lord was watching over them as no one was coming, and they didn't hit anything.

Once while the group was on the road traveling, they had parked several of their cars in Dall's yard. While they were gone, Naomi made up For Sale signs and put them on all the cars.

In 1986, Darrell Webb started singing with the Southern-Aires. Previously, in 1970, Darrell had organized the Harbinger Quartet, and they continued until about 1985. Prior to marrying Darrell, Wanda Malony sang with the Chapel Keys Trio.

In the winter of 1978, the Harbingers were scheduled to sing in Newton, West Virginia, at the home church of Squire Parsons. Wanda had not been singing because of her recent pregnancy, and she had just given birth to their youngest son. As they were making final preparations for the trip, the tenor singer who was filling in for Wanda called, indicating he would not be making the trip. Having no time to find a replacement, Wanda agreed to make the trip. On the way to West Virginia, the heater on the bus quit working. It was a long cold trip, but they made it to Newton, singing for three services. But it was so cold on the bus while traveling home that at about three on Monday morning, they had to stop in Wilmington at the police station to heat up the baby bottle, so they could feed the baby.

One summer, the Harbingers were scheduled to sing at a church that was building a new sanctuary in Booneville, Kentucky. The pastor told them to plan on singing in the new sanctuary. Upon arrival, they were informed the new building was not finished, but the singing would go on. The church had put together some temporary seats using concrete blocks and wooden planks. A good crowd came out, and the singing was going well. Dave Reynolds, who was filling in for Wanda, was singing a very moving song written by Gordon Jenson when suddenly a bat flew inside the building. Then because of the way the light was reflecting off of Dave's head, the bat began attacking Dave. The pastor's wife quickly started chasing the bat around with her songbook. All the commotion made it very difficult to sing.

In 1983, the Harbingers were touring Florida for a few weeks. The last week, they had to travel down to Key West, and one of the bridges they had to cross was under construction. Entering the bridge, they slowly worked their way across the bridge. The bus wheels along the driver's side scraped against the edge of the bridge, and the mirrors were repeatedly scrapped by semis as they attempted to pass the bus headed the other direction. That's too close for me!

For a while, Darrell was traveling in two directions because in 1984 before the Harbingers stopped singing, Darrell was also singing with the Anchormen in Ashland, Kentucky, and he continued traveling with them until 1987, about a year after he started singing with the Southern-Aires. While with the Anchormen, they sang at such places as the Paramount Theatre in Ashland, Kentucky, Gatlinburg, Tennessee, and Boston, Massachusetts. While in Boston, they spent some time with Boston Red Sox chaplain Ernie Trivila.

After leaving the Anchormen, Darrell and his wife, Wanda, sang with the Charles Feltner Singers for a while. In 1994, Darrell and Wanda along with their two sons, Jason and Shawn, started traveling together as the Webb Family for a period of about three years. Shortly thereafter, as they had previously sung with the Southern-Aires, Darrell and his wife worked out an arrangement with Dall Miller and returned to the Southern-Aires where they continue to minister today.

Jason Webb began his musical studies at age five and began playing professionally at age fourteen. Jason played piano for his family group and the Southern-Aires while in high school and currently produces most of the sound tracks for the Southern-Aires. At age eighteen, Jason turned down an offer to play for the Kingsmen Quartet as he wanted to finish his schooling. After high school, Jason went on to earn a degree in jazz performance at the Cincinnati Conservatory of Music. Jason later played for the Dixie Melody Boys and the Down East Boys. In 2000, Jason moved to Hendersonville, Tennessee, and his compositions and arrangements have been recorded by artists all over the world. In 2003, Darrell Webb sang on a Stamps-Baxter promotional CD with Terry Franklin who previously sang with the Gaither Vocal Band and Jason Webb.

Duane Early started singing with the Southern-Aires in 2005. In 1970, Duane helped form a quartet in Dayton called the Royal Heirs, and the group stayed together for about five years. Then in 1978, Duane agreed to fill the tenor position for the Victors Quartet in Middletown.

Leaving the Victors Quartet in 1981, Duane, Curtis Williams, and Lowell Riegal formed a group called the Riegal Brothers, a trio based in Dayton. Daryl Strickler, a prior member of the Southern-Aires, also sang with the Riegal Brothers for a while. Then while traveling in Michigan with the Riegal Brothers, he met the love of his life and soon left the group. Over the years, the tenor position was filled by a number of people, and the group altered back and forth from a trio to a quartet, finishing their last year as a quartet in 1999. Jeff Christmas also sang with them for a while, nothing like having "Christmas" around all year.

Eddie Miller started singing bass when he was fourteen, and Randy Miller started playing when he was thirteen, and they did a little bit of reminiscing at the Southern-Aires fiftieth anniversary. Eddie shared the story about the time they left Randy asleep in the seat of a church they were singing at in Indianapolis, Indiana. They had left the church and were headed to an afternoon sing at another church. Someone said something about Randy, and

Naomi responded, "Isn't he back there on the bunk?" They looked around and discovered that he was not on the bus. They couldn't wait to get back to the church. Arriving back at the church, there was still someone there, and they were able to get in only to find Randy sound asleep on the pew.

The Dayton Ambassadors, sharing a close relationship with the group, commend them for their many years of dedication and counted it an honor to share the stage with the Southern-Aires during their fiftieth anniversary celebration. Throughout the years, a number of members have come and gone. Many of these members have come from other groups or went on to be with other groups and include such people as Cliff Chamblin, Ricky Todd, Chip and Marilyn Bowling, Gary Cohn, Wendall Davis, Tim McNeal, Allen Law and others. The Southern-Aires continue to travel for the Lord, and after completing about fifty recordings, Dall says, "Perhaps one of my favorite songs would have to be Jim Hill's song, 'What a Day That Will Be.'"

* * *

John Vaughn was eighteen, and Joyce New was seventeen when they got married. Joyce was raised in a Holiness Church of God, and her mother thought their church was the only one that was going to make it. Knowing how her mother felt, Joyce was frightened at the thought of marrying a Baptist guy, but she did it anyway. In 1964, leaving their hometown of Somerset, Kentucky, Joyce and John loaded up their things and moved to Dayton where John became employed at a local Chrysler plant. Several years later, they began singing as a duet, and in 1969, with the help of Joe Hunter, Dave Baker, and Peggy O'Bryant, they formed the Homegate Quartet. When they first started, John was shy and wouldn't talk. Their pastor, Jack Combs, told John, "You've got to learn to talk. Just talk about Jesus, leave the denomination out of it. Just testify about how good God is to you, and it'll go."

Once after singing at a little country church near London, Kentucky, they had packed all their equipment in the van and were ready to head home. Suddenly, John noticed the gas cap was missing, and there was sand all around the gas tank opening. One of the men of the church spotted Darrell and John looking at the van and came over to find out what was wrong. Some of the people in the church began asking questions, and soon they determined that a young boy, who was just playing, had put sand in the gas tank. Afraid of the damage that might result, one of the men told them they could not start the engine until the problem was resolved. The man owned an auto parts store, and he went over to his store and picked up a filter. Upon returning from the store, without even taking off his suit, the man pulled off the fuel line, drained and flushed out the gas tank, and soon had them back on the road. Someone later found the gas cap in the outhouse of the church.

Dave Baker later became a therapist and, because of his work schedule, had to drop out of the group. Joe quit singing with the group for about a year, but after returning, he remained with the group until he passed away.

The group often sang with the Dayton Ambassadors and enjoyed a close fellowship with them. Some time in the 1980s, the Homegate Quartet was visiting someone at the hospital and had parked in the preacher's parking space. Tom Lawson, having his police uniform on and wanting to have some fun, quickly came up to them and said, "You can't park there, don't you know better than that?" John told him they were just going to run up and visit their bass singer and would be right back. About that time, Tom doubled over in laughter.

Another member, Carl Fiffe, remained with the group about thirty years until dropping out in 2005 because of health problems.

John worked second shift, and often after singing in Illinois, he would drive home, change clothes, and go to work. Don Jaquish sang bass for a while. His dad used to sing with Cecil Hickman and the Kings Highway Quartet from Dayton. Their youngest daughter came to the altar one evening while they were singing. Paul Wallin used to help them learn their songs. Paul sang with the Rock of Ages Quartet for years. They sang with no music.

The Homegate Quartet was privileged to be part of a six-week revival held by Norm Livingston and Jack Combs at a popular church in Dayton located on Blueberry Avenue.

Working at Chrysler daily and singing nightly at the revival proved to be a bit much for John as one evening near the end of the revival, John was sitting on the front pew, and some time during the service, he drifted off to sleep and fell out of his seat almost falling onto the floor. And soon, everyone was cracking up laughing.

The biggest crowd they ever sang for was a Sunday school class of about eight hundred people at the Detroit Baptist Temple, and they were petrified. Several times promoter Norm Livingston tried to get the Homegate Quartet to sing for one of his concerts held at Memorial Hall, but John would always refuse, believing they were not of the same quality as the other groups and would certainly be laughed off the stage.

Singing in the current group are Joyce and John's two sons Scott and Darrell. Scott's son, Doug, goes with them sometimes and plays the guitar. Joyce says, "We try to work the grandkids in there as much as we can. So somebody can take over when we are gone."

Boyd Lamb has played for them off and on for years. He plays lead guitar from a wheelchair. Only forty-six years old, Boyd is also being treated for cancer.

As they were preparing to leave a church somewhere in Kentucky, they had a flat tire. After taking the tire off, they realized their new spare was flat also. Soon a man from the church stopped to offer his help, and discovering the problem, he took the spare off of his pickup truck and put in on their van. He told them, "If you're ever down through here, you can drop it off. About two weeks later, they were going to Somerset and stopped on the way to return the man's tire.

John sees the group winding down because of health reasons, but their son Scott wants to keep singing. Joyce believes they are holding Scott back as several groups have asked him to go with them, but he won't leave mom and dad. Scott said, "My parents brought me up in church, they taught me what I know, and I feel comfortable right here."

* * *

The Littlejohn Brothers known simply as the "Brothers," were members of the same church when the group formed in 1979 as an a cappella trio through the diplomatic encouragement of their mother. The group started singing in local churches patterning their ministry after such influences as the Mighty Clouds of Joy, the Williams Brothers, the Winans and James Cleveland. The group has traveled throughout the United States singing with such greats as the Charles Fold Singers.

The Brothers were traveling to an engagement somewhere in the south, and while traveling, they were engaged in a card game for fun when a tire blew out. After changing the tire, they were soon back on the road and back to their card game, but it wasn't long before they blew another tire. Needless to say, they changed the tire, but after getting back on the road, the card game never resumed throughout that or any other trip, and they have never experienced another flat tire while traveling down the road. Superstitious? No, just wise!

The group is also known for their community work, receiving recognition from Ohio Governor George Voinovich for their Young People's Interdenominational Mass Musical (YIMM) initiated in 1985. In the period of ten years, the YIMM grew from one hundred participants to over four hundred. Over the years, several of the other brothers joined the group, and the Littlejohn Brothers continue today combining their close-knit harmony, that is a by-product of their family relationship, with a blend of traditional and contemporary gospel to produce a style that is all their own.

* * *

Randall Clay was born in Mullens, West Virginia. His first ambition was to be a shop teacher until the school introduced photography, and he had found his nitch. First introduced to gospel music as a young boy by the Laurel Valley Quartet, Randall found another great interest in his life, and Randall soon developed a love for gospel music.

Randall became a news photographer, and in 1955, he was working at a TV station in Bluefield, West Virginia. Although he had started buying quartet records, he had never met any of the groups. Then one day, the director told him to get the piano set up because they had a quartet coming in. When he told him it was the Blue Ridge Quartet from Spartansburg, South Carolina, Randall just about flipped as he really liked them and had been buying their records. He soon became friends with them and went to Spartansburg, South Carolina, several times to be with them. After George Younce joined them, they became close friends and remained good buddies until he passed away. The next group to come through was the Blackwood Brothers, right after the plane crash. They had just reorganized, hiring J. D. Sumner and Cecil Blackwood. While working for the TV station, he met several other groups such as the "old" Oak Ridge Quartet and the Foggy River Boys who moved from Springfield, Missouri to Dayton. Prior to moving to Dayton, they had been doing the *Red Foley Show*. The group members at that time were Don Taylor, Danny Koker, Earl Terry, who had a sweet voice, and Jim Hamill.

Randall wasn't making much money in West Virginia even though he traveled with John Kennedy for three days, former president Truman for two days, and a number of show business people. His sister had moved to Dayton and on one trip to visit her, he decided to look around for a job. He found a job in a studio paying double what he was making in West Virginia, so he took the job. He knew nothing about portrait work, but soon he became a good portrait photographer.

Some time later, he was at the fairgrounds in Dayton, and his buddies, the Blue Ridge Quartet, were there along with some other gospel groups. He was standing in the lobby watching them through the door when a man walked up beside him. They started talking, and he asked if Randall sang. The man said, "You sound like you would be a bass singer, and we just lost our bass singer. Would you like to try out?" The man was Bob Michaels. So Randall, agreeing to meet with them, went over and tried out with those guys. They scared him to death because the first thing they did was to get down and started praying, and he wasn't even a Christian. He thought, *Holy cow, what have I gotten into?* Before long, he came under conviction, and Jim Hill said something in a concert that really touched his heart, causing him to give his life to the Lord, and that's when things started turning around.

In 1950, the Reverend Loren Kolb had an idea that there should be a Gospel television program covering Southwestern Ohio. He tried several different formats until the program *Good Ship Zion* evolved and was accepted for public service programming by station WHIO-TV. "Captain" Kolb found a gospel quartet from Dayton and named them the Gospel Mariners. The program, presented as though it originated on board a ship, consisted of three or four songs by the quartet and a short message by Captain Kolb. The *Good Ship Zion* program was one of the longest sustained programs in the country.

The popularity of the group grew to such an extent that in the fall of 1963, four out of the five members decided to go full time. At the same time it was necessary to limit the number of appearances on *Good Ship Zion* as the program was carried live on Sundays at noon. It was very difficult to get back from their personal appearances to Dayton in time for the program, but this problem was resolved by adding another quartet to the staff. Loren Kolb wanted to continue using the group name, the Gospel Mariners, so the full time group called themselves the Mariners.

One of the original members, Ray Seaman, was born in 1943 and was off to a head start in music as his father was already an accomplished musician. By the time Ray was five years old, he had begun singing with his family. He accepted Christ at the tender age of seven, and by age twelve, he was traveling with the Calvary Quartet and remained with them until he was seventeen.

In 1962, Ray moved to Dayton where he met and married the love of his life, Janet. During these years, Ray was singing lead with the Gospel

Crusaders Quartet, the Mariners Quartet, and then his baritone voice would be joined with the Notemen Quartet. From Dayton, Ray and his family headed south to Kenner, Louisiana, where they lived until 1974. In Kenner, Ray sang tenor with the Directors, a male trio and finally a mixed quartet, the Trinity Singers that would include Janet's beautiful voice. This is also a time when their children Rodney and Rhonda started singing with their parents from time to time. Garland, Texas, was the next stop where in 1975, singing lead with the Nobelmen, they won the Walley Fowler Talent Contest. Their compensation was to open for J. D. Sumner and the Stamps Quartet during several concerts that year in the Texas area.

In 1977, it was back to Dayton for a year where Ray once again sang in a trio that included Janet. Then it was on to Hollywood, Florida, where the trio would sing for the church's radio and television programs. Indiana became home in 1981, and 2003 brought about the reuniting of the Mariners Quartet and Ray's singing schedule currently alternates between a quartet known as His Voice Through Us and the reunited Mariners Quartet.

Another original member, Ned Williams, was born in Van Wert, the last of ten children. He worked along with the rest of the family in their supermarket business, and Christ came into his life at age six. In high school, he sang with a barbershop quartet called the Kings Quartet. After high school, he married Marilyn, the girl of his dreams, and sang with the Sons of Harmony on WLW radio. He had to leave this group in 1953 when he was drafted into the U.S. Army. During his two-year tour of duty he met a group from a television program he was watching called the Kingsmen. He sang with this quartet until he finished his tour of duty. After returning home, he received a letter from the Gospel Mariners and sang with them for about two years.

Ned was living in Indianapolis, Indiana, when they first went on the road full-time, so when they would drive through Indianapolis on old U.S. 40, if Ned was in bed, he would always tell the guys to wake him up so he could call his wife. Once they were traveling, and Ned told them, "You guys, wake me up when we get to Indianapolis." He then went to the back of the bus, climbed into the top bunk and went to sleep. Just a few miles outside of Indianapolis, Randall very quietly went back to where Ned was soundly sleeping, took a necktie, and looping it around Ned's feet, tied it to the foot of the bed. After traveling a couple miles down the road, one of the guys hollered, "Hey, Ned, we're coming into Indianapolis." About that time, everything came out of the bed but his feet. It was a horrible sound.

After his time with the Mariners, Ned joined the Swanee River Boys Quartet when they were regulars on the *Cadle Tabernacle* radio and television programs. After singing with them for five years, he returned to Dayton to once again sing with the Mariners Quartet. Ned was forced to come off the road when his daughter was diagnosed with a serious kidney disease. Thanks to a touch from heaven, after suffering for seventeen years, she was healed. During this period, Ned joined Roark Furniture as a sales representative and also did their radio and television commercials. After leaving Roark, Ned and his family went into the fried chicken business, and for the past twenty-eight years, his family has been feeding thousands of people at the Darke County Fair in Greenville. And if you haven't tried Ned's sweet barbecue sauce, you don't know what you're missing.

The Mariners spent their full-time traveling and making personal appearances at churches, revivals, and all-night sings. They appeared on many TV programs including *Hootinnati* (WKRC-TV Cincinnati), *Dialing for Dollars* (WTVN-TV Columbus), and *Easter's Parade* (WIMA-TV Lima) to name a few. When they started traveling full-time, they didn't do much work in Ohio. One of their first long tours was with the Stamps when Jim Hill, Big John, Hall and Roger McDuff were traveling with the group. The Stamps booked the Mariners with them all across Oklahoma, Texas, and throughout that part of the country.

One of Randall's idols was George Younce, and while many groups were trying to see how high their tenor could sing and how low their bass could go, the Mariners simply tried to work on maintaining close harmony. Randall says, "Our whole emphasis was trying to win souls because the guys were really dedicated Christians."

They worked frequently with the Cathedrals, and the Mariners did a special recording for a company along with the Cathedrals, the Rangers, and a group called the Christian Troubadours from Washington. They sent them all to Nashville, and they furnished the musicians. David Reese played the piano for them, and part of Jim Reeves's band played. The company recorded the albums, took their pictures, paid for the studio, and sold them the albums for $0.50 a piece. Randall said, "We were on cloud nine, and selling them for $2.00, we thought we were making big money."

The Mariners had some neat experiences working with some of the other guys. The Statesmen were always good to them and were responsible for their first tour in Canada. They had a guy managing them at that time who was an outstanding gospel singer. His name was Don Butler, and he had previously sung with the Sons of Song. One night, Don called Randall and told him he had talked with Hovie, and they needed another group to go to Canada. Don told him they would recommend them and have the promoter call him.

Soon they received a call from Toronto, Canada, and were scheduled to sing. It was their first trip to Canada, and they were worried about getting through customs. Randall told the guys, "I've heard all kinds of stories, sometimes you go through like a breeze, and sometimes they just harass you to death." It was about two o'clock in the morning when they crossed the Ambassador Bridge into Canada from Detroit. Randall was sitting up front talking and said, "Here comes a bus." When the bus reached, them it was the Stamps Quartet, so Randall jumped out and started motioning to them to stop. He ran over and told Jim Hill they didn't know how to get through customs. Jim said, "When we get there, you get out, and just do everything I do." They went through like a breeze because Jim had been up there several times. It was an exciting trip and probably one of the biggest things they had done. They sang with the Statesmen, the Junior Blackwoods, and the Sego Brothers & Naomi. The auditorium had three levels of balconies, and they filled it for two nights in a row. Almost everybody that came to their table would buy two of everything in case the group didn't come back.

They did go back to Canada again. In fact, they started touring up there and did a string of dates in Canada with the Goodman Family. Randall and Rusty were good friends, and once, they went to Quebec to sing with The Goodmans. This is before the Goodmans bought their new Silver Eagle bus. When the concert was over, Rusty said, "Hey, Randall why don't you ride back to Toronto with me?" So he told the guys he would see them back at the hotel. On the way back, the Goodmans had trouble with their bus. They couldn't get the heater to work in it, so Howard and Vestal were sitting over there all night wrapped up in a blanket. Sam and Rusty messed with the bus, and finally, they got to the hotel in Toronto at the time his group members were getting out of bed and having breakfast. They had been up all night but right after that the Goodmans bought a brand new Silver Eagle.

One day, Randall had stopped at the little record shop located on East Third Street in Dayton. While he was there, Charles Feltner came by and gave him a copy of a song he had written. They were living in Huber Heights at the time, and when Randall arrived home, he tossed the sheet music on the TV set. Carolyn said, "What's that?"

And he said, "Oh, Charlie Feltner wrote a song, and gave me a copy of the music." She picked it up and did something with it. Some time later, he heard a song on the radio, and it sounded familiar. He asked his wife, "What did you do with that sheet of music that Charlie Feltner gave me?" She told him where it was, and when he dug it out, it was the song "I'll See You in the Rapture."

On the road, the Mariners had some unique situations. One night, they were coming in, and Randall was driving. The guys were all in their bunks asleep. Ned got up and came to the front and told Randall to be careful. He said, "Denny, our tenor singer, is trying to go to sleep and said he envisioned a wreck, just like a vision came to him."

Randall said, "Okay" and didn't think anything more about it. They hadn't gone two miles until he drove into a patch of fog that was so heavy he had to slam on the brakes and slow down. It was a two-lane road, and he pulled over until he felt the wheels go off the pavement. All of a sudden, an eighteen-wheeler popped through, and it was driving right in the middle of the road. Had they not slowed down and gotten over, there would have been a horrible head-on crash, and Randall might have been killed. Randall believes God really spoke to Denny and Ned in an effort to warn him.

One other time, they were headed to Kentucky to do a tent revival with a young preacher. They were driving an old Silverside bus that had seating up front with a door that swung into the back area where they had six beds and six closets. They were running late, coming down through the mountains, and Randall was driving, and he said, "Guys, why don't you all go back there and get dressed. That way, you can start setting up the sound equipment as soon as we arrive while I get suited up, and we will be ready to go."

While everyone was in the back changing, they started down a hill on a two-lane road. They were approaching a little bridge located in a curve when he spotted a big truck loaded with logs creeping up ahead. He could tell they were going to meet on the bridge, so he swung out and tried to cut back at the last minute without hitting the bridge. Soon lumber was flying all over, bouncing around his head. When he hit the brakes, Ned come flying through the door backward, coming all the way to the dashboard with his pants down around his ankles. Despite this incident, they arrived safely to their destination, had a wonderful service, and saw many people saved.

They sung for about ten years on the road full-time, working often in Pennsylvania with the Couriers, and the furthest the Mariners ever traveled was to Jerusalem. Then different ones started wanting to get off the road, so Randall took his wife and children and started a family ministry that included both music and teaching. They were called the Randall Clay Family, and their three children, twin boys and a daughter, were part of the group. Randall and Carolyn are still in full-time family ministry, singing and teaching marriage and family seminars. All three of their children are in ministries in other places now, and for the past ten years, it has been Randall and his wife. Randall and Jim Hill talk almost every week. Randall tells him over and over, "When we sing the song 'What a Day That Will Be,' it doesn't matter if they are in a Pentecostal church, a Nazarene church, a Church of God, or Baptist. People lift their hands and praise the Lord more during that song than any other. People like songs that they can identify with."

In 2003, the old group got together for dinner, the same four that went on the road full-time, and someone said, "Why don't we get together and see if we can still sing, just for fun?" It wasn't long after that until they were back doing concerts. On Friday, January 14, 2005, at age seventy-three, Denny Sullivan, their tenor singer, unexpectedly passed away. His wife had a stroke and was in the hospital. The nurse came in to check on her and found Denny sitting there, leaned over against her—he had passed away. It was quite a shock to the group. He had a beautiful Irish tenor voice, and both the Cathedrals and Bill Gaither had approached Denny about singing with them. The Mariners later hired Tommy Linder, Jr. who was born in Baton Rouge, Louisiana, in 1949 and grew up in Moss Point, Mississippi.

At age five, Tommy would begin to apply his musical interests with piano lessons. By the time he was nine, he began singing in the local Presbyterian Church Choir at the church where his family attended. During Vacation Bible School (at age twelve), Tommy made a profession of faith joining First Baptist Church of Moss Point. His family soon followed, and from age twelve to seventeen, he participated in youth choirs, small group ensembles, solos, and state choir festivals and competitions.

In 1967, the family moved to Beans Corner, Maine, where Tommy attended The University of Maine and was a founding member of the Designed Xpression, a choral group that traveled six months in Europe as part of winning a USO tour. The group performed at over two hundred locations throughout Europe where American armed forces men and women were stationed. As part of the Designed Xpression, Tommy also sang in men's quartet called the Grimaces Four and developed his hidden talent as being a real *ham*.

While attending Naval Flight Officers Candidate School in Pensacola, Florida, from 1972 to 1973, Tommy sang with the nondenominational Pensacola Naval Air Station Church. Tommy was a member of the Thomas

Road Baptist Church in Lynchburg, Virginia, from 1973 to 1977. He traveled around the country with the Liberty Four Quartet and sang on *The Old Time Gospel Hour* television program. This allowed Tommy the opportunity to sing backup vocals with Christian recording artist Robie Hiner at numerous Christian concerts. While teaching at Liberty Bible College, Tommy had the privilege to teach both Robie Hiner and Mark Lowry. He has been singing with Ray and Janet Seaman since 1995 as the Trio and has also been part of a men's quartet since 1997. Both groups have been blessed with multiple opportunities to spread the gospel through song during Indiana Christmas pageants.

Shortly before George Younce passed away, Randall and Carol were at the mall in Lafayette, Louisiana. He told Carol he was going out to the motor home to check his voice mail. There was a message from George. He simply said, "Felt like singing today." He was getting pretty weak, and he said, "Thought I would call somebody I love and sing to them." He then sang a verse and a chorus of an old song while Randall sat there and cried his eyes out. Randall was very close to George. He would often call Randall up and give him a hard time about being uglier than him. Wally Fowler had been dead for years, but George called one night when Randall was up on a ladder remodeling his kitchen. When the phone rang, he got down off the ladder, and when he answered the phone, George said, "Randall, Wally Fowler just called me and wants me and you up in Alabama next Saturday night." George was always doing stuff like that.

Randall says, "George is a man that loved everybody, he always had time for everybody, and was just a super guy."

Randall believes there have been a number of people who influenced him over the years. He says, "Rex Nelon was a super guy, and I was always impressed with the life of Jake Hess." Randall and his wife retained a close relationship with the Weatherfords, and Randall says, "Lily is a sweetheart." The Weatherfords would often spend time at their house when in the area. Jim Hill has always been a close friend and has just bent over backward to help the group. Randall remains close friends with Ed Spraggs, who sang with the Blue Ridge Quartet and, at eighty-four, is still singing in a quartet. Kenny Gates also of the Blue Ridge Quartet has remained a good friend.

The Mariners are taking choice dates and not just running everywhere. The last bus they had was one of the old Greyhound Scenic Cruisers, but they usually travel in two motor homes. Most are retired now, so they don't have to pay big salaries. They like to reminisce and always have prayer together.

It's the "hugginest" four guys you've ever seen. They hug each other's necks every time they see each other.

* * *

At age five, Toby Siler started singing that old Kingsmen song "Excuses." Later, singing with Rick Doran's son, Richard Matthew and two other young men, they took first place at the 1992 Top Flight competition. In 1994, Toby Siler, along with several members from his church, organized a male quartet called New Life. Then in 1999, when Toby's wife, Christi, joined the group, New Life became a mixed trio. A young man named Justin traveled with the group for a while. He had been playing the piano since he was ten years old. He was raised a preacher's son, and he sang in church with his mother. Justin once fell off the stage in the middle of a song, and another time, he was up singing and broke a tooth when his microphone hit him in the face. On March 4, 2006, Justin married Elizabeth (Liz). Liz traveled with the group helping set up the sound equipment and working at their product table. She also took care of the twins during some of the concerts.

Phil Sowders traveled with the group for about nine years. In 2003, Phil started traveling with the Toney Brothers in Gallatin, Tennessee, remaining with them for two years. Another current member of the group, Aaron Ballard, previously sang with a group called Lighthouse in southern Ohio.

In conjunction with Victor Seaton, president of Encore Productions, Toby has held some very successful concerts at his home church featuring such groups as Legacy Five and Greater Vision. Traveling on the road with their five-year-old twins, Jarrod and Jewell, there is never a dull moment on the bus. Toby desires to instill within his children the same love for southern gospel music that God placed within his heart. When Toby sings the song "Christmas Shoes" with the help of his boys, the crowd is truly blessed.

* * *

The Notemen Quartet was started in 1956 by Bill Neal as an offspring of the Bowman Brothers Quartet based in Dayton. Uncle Charlie Bowman later sang with the Miami Valley Quartet and was the founder of the Montgomery County Singing Convention (MCSC). The Notemen started out traveling in an old Cadillac limousine pulling a one-wheel trailer and later purchased an old Flex Bus.

Keith Chapman started with the group at age twenty-five. He previously sang with the Happy Rhythm Boys in West Virginia. He later sang with his brother in the Victors Quartet in Middletown.

Once while they were traveling, the engine lost its power, forcing them to pull off to the side of the road. Keith put on his coveralls, and pulling off the distributor, he determined the rotor was busted. While he was looking at the engine, some people from the church where they were scheduled to sing stopped to help them get their equipment to the church. Before they returned to pick him up, he walked to a nearby house and asked if they could take him to where he could get some parts to fix the bus. They agreed to take him to a nearby Sinclair Service Station in exchange for one album. He fixed the bus, and after the service, they headed down the road toward home.

Buddy Liles, who had sung with several groups and eventually went on to sing with the Florida Boys, sang bass for the Notemen for two years. When Buddy Liles left the group he was replaced by Ronnie Parks who currently sings with the Victors in Middletown.

The Notemen sang mostly in churches and had a radio program on WPFB. A premier group, they were the first local group that promoter Lloyd Orrell featured at Memorial Hall in Dayton. Some time in the late 1960s, after the group has lost several of its members, Keith also left the group to join Middletown's the Victors Quartet. After Keith left, the group never reorganized.

* * *

Royalty began singing as a trio in the summer of 1999. Baritone singer and pianist Mike Gibson, a native of Dayton, has been involved in Christian music since he was twelve years old. Mike says, "I am very thankful for the opportunity to sing southern gospel music. It is truly a dream coming true for me." First tenor Jeff Gibson was called into the singing ministry at a young age. Blue Creek resident, Jason Cooper, is the second lead singer for Royalty. He won a talent show singing "The Lighthouse" when he was twelve years old, which sparked his interest in the music ministry. He continually strives to be the best he can and has not forgotten who sends the blessings.

Their mission is one that is very simple in its concept. One must be consistent and forever have a servant's heart to truly feel the approval that is necessary each and every weekend on the road. When you saw Royalty in person, you witnessed three men who loved the gospel and counted it a privilege to sing for Him.

* * *

David Folenius was born in the Cincinnati area on July 31, 1972. Dave was saved at age twelve and, soon after, started leading the singing in his father's church. Once after the Southern-Aires had sung at David's church, his father received a call from Dall Miller inquiring as to whether Dave would be permitted to sing with the group. Dave started with the Southern-Aires at age fifteen. His brother Steven Folenius started singing lead for the Southern-Aires a year later.

They remained with the group several years until one day when on their way to make a videotape, they were involved in a very bad accident due to flooding caused by a heavy rainstorm. They suffered severe injuries, but thank God, they both survived. As a result, their father decided they should step down from the group and focus on schoolwork for a while. They later filled in for a while with a group called Higher Dedication located in Hamilton. Then Dave and his brother Steven formed a group called Steadfast Ministries. The group continues today, but Dave left them in 2004.

In 2005, Dave started singing with the Promised-Aires in Greenville. He had been with them a little less than one year when he took an offer to travel full-time with Ed Crawford and the Mystery Men from Nashville, Tennessee. He traveled with them for one year. Then in 2006, he joined the Worley Brothers in Florence, Kentucky. Dave says, "When I was young and starting out, it was important for me to be seen, but I now view my ministry through different eyes, looking forward to that day when I will see the faces of those to whom I have witnessed, this will make it all worthwhile."

* * *

Some time around 1909, Ira Wilson, composer, arranger and editor for the Lorenz Publishing Company in Dayton penned the words to the song "Make Me a Blessing." The song was first sung at the International Sunday School Convention held in Cleveland. The song was published in 1924 and has been included in many songbooks.

* * *

Kenneth Eugene Shiveley was born May 22, 1923, in Adams County by the Ohio River in Rome, just three miles down the road from the famous Cowboy Copus, better known as Floyd Copus, who later became his personal acquaintance. At the age of three, he had nineteen carbuncles, large boils, on his neck that closed in on his windpipe bringing him near death. At age five, his father began teaching him to work on their Model T Ford. His first bicycle, a used one, had one pedal and a burlap bag for a seat. He later got a new bike, an Elgin from Sears, paying a monthly payment of $3.00.

As a young boy, he walked down to Westfork Church. After walking four miles, and entering the church, he discovered no one was there. They were all in the choir room. The next Sunday, he rode his bicycle to church, but someone stole it during the service. He was just a young boy with fire engine red hair and freckles, but they liked him, and they were going to make him a bass singer. They showed him the notes and how to read music. One person would elbow him when he was supposed to sing low, and another would elbow him when he was supposed to sing high. Before long, they had him on the radio in Maysville, Kentucky, singing bass for the choir. By age nine, he was singing bass with Fred Tacket, who was the lead singer in his parent's group called the Shiveley Quartet. When Kenny was eleven, a man named Pat O'Brien was at their homecoming, and he told Kenny he had a great bass voice, and he offered him a job singing bass. Despite being told he could see the world at no cost, he didn't take the offer.

He purchased his first guitar from Spiegel May Stern as a catalog order. He paid $14.99 and rowed a skiff (boat) six miles up the river to Vanceburg, Kentucky to pick it up, and then rowed back to Rome. He lost the guitar in the 1937 Flood.

As a young teenager, Kenny had a crush on Carl Shiveley's sister. They would often meet outside while the service was taking place. While carrying her little brother Gene, she would pinch him and make him cry, so she would have to take him outside so he wouldn't disrupt the service. Then she and Kenny could be together.

Some time later, he traded a bicycle for a 1928 Model A Ford ragtop pickup giving $8.00 extra. He drove it home as they did not require a driver's license in those days. He would borrow mom's Model A Ford coupe when going on a double date as there wasn't room in his pickup. Learning to drive an old dump truck out in the pasture field, he got the dump bed up and couldn't get it down. Kenny still cannot recall exactly how he was able to get the bed back down.

Kenny had a 1937 Ford, which had many lights, squirrel tails everywhere, mud flaps, a dual exhaust and fake, painted white sidewall tires. One evening in 1939, hearing there were plenty of pretty girls in Buena Vista in Scioto County, Kenny and his friend Wilbur took a drive through the city, and after driving around four or five blocks, they hadn't seen any girls. Making one more round, there on the corner they spotted three beautiful girls. In the middle was a little short girl, who had a red sweater on with a black skirt. Kenny quickly said, "Wilbur, stop!" He pointed to the little one in the middle and said, "That's going to be my wife." Talk about love at first sight!

He attended high school in Manchester, and as times were hard, he was soon working in construction. Uncle Sam sent him a greeting letter, so he moved to Dayton to work at the defense plant in 1941. Then on September 29, 1945, at a Methodist church in Rome (Ohio), that young lady from Buena Vista became Betty Louis (Hazelbaker) Shiveley, and sixty-two years later, she still holds that title. He quit working in Dayton and went back to Rome where he opened a used car lot. After holding several jobs, including a franchise from Ferguson Equipment, he moved back to Dayton in 1955 and went to work as a mechanic for White Allen Chevrolet.

At the age of eighteen, he drank his first beer, Burger Beer. It tasted terrible, but his brother, Basil told him he'd get use to it. He ended up drunk, and soon it was whiskey every day at noon plus a twelve-pack of beer. He even started drinking moonshine and chasing it with cider, and that's really bad. But one New Year's celebration at Lee's Bar on Main Street in Dayton, he told the bartender, "I want a two double please."

Lee looked at him and said, "I don't want to give it to you, it will kill you."

Ken said, "I want to quit drinking or die."

Red Runner, Indianapolis race car driver, laughed at him. That was in 1956, and no more drinking. That ended eleven years of drunkenness for Ken. Then in 1957, after developing a friendship with Vernon B. Collins and his brother, Delbert, Kenny got saved, and soon they started singing with Vernon's wife, Bea, in a group called the Travelers Trio.

Sanford Wood and Kenny Shiveley had a group with Dorsel Stewart called the Stewart Jordan Quartet. Soon he formed the Songsters Quartet—Sanford Wood sang tenor, LB Taulbee sang baritone, Russell Strong sang lead and played piano, and of course, Kenny continued to sing bass. He later took several different music courses, but it didn't last long as he wanted to create a style of his own. Kenny says, "I wanted it my way." In 1964, he and Carl Shiveley got together and traveled as Kenny Shiveley and the Cadets for about five years, having quite a time together. They sang on the WHIO *Good Ship Zion* program.

When Carl was singing with Kenny Shiveley one time, it was him and a guy named Henry Banner. Henry was a good singer and played the guitar, and Carl was singing and usually played the banjo. They were doing a program in a high school, and they decided that Kenny was not going to talk all the way through. They had the songs laid out so they could go from one song to another and never have to change capos or anything. They walked up on stage and started singing, and for almost forty-five minutes, Kenny didn't speak a word—he just sang. Coming down off the platform, somebody said, "What's wrong with Kenny?"

In 1971, Kenny was elected president of the Montgomery County Singing Convention. Soon after he became president, Hopkins Chevrolet presented Kenny with a new van. Ken has held the position ever since. Under Kenny's direction, they held some great events at UD Arena, the Dayton Convention Center, and Memorial Hall. In 1973, an up-coming group known as the Cathedrals sang for the MCSC, and in that same year, the convention choir won a first-place award and opened for several of the Lloyd Orrell gospel concerts held at Memorial Hall in Dayton. He directed the *Cross County Jubilee* program on TV for almost two years.

Recording a live album at Bethel Temple by WFCJ, Ed Boston, owner of Queen City Recording Studios, jokingly presented Kenny with a gold record for not selling a million copies.

Ann (Feltner) Stacey attended Kenny Shiveley's church for a long time and sang in a group with Kenny for a while. In 1985, the Old-Timers Quartet was formed by Kenny Shiveley, "Pappy" Helmick, Charles Feltner, and two other close friends. Later when Jack Barrett and Paul Barnhart joined the group, the name was changed to the Zionheirs. In 1989, Dayton mayor Clay Dixon proclaimed November 5 as Montgomery County Singing Convention Day. When "Pappy" was ninety-six years old, he and Kenny sang with two other elderly men in a quartet called the Antiques, and they sang for three years.

At one time, Kenny nearly drowned in Ohio River, but Harry Pott helped him out. Leaving Davis Buick, he opened his own car shop and worked as a mechanic for fifty-nine years. He has had seven cars to fall on him, wrecked a Harley Davidson motorcycle, wrecked three automobiles, but at age eighty-four, he's never had a bone broken in his body, not even a finger. Kenny has been pastor of a Christian Union Church for thirty-four years and is still singing.

Returning Home

Leaving Dayton, we continue east on First Street passing the Dayton Dragons' Baseball Field. Then bearing left onto Springfield Street, we travel east to the village of Riverside where we take Harshman Road north. While entering Harshman Road, we can view, off to the right, the famous Air Force Museum, and we soon pass Eastwood Park on the left where annually Kenny Shiveley holds a big gospel extravaganza. Crossing the Mad River, we continue along Harshman (Needmore) Road to Dixie Drive where we turn right and head to Vandalia ending Tour 8.

KING'S JOURNEYMEN

NORTHERNAIRES

BUCKEYE TRIO

WELLS OF SALVATION

WELLS OF SALVATION

FAITHFUL FOUR

STILLWATERS

CARL SHIVELEY FAMILY

BLESSINGS UNLIMITED

ONEY FAMILY

ONEYS

DAYTON AMBASSADORS

DAYTON AMBASSADORS

DAYTON AMBASSADORS

DAYTON AMBASSADORS BAND

DAYTON GALILEANS

O'BYRANT FAMILY

DAYTON HARVESTERS

Rusty Ballinger

Rod Burton

GOSPEL MELOTONES

GOSPELAIRES OF DAYTON

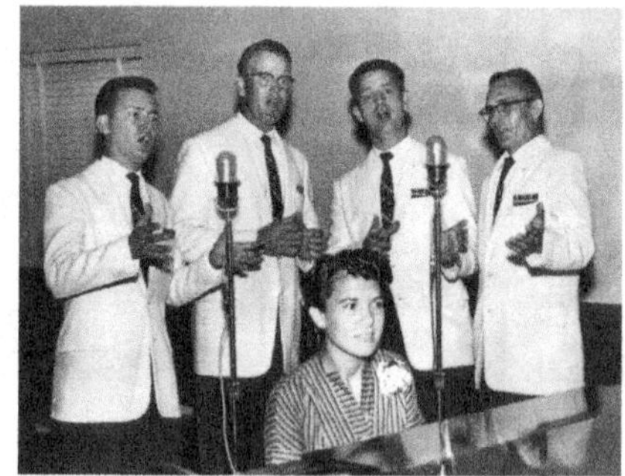

SOUTHERN-AIRES

SOUTHERN-AIRES

CHARLES FELTNER SINGERS

CHARLES FELTNER SINGERS

HARBINGERS

HOMEGATE QUARTET

LITTLEJOHN BROTHERS

LITTLEJOHN BROTHERS

CAMPMEETING SINGERS

GOSPEL MARINERS

MARINERS

NEW LIFE TRIO

NOTEMAN

Kenny Shiveley with the CADETS

Chapter IX

Passing the Torch

Just One More Soul

The preachers are weary, the singers are tired
The church as we know it is losing its fire
Some are discouraged from bearing the load
But we must determine to keep pressing on

So preachers, keep preachin' and singers, go sing
Laymen, keep sharing that Jesus is King
The angels have gathered, they're surrounding the throne
And they'll start rejoicing for just one more soul

'Cause if just one more soul were to walk down the isle
It would be worth every struggle, it would be worth every mile
A lifetime of labor is still worth it all
If it rescues just one more soul

—Rodney Griffin
(Used with permission)

I trust in reading this book you now possess a greater appreciation for those who have committed all, or a portion of, their life to spreading the gospel of Jesus Christ through southern gospel music. Being on the road is not all fun and glamour as one may think. These groups have experienced the chill of traveling down the road on a freezing bus; they've had to push that big old bus to jump start the engine; they've rolled in during those early morning hours, after a long weekend on the road, often going to work without having any sleep; they've carried and set up that heavy equipment time after time; they've sung when their voices could only produce a whisper, and their families have made unending sacrifices to keep them on the road.

No doubt many of them have asked the question, "Is it worth it?" and "Can I go on?" But Rodney Griffin, in his song "Just One More Soul," reminds us that the work is not over, and I would encourage each one to continue walking the path that God has placed before you. As such, I would like to pass on a few words of wisdom from those who have been called to carry on this great heritage of southern gospel music.

STUDY TO SHOW THYSELF APPROVED

The vocal training Glen Payne received during his early days established a vocal foundation, and that powerful voice remained in the forefront for a number of years. What an experience as I sat there that evening in Freedom Hall during the 1999 NQC and listened to Glen Payne's last public performance, via telephone. It was truly an evening to be remembered.

MAKE CERTAIN OF YOUR CALLING

Joe Bonsall tells us, George Younce and Glen Payne were devout family men and that definitely raised their level of sacrifice. They were blessed with beautiful, loving, supportive wives, children, and grandchildren who spent an eternity of nights alone while daddy was singing at a civic arena, a high school auditorium, or at the First Church of Somewhere in America. Although constantly surrounded by people (promoters, preachers, radio guys, and gospel music fans by the thousands), you still find yourself amazingly alone most of the time. Whether it be in a motel room, backstage, on a plane, or curled up safely in your bunk of the bus with the curtains pulled closed, you are always reflecting upon the years behind and the miles up ahead. You love to sing, but "Oh, how you miss those kids!"

This is where men of God such as Glen Payne and George Younce have had a tremendous advantage. They knew they'd been called to sing. They knew their lives and talents had been totally responsible for drawing people, both young and old, to Jesus Christ. They were more aware of the constant presence of God's mighty angels who protected them, and of the Holy Spirit who constantly guided their hearts and anointed their music. These were men who walked the walk and talked the talk. They knew that God had a keen understanding of their humanity and loved them dearly, and had blessed them and their families tremendously for the sacrifices made, "*to sing for him*!"

REMEMBER THE REASON YOU GO

Walley Fowler encourages us to express ourselves with music, through singing, playing instruments, and blending our voices together in harmony, melody, and rhythm. Provide enough Gospel in song that any one who has not accepted Christ as Lord and Savior may learn enough to accept the plan of salvation.

ALWAYS EVALUATE YOUR APPEARANCE

Jim Hill warns us, "I believe any time you walk on a platform in a sanctuary, behind the sacred desk where His message is sent to a lost and dying world, you are in His presence, and you should look the best you can and give your best to Him. I am concerned about the future of worship and believe if churches in America today don't change direction, choosing a place of Sunday morning worship will soon be the same as choosing a restaurant."

CARRY YOUR SHARE OF THE LOAD

Bill Gaither reminds us, "The more we get treated like royalty, the more we enjoy it, get used to it, expect it, and eventually demand it . . . At my age and station in life, I'm sure no one would raise a critical brow if I went from the stage to the bus and relaxed while the crew packed and loaded the equipment. But am I really more important than those people? I can't justify that biblically. I carry equipment, not to shame anybody or to show off my humility. I do it mainly because of my work ethic, but also to get going. I want to get home!"

STAY IN HARMONY

George Younce offers a prayer, "May you not only have harmony when you sing, but in every aspect of your lives on the road together! Stay in harmony with Jesus, harmony with family, harmony with each other, harmony in traveling, harmony in decisions, harmony in rehearsal, harmony in material, looks, speech, and presentation. Harmony is easy on the ears, discord is heavy on the heart. Rest, abide, enjoy, worship, and *sing, sing, sing*!"

REMAIN OPEN TO CHANGE

Charles Novell advises us, "It's becoming harder to get bookings as a result of the changes taking place within gospel music. We have to accept the fact that gospel music is continually changing. Those groups that are to continue will need to adjust to the changes. Today's congregation no longer wants to sit back and simply listen, they want to be a part of the worship."

REMEMBER THE OLD HYMNS

Ron McNeal pleads with us, "Don't forget those great old hymns!" He tells us, "As a young boy, we would go to church, and hearing the words to those hymns was absolutely powerful. I was often overwhelmed to the point that I would sing those songs at the top of my lungs. They would bring tears to my eyes and conviction to my heart. Not having a car, we had to walk everywhere, and as a young child, no matter how dark it got at night or how far I had to walk, I wasn't afraid because while whistling a tune or singing one of those hymns, I was indestructible. Growing up, I memorized nearly the whole entire hymnal. Knowing all the help I received from those hymns as a young Christian, I feel like we are letting the boat get away from us by not keeping those old hymns in front of people. They can show them on the wall if they want, but there was just something special about holding that hymnal in my hands even though I had the song memorized. And even today, when a minister or a Sunday school teacher wants to make an impact with a statement, they often pick up the hymnal and say, 'Listen to what this song says.' My heart literally aches for the young people because of the fact that the hymnals are put aside. We need to keep that type of literature in front of the young people."

AVOID PRIDE AT ALL COST

Mark Trammell challenges us, "We are to be ministers of the Gospel of Jesus Christ living, preaching, and singing in such a manner that no one feels or thinks we're trying to be something we are not. We are to be trusted stewards of God's blessings in our lives. We are to be faithful and obedient to God's leadership directing our ministry with integrity based on sound godly principles. The bottom line is for our families to be able to say, 'We're glad we lived in the home of a gospel singer.'"

Randall Clay & Rick Doran

Rick Doran & DALTON GANG

Lily Isaacs & Rick Doran

Jimmy Dooley & Rick Doran

Lorne Matthews & Rick Doran

Rick Doran & O'Bryants

Rick Doran & VICTORS

Rick Doran & John Pfeifer

Harold Reed & Rick Doran

Rick Doran & Sanya Isaacs

Rick Doran & SONGSTERS

Steve Ladd & Rick Doran

Rick Doran & Singing Weavers

Rick Doran & Roy Webb

Rick Doran & Lawrence Bishop

Rick Doran & HEARTS OF FAITH

Chris Freeman & Rick Doran

Jerry Coulter & Rick Doran

Rick Doran & Carroll Rawlings

Rick Doran & MURPHYS

Rick Doran, Lilly Weatherford & Rita Doran

Rick Doran & George Amon Webster

Rick Doran & FORGIVEN

Ronnie Booth & wife, Michael Booth, Rita Doran and Scott Fowler

Mike Allen and Rick Doran

Rick Doran & Jim Hill

Francis Chamberlain & Rick Doran

Rick Doran & the GIBBONS
(Gayle and Dale)

Big John Hall (The man who inspired
Rick to sing) & Rick Doran

Rick Doran's Family
(Three generations)

Group Directory

I'm certain, even with the extensive research completed, that a number of Ohio-based groups and artist have not been identified. If your group or ministry was not mentioned I apologize and please know that I commend every group and artist for their efforts to spread the gospel through southern gospel music. In an effort to identify as many groups as possible I have created the following list of Ohio based groups who, even though I was unable to gather enough information to address them properly within the body of this book, have contributed to the ministry of southern gospel music.

Allen Family—Livingston
Apostolic Gospel Trio—Beavercreek
Back To Calvary Trio—Dayton
Bethel-Aires—Dayton
Blessed Hope Trio—Washington Court House
Bluegrass Gospel Roundup—Canton
Brewer Singers—Vaughnville
Brothers Quartet—Columbus
Burt Family—Cambridge
Calvary Quartet—Cincinnati
Calvary Trio—Dayton
Calvarymen Quartet—Toledo
Chestnut Ridge—Mount Vernon
Chosen Generation—Chillicothe
Conquerers Quartet—Dayton
Country Gospel-Aires—Dayton
Crusaders—Dayton
Dawn of Praise—Hamilton
Deliverance—Mt Vernon
Foundation—Dublin

Freedom Chapel Bluegrass—Cambridge
Glory Gospel Group—Van Wert
Gospel Air Quartet—Medina
Gospel Cadence—Newark
Gospel Heralds—Canton
Gospel Singers—Cincinnati
Gospel Trio—Norton
Grace 4 Faith—Mechanicsburg
Grace Gospel-Aires—Dayton
Graceway—Columbus
Harmony—Dayton
Hearts of Praise—Canton
Humble Gospel Singers—Cleveland
Jackson Family—Troy
Jubilee Four—Cleaveland
Just Us—Brookville
King's Messengers—Greentown
King's Trio—Akron
Little Country Trio—Cincinnati
Lowell Mason Trio—Ripley
Masters Trio—Trenton
McDonalds—Marion
Morning Light—Dayton
New Found Road—Franklin
New Haven Quartet—Cincinnati
New Mercy—Reynoldsburg
Oak Grove Singers—South Amherst
Old Time Religion Singers—Springfield
One Way Express—Brookville
Orner Trio—Dayton
Patrick Family—Cincinnati
Pilgrims Quartet—Spring Valley
Privett Family—Streetsboro
Pure Heart—Fairborn
Ray Anderson Gospel Trio—Richmond Dale
Rhythm-Aires—Batavia
Rose Family—Canton
Royal Harmonizers—Dayton

Scioto Ridge Boys—Hilliard
Scott Countians—Milford
Singing Flanneys—Fairfield
Singing Hymnals—South Amherst
Singing Reids—Painesville
Singing Roars—Piketon
Sons of Joy—Canton
Sounds of Gospel—Maineville
Souns of Victory—Sandusky
Sunrise Quartet—Portsmouth
Tabernacle Gospel Singers—Fairborn
Temple Quartet—Akron
Temple Tones—Franklin
The Disciples—Grove City
The Mighty Miracles—Dayton
Tru Anointing—Monroe
Voices of Love—Cleveland
Voices of Victory—Sunbury
Wesley Singers—Cincinnati
Willing Four Quartet—Akron
Workman Quartet—Sidney

Resources

INTRODUCTION

JAMES D. VAUGHAN—*The Music Men*, Bob Terrell, Bob Terrell Publisher, 1990, Pg 14-16

JAMES D. VAUGHAN—*Music In The Air*, Mark Ward, Sr., Ambassador International, 2005, Pg 70-71

VICTOR TALKING MACHINE—*Music In The Air*, Mark Ward, Sr., Ambassador International, 2005, Pg 121

WHY SHOULD THE DEVIL HAVE ALL THE GOOD TUNES?—*Time Magazine*, Nov. 7, 1949

J.D. SUMNER—*The Music Men*, Bob Terrell, Bob Terrell Publisher, 1990, Pg 268

CHAPTER I

1— BLUEGRASS GOSPELAIRES—Personal interview with Talmadge Clark

1— CHRISTIAN FAMILY SINGERS—Personal interview with Wilma Jackson

2— SHEPHERDS—Personal interview with Ernie DeWaters

2— GIBBONS FAMILY—Personal interview with Dale & Gayle Gibbons

3— RODNEY GRIFFIN—Personal interview with Rodney Griffin

4— GOSPEL AMBASSADORS—Personal interview with Tim Means

5— KUHN SISTERS—Personal interview with Leora Minnich

5— APOSTLES—Personal interview with Betty Kuhns

5— ACCLAIM—Personal interview with Gaylen Blosser

6— VIRGIL BROCK—*Music In The Air*, Mark Ward, Sr., Ambassador International, 2005, Pg 286-287

7— DENOMINATIONS—Personal interview with June ????

8— TRINITY—Personal interview with Gary Adams
9— RANDY LONG—Personal interview with Randy Long
10— MESSENGERS QUARTET—Personal interview with Lamar Yoder
11— TOLEDO—*Ohio: A Guide To Some Really Strange Places*, Pholen, Jerome, Oddball, Chicago Review Press, Chicago, 2004
11— CAROLYN CONNOR—*Precious Memories Magazine*, January/February 1989, Page 19)
11— GARY HERRON—Personal interview with Gary Herron
11— SOUL SEEKERS—Personal interview with Wardell Langston
11— LARRY ORRELL—Personal interview with Larry Orrell
11— PILGRIM WONDERS—Personal interview with Henry Newsome
12— CLYDE—*Ohio: A Guide To Some Really Strange Places*, Pholen, Jerome, Oddball, Chicago Review Press, Chicago, 2004
12— FISHERMEN QUARTET—Personal interview with Larry Kessler, Mike Allen
13— FINDLAY—*Ohio: A Guide To Some Really Strange Places*, Pholen, Jerome, Oddball, Chicago Review Press, Chicago, 2004
13— GOSPEL MESSENGERS—Information from Album Cover
13— EVANGELS—Personal interview with Jeff Arn
13— JERICHO ROAD—Personal interview with Russ Brauneller
13— HEARTFELT—Personal interview with Daryl Walker
13— SOJOURNER—Personal interview with Mark May
14— NANCY KEETON—Personal interview with Nancy Keeton
15— BUD MOTTER—Personal interview with Bud Motter
15— DIXIE GOSPELAIRES—Personal interview with Lillie Mae Whitaker
16— BERRY MAUST—Personal interview with Berry Maust
17— STEVE ADAMS—Personal interview with Steve Adams
17— MARION MONROE—Personal interview with Marion Monroe
18— FIRST BORN—Personal interview with Allen Law
18— MASTER SINGERS—Personal interview with Ralph Royse
19— MILLS BROTHERS—Mills Brothers Website
20— HENRY SHOWALTER—*Precious Memories Magazine*, January/February 1989, Pg 17
20— LAFONTAINE FAMILY—Personal interview with Sheri
21— JONES FAMILY—Personal interview with Betty Jones
21— KINGSWAY—Personal interview with Eric King
22— BURRESS FAMILY—Personal interview with Tom Burress

CHAPTER II

1— JOHN BURKE & LAYMAN TRIO—Personal interview with Talmadge Clark

1— GRACE BROTHERS—Personal interview with Larry Polley

2— GLORYLANDERS QUARTET—Personal interview with Dave Marquette

2— STEVE LADD—Personal interview with Steve Ladd

3— KEGLEY SISTERS—Personal interview with Mary Bieker

3— MELODY-ETTES—Personal interview with Glenda Washburn

3— PARKS QUARTET-Fracis Chamberlain, Mary Parks

3— UNITED GOSPEL SINGERS—Personal interview with Loretta Harris

4— BLENDWRIGHTS—Personal interview with Alice ThomasLarry Blackwell

4— SOUND OF PRAISE—Personal interview with Loretta Carter

4— HYMN TRIO—Personal interview with Rick Todd

5— MARK CRARY—Personal interview with Mark Crary

5— HOSKINS FAMILY—Personal interview with Angie Hoskins

5— TOUCH OF GRACE—Personal interview with Ken Ankney

5— DOUG OLDHAM—Personal interview with Doug Oldham

5— WAYMAKERS—Personal interview with Martin Neal

5— NEW HAPPINESS—Personal interview with Gary Bates

6— MCGUIRE SISTERS—*The Legacy Of The Blackwood Brothers*, Paul Davis, Blue Ridge Publishing 2000, Pg 61-62

6— MCGUIRE SISTERS—*Close Harmony*, James R. Goff Jr., The North Carolina Press, Pg 173

6— MCGUIRE SISTERS—*The Music Men*, Bob Terrell, Bob Terrell Publisher, 1990, Pg 142

6— MCGUIRE SISTERS—*GMA Good News Magazine*, March 1971

6— RONNIE MERRILL—Personal interview with Ronnie Merrill

6— PROFITTS—Personal interview with James & Shirley Profitt

6— REVELERS—Personal interview with Wendell Davis

6— VICTORS QUARTET—Personal interview with Roy Parks and Gary Crawley

7— MCCRARYS—*Unclouded Days*, The Gospel Music Encyclopedia, Bill Carpenter, Pg 287-88

8-441—Personal interview with Rhonda Hall

8— DON BLADWIN—*Southern Gospel History 101*, Don Baldwin

8— DON BLADWIN—*Close Harmony*, James R. Goff Jr., The North Carolina University Press, Pg 250
8— BENGE FAMILY—Personal interview with Jeff Benge
8— BURTON FAMILY—Personal interview with Grady Burton
8— CHANCELLOR GOSPEL QUARTET—Information from Album Cover
8— JOHN JARVIS—*Encyclopedia of American Gospel Music*, Routledge, 2005, Pg 203
8— THOMPSONS—Personal interview with Anna Thompson
9— UNDIVIDED HEARTS—Personal interview with Greg Duncan
10— EASTMEN TRIO—Information from Album Cover
11— LAWRENCE BISHOP—Personal interview with Lawrence Bishop
11— ISAACS—Personal interview with Lily Isaacs
12— DENVER LAMB—Personal interview with Denver Lamb
12— MIAMI VALLEY BOYS—Personal interview with Bonnie Smith
12— LIGHTHOUSE QUARTET—Personal interview with David Griffeth
12— SKYWARD BOUND—Personal interview with Mary Jo Clouse
13— THEM BOWMANS—Personal interview with Blaine Bowman
14— WAYNESVILLE—*Ohio: A Guide To Some Really Strange Places*, Pholen, Jerome, Oddball, Chicago Review Press, Chicago, 2004
14— HEARTS OF FAITH—Personal interview with Brenda Messaros
15— GARY COHN TRIO—Personal interview with George Kidd
15— HANINGS—Personal interview with David Hanings
16— CHARIOTEERS—*Encyclopedia Of American Gospel Music*, Routledge, 2005, Pg 74
17— PHIL BROWER—*Singing News Magazine*, September 2006, Vol 38, Issue 5, Pg 26

CHAPTER III

1— GOD'S AMBASSADORS—Personal interview with Judy Spires
1— HAMILTON ROAD GOSPEL—Personal interview with Rick Hinkle
2— NEW PRESENCE—Personal interview with Virgil Hager
2— NEW PRESENCE—*Columbus Dispatch*, Dana Wilson, July 4, 2008
3— FREEDOM VOICE—Personal interview with Ron Roesink
4— ORRVILLE—*Ohio: A Guide To Some Really Strange Places*, Pholen, Jerome, Oddball, Chicago Review Press, Chicago, 2004
4— COGAR'S SINGING JUBILEE—Personal interview with Wanda Cogar
4— SLABACH SISTERS—Information from Album Cover

5— MASSILLON—*Fun With The Family In Ohio,* Zimmeth, Khristi S. The Globe Pequot Press, Guiliford, Ct, 1996-2002
5— GLICK FAMILY—Personal interview with Lanette Glick
5— MOLLY ODELL—*The Comprehensive Country Music Encyclopedia*, Dwight Yoakum, Times Books In 1994, Pg 271
5— MOLLY ODELL—*Precious Memories Magazine*, January/February 1989, Pg 7-15
5— MOLLY ODELL—Information from Album Cover, A Sacred Collection, 1975
5— MOLLY ODELL—*Encyclopedia Of American Gospel Music*, Routledge, 2005, Pg 260
6— COLE FAMILY—Personal interview with Faran Cole
7— CHRIST UNLIMITED—Personal interview with Beverly Nieminen
7— PARKER TRIO—Personal interview with Shannon Parker
8— AKRON—*Ohio: A Guide To Some Really Strange Places*, Pholen, Jerome, Oddball, Chicago Review Press, Chicago, 2004
8— EMBERS—Personal interview with Edward Hawks
8— EMMANUELS—Personal interview with Joe Knight
8— EVANGELAIRES—Personal interview with Jim Buckner
8— HEAVENLY GOSPEL SINGERS—*Encyclopedia Of American Gospel Music*, Routledge, Pg 183-184
8— REX HUMBARD—*Music In The Air*, Mark Ward, Sr., Ambassador International, 2005, Pg 320
8— ROYAL ANGELETTES—*Beacon Journal*, Colette M. Jenkins, Beacon Journal Staff Writer
8— SHARON TAWNEY—Personal interview with Sharon Tawney
8— THE BROTHERS—Personal interview with George Amon Webster, Lorne Matthews, Roy Tremble
8— WEATHERFORDS—Personal interview with Lily Weatherford, Armon Morales, Henry Slaughter
9— SONGSTERS—Personal interview with Jerry & Sharon Waldrop
9— GOSPEL ECHOES—Personal interview with David Lemon
10— MIKE ABERNATHY—Personal interview with Mike Abernathy
11— SINGING WEAVERS—Personal interview with Weaver Family
12— FRAME FAMILY—Personal interview with Duane Frame
13— KENT—2000-2003 *The Kent Historical Society*
13— KENT—*Ohio Oddities: A Guide To The Curious Attractions Of The Buckeye State,* Zurcher, Neil, Gray & Company, Publishers, Cleveland, 2001-2002

13— ONE WAY RIDER—Personal interview with David Mayfield

14— CATHEDRALS—*Encyclopedia Of American Gospel Music*, Routledge, 2005, Pg 70-71

14— CATHEDRALS—*The Music Men*, Bob Terrell, Bob Terrell Publisher, 1990, Pg 48, 52, 205, 274, 285, 294, 296

14— CATHEDRALS—*Murry's Encyclopedia of Southern Gospel Music*, David Bruce Murray, Musicscribe Publishing, 2005, Pg 105-6, 163

14— CATHEDRALS—*Singing News Magazine*, March 2006, Pg 53

14— CATHEDRALS—*Singing News Magazine*, July 2006, Pg 26

14— CATHEDRALS—*This Is My Story*, David Liverett, Thomas Nelson Publishers, 2005, Pg 103

14— CATHEDRALS—*Music In The Air*, Mark Ward, Sr., Ambassador International, 2005, Pg 124

14— CATHEDRALS—Article: "A Tribute To The Cathedral Quartet", Joseph S Bonsall, May 19, 1999

14— CATHEDRALS—*Gospel Singing World*, October-November-December, Vol 2, No. 4, Grc A Trust

14— CATHEDRALS—*Homecoming*, Bill Gaither with Jerry Jenkins, Zondervan Publishing House, 1997, Pg 188

14— CATHEDRALS—*I Was A Gospel Singer*, Sammy Capps

14— CATHEDRALS—Personal interview with Gerald Wolfe, Lorne Matthews, Roy Tremble, George Amon Webster, Scott Fowler, Mark Trammell, Haskell Cooley, Bill Dykes

14— SIGNATURE SOUND—*Singing News Magazine*, July 2005, Vol 37, Issue 3, Pg 58-59

14— SIGNATURE SOUND—*Singing News Magazine*, July 2006, Vol 38, Issue 3, Pg 86

14— SIGNATURE SOUND—*Singing News Magazine*, January 2007, Vol 38, Issue 9, Pg 41, 44-45

14— SIGNATURE SOUND—*Singing News Magazine*, February 2007, Vol 38, Issue 10, Pg 36

14— SIGNATURE SOUND—Article—"Get Away Jordan", Joe Bonsall, Rick Hendrix Company

14— SIGNATURE SOUND—Personal interview with Roy Webb

15— JOSEPH HABEDANK—Personal interview with Joseph Habedank

16— CIRCLE OF FRIENDS—Personal interview with Lisa Pierce

17— PHILIP BLISS—*Encyclopedia Of American Gospel Music*, Routledge, 2005, Pg 39

17— PHILIP BLISS—*The Story Of The American Hymn*, Edward S. Nindle / Abingdon Press, 1921
18— EVERLASTING HOPE—Personal interview with Amanda Kuszmul
18— STEVENS FAMILY—Personal interview with Rich Stevens
19— WILLIAM MCKINLEY-Christian History Magazine, Issue 99, Summer 2008, Richard V. Pierard, Pg 24
19— ABRAHAM BROTHERS—Personal interview with David Hamilton
19— GEORGE BENNARD—*50 Southern Gospel Favorites*, Pg 154 / 101 Hymn Stories, Kenneth Osbeck, Kregel Publishers, 1982
19— LINDA MCCRARY—*Decision Magazine*, March 2007, Jerri Menges, Copy Editor For Decision Magazine, Billy Graham Evangelistic Association
19— CHORDS—Personal interview with Lynn Royce Taylor
20— JUDSON VAN DEVENTER—*50 Southern Gospel Favorites*, Linday Terry, Kregel Publications 2002, Pg 168
21— MATT FELTS—Personal interview with Matt Felts

CHAPTER IV

1— HIGHER CALL—Personal interview with Scott Madden
1— PFEIFERS—Personal interview with John Pfeifers
2— SINGING DISCIPLES—Personal interview with Lanny Bryant, Cliff Chablin
3— GUARDIANS—Personal interview with Dale Uhrig
3— SPIRIT OF PRAISE—Personal interview with Jamie Bacenhaster
3— SINGING DIEHLS—Personal interview with Joe Diehl
3— SOUND OF LATTER REIGN—Personal interview with Norma Hutton
3— PAUL MINNEY MINISTRIES—Personal interview with Paul Minney
4— WAVERLY—*Ohio Oddities: A Guide To The Curious Attractions Of The Buckeye State*, Zurcher, Neil, Gray & Company, Publishers, Cleveland, 2001-2002
4— GOSPEL TONES—Personal interview with Verlin Kritzwiser
5— ATONEMENT—Personal interview with Jim Daulton
6— TRACE FAMILY TRIO—*Encyclopedia Of American Gospel Music*, Routledge, 2005, Pg 402
7— PORTHSMOUTH—*Ohio Oddities: A Guide To The Curious Attractions Of The Buckeye State*, Zurcher, Neil, Gray & Company, Publishers, Cleveland, 2001-2002
7— GOLDEN KEYS—Personal interview with James Hill
7— GOOD NEWS TRIO—Personal interview with Ray Meginnis

7— RADIENT HEART—Personal interview with Lori Reed
7— MARILYN BOWLING—Personal interview with Marilyn Bowling
7— GREG TINGLER—Personal interview with Greg Tingler
8— TRUE GOSPEL SOUNDS—Personal interview with Rick Schweinsberg
8— DAY3—Personal interview with Sheri Noel
9— RICH ADKINS—Personal interview with Rich Adkins
9— GOSPEL RIVER BOYS—Personal interview with Gary Morgan
10— FORGIVEN 4—Personal interview with Willie Church
11— CONCORDS—Personal interview with Doug Miller
12— FAMILY HERITAGE—Personal interview with Sandy Davis
13— SIDNEY WHEELER—Personal interview with Sidney Wheeler
14— HOMER RODEHEAVER—*Music In The Air*, Mark Ward, Sr., Ambassador International, 2005, Pg 57-63, 125)
14— HOMER RODEHEAVER—*Encyclopedia Of American Gospel Music*, Routledge, 2005, Pg 320-322
14— HOMER RODEHEAVER—*Gospel Music Encyclopedia*, Robert Anderson & Gail North, Sterling Publishing Company, 1979, Pg 202
14— HOMER RODEHEAVER—*Singing News Magazine*, July 2003, Pg 52
15— CIRCLEVILLE—*Ohio: A Guide To Some Really Strange Places*, Pholen, Jerome, Oddball, Chicago Review Press, Chicago, 2004
15— CIRCLEVILLE—*Ohio Historical Society*, 2005, "Circleville", *Ohio History Central: An Online Encyclopedia Of Ohio History.*
15— HOMELIGHTERS—Personal interview with Kermit Haddox
15— MASTER'S MEN—Personal interview with Don Kontner
15— MASTER'S FOUR—Personal interview with Rob Watson
15— ROYALAIRES—Personal interview with Jerry Metzler

CHAPTER V

1— BURTON FAMILY SINGERS—Personal interview with Marlene Burton
1— MASTER SOUNDS—Personal interview with Rhonda Moore, Marla Conrad
1— BLAKE POWELL—Personal interview with Blake Powell
1— RESCUED—Personal interview with Janie Kenerly
2— COLUMBUS—*Ohio: A Guide To Some Really Strange Places*, Pholen, Jerome, Oddball, Chicago Review Press, Chicago, 2004
2— CHALLENGERS—Personal interview with Chuck Larkin
2— DANNY WHITE—Personal interview with Danny White
2— GOSPEL CLOUDS OF JOY—Personal interview with Anthony Byrd

2— GOSPEL TRUMPETS—Personal interview with Edward Saunders
2— GRACE HARBOR—Personal interview with Randy Snodgrass
2— FIVE STAR HARMONIZERS—Personal interview with Bruce Fletcher
2— HEAVEN BOUND SINGERS—Personal interview with Ruth Meadows
2— JUST JOY—Personal interview with John Garnes
2— LAYMAN—Personal interview with Elliott McCoy
2— NEW JERUSALEM—Personal interview with Diana Boggs
2— PATHFINDERS—*The Legacy Of The Blackwood Brothers*, Paul Davis, Blue Ridge Publishing 2000, Pg 130-31
2— PATHFINDERS—*It's More Than The Music*, Bill Gaither, Warner Faith, 2003, Pg 41-44
2— PATHFINDERS—*Music In The Air*, Mark Ward, Sr., Ambassador International, 2005, Pg 266, 274-275
2— PATHFINDERS—*I Almost Missed The Sunset*, Bill Gaither With Jerry Jenkins, Thomas Nelson Publishers, 1992
2— PATHFINDERS—*Me'n Elvis*, Charlie Hodge, Castle Books
2— PATHFINDERS—Personal interview with Jennifer Hodge
2— REVELATORS—Personal interview with Diana Boggs
2— KATY VAN HORN—Personal interview with Katy Peach
2— LANNY WOLFE—Personal interview with Lanny Wolfe
2— SIDE BY SIDE—Personal interview with Gary Brown
3— MT VERNON—*Ohio: A Guide To Some Really Strange Places*, Pholen, Jerome, Oddball, Chicago Review Press, Chicago, 2004
3— VANSCYCOS—Personal interview with Helen Vanscycos
4— PEARLY GATES—Personal interview with Stacy Shaw
5— COPENHAVERS—Personal interview with Karen Copenhaver
6— REGENTS—Personal interview with Larry McElroy
7— GLORIOUS GOSPEL HEIRS—Personal interview with Mark Payne
8— CLEVELAND—*Ohio: A Guide To Some Really Strange Places*, Pholen, Jerome, Oddball, Chicago Review Press, Chicago, 2004
8— SHERRI FARMER—Personal interview with Sherri Farmer
8— MARKSMEN—Personal interview with Randall Clay
8— DAVID YOUNG—Personal interview with Randall Clay
8— FOGGY RIVER BOYS—*Singing News Magazine*, January 2003, Pg 44
8— FOGGY RIVER BOYS—Information from Album Cover, Foggy River Boys—My God Is Real
8— FOGGY RIVER BOYS—*Encyclopedia Of American Gospel Music*, Routledge, 2005, Pg 219

8— FOGGY RIVER BOYS—Personal interview with Randall Clay
8— LOREN HARRIS—Personal interview with Loren Harris
8— JOHN NORQUIST—Information from Album Cover
8— SALLIE MARTIN SINGERS—*Encyclopedia Of American Gospel Music*, Routledge, 2005, Pg 243-44
8— WOMACK BORTHERS—*Cleveland's Gospel Music*, Frederick Burton, Arcadia Publishing 2003
8— FRIENDLY BROTHERS—*Cleveland's Gospel Music*, Frederick Burton, Arcadia Publishing 2003, Page 34, 50, 92, 107-108
8— SHIELDS BROTHERS—*Cleveland's Gospel Music*, Frederick Burton, Arcadia Publishing 2003, Page 11-12, 26
9— SANDUSKY—*Ohio: A Guide To Some Really Strange Places*, Pholen, Jerome, Oddball, Chicago Review Press, Chicago, 2004
9— PATHWAYS—Personal interview with Daryl & Chris Freeman
9— ONE LESS STONE—Personal interview with Eric Anderson
10— FISK JUBILEE SINGERS—*The History Of Gospel Music*, Rose Blue And Corinne J. Naden, Chelsea House Publishers 2001, Pg 56-57
10— FISK JUBILEE SINGERS—*Dark Midnight When I Rise: The Story of the Jubilee Singers Who Introduced the World to the Music of Black America*, Andrew Ward, New York: New York University Press, 1988, Pg 139
11— MANSFIELD—*Ohio: A Guide To Some Really Strange Places*, Pholen, Jerome, Oddball, Chicago Review Press, Chicago, 2004
11— COLONIAL CITY—Personal interview with Karen Campbell
11— ADKINS BROTHERS—Personal interview with Asbury Adkins
11— SPENCERS—Personal interview with JD & Barbara Spencer, Kevin Spencer, Wade Spencer, Geniece Ingold
12— HALL FAMILY—Personal interview with Tony Hall

CHAPTER VI

1— WILMINGTON—*Ohio: A Guide To Some Really Strange Places*, Pholen, Jerome, Oddball, Chicago Review Press, Chicago, 2004
1— EASTERN SKY—Personal interview with Kyle Parker
2— NEW CREATION—Personal interview with Steve ??
3— DALTON GANG—Personal interview with Cheryl Dalton
5— NORTH FAMILY—Personal interview with Karen Foster
6— SOUL'D OUT QUARTET—Personal interview with Matt Rankin
7— JIM BOGGS—Personal interview with Jim Boggs

7— JIMMY DOOLEY—Personal interview with Jimmy Dooley
8— TRINITY—Personal interview with Todd Kritzwiser
9— SONMEN—Personal interview with Berry Woodruff
10— BRIDGES—Personal interview with Scott Bridges
11— CINCINNATI—*Ohio: A Guide To Some Really Strange Places*, Pholen, Jerome, Oddball, Chicago Review Press, Chicago, 2004
11— BROWNS FERRY FOUR—*The Comprehensive Country Music Encyclopedia*, Dwight Yoakum, Times Books In 1994, Pg 42
11— BROWNS FERRY FOUR—*A History And Encyclopedia Of Country, Western, And Gospel Music*, Second Addition (Completely Revised), Linnell Gentry, Clairmont Corp. 1969, Pg 383
11— KEITH WAGGONER—Personal interview with Keith Waggoner
11— CHARLES FOLD SINGERS—*Uncloudy Days, The Gospel Music Encyclopedia*, Bill Carpenter, Backbeat Books 2005, Pg 77
11— CROWNSMEN—Personal interview with Glen Steely
11— DIXIELAND QUARTET—Personal interview with Nelson Ball
11— TENNESSEE ERNIE FORD—*Gospel Music Encyclopedia*, Robert Anderson & Gail North, Sterling Publishing Company, 1979, Pg 72-74
11— FORGIVEN—Personal interview with Cloid Baker
11— JULIE GREATOREX—Personal interview with Julie Greatorex
11— ISLEY BROTHERS—www.Classicbands.Com/Isley.Html
11— MASON BROTHERS—Personal interview with Bill Mason
11— OHIO VALLEY BOYS—Personal interview with Steve Wilson
11— HARPERS—Personal interview with Don Harper
11— HAROLD REED—Kingsmen Quartet website
11— REGENTS—Personal interview with Charles Novell
11— KAY FRANCIS BARKSDALE—"LWF Communications," 1998 Article by Bennie J. McRae, Jr.
11— ACE RICHMAN—*Precious Memories Magazine*, January/February 1989, Page 24-25
11— ACE RICHMAN—*The Music Men*, Bob Terrell, Bob Terrell Publisher, 1990, Pg 156, 162-63, 188-191
11— ACE RICHMAN—*A History And Encyclopedia Of Country, Western, And Gospel Music*, Second Addition (Completely Revised), Linnell Gentry, Clairmont Corp. 1969, Pg 528-29
11— ROY ROGERS—*A History And Encyclopedia Of Country, Western, And Gospel Music*, Second Addition (Completely Revised), Linnell Gentry, Clairmont Corp. 1969, Pg 536

11— ROY ROGERS—*Encyclopedia Of American Gospel Music*, Routledge, 2005, Pg 322-323
11— ROY ROGERS—*The Story of Roy Rogers and Dale Evans—Happy Trails*, Carlton Stowers, Word Books, 1979
11— ROY ROGERS—*The Comprehensive Country Music Encyclopedia*, Dwight Yoakum, Times Books In 1994, Pg 6, 338-39
11— RUTH SESS—Information from Album Cover
11— SHULERS—Personal interview with Jim Brady
11— AYCEL SOWARD—*The Music Men*, Bob Terrell, Bob Terrell Publisher, 1990, Pg 186-87
11— SWANEE RIVER BOYS—*The Music Men*, Bob Terrell, Bob Terrell Publisher, 1990, Pg 151-53, 304
11— SWANEE RIVER BOYS—*Encyclopedia Of American Gospel Music*, Routledge, 2005, Pg 388
11— SWANEE RIVER BOYS—*Singing News Magazine*, July 2002, Pg 44
11— SWANEE RIVER BOYS—*Close Harmony*, James R. Goff Jr., The Unerversity of North Carolina Press, Pg 168
11— SWANEE RIVER BOYS—*Murry's Encyclopedia Of Southern Gospel Music*, David Bruce Murray, Musicscribe Publishing, 2005, Pg 151-152
11— DANIEL TOWNER—*Encyclopedia Of American Gospel Music*, Routledge, 2005, Pg 401
12— BILL PHELPS—Personal interview with Bill Phelps
13— LANDMARK—Personal interview with Carroll Rawlings, Dennis Whitaker
13— BUDDY LILES—*Singing News Magazine*, February 2005, Pg 26
14— GOSPEL JOURNEYMEN—Personal interview with Tookie Wilson

CHAPTER VII

1— CANAL WINCHESTER—*Ohio: A Guide To Some Really Strange Places*, Pholen, Jerome, Oddball, Chicago Review Press, Chicago, 2004
1— MARSHALL FAMILY—Personal interview with Judy Marshall
1— MERE IMAGE—Personal interview with Donna (Marchell)
2— CORNERSTONE—Personal interview with Mel Meloy
3— GENERATION OF FAITH—Personal interview with Robby Kirk
3— KING FAMILY—Personal interview with Jonathan King
3— SONGSMEN—Personal interview with Debbie Bibler
4— LEE & SADDLER—Personal interview with Rhonda Lee

5— LOGAN—*Ohio Oddities: A Guide To The Curious Attractions Of The Buckeye State*, Zurcher, Neil, Gray & Company, Publishers, Cleveland, 2001-2002
5— ANDY GOOD—Personal interview with Andy Good
5— SHARON HARDMAN—Personal interview with Sharon Hardman
6— DAYSPRING—Personal interview with Mike Douglas
7— ATHENS—*Fun With The Family In Ohio*, Zimmeth, Khristi S. The Globe Pequot Press, Guiliford, Ct, 1996-2002
7— DELIVERED—Personal interview with Shirley Nutter
8— BELPRE—*Fun With The Family In Ohio*, Zimmeth, Khristi S. The Globe Pequot Press, Guiliford, Ct, 1996-2002
9— SPIRITUAL ROAD—Personal interview with Carolyn Richards
10— CONNIE SMITH—*Singing News Magazine*, April, 1973
11— CLARK FAMILY—Personal interview with Marvin Clark
12— CHAPEL-AIRES—Personal interview with Jim Blair
13— DARLA WHEELER—Personal interview with Darla Wheeler
14— CAMBRIDGE—*Ohio: A Guide To Some Really Strange Places*, Pholen, Jerome, Oddball, Chicago Review Press, Chicago, 2004
14— DENISE EDWARDS—Personal interview with Denise Brown
14— QUINCY EDWARDS—Personal interview with Quincy Edwards
15— COLE FAMILY—Personal interview with Jim Coleman
16— BELIEVERS—Personal interview with Jack Palmer
17— DAVID MATHES—Personal interview with David Mathes
18— GOSPEL H.I.M.S.—Personal interview with Joe Pena
19— JONATHAN WHITE—Personal interview with Jonathan White
20— FRIENDSHIP FOUR—Personal interview with Tim Thomas
21— SINGING GRANNYS—Personal interview with Wava Shuster
22— RAMBOS—*The Legacy Of Buck & Dottie Rambo*, Buck Rambo, Starsong Publishing Group 1992, Pg 65-66
22— RAMBOS—*50 Southern Gospel Favorites*, Linday Terry, Kregel Publications 2002, Pg 101
22— RAMBOS—*The Legacy Of Buck & Dottie Rambo*, Buck Rambo, Starsong Publishing Group 1992, Pg 94-95
24— PAMELA KAY—Personal interview with Pamela Kay
25— BILL DYKES—Personal interview with Bill Dykes
25— CRUSADERS—Personal interview with Ron McNeal
25— MERCY'S MARK—Personal interview with Gary Jones
25— SOUL PURPOSE—Personal interview with Judy Clapsaddle

CHAPTER VIII

1— KING'S JOURNEYMEN—Personal interview with LD King
1— SINGING NORTHERNAIRES—Personal interview with Jim Clayton
1— WELLS OF SALVATION—Personal interview with Mick Wells
2— FAITHFUL FOUR—Personal interview with Barb Lemaster
3— STILLWATERS—Information from Album Cover
3— CARL SHIVELEY FAMILY—Personal interview with Carl Shiveley Family
4— DAYTON—*Ohio: A Guide To Some Really Strange Places*, Pholen, Jerome, Oddball, Chicago Review Press, Chicago, 2004
4— THE OLD COUNTRY CHURCH—*Singing News Magazine*, August, 1997, Pg 33
4— THE OLD COUNTRY CHURCH—*Homecoming*, Bill Gaither With Jerry Jenkins, Zondervan Publishing House, 1997, Pg 159
4— BELIEVERS TRIO—Personal interview with Durard Brown
4— BLESSINGS UNLIMITED—Personal interview with Gerald Coulter
4— DAVID ONEY FAMILY—Personal interview with David & ??? Oney
4— DAYTON AMBASSADORS—*Lest The Memories Be Forgotten*, Richard L. Doran, 1998
4— DAYTON AMBASSADORS—Personal interview with Tony Rankin & Tom Lawson
4— DAYTON GALILEANS—Personal interview with O'Bryant Family
4— O'BRYANT FAMILY—Personal interview with O'Bryant Family
4— RUSTY BALLINGER—Personal interview with Rusty Ballinger
4— DAYTON HARVESTERS—Personal interview with Pearl Ford
4— ROD BURTON—Personal interview with Rod Burton
4— GOSPEL MELOTONES—Personal interview with George Walker
4— GOSPELAIRES—Personal interview with Bill Allen
4— SOUTHERN AIRES—Personal interview with Dall Miller
4— CHARLES FELTNER—Personal interview with Betty & Sherman Feltner
4— HARBINGERS—Personal interview with Darrell Webb
4— RIEGAL BROTHERS—Personal interview with Duane Early
4— HOMEGATE—Personal interview with John & Joyce Vaughn
4— LITTLEJOHN BROTHERS—Personal interview with Daryll Littlejohn
4— MARINERS—Personal interview with Randall Clay
4— NEW LIFE TRIO—Personal interview with Toby Siler
4— NOTEMAN—Personal interview with Keith Chapman
4— ROYALTY—Article by Mike Gibson

4— DAVID FOLENIUS—Personal interview with David Folenius
4— IRA WILSON—*Music In The Air*, Mark Ward, Sr., Ambassador International, 2005, Pg 309
4— ZION AIRES—Personal interview with Kenny Shiveley

CHAPTER IX

STUDY TO SHOW THYSELF APPROVED—Live performance by Glen Payne at 1999 NQC
MAKE CERTAIN OF YOUR CALLING—"A Tribute To The Cathedral Quartet," Joseph S Bonsall, May 19, 1999
REMEMBER THE REASON YOU GO—Charlie Fowler—Proclamation To The "All Nite Singing Family" Over 50 Years Ago.
ALWAYS EVALUATE YOUR APPEARANCE—Personal interview with Jim Hill
CARRY YOUR SHARE OF THE LOAD—*I Almost Missed The Sunset*, Bill Gaither With Jerry Jenkins, Thomas Nelson Publishers, 1992, Pg 190
STAY IN HARMONY—George Younce—
REMAIN OPEN TO CHANGE—Personal interview with Charles Novell
REMEMBER THE OLD HYMNS—Personal interview with Ron McNeal
AVOID PRIDE AT ALL COST—Personal interview with Mark Trammell

Index

C

D

E

F

H

J

K

L

M

N

O

Q

R

S

U

V

Y